One World Archaeology

More information about this series at http://www.springer.com/series/8606

Thomas E. Levy • Ian W.N. Jones
Editors

Cyber-Archaeology and Grand Narratives

Digital Technology and Deep-Time Perspectives on Culture Change in the Middle East

Springer

Editors
Thomas E. Levy
University of California, San Diego
La Jolla, CA, USA

Ian W.N. Jones
University of California, San Diego
La Jolla, CA, USA

One World Archaeology
ISBN 978-3-319-65692-2 ISBN 978-3-319-65693-9 (eBook)
https://doi.org/10.1007/978-3-319-65693-9

Library of Congress Control Number: 2017953786

Printed on acid-free paper

This Springer imprint is published by Springer Nature
The registered company is Springer International Publishing AG
The registered company address is: Gewerbestrasse 11, 6330 Cham, Switzerland

Preface

This volume focuses on cyber-archaeology in the Middle East, particularly the Seventh World Archaeology Congress (WAC-7), held along the beautiful shores of the Dead Sea in Jordan between 14 and 18 January 2013. The meetings took place at the palatial King Hussein Bin Talal Convention Centre at the Dead Sea in the most relaxed, efficient, and hospitable context that can only occur in Jordan. The general theme of WAC-7 was "Preservation and Heritage Identities in Times of Conflict." WAC-7 happened before the advent of the Islamic State (ISIS) targeting of UNESCO World Heritage Sites and the recent destruction of so many archaeological and cultural heritage sites in Iraq, Syria, and other parts of the Arab world. The chapters in this volume have evolved since 2013 and include papers that were not presented at the WAC-7 conference. However, they all reflect a concern with the preservation of Middle Eastern archaeological sites and the application of the digital data capture, curation, analysis, and dissemination tools of cyber-archaeology — the marriage of archaeology, computer science, engineering, and the natural sciences (Levy 2013). My own time spent on preparing this publication has been a result of a University of California Office of the President (UCOP) Catalyst grant that deals with "At-Risk World Heritage and the Digital Humanities," for which I serve as the principal investigator. This UCOP Catalyst project focuses specifically on at-risk archaeological sites in the Middle East. Unfortunately, this is an ever-evolving problem for our region, and all the contributors to this volume are using cyber-archaeology not only to preserve Middle East cultural heritage but also for scientific storytelling to create grand narratives of culture change in the region.

At the WAC-7 conference, the organizers asked those of us who work in Jordan to highlight the scientific methods we develop and employ in that country. In our WAC-7 sessions, there were a number of papers from the University of California, San Diego, Edom Lowlands Regional Archaeology Project (ELRAP), which I co-direct with my friend and colleague Mohammad Najjar. Over the years since WAC-7, we published those papers in a wide range of publications, including peer-reviewed journals (Levy et al. 2014a; Ben-Yosef and Levy 2014; Gidding et al. 2014; Howland et al. 2014a, 2014b; Jones et al. 2014; Knabb et al. 2014; Levy 2014; Levy et al. 2014c; Petrovic et al. 2014; Savage and Levy 2014; Smith and Levy 2014; Smith et al. 2014; Vincent et al. 2014a, 2014b) and a large two-volume study (Levy et al. 2014b) of Iron Age metal production and social evolution in Jordan's Faynan region. Thus, those WAC-7 papers are not presented in this volume as they have been published elsewhere.

It is important to highlight that our UC San Diego–Department of Antiquities of Jordan project in Faynan began in 1997 as an analogue project with excavations at the WFD 40 Iron Age Cemetery and Early Bronze I WFD 4 sites (Levy et al. 1999). By 1998, we carried out an archaeological survey along the Wadi Fidan where we began to implement some aspects of digital recording linked to the use of a Total Station (Levy et al. 2001a). However, it was in the fall of 1999 (Levy et al. 2001b) when our team went totally "paperless" and relied entirely on a digital recording system for the excavation of the Pre-Pottery Neolithic site at Tell Tifdan (WFD 001) and the Early Bronze Age III–IV copper production site at Khirbat Hamra Ifdan (Levy et al. 2002). The transition from analogue archaeology to digital archaeology was painful to say the least. There were sleepless nights and endless troubleshooting. However, the system worked and provided the basis for what has become a seamless digital data recording, curation, and dissemination excavation program. I did not know it then in 1999, but by "going digital" and using a geo-spatial database founded on the recording of X, Y, and Z (elevation) coordinates for every artifact and piece of data recorded in our Faynan region excavations, our research was "pre-adapted" to the world of scientific visualization at Qualcomm Institute, California Institute for Telecommunications and Information Technology (Calit2), University of California–San Diego (http://calit2.net/). This has led to our UC San Diego team playing a significant role in the development of cyber-archaeology on the world scene (Forte 2008, 2010; Forte et al. 2012, 2015; Levy 2013, 2014; Levy et al. 2010, 2012, 2013; Lercari et al. 2016), as highlighted by this WAC-7 publication.

WAC-7's Academic Secretary, Talal Akasheh, and WAC's International Academic Secretary, Claire Smith, are to be congratulated for the excellent organization of the conference that welcomed participants from all the countries of the Middle East and world community. I would like to personally thank Anne Pyburn and Arwa Badran, the editors of the WAC-7 publication series, for their support in publishing this volume. Special thanks go to Teresa M. Krauss, the senior editor for Social Sciences at Springer in New York, for all her advice and help during the production of this book. I would also like to thank my colleagues from Calit2's Qualcomm Institute at UC San Diego for their support in the activities of the Center for Cyber-Archaeology and Sustainability: Ramesh Rao, Larry Smarr, Tom DeFanti, Margie Burton, Jurgen Schulze, Falko Kuester, Joe Keefe, Greg Dawe, Lisa Tauxe, Steve Savage, Philip Weber, and Chris McFarland. Special thanks also go to my former and current graduate students who have helped to develop cyber-archaeology in Jordan: Adolfo Muniz, Margie Burton, Yoav Arbel, Neil Smith, Marc Beherec, Erez Ben-Yosef, Kyle Knabb, Aaron Gidding, Kathleen Bennallack, Matt Vincent, Sowparnika Balaswaminathan, Matt Howland, Ian Jones (especially with regard to this volume), Brady Liss, Craig Smitheram, and Tony Tamberino. Finally, I am grateful to Mohammad Najjar and Alina Levy for making cyber-archaeology possible in Jordan and at home.

San Diego, CA, USA Thomas E. Levy

References

Ben-Yosef, E., & Levy, T. E. (2014). A 'small town' discovered twice: A forgotten report of major H.H. Kitchener. *Palestine Exploration Quarterly, 146*(3), 179–184.

Forte, M. (2008). Cyber-archaeology: An eco-approach to the virtual reconstruction of the past. In *14th international conference on virtual systems and multimedia, Larnaca, Cyprus*. Larnaca.

Forte, M. (Ed.). (2010). *Cyber-archaeology*. Oxford: Archaeopress.

Forte, M., Dell'Unto, N., Issavi, J., Onsurez, L., & Lercari, N. (2012). 3D archaeology at Çatalhöyük. *International Journal of Heritage in the Digital Era, 3*, 351–378.

Forte, M., Dell'Unto, N., Kristina, J., & Lercari, N. (2015). Interpretation process at Çatalhöyük using 3D. In I. Hodder, & M. Arkadiusz (Eds.), *Assembling Çatalhöyük* (pp. 43–57). Leeds: Maney Publishing.

Gidding, A., Levy, T. E., & DeFanti, T. A. (2014). ArchaeoSTOR: The development and utilization of a web-based database for the field and lab. *Near Eastern Archaeology, 77*(33), 198–202.

Howland, M. D., Kuester, F., & Levy, T. E. (2014a). Photogrammetry in the field: Documenting, recording, and presenting archaeology. *Mediterranean Archaeology and Archaeometry, 14*(4), 101–108.

Howland, M. D., Kuester, F., & Levy, T. E. (2014b). Structure from motion: Twenty-first century field recording with 3D technology. *Near Eastern Archaeology, 77*(3), 187–191.

Jones, I. W. N., Najjar, M., & Levy, T. E. (2014). "Not found in the order of history": Toward a "medieval" archaeology of Southern Jordan. In S.D. Stull (Ed.), *From West to East: Current Approaches to Medieval Archaeology* (pp. 179–205). Newcastle-upon-Tyne: Cambridge Scholars Publishing.

Knabb, K. A., Schulze, J. P., Kuester, F., DeFanti, T. A., & Levy, T. E. (2014). Scientific visualization, 3D immersive virtual realtiy environments, and archaeology in Jordan and the Near East. *Near Eastern Archaeology, 77*(3), 228–232.

Lercari, N., Shulze, J., Wendrich, W. Z., Porter, B., & Levy, T. E. (2016). 3-D Digital preservation of at-risk global cultural heritage. In C.E. Catalano, & L. De Luca (Eds.), *Eurographics workshop on graphics and cultural heritage, 2016*. Aire-la-Ville: Eurographics Association. doi: 10.2312/gch.20161395.

Levy, T. E. (2013). Cyber-archaeology and world cultural heritage: Insights from the Holy Land. *Bulletin of the American Academy of Arts and Sciences, LXVI*, 26–33.

Levy, T. E. (Ed.). (2014). Cyber-archaeology [Special issue]. *Near Eastern Archaeology, 77*(3).

Levy, T. E., Adams, R. B., & Shafiq, R. (1999). The Jabal Hamrat Fidan Project: Excavations at the Wadi Fidan 40 Cemetery, Jordan (1997). *Levant, 31*, 293–308.

Levy, T. E., Adams, R. B., Witten, A. J., Anderson, J., Arbel, Y., Kuah, S., et al. (2001a). Early metallurgy, interaction, and social change: The Jabal Hamrat Fidan (Jordan) research design and 1998 archaeological survey: Preliminary report. *Annual of the Department of Antiquities of Jordan, 45*, 159–187.

Levy, T. E., Anderson, J. D., Waggoner, M., Smith, N., Muniz, A., & Adams, R. B. (2001b). Interface: Archaeology and technology – Digital archaeology 2001: GIS-based excavation recording in Jordan. *The SAA Archaeological Record, 1*(3), 23–29.

Levy, T. E., Adams, R. B., Hauptmann, A., Prange, M., Schmitt-Strecker, S., & Najjar, M. (2002). Early bronze age metallurgy: A newly discovered copper manufactory in Southern Jordan. *Antiquity, 76*(292), 425–437.

Levy, T. E., Petrovic, V., Wypych, T., Gidding, A., Knabb, K., Hernandez, D., et al. (2010). On-site digital archaeology 3.0 and cyber-archaeology: Into the future of the past – New developments, delivery and the creation of a data avalanche. In M. Forte (Ed.), *Introduction to cyber-archaeology* (pp. 135–153). Oxford: Archaeopress.

Levy, T. E., Smith, N. G., Najjar, M., DeFanti, T. A., Yu-Min Lin, A., & Kuester, F. (2012). Cyber-archaeology in the Holy Land: The future of the past. Washington, DC: Biblical Archaeology Society eBook.

Levy, T. E., Tuttle, C. A., Vincent, M., Howland, M., Richter, A., Petrovic, V., et al. (2013). The 2012 petra cyber-archaeology cultural conservation expedition: Temple of the winged lions and environs, Jordan. *Antiquity (Project Gallery)*, http://antiquity.ac.uk/projgall/levy335/

Levy, T. E., Munger, S., & Najjar, M. (2014a). A newly discovered scarab of Sheshonq I: Recent iron age explorations in southern Jordan. *Antiquity, 341*. http://journal.antiquity.ac.uk/projgall/levy341

Levy, T. E., Najjar, M., & Ben-Yosef, E. (Eds.). (2014b). *New insights into the iron age archaeology of Edom, Southern Jordan — surveys, excavations and research from the Edom Lowlands regional archaeology project (ELRAP)*. Los Angeles: Cotsen Institute of Archaeology Press.

Levy, T. E., Vincent, M. L., Howland, M., Kuester, F., & Smith, N. G. (2014c). The art of implementing SfM for reconstruction of archaeological sites in Greece: Preliminary applications of cyber-archaeological recording at Corinth. *Mediterranean Archaeology and Archaeometry, 14*(4), 125–133.

Petrovic, V., Vanoni, D. J., Richter, A. M., Levy, T. E., & Kuester, F. (2014). Visualizing high resolution three-dimensional and two-dimensional data of cultural heritage sites. *Mediterranean Archaeology and Archaeometry, 14*(4), 93–100.

Savage, S., & Levy, T. E. (2014). DAAHL – The digital archaeological atlas of the Holy Land: A model for mediterranean and world archaeology. *Near Eastern Archaeology, 77*(3), 243–247.

Smith, N. G., & Levy, T. E. (2014). ArchField in Jordan: Real-time GIS data recording for archaeological excavations. *Near Eastern Archaeology, 77*(3), 166–169.

Smith, N. G., Passone, L., al-Said, S., al-Farhan, M., & Levy, T. E. (2014). Drones in archaeology: Integrated data capture, processing, and dissemination in the al-Ula Valley, Saudi Arabia. *Near Eastern Archaeology, 77*(3), 176–181.

Vincent, M. L., Kuester, F., & Levy, T. E. (2014a). OpenDig: Contextualizing the past from the field to the web. *Mediterranean Archaeology and Archaeometry, 14*(4), 109–116.

Vincent, M. L., Kuester, F., & Levy, T. E. (2014b). OpenDig: Digital field archaelogy, curation, publication, and dissemination. *Near Eastern Archaeology, 77*(3), 204–208.

Contents

Contributors

Silvia Blanco-Pons Department of Cartographic Engineering, Geodesy and Photogrammetry Photogrammetry & Laser Scanning Research Group (GIFLE), Universitat Politècnica de València, Valencia, Spain

Miriam Cabrelles Department of Cartographic Engineering, Geodesy and Photogrammetry, Photogrammetry & Laser Scanning Research Group (GIFLE), Universitat Politècnica de València, Valencia, Spain

Berta Carrión-Ruiz Department of Cartographic Engineering, Geodesy and Photogrammetry Photogrammetry & Laser Scanning Research Group (GIFLE), Universitat Politècnica de València, Valencia, Spain

D. Christodoulou University of Patras, Department of Geology, Lab of Marine Geology and Physical Oceanography, Patras, Greece

Steven E. Falconer Department of Anthropology, University of North Carolina Charlotte, Charlotte, NC, USA

Patricia L. Fall Department of Geography & Earth Sciences, University of North Carolina Charlotte, Charlotte, NC, USA

E. Fikos Aristotle University of Thessaloniki, Exploration Geophysics Lab, School of Geology, Thessaloniki, Greece

M. Garaga University of Patras, Department of Geology, Lab of Marine Geology and Physical Oceanography, Patras, Greece

A. Georgopoulos National Technical University of Athens, Laboratory of Photogrammetry, School of Rural & Surveying Engineering, Athens, Greece

Moti Haiman Israel Antiquities Authority, Jerusalem, Israel

M. Howland University of California, San Diego, Department of Anthropology, Center for Cyber-Archaeology and Sustainability, Scripps Center for Marine Archaeology, La Jolla, CA, USA

Matthew D. Howland University of California, San Diego, CA, USA

Ian W.N. Jones Department of Anthropology, Center for Cyber-Archaeology and Sustainability, University of California, San Diego, CA, USA

Adi Keinan-Schoonbaert University College London, London, UK

José Luis Lerma Department of Cartographic Engineering, Geodesy and Photogrammetry Photogrammetry & Laser Scanning Research Group (GIFLE), Universitat Politècnica de València, Valencia, Spain

Thomas E. Levy Department of Anthropology, Center for Cyber-Archaeology and Sustainability, University of California, San Diego, CA, USA

B. Liss University of California, San Diego, Department of Anthropology, Center for Cyber-Archaeology and Sustainability, Scripps Center for Marine Archaeology, La Jolla, CA, USA

I. Liritzis University of the Aegean, Department of Mediterranean Studies, Lab of Archaeometry and Lab of Environmental Archaeology, Rhodes, Greece

Aren M. Maeir The Tell es-Safi/Gath Archaeological Project, Bar-Ilan University, Ramat-Gan, Israel

Chris McKinny Texas A&M University Corpus Christi, Corpus Christi, Texas, United States

R. Norris University of California, San Diego; Scripps Center for Marine Archaeology, Scripps Institution of Oceanography, La Jolla, CA, USA

G. Papatheodorou University of Patras, Department of Geology, Lab of Marine Geology and Physical Oceanography, Patras, Greece

Elizabeth Ridder Department of Liberal Studies, California State University San Marcos, San Marcos, CA, USA

I. Rivera-Collazo University of California, San Diego, Department of Anthropology, Center for Cyber-Archaeology and Sustainability, Scripps Center for Marine Archaeology, La Jolla, CA, USA

Itzhaq Shai Israel Heritage Department, Ariel University, Ariel, Israel

T. Sideris University of the Aegean, Department of Mediterranean Studies, Lab of Archaeometry and Lab of Environmental Archaeology, Rhodes, Greece

A. Stambolidis Aristotle University of Thessaloniki, Exploration Geophysics Lab, School of Geology, Thessaloniki, Greece

Mariela Soto-Berelov School of Mathematical and Geospatial Sciences, RMIT University, Melbourne, VIC, Australia

G. Tsokas Aristotle University of Thessaloniki, Exploration Geophysics Lab, School of Geology, Thessaloniki, Greece

P. Tsourlos Aristotle University of Thessaloniki, Exploration Geophysics Lab, School of Geology, Thessaloniki, Greece

G. Vargemezis Aristotle University of Thessaloniki, Exploration Geophysics Lab, School of Geology, Thessaloniki, Greece

About the Editors

Thomas E. Levy is a distinguished professor and holds the Norma Kershaw Chair in the Archaeology of Ancient Israel and Neighboring Lands at the University of California, San Diego. He is a member of the Department of Anthropology and Judaic Studies Program and leads the cyber-archaeology research group at the Qualcomm Institute, California Institute for Telecommunications and Information Technology (Calit2).

Ian W.N. Jones is a Ph.D. candidate in the Department of Anthropology at the University of California, San Diego. His research focuses primarily on copper production during the Islamic period in southern Jordan and the economy of the southern Levant in the early 2nd millennium CE. As part of his work with UCSD's Center for Interdisciplinary Science in Art, Architecture, and Archaeology (CISA3), he is also interested in the integration of spatial technologies such as GIS and satellite remote sensing with traditional archaeological field methods for investigating processes of settlement and landscape change.

Chapter 1
Cyber-archaeology and Grand Narratives: Where Do We Currently Stand?

Ian W.N. Jones and Thomas E. Levy

Introduction

The digital "data avalanche" in archaeology is a result of the relatively inexpensive plethora of digital data capture tools (digital cameras, GPS units, mobile phones, laptop computers, external hard drives, drones, and more) that are rapidly becoming part of the archaeologist's toolbox. How do field archaeologists and their teams grapple with the exponential growth in using these digital tools for effective research? The adoption of digital methodologies by these researchers has led to the emergence of a new subfield that may be called "cyber-archaeology" (see below). This volume brings together contributions by a number of authors exploring the potential of cyber-archaeology in the Middle East to answer large-scale research questions of anthropological and historical concern. In this sense, this volume is not about the most effective methods for curating digital cultural heritage data or developing the next best program for a Web-based database for archaeological field research. Instead, it demonstrates how archaeologists working in a variety of countries in the eastern Mediterranean—primarily Israel, Jordan, and neighboring countries—apply cyber-archaeology methods to help create "grand narratives" to explain what happened in the past in one of the world's most complex historical and cultural regions.

I.W.N. Jones • T.E. Levy (✉)
Department of Anthropology, Center for Cyber-Archaeology and Sustainability, University of California, San Diego, CA, USA
e-mail: iwjones@ucsd.edu; tlevy@ucsd.edu

T.E. Levy, I.W.N. Jones (eds.), *Cyber-Archaeology and Grand Narratives*, One World Archaeology, https://doi.org/10.1007/978-3-319-65693-9_1

Cyber-archaeology

In this volume, the term "cyber-archaeology" is defined, following Levy (2013: 28), as "the integration of the latest developments in computer science, engineering, science, and archaeology" (see also Levy et al. 2012). This use of the term is different from that of Forte (2010, 2016), who envisions cyber-archaeology as a Deleuzean revision of "virtual archaeology" (Forte and Siliotti 1997), aimed primarily at simulating "a potential past" in a 3D "cyber-environment" (Forte 2011: 8). Instead, cyber-archaeology is used in a broader sense here, closer to the more general term "digital archaeology" (see Averett et al. 2016; Evans and Daly 2006; Kansa et al. 2011; Levy et al. 2001; Levy and Smith 2007). Cyber-archaeology is a preferable term in the context of this volume, however, because it emerged as a way of describing collaborative efforts between digital archaeologists and computer scientists to develop cyberinfrastructure for archaeology (Levy et al. 2010), with cyberinfrastructure, in this case, referring to linked regional archaeological databases (see also Kansa and Kansa 2011; Kintigh 2006; Snow et al. 2006). This effort led to the creation of the Mediterranean Archaeology Network (MedArchNet; Savage and Levy 2014b) and, in particular, its active Levantine node, the Digital Archaeological Atlas of the Holy Land (DAAHL; Savage and Levy 2014a) with Stephen Savage. In short, cyber-archaeology emphasizes digital data acquisition, curation with Web-based cyberinfrastructure (Fig. 1.1; cf. Levy 2013), analyses and dissemination over the Internet, and access across more protected high-speed fiber-optic networks and in 3D visualization platforms.

In recent years, digital and cyber-archaeology have become robust, interdisciplinary fields concerned with collecting, curating, and displaying data at all points of the archaeological research process. Much attention, naturally, has been given to the recovery and management of archaeological data in the field and laboratory (e.g., Averett et al. 2016; Berggren et al. 2015; Cascalheira et al. 2014; Fee et al. 2013; Gidding et al. 2013; Levy et al. 2001; Roosevelt et al. 2015; Smith and Levy 2014a, 2014b; Vincent et al. 2014). As tablet computers, handheld computers, and smartphones have become increasingly powerful and affordable, they have also become standard parts of archaeologists' field toolkits, and a body of literature has developed around how best to integrate these devices into field and laboratory workflows. This a recurrent theme among the chapters in this volume, as well—in particular Howland (Chap. 2), Maeir (Chap. 3), McKinney and Shai (Chap. 4), Cabrelles, Blanco-Pons, Carrión-Ruiz, and Lerma (Chap. 5), and Levy et al. (Chap. 9)—as the shift to digital recording practices no doubt affects the way archaeologists interpret a site (Huggett 2015: 89–90), and the types of data being recorded have implications for the types of questions that can later be asked.

Another key consideration, however, is the management of the rapidly increasing quantities of digital data being generated—a problem that has been referred to as archaeology's "data avalanche" (Levy et al. 2010; Petrovic et al. 2011)—particularly given the instability of many digital storage solutions (Jeffrey 2012), as well as the dissemination of these data, for which traditional publication is often inadequate

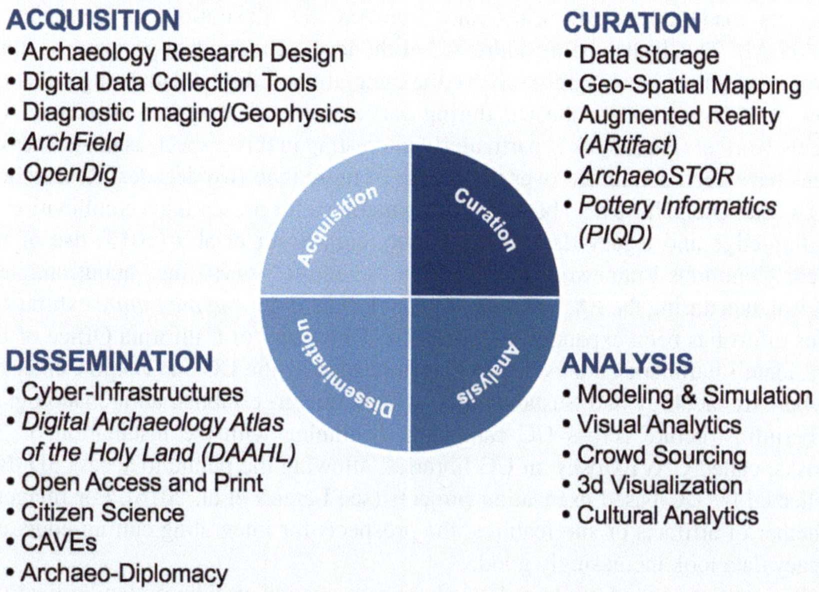

Fig. 1.1 A chart representing the UC San Diego Center for Cyber-Archaeology and Sustainability workflow (after Levy 2013)

(see Kansa and Kansa 2013; Kansa et al. 2014). A number of potential solutions to these problems have emerged, including regional site databases, such as MedArchNet, discussed above; state site inventories, such as the Middle Eastern Geodatabase for Antiquities (MEGA) project (Myers and Dalgity 2012; Palumbo 2012); and larger, worldwide databases archiving a wider range of archaeological data, such as the Digital Archaeological Record (tDAR; Kintigh and Altschul 2010; McManamon and Kintigh 2010), Open Context (Kansa et al. 2007; Kansa 2010; Kansa and Kansa 2011), and the Online Cultural and Historical Research Environment (OCHRE; Schloen and Schloen 2012). These projects represent an important step toward a culture of data sharing that will allow archaeologists to ask large-scale questions.

Several problems become evident when attempting to link data from numerous projects and regions in this way, however. First, how do practices of data collection and the types of data that are shared affect potential analyses? Shott (2014: 3), for example, notes that despite the proliferation of 3D imaging technologies, 2D documentation has remained the norm in lithic studies. Even if 3D models are freely shared, can these be easily analyzed alongside 2D data? More generally, even if data collected using new methods and "legacy" data can be stored together, can they be analyzed alongside one another? While certainly dependent on the analysis and the types of data on which it is conducted, in at least some cases the answer seems to be yes. Smith et al. (2012), for example, have developed a method for analyzing mixed datasets made up of 3D scans and digitized 2D illustrations of ceramics in MATLAB. This is also being addressed at the level of individual projects, as long-term excavations increasingly involve the integration of digital data being collected now with legacy data collected during earlier seasons. Berggren et al.'s (2015) recent work at Çatalhöyük is particularly interesting in this respect, as those excavations have been conducted over the course of more than two decades. Researchers at UC San Diego have also been exploring methods for presenting a combination of cutting-edge and legacy data to the public, e.g., Srour et al.'s (2015) use of the MediaCommons Framework to engage in "scientific storytelling" about archaeological data during the *EX3: Exodus, Cyber-Archaeology and the Future* exhibition. This effort has been expanded as part of the University of California Office of the President's hallmark Catalyst Project, spearheaded by the UC San Diego Center for Cyber-Archaeology and Sustainability, which aims to establish an archaeological cyberinfrastructure across UC campuses, beginning with the installation of 3D kiosks, called CAVEkiosks, in UC libraries, allowing the public to access 3D data collected by UC-based excavation projects (see Lercari et al. 2016). For imagery, whether of artifacts or site features, the prospects for integrating cutting-edge and legacy data look increasingly good.

For other types of artifact data, there is a second problem: standardization. Kansa and Kansa (2013) encapsulate this problem in their title, drawn from an interview with an archaeologist: "We all know that a 14 is a sheep." Methods for recording data are often idiosyncratic, which makes data sharing and the development of cyberinfrastructure difficult. This is not a new problem in digital archaeology. Indeed, it has been a concern for the discipline since its earliest days, dating back to the Ban Chiang Project's use of a punchcard-based IBM System/370 mainframe in the late 1970s and early 1980s (Hastings 1982) and even earlier experiments with "computer archaeology" in the 1950s and 1960s (Chenhall 1967; Cowgill 1967; Gardin 1958; Gardin 1967). Kansa and Kansa (2013: 89) suggest that the solution is a "model of 'data sharing as publication,'" where archaeologists assume that other researchers will have access to their data and adhere to certain standards in order to facilitate use beyond a single lab. This model of publication has the potential to encourage sharing of data that might otherwise remain unpublished (E. C. Kansa et al. 2010), and this model of standardization has been identified as one key advantage of Open Context for academic archaeologists (Sheehan 2015: 208).

For certain types of data, where most researchers agree upon standards, this is an excellent solution. It is not surprising, in this respect, that many of the studies that have been conducted using Open Context have focused on faunal data (Arbuckle et al. 2014; Kansa et al. 2014; Kansa and MacKinnon 2014; Kansa 2015). Even in these cases, problems with legacy datasets have been noted (Atici et al. 2013). For other types of data, this problem is more difficult to resolve. Labrador (2012: 241–241), following Bowker (2000a: 653), notes the problem of "local data cultures' … wherein point typologies for the same region may use differing terms depending upon author, locale, or whim." Snow et al. (2006: 958) identify the same problem for a variety of project data: "Data classifications and terminology vary, are regionally and temporally specific, and are inconsistently applied." This is particularly the case for spatial data, which is a key focus for several of the authors in this volume, including Fall, Soto-Berelov, Ridder, and Falconer (Chap. 6), Haiman (Chap. 7), and Keinan-Schoonbaert (Chap. 8). The same period may be glossed by different terms in different regions, but even more problematically, the same term may be used to refer to different periods. As an example, in Anatolia, the term "Late Byzantine" refers to a period up to 1000 years later than the period glossed by the same term in the southern Levant (Jones et al. 2014: 174). While some of these issues can be resolved by adopting different metadata standards—for example, the use of "fuzzy dates" in spatial databases (Belussi and Migliorini 2014), in addition to or as a replacement for regionally specific temporal terms—the ideal solution is unclear. Bowker (2000b) suggested nearly 20 years ago, in the context of biodiversity studies, that forcing the issue of standardization might be misguided, and that analysts should account for variation due to "local data cultures," rather than trying to eliminate this variation. In the context of the development of archaeological cyberinfrastructure, Huggett (2012) and Dallas (2015) have more recently argued that standards are necessary, but must be developed with the practices of archaeological data collection and curation in mind, and even then are unlikely to ever be truly satisfactory. One attractive solution is Labrador's (2012: 241) suggestion that multiple tags could be given to data in addition to standardized metadata, which could also have the added benefit of making this data more open for use in public archaeology and crowdsourcing projects (Lake 2012; for an example of this type of project, see Lin et al. 2014). Many of the authors in this volume take a pragmatic approach—one also recently used by Bradbury et al. (2016) for mortuary data—developing regional databases to fit the needs of a particular project or analysis. As archaeological cyberinfrastructure continues to develop, however, these databases can be linked and the methods used in the projects described in this volume applied to increasingly large and complex datasets.

The third problem relates to the reliability of the disparate datasets brought together into larger databases. One of the primary uses of spatial databases is the analysis of settlement patterns and particularly changes in settlement patterns over time (Kowalewski 2008). These studies are inherently limited by the quality and reliability of available data. Answering questions about sociopolitical organization and site hierarchy often requires the use of site size estimates, but these estimates can vary considerably depending on the methodology and criteria used (for an example of this, see Iacovou 2007: 6–7). At an even more basic level, the reconstruction of any settlement pattern is dependent not only on survey methodology and quality but on the reliability of the underlying chronological indicators and particularly regional ceramic typologies.

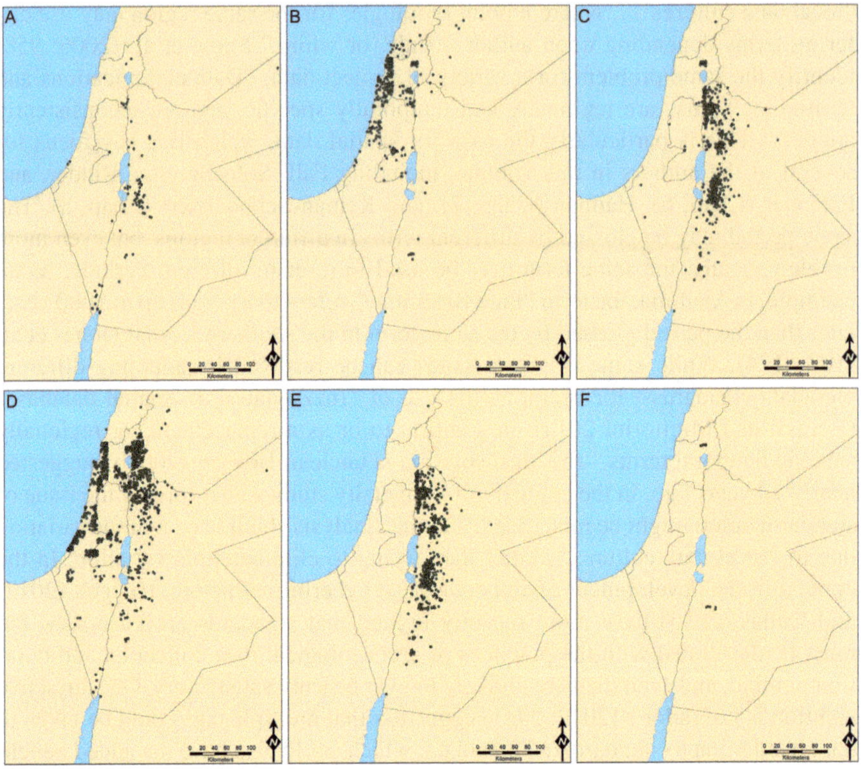

Fig. 1.2 Map of site distributions for six periods from the Digital Archaeological Atlas of the Holy Land (DAAHL). (**a**) Sites attributed to the Fatimid period (970–1099 AD); (**b**) sites attributed to the Crusader period (1099–1291 AD); (**c**) sites attributed to the Ayyubid period (1187–ca. 1260 AD); (**d**) sites attributed to the Mamluk period (ca. 1260–1516 AD); (**e**) sites attributed to the Ayyubid/Mamluk period (1187–1516 AD); (**f**) sites attributed to the Middle Islamic period (1000–1400 AD). Data: DAAHL (http://daahl.ucsd.edu)

A Brief Example

Considering an example from the *Digital Archaeological Atlas of the Holy Land* (DAAHL) will illustrate this point (Fig. 1.2). Figure 1.2 shows six distribution maps for sites listed in the DAAHL. The first four represent periods in a dynastic chronology: the Fatimid (Fig. 1.2a; 970–1099 AD), Crusader (Fig. 1.2b; 1099–1291 AD), Ayyubid (Fig. 1.2c; 1187–ca. 1260 AD), and Mamluk (Fig. 1.2d; ca. 1260–1516 AD) periods. The remaining two represent broader periods: the "Ayyubid/Mamluk" period (Fig. 1.2e; 1187–1516 AD)—a term once commonly used on surveys due to the difficulty of dating the common handmade ceramics of these periods (Walker 1999: 207)—and the Middle Islamic period (Fig. 1.2f; 1000–1400 AD).

The first four maps appear to show fairly major geographic shifts in site concentration, with a gradual increase in the number of sites from a trough during the Fatimid period to a peak in the Mamluk period. Several problems with this data complicate this picture, however. Schick (1997: 81–82) noted the difficulty of distinguishing Fatimid ceramics from those of earlier and later periods, particularly in southern Jordan. While the situation has improved somewhat since the publication of that article, this remains a problem—again, particularly in southern Jordan—and has no doubt affected many of the older surveys entered into the DAAHL.

The Crusader period map is likely more accurate, but does not represent the same period throughout the entire map. While the Crusaders entered Jerusalem in 1099 AD, the Crusader settlements in southern Jordan were not established until at least 1115 (Mayer 1987: 199). Likewise, while the Crusaders were ousted from Jordan in 1189 AD, they were able to reconquer Acre and much of coastal Israel in 1191, and did not lose these holdings until 1291 (Boas 1998: 141). The lack of Ayyubid period settlements in northwestern Israel, then, is not due to a decrease in settlement in this region after the late twelfth century, but instead to differences in dynastic chronological terms (see also Jones et al. 2014: Fig. 12.69).

The similarity of the Ayyubid and "Ayyubid/Mamluk" settlement patterns in Jordan is also suspect, particularly given the historical difficulty of separating Ayyubid and Mamluk ceramics—a problem now largely resolved—which made the identification of distinct Ayyubid period occupations difficult to identify (Walker 1999: 211, 219). While many of these sites were without doubt occupied in the Ayyubid period, the similarity of Figs. 1.2c and e, particularly compared to Fig. 1.2d, suggests that many sites dated "Ayyubid/Mamluk" on survey have also been entered into the DAAHL as Ayyubid. All Ayyubid/Mamluk sites listed for the Archaeological Survey of the Karak Plateau (Miller 1991), Wadi al-Hasa Survey (MacDonald 1988), and Edom Survey (Hart and Falkner 1985), to give several examples, have also been entered into the DAAHL as Ayyubid sites, despite the fact that none of these surveys distinguished between these two periods.

This may also explain the apparent decrease in settlement in these survey areas, particularly central Jordan, during the Mamluk period, as these Ayyubid/Mamluk sites have also been entered as Ayyubid, but not as Mamluk. While the sharp increase in Mamluk period settlement on the coast is due, as mentioned above, to the length of the Crusader settlement there, in other regions this may be related to surveyors using the term "Mamluk" to refer to the entire Middle Islamic period. This is particularly likely for the Golan Heights and Jerusalem region, which were both without doubt settled during the Ayyubid period.

The most interesting maps are Figs. 1.2e and f, which show broader, nondynastic periods. Sites identified as Ayyubid/Mamluk are limited almost entirely to modern Jordan, reflecting regional practices in archaeological survey and terminology. Most problematically, the map of Middle Islamic period settlement, which should include most of the sites from the other maps, instead shows only two small clusters, which suggests that this term is only used in the database for a small number of surveys that have adopted a nondynastic chronology. It is also worth noting the absence, on all of these maps, of sites in the West Bank, an issue discussed by Keinan-Schoonbaert (Chap. 8).

These issues would make it difficult to accurately discuss settlement pattern changes in the first half of the second millennium AD without first revisiting much of the underlying data and perhaps even reanalyzing some of the material from these surveys in person. This is not a specific critique of the DAAHL. Walker (2011: 162–163, 175, Figs. 1–2) has made a similar argument about the apparent decrease in settlement during the Ottoman period (1516–1918 AD) seen in the Jordan Antiquities Database and Information System (JADIS), the predecessor to MEGA-Jordan, mentioned above, and these are only two of many examples. Any archaeological database or cyberinfrastructure bringing together legacy data from many projects will reveal inconsistencies in how the data was collected and described. These projects are still quite worthwhile, but the limitations described above place constraints on the types of questions that can be productively asked of the data. While the chronological resolution of the data in the DAAHL poses problems for identifying settlement pattern shifts during the early second millennium AD, with some manipulation the data could be used to investigate shifts on longer, coarser timescales.

Grand Narratives and Theory

It has often been noted, both by archaeologists (e.g., Sherratt 1995: 1) and scholars in related disciplines (e.g., Braudel 1970: 149), that a key advantage of archaeology is its ability to reconstruct human history on long timescales. Because of this, archaeology is uniquely placed to address questions concerning "grand narratives" of human history, defined by Andrew Sherratt (1995: 1) as "a sense of the architecture of the human past, why parts of it are different from others, and how they all fit together." Levy (2006) has suggested a view of grand narratives as explanations of long-term change and draws on Childean concepts such as technological stages (Childe 1944), e.g., the Stone Age, the Bronze Age, and the Iron Age, and technological revolutions, e.g., the Neolithic Revolution, the Urban Revolution (Childe 1950), and the Secondary Products Revolution (Sherratt 1983), to define them. Grand narratives explain specific, durable shifts in technology, economy, and sociopolitical organization. In this sense, grand narrative explanations are similar to Sewell's (1996: 843) "events," which he defines as "sequences of occurrences that result in transformations of structures." Sewell's conception of the "event" has, within the last decade, seen some adoption in archaeology (Bolender 2010), but this usage is also paralleled in Childe's (1952: 1) later work on technological revolutions, demonstrating that archaeology is well suited to this scale of analysis.

This was, however, challenged by the postmodern turn in the social sciences and humanities. Lyotard (1984: xxiv), for example, "define[d] *postmodern* as incredulity toward metanarratives" or grand narratives (see also Rosenau 1992: 85). While the place of Marxian—and, by extension, Childean—thinking was debated among scholars with differing views of postmodernism, Marxism was generally viewed with some skepticism, particularly due to its reliance on grand narratives (Rosenau 1992: 160–164). In archaeology's post-modern school—post-processualism—this played out similarly. While works exploring long-term approaches were published even during the height of post-processualism (e.g., Bintliff 1991; Hodder 1987; Knapp 1992), these were generally exceptions to the overall trend, and, by 1995, Sherratt (1995: 4) was lamenting "[t]he current lack of thinking about the large scale and long term" and calling for a revival of grand narratives.

At the turn of the millennium, the development of post-Braudelian thought in a number of disciplines—whether in the form of revisitations of Braudel's Mediterranean, as in Horden and Purcell's (2000) influential *The Corrupting Sea*, or rapprochement with postmodernism (e.g., De Landa 1997)—revived interest in long-term thinking. In archaeology, the past decade has seen the publication of a number of volumes exploring long-term narratives of human history and theorizing archaeological conceptions of timescales (e.g., Bolender 2010; Emberling 2016; Lucas 2005; Robb and Pauketat 2013). This has especially been the case for the eastern Mediterranean. In addition to a recent edited volume (Concannon and Mazurek 2016) explicitly engaging Horden and Purcell's (2000) work, scholars have proposed several other approaches to the long term, including "global moments" (Manger and LaBianca 2009), a concept recalling Sewell's "events"; LaBianca's (2007) revival of Redfield's (1955) "great and little traditions" framework, with the persistence of local "little traditions" over time proposed as an alternative to Braudelian approaches to the *longue durée*; and "grand narratives" of social and technological change (Levy 2006).

This revival of interest in long-term change and grand narratives has been quite productive. As Hodder (2000: 21) has pointed out, however, "archaeological understanding of the long term is built up from traces of the smallest and least significant of acts." Answering questions concerning long-term change requires access to a range of data beyond the level of individual projects. Given the revival of interest in grand narratives and long-term change, and the increasing success with which cyber-archaeologists are integrating disparate datasets into regional databases and cyberinfrastructure, it is appropriate to ask explicitly what contributions cyber-archaeology can make to the study of grand narratives, and what barriers still remain to be overcome. The chapters in this volume are dedicated primarily to this task, and can be broadly divided into three categories.

3D Recording and Documentation

Two of the chapters in this volume explore the potential contributions of the "subtle revolution" (Shott 2014) of 3D recording in archaeology to grand narratives. Howland (Chap. 2) provides a welcome critical review of common 3D recording techniques, including aerial and terrestrial laser scanning and image-based modeling. Although he takes a skeptical approach to the question of whether these techniques provide "style without substance," he ends on a "cautiously optimistic" note, arguing that these technologies do, in fact, have the ability to contribute to grand narratives of social change.

Cabrelles, Blanco-Pons, Carrión-Ruiz, and Lerma (Chap. 5) focus instead on a specific example: the documentation of Djinn Block No. 9, a Nabataean monument in the Petra Archaeological Park in southern Jordan. They describe the impressive range of 2D and 3D recording techniques that they have applied to the monument, as well as a smartphone app they have developed to disseminate this data to visitors at Petra. They argue that this type of dissemination allows tourists at Petra to engage with archaeological narratives through "self-learning" and that the tourists' feedback on the app can provide information to archaeologists and site managers as to how visitors to the site interact and engage with this data as they explore the park.

Excavation Recording and Documentation

Two of the chapters in this volume address the adoption of cyber-archaeology to record excavation at large, multiperiod sites. Maeir (Chap. 3) describes the integration of microarchaeology and macroarchaeology at Tell es-Safi in the Shephelah, or foothills, of central Israel. The adoption of microarchaeological techniques allows archaeologists working at the site to identify what are without doubt the "traces of the smallest and least significant of acts" (Hodder 2000: 21), and this, combined with precise macroarchaeological and dating techniques, provides a robust database for understanding changes in how the site was used over time.

McKinny and Shai (Chap. 4) describe the adoption of a specific digital tool, PlanGrid, to record excavations at Tel Burna, another site in the Shephelah, ca. 8 km southeast of Tell es-Safi. Some projects have developed purpose-built excavation recording software, e.g., the Edom Lowlands Regional Archaeology Project's ArchField program (Smith and Levy 2014a, 2014b), which has successfully been implemented on a number of excavations in southern Jordan and recently in Greece (Sideris et al. 2017). At Tel Burna, however, McKinny and Shai have adapted a program designed for a different task. PlanGrid was originally developed as a tool for construction workers, but McKinny and Shai describe using it "in ways … not intended," as a replacement for traditional paper forms. They describe their successful integration of PlanGrid into the archaeological workflow at Tel Burna, and end their chapter by stating their plans to store the data they have collected using PlanGrid in the Codifi database. Codifi's adherence to linked open data standards (Prins et al. 2014: 196) makes this especially promising, as this ensures that the data can be easily integrated into larger databases.

A third, Levy et al. (Chap. 9), instead takes a transdisciplinary, cyber-archaeological approach to regional archaeology, focusing on the Antikyra Bay region in eastern Phokis, Greece, on the northern Gulf of Corinth. Their research integrates excavation and geophysical survey of a Mycenaean tomb at Kastrouli with marine archaeology in the bay itself, investigating how coastal zones provide ideal sediment and cultural "traps" for studies of historical ecology and the roles played by exchange, climate, and environmental change in long-term cultural change. The transdisciplinary team included experts in archaeometry, archaeology, terrestrial and marine geophysics, paleo-marine biology, geomorphology, and more. This approach is linked to broader issues in Mediterranean archaeology, such as the Late Bronze Age collapse of civilizations including the Hittites in Anatolia, New Kingdom Egypt, and the Mycenaeans in Greece, the importance of which has recently been stressed by Cline (2014). They explicitly take up the challenge of Thomas F. Tartaron (2013) to develop methodologies and carry out research concerning the identification and analyses of longneglected "Mycenaean coastal worlds," focusing on local interaction between Late Bronze Age settlements and their anchorages. This project should become a model for the integration of cyber-archaeology and marine archaeology in coastal studies around the Mediterranean basin.

Surveys and Databases

The three remaining chapters are concerned with the collection, compilation, and management of data at the regional level. Fall, Soto-Berelov, Ridder, and Falconer (Chap. 6) present the results of a project modeling patterns of vegetation between 5500 and 3000 BP, roughly corresponding to the Bronze Age, in the Jordan Valley and surrounding areas. This project directly explores the Childean grand narrative of the Urban Revolution. Using a database of almost 1700 points at which plant species were observed and recorded, they argue that the formation of towns at the beginning of the Early and Middle Bronze Ages correspond to "sudden shifts in vegetation," while the collapses at the end of the Early and Late Bronze Ages were instead the result of longer-term trends. Their study demonstrates the great potential of GIS and statistical modeling software to provide a more nuanced picture of how grand narratives play out.

Haiman (Chap. 7) considers issues with the recording and management of survey data, using Byzantine (fourth to early seventh centuries AD) and Early Islamic (seventh to tenth centuries AD) period agricultural sites in the Negev of southern Israel as examples. He argues that the common method of entering sites as "points" in databases obscures information about their associated features necessary for evaluating changes in agricultural landscape use over time, echoing McCoy and Ladefoged's (2009: 280) concerns about the inability of many databases to adequately deal with data from "siteless" surveys. This is the motivation for this Ancient Desert Agriculture Systems Revived and Mapping Agricultural Systems Projects, which have the goal of recording high-resolution spatial data at sites previously recorded only as points in order to investigate shifts in patterns of land use in the Negev between the fourth and tenth centuries AD.

Keinan-Schoonbaert (Chap. 8) discusses the compilation of the West Bank and East Jerusalem Archaeological Database, which documents Israeli archaeological activities in the West Bank between 1967 and 2007. While the database is the most complete archive of these sites, its creation highlighted many issues familiar from the discussion of the DAAHL, mentioned above. Much of the data was difficult to find, some of it remains unpublished, and different sources occasionally had contradictory data. Additionally, the data reveals the biases of the surveyors who were primarily interested in Bronze Age-Roman period sites; the Paleolithic-Neolithic and Islamic periods were generally not a focus, and this is represented in the data. The political issues lurking in this chapter, particularly concerning Israeli archaeologists working in the occupied territories and the lack of recognition of the Green Line by some of these researchers, likewise highlight the importance of and controversies surrounding heritage in the present, and force consideration of whose grand narratives are being told.

Conclusion

Overall, the contributors to this volume make a compelling, if occasionally cautious, case for the ability of cyber-archaeology to contribute to the revival of grand narratives. The limitations of new techniques and the problems of disparate legacy datasets must, of course, be kept in mind. Recognizing these limitations should not, however, prevent archaeologists from using innovative technologies and large databases to ask questions about sociopolitical and technological change on a large scale and in the long term. The chapters in this volume demonstrate that it is possible to ask new questions of old data and show a concern with data standardization and openness that promises to make addressing large-scale questions increasingly easy in the future.

References

Arbuckle, B. S., Kansa, S. W., Kansa, E., Orton, D., Çakırlar, C., Gourichon, L., et al. (2014). Data sharing reveals complexity in the westward spread of domestic animals across Neolithic Turkey. *PloS One, 9*(6), e99845. doi:10.1371/journal.pone.0099845.

Atici, L., Kansa, S. W., Lev-Tov, J., & Kansa, E. C. (2013). Other people's data: A demonstration of the imperative of publishing primary data. *Journal of Archaeological Method and Theory, 20*(4), 663–681. doi:10.1007/s10816-012-9132-9.

Averett, E. W., Gordon, J. M., & Counts, D. B. (Eds.). (2016). *Mobilizing the past for a digital future: The potential of digital archaeology*. Grand Forks: The Digital Press at the University of North Dakota.

Belussi, A., & Migliorini, S. (2014). A framework for managing temporal dimensions in archaeological data. In *21st international symposium on temporal representation and reasoning* (pp. 81–90). Verona: IEEE.

Berggren, Å., Dell'Unto, N., Forte, M., Haddow, S., Hodder, I., Issavi, J., et al. (2015). Revisiting reflexive archaeology at Çatalhöyük: Integrating digital and 3D technologies at the trowel's edge. *Antiquity, 89*(344), 433–448. doi:10.15184/aqy.2014.43.

Bintliff, J. (Ed.). (1991). *The Annales school and archaeology*. Leicester: Leicester University Press.

Boas, A. J. (1998). Archaeological sources for the history of Palestine: The Frankish period: A unique medieval society emerges. Near Eastern. *Archaeology, 61*(3), 138–173.

Bolender, D. J. (Ed.). (2010). *Eventful archaeologies: New approaches to social transformation in the archaeological record*. Albany: State University of New York Press.

Bowker, G. C. (2000a). Biodiversity datadiversity. *Social Studies of Science, 30*(5), 643–683.

Bowker, G. C. (2000b). Mapping biodiversity. *International Journal of Geographical Information Science, 14*(8), 739–754.

Bradbury, J., Davies, D., Jay, M., Philip, G., Roberts, C., & Scarre, C. (2016). Making the dead visible: Problems and solutions for "big" picture approaches to the past, and dealing with large "mortuary" datasets. *Journal of Archaeological Method and Theory, 23*, 561–591. doi:10.1007/s10816-015-9251-1.

Braudel, F. (1970). History and the social sciences: The long term. *Social Science Information, 9*(1), 144–174.

Cascalheira, J., Gonçalves, C., & Bicho, N. (2014). Smartphones and the use of customized apps in archaeological projects. *The SAA Archaeological Record, 14*(5), 20–25.

Chenhall, R. G. (1967). The description of archaeological data in computer language. *American Antiquity, 32*(2), 161–167.

Childe, V. G. (1944). Archaeological ages as technological stages. *The Journal of the Royal Anthropological Institute of Great Britain and Ireland, 74*(1/2), 7–24.

Childe, V. G. (1950). The urban revolution. *The Town Planning Review, 21*(1), 3–17.

Childe, V. G. (1952). The birth of civilisation. *Past & Present, 2*, 1–10.

Cline, E. H. (2014). *1177 B.C.: The year civilization collapsed*. Princeton: Princeton University Press.

Concannon, C., & Mazurek, L. A. (Eds.). (2016). *Across the corrupting sea: Post-Braudelian approaches to the ancient eastern Mediterranean*. London/New York: Routledge.

Cowgill, G. L. (1967). Computer applications in archaeology. In *AFIPS'67: Proceedings of the fall joint computer conference, november 14–16, 1967, AFIPS conference proceedings* (Vol. 31, pp. 331–337). Washington, DC/London: Thompson Books/Academic Press.

Dallas, C. (2015). Curating archaeological knowledge in the digital continuum: From practice to infrastructure. *Open Archaeology, 1*, 176–207.

De Landa, M. (1997). *A thousand years of nonlinear history*. Brooklyn: Zone Books.

Emberling, G. (Ed.). (2016). *Social theory in archaeology and ancient history: The present and future of counternarratives*. New York: Cambridge University Press.

Evans, T. L., & Daly, P. (Eds.). (2006). *Digital archaeology: Bridging method and theory*. London/New York: Routledge.

Fee, S. B., Pettegrew, D. K., & Caraher, W. R. (2013). Taking mobile computing to the field. *Near Eastern Archaeology, 76*(1), 50–55.

Forte, M. (Ed.). (2010). *Cyber-archaeology*. Oxford: Archaeopress.

Forte, M. (2011). Cyber-archaeology: Notes on the simulation of the past. *Virtual Archaeology Review, 2*(4), 7–18.

Forte, M. (2016). Cyber archaeology: 3D sensing and digital embodiment. In M. Forte & S. Campana (Eds.), *Digital methods and remote sensing in archaeology: Archaeology in the age of sensing* (pp. 271–289). Cham: Springer. https://doi.org/10.1007/978-3-319-40658-9_12.

Forte, M., & Siliotti, A. (Eds.). (1997). *Virtual archaeology: Re-creating ancient worlds*. New York: H. N. Abrams.

Gardin, J.-C. (1958). Four codes for the description of artifacts: An essay in archaeological technique and theory. *American Anthropologist, 60*(2), 335–357.

Gardin, J. C. (1967). Methods for the descriptive analysis of archaeological material. *American Antiquity, 32*(1), 13–30.

Gidding, A., Matsui, Y., Levy, T. E., Defanti, T., & Kuester, F. (2013). ArchaeoSTOR: A data curation system for research on the archeological frontier. *Future Generation Computer Systems, 29*(8), 2117–2127. doi:10.1016/j.future.2013.04.007.

Hart, S., & Falkner, R. K. (1985). Preliminary report on a survey in Edom, 1984. *Annual of the Department of Antiquities of Jordan, 29*, 255–277.

Hastings, J. (1982). Potsherds into printouts: The ban chiang computer project. *Expedition, 24*(4), 37–41.

Hodder, I. (Ed.). (1987). *Archaeology as long-term history*. Cambridge: Cambridge University Press.

Hodder, I. (2000). Agency and individuals in long-term processes. In M.-A. Dobres & J. E. Robb (Eds.), *Agency in archaeology* (pp. 21–33). London: Routledge.

Horden, P., & Purcell, N. (2000). *The corrupting sea: A study of Mediterranean history*. Malden: Blackwell.

Huggett, J. (2012). Lost in information? Ways of knowing and modes of representation in e-archaeology. *World Archaeology, 44*(4), 538–552. doi:10.1080/00438243.2012.736274.

Huggett, J. (2015). A manifesto for an introspective digital archaeology. *Open Archaeology, 1*, 86–95.

Iacovou, M. (2007). Site size estimates and the diversity factor in late Cypriot settlement histories. *Bulletin of the American Schools of Oriental Research, 348*, 1–23.

Jeffrey, S. (2012). A new digital dark age? Collaborative web tools, social media and long-term preservation. *World Archaeology, 44*(4), 553–570. doi:10.1080/00438243.2012.737579.

Jones, I. W. N., Najjar, M., & Levy, T. E. (2014). "Not found in the order of history": Toward a "medieval" archaeology of southern Jordan. In S. D. Stull (Ed.), *From west to east: Current approaches to medieval archaeology* (pp. 179–205). Newcastle-upon-Tyne: Cambridge Scholars.

Kansa, E. C. (2010). Open context in context: Cyberinfrastructure and distributed approaches to publish and preserve archaeological data. *The SAA Archaeological Record, 10*(5), 12–16.

Kansa, S. W. (2015). Using linked open data to improve data reuse in zooarchaeology. *Ethnobiology Letters, 6*(2), 224–231. doi:10.14237/ebl.6.2.2015.467.

Kansa, E. C., & Kansa, S. W. (2011). Toward a do-it-yourself cyberinfrastructure: Open data, incentives, and reducing costs and complexities of data sharing. In E. C. Kansa, S. W. Kansa, & E. Watrall (Eds.), *Archaeology 2.0: New approaches to communication and collaboration* (pp. 57–91). Los Angeles: Cotsen Institute of Archaeology Press.

Kansa, E. C., & Kansa, S. W. (2013). We all know that a 14 is a sheep: Data publication and professionalism in archaeological communication. *Journal of Eastern Mediterranean Archaeology and Heritage Studies, 1*(1), 88–97.

Kansa, S. W., & MacKinnon, M. (2014). Etruscan economics: Forty-five years of faunal remains from Poggio Civitate. Etruscan. *Studies, 17*(1), 63–87.

Kansa, S. W., Kansa, E. C., & Schultz, J. M. (2007). An open context for Near Eastern archaeology. *Near Eastern Archaeology, 70*(4), 188–194.

Kansa, E. C., Kansa, S. W., Burton, M. M., & Stankowski, C. (2010). Googling the grey: Open data, web services, and semantics. *Archaeologies, 6*(2), 301–326. doi:10.1007/s11759-010-9146-4.

Kansa, E. C., Kansa, S. W., & Watrall, E. (Eds.). (2011). *Archaeology 2.0: New tools for communication and collaboration*. Los Angeles: Cotsen Institute of Archaeology Press.

Kansa, E. C., Kansa, S. W., & Arbuckle, B. (2014). Publishing and pushing: Mixing models for communicating research data in archaeology. *International Journal of Digital Curation, 9*(1), 57–70.

Kintigh, K. (2006). The promise and challenge of archaeological data integration. *American Antiquity, 71*(3), 567–578.

Kintigh, K. W., & Altschul, J. H. (2010). Sustaining the digital archaeological record. *Heritage Management, 3*(2), 264–274.

Knapp, A. B. (Ed.). (1992). *Archaeology, annales, and ethnohistory*. Cambridge: Cambridge University Press.

Kowalewski, S. A. (2008). Regional settlement pattern studies. *Journal of Archaeological Research, 16*, 225–285.

LaBianca, Ø. S. (2007). Great and little traditions: A framework for studying cultural interaction through the ages in Jordan. In F. al-Khraysheh (Ed.), *Studies in the history and archaeology of Jordan IX: Cultural interaction through the ages* (pp. 275–289). Amman: Department of Antiquities of Jordan.

Labrador, A. M. (2012). Ontologies of the future and interfaces for all: Archaeological databases for the twenty-first century. *Archaeologies, 8*(3), 236–249. doi:10.1007/s11759-012-9203-2.

Lake, M. (2012). Open archaeology. *World Archaeology, 44*(4), 471–478. doi:10.1080/00438243.2012.748521.

Lercari, N., Schulze, J., Wendrich, W., Porter, B., Burton, M., & Levy, T. E. (2016). 3-D digital preservation of at-risk global cultural heritage. In C. E. Catalano & L. De Luca (Eds.), *Eurographics workshop on graphics and cultural heritage, 2016*. Aire-la-Ville: Eurographics Association. doi:10.2312/gch.20161395.

Levy, T. E. (2006). Grand narratives, technological revolutions and the past: Deep-time studies of metallurgy and social evolution in the eastern Mediterranean. In Ø. S. LaBianca & S. A. Scham (Eds.), *Connectivity in antiquity: Globalization as a long-term historical process* (pp. 10–25). London: Equinox.

Levy, T. E. (2013). Cyber-archaeology and world cultural heritage: Insights from the holy land. *Bulletin of the American Academy of Arts and Sciences, 66*(3), 26–33.

Levy, T. E., & Smith, N. G. (2007). On-site GIS digital archaeology: GIS-based excavation recording in southern Jordan. In T. E. Levy, P. M. M. Daviau, R. W. Younker, & M. Shaer (Eds.), *Crossing Jordan: North american contributions to the archaeology of Jordan* (pp. 47–58). London: Equinox.

Levy, T. E., Anderson, J. D., Waggoner, M., Smith, N., Muniz, A., & Adams, R. B. (2001). Interface: Archaeology and technology – Digital archaeology 2001: GIS-based excavation recording in Jordan. *The SAA Archaeological Record, 1*(3), 23–29.

Levy, T. E., Petrovic, V., Wypych, T., Gidding, A., Knabb, K., Hernandez, D., et al. (2010). On-site digital archaeology 3.0 and cyberarchaeology: Into the future of the past – New developments, delivery and the creation of a data avalanche. In M. Forte (Ed.), *Cyberarchaeology* (pp. 135–153). Oxford: Archaeopress.

Levy, T. E., Smith, N. G., Najjar, M., DeFanti, T. A., Lin, A. Y.-M., & Kuester, F. (2012). *Cyber-archaeology in the holy land: The future of the past*. Washington, DC: Biblical Archaeology Society.

Lin, A. Y.-M., Huynh, A., Lanckriet, G., & Barrington, L. (2014). Crowdsourcing the unknown: The satellite search for genghis khan. *PLoS One, 9*(12), e114046. https://doi.org/10.1371/journal.pone. 0114046.

Lucas, G. (2005). *The archaeology of time*. London/New York: Routledge.

Lyotard, J.-F. (1984). *The postmodern condition: A report on knowledge* (trans: Bennington, G. & Massumi, B.). Minneapolis: University of Minnesota Press.

MacDonald, B. (1988). *The Wadi el Hasa archaeological survey 1979–1983, west-Central Jordan*. Waterloo: Wilfrid Laurier University Press.

Manger, L., & LaBianca, Ø. S. (Eds.). (2009). *Global moments in the Levant: A Unifob global research project*. Bergen: Unifob Global.

Mayer, H. E. (1987). The Crusader lordship of Kerak and Shaubak: Some preliminary remarks. In A. Hadidi (Ed.), *Studies in the history and archaeology of Jordan III* (pp. 199–203). Amman: Department of Antiquities of Jordan.

Mccoy, M. D., & Ladefoged, T. N. (2009). New developments in the use of spatial technology in archaeology. *Journal of Archaeological Research, 17*(3), 263–295. https://doi.org/10.1007/s10814-009-9030-1.

McManamon, F. P., & Kintigh, K. W. (2010). Digital antiquity: Transforming archaeological data into knowledge. *The SAA Archaeological Record, 10*(2), 37–40.

Miller, J. M. (Ed.). (1991). *Archaeological survey of the Kerak Plateau*. Atlanta: Scholars Press.

Myers, D., & Dalgity, A. (2012). The middle eastern geodatabase for antiquities (MEGA): An open source GIS-based heritage site inventory and management system. *Change Over Time, 2*(1), 32–57.

Palumbo, G. (2012). Twenty-five years of archaeological site inventories in the Middle East: Challenges and perspectives. *Change Over Time, 2*(1), 20–31.

Petrovic, V., Gidding, A., Wypych, T., Kuester, F., DeFanti, T. A., & Levy, T. E. (2011). Dealing with archaeology's data avalanche. *Computer, 44*(7), 56–60. doi:10.1109/MC.2011.161.

Prins, A. B., Adams, M. J., Homsher, R. S., & Ashley, M. (2014). Digital archaeological fieldwork and the Jezreel Valley regional project, Israel. *Near Eastern Archaeology, 77*(3), 192–197.

Redfield, R. (1955). The social organization of tradition. *Far Eastern Quarterly, 15*(1), 13–21.

Robb, J., & Pauketat, T. R. (Eds.). (2013). *Big histories, human lives: Tackling problems of scale in archaeology*. Santa Fe: School for Advanced Research Press.

Roosevelt, C. H., Cobb, P., Moss, E., Olson, B. R., & Ünlüsoy, S. (2015). Excavation is ~~destruction~~ digitization: Advances in archaeological practice. *Journal of Field Archaeology, 40*(3), 325–346. doi:10.1179/2042458215Y.0000000004.

Rosenau, P. M. (1992). *Post-modernism and the social sciences: Insights, inroads, and intrusions*. Princeton: Princeton University Press.

Savage, S. H., & Levy, T. E. (2014a). DAAHL—The digital archaeological atlas of the holy land: A model for Mediterranean and world archaeology. *Near Eastern Archaeology, 77*(3), 243–247.

Savage, S. H., & Levy, T. (2014b). The Mediterranean archaeological network – a cyberinfrastructure for archaeological heritage management. *Mediterranean Archaeology and Archaeometry, 14*(4), 135–141.

Schick, R. (1997). Southern Jordan in the Fatimid and Seljuq periods. *Bulletin of the American Schools of Oriental Research, 305*, 73–85.

Schloen, J. D., & Schloen, S. R. (2012). *OCHRE: An online cultural and historical research environment*. Winona Lake: Eisenbrauns.

Sewell, W. H., Jr. (1996). Historical events as transformations of structures: Inventing revolution at the bastille. *Theory and Society, 25*, 841–881.

Sheehan, B. (2015). Comparing digital archaeological repositories: tDAR versus open context. *Behavioral and Social Sciences Librarian, 34*(4), 173–213. https://doi.org/10.1080/01639269.2015.1096155.

Sherratt, A. (1983). The secondary exploitation of animals in the old world. *World Archaeology, 15*(1), 90–104.

Sherratt, A. (1995). Reviving the grand narrative: Archaeology and long-term change. *Journal of European Archaeology, 3*(1), 1–32.

Shott, M. (2014). Digitizing archaeology: A subtle revolution in analysis. *World Archaeology, 46*(1), 1–9. doi:10.1080/00438243.2013.879046.

Sideris, A., Liritzis, I., Liss, B., Howland, M. D., & Levy, T. E. (2017). At-risk cultural heritage: New excavations and finds from the mycenaean site of kastrouli, phokis, Greece. *Mediterranean Archaeology and Archaeometry, 17*(1), 271–285. doi:10.5281/zenodo.163772.

Smith, N., & Levy, T. (2014a). ArchField: A digital application for real-time acquisition and dissemination – From the field to the virtual museum. *Mediterranean Archaeology and Archaeometry, 14*(4), 65–74.

Smith, N. G., & Levy, T. E. (2014b). ArchField in Jordan: Real-time GIS data recording for archaeological excavations. *Near Eastern Archaeology, 77*(3), 166–170.

Smith, N. G., Karasik, A., Narayanan, T., Olson, E. S., Smilansky, U., & Levy, T. E. (2012). The pottery informatics query database: A new method for mathematic and quantitative analyses of large regional ceramic datasets. *Journal of Archaeological Method and Theory, 21*, 212–250. https://doi.org/10.1007/s10816-012-9148-1.

Snow, D. R., Gahegan, M., Giles, C. L., Hirth, K. G., Milner, G. R., Mitra, P., et al. (2006). Cybertools and archaeology. *Science, 311*(5763), 958–959.

Srour, D., Mangan, J., Hoff, A., Margolis, T., Block, J., Vincent, M. L., et al. (2015). MediaCommons framework: An immersive storytelling platform and exodus. In T. E. Levy, T. Schneider, & W. H.

C. Propp (Eds.), *Israel's exodus in transdisciplinary perspective: Text, archaeology, culture, and geoscience* (pp. 173–184). Cham: Springer. https://doi.org/10.1007/978-3-319-04768-3_13.
Tartaron, T. F. (2013). *Maritime networks in the Mycenaean world.* New York: Cambridge University Press.
Vincent, M. L., Kuester, F., & Levy, T. E. (2014). OpenDig: Digital field archaeology, curation, publication, and dissemination. *Near Eastern Archaeology, 77*(3), 204–208.
Walker, B. J. (1999). Militarization to nomadization: The middle and late Islamic periods. Near Eastern. *Archaeology, 62*(4), 202–232.
Walker, B. (2011). The phenomenon of the "disappearing" villages of late medieval Jordan, as reflected in archaeological and economic sources. *Bulletin d'etudes orientales, 60*, 161–176.

Chapter 2
3D Recording in the Field: Style Without Substance?

Matthew D. Howland

Introduction

Three-dimensional field recording is one of the fastest-growing applications in archaeology today. Increasing numbers of archaeological field projects are applying 3D methods, including laser scanning and image-based modeling. 3D recording's proponents have cited its precision and accuracy for making measurements, its efficiency in the field, and its cost-effectiveness for some applications (De Reu et al. 2014; Doneus et al. 2011: 84; Forte 2014: 13; Jorayev et al. 2016; Lambers et al. 2007; Magnani and Schroder 2015; Quartermaine et al. 2014; Reshetyuk and Mårtensson 2016; Roosevelt 2014; Sapirstein 2016; Verhoeven 2011). Criticisms or cautions aimed at the "3D revolution" have warned that certain applications of these methods may prioritize their aesthetics over their usefulness to legitimate research inquiry (Forte 2014: 2). Uncritical application of developing technology is not a phenomenon new to archaeology—similar criticisms have been leveled at GIS (Church, Brandon, and Burgett 2000; Fletcher and Winter 2008: 2; Kvamme 1999: 174; McCoy and Ladefoged 2009: 282). Yet the intervening decades have shown GIS to be a powerful tool, allowing for methodological advances and new types of analysis to be performed. The utility of 3D recording techniques to archaeology has not been similarly resolved yet, despite recognition of the importance of this issue (Olson and Placchetti 2015; Opitz 2015).

Ultimately, widespread adoption of three-dimensional approaches will depend on whether or not these methods have the potential to aid in answering archaeological research questions. The usefulness of any technology to archaeologists can be understood in three ways, ranging from most useful to least: first, that the technique will be applicable to understanding the social and ideological structures of the past, ancient lifeways, and culture change. The investigation of these concepts is the basis

M.D. Howland (✉)
University of California, San Diego, CA, USA
e-mail: mdhowlan@ucsd.edu

T.E. Levy, I.W.N. Jones (eds.), *Cyber-Archaeology and Grand Narratives*,
One World Archaeology, https://doi.org/10.1007/978-3-319-65693-9_2

of much current archaeological research, and as such, any emergent technology's usefulness in shedding light on these aspects of the past must be considered in its adoption by archaeologists. A secondary form of utility for the technique could be found in the realm of a purely methodological advance. An approach that cannot directly shed light on the past might still prove useful to archaeologists by allowing for an improvement in already applied methods, such as an increase in the precision and/or accuracy of spatial recording. A third scenario for the usefulness of 3D technology is the bleakest for its future: that these techniques are not applicable to relevant archaeological research questions and that they do not represent a methodological improvement. In such a case, we would expect reports of a "3D revolution" in archaeology to be greatly exaggerated. Three-dimensional field recording might then be relegated to party-trick status, applied only to impress onlookers, donors, or students with 3D models. We can thus expect the future of 3D modeling to resemble one of these scenarios: that it is useful for examining ancient culture and society, useful in the day-to-day practice of archaeological excavation or investigation, or, lastly, that it is ultimately not worth bothering with. These options, running the gamut from critical tool to flash in the pan, define the best- and worst-case scenarios for the utility of 3D archaeology. A discussion of to what extent 3D field recording can put meat on the bones of the archaeological record and provide insight into relevant research questions is important to have, especially at a time when many archaeologists are considering its use.

Background

Two main 3D field recording technologies are most often applied in archaeology: laser scanning and image-based modeling (henceforth IBM). To be clear, these are not the only three-dimensional technologies applied to archaeology, nor do they account for the rapidly expanding category of 3D–based lab analysis of artifacts (e.g., Bretzke and Conard 2012; Karasik and Smilansky 2008). However, this discussion will focus on 3D recording in the field, which is primarily done through laser scanning and IBM. These two methods have emerged, hand in hand, in recent years as the most widely applied techniques of three-dimensional field recording. Each of these techniques has different advantages and disadvantages, justifying a short introduction.

Laser scanning, broadly, refers to the collection of tens of thousands to millions of data points through shooting lasers onto an object and recording its position in 3D space (relative to the scanner). Points from laser scanning, in addition to spatial coordinates, also can contain limited color values, originating from a camera often included in the laser scanner. Laser scanning is performed through one of three main measurement techniques: the time-of-flight method, the phase comparison method, and the triangulation method. In time-of-flight scanning, the most popular variety for application at archaeological excavations, a laser pulse is emitted from the scanner and reflected from the target object back to the scanner, at which point the amount of time the reflection took and the angle of the initial pulse are used as the basis to calculate the location of the reflecting object (Boehler and Marbs 2002; Lerma et al. 2010: 501). The phase comparison method works similarly to the time-of-flight method, though the scanner also records the difference in between the wavelength of the emitted beam and the reflected light. This can result in more accurate point detection, though the range of the scanner and the number of successfully recorded points may suffer (Boehler and Marbs 2002). Lastly, the triangulation method separates the laser emitter from the camera, which identifies the position of the laser on the object. This final approach can be more useful for short-range scanning (Boehler and Marbs 2002; Lerma et al. 2010: 501). Our discussion of laser scanning will be limited to time-of-flight methods, as these are most common in field archaeology. This approach can be applied with a terrestrial scanner or a scanner mounted on a plane, referred to as aerial laser scanning (ALS) or LiDAR (**Li**ght **D**etection **A**nd **R**anging; an excellent overview of LiDAR as a technology is available in White 2013). In general, laser scanning has been praised for its ability to record highly precise and accurate point data, with millimeter or submillimeter precision possible depending on the specific equipment (Yastikli 2007: 424). As such, the technique is the gold standard of precision and accuracy in 3D field recording of archaeological excavation (Boehler and Marbs 2004: 297). However, laser scanners also rely on line-of-sight recording, meaning that occlusions in recorded datasets can be common, especially at topographically complex archaeological sites. Resolving this issue requires the taking of multiple scans and the co-registration of these separate point cloud datasets (Al-Kheder et al. 2009: 540–2). This can be a potentially lengthy and difficult process, depending on how many scans are required (Lerma et al. 2010: 501; Levy et al. 2010: 140). A laser scanner is also an unwieldy piece of equipment, the price of which can run well beyond the reach of smaller archaeological projects at tens or hundreds of thousands of dollars (Boehler and Marbs 2004: 292).

Image-based modeling is a second option for three-dimensional archaeological field recording. IBM refers to the creation of 3D models from photography taken of a target object from multiple directions, a process of digital photogrammetry. The method of data capture for IBM must necessarily be adapted to the size and shape of the object of interest in each case, but the basic principles are similar regardless of exact approach. IBM requires that many (ranging from tens to thousands) photos be taken of the target and that each image share a considerable overlap with adjacent images (the user's manual for Agisoft Photoscan, one IBM program, suggests >60% overlap between images [Agisoft 2017]). This is due to the fact that reconstruction of the object occurs through identification of the same point in multiple images. As such, any part of the object or area of interest must be present in at least two images in order to be reconstructed (Agisoft 2017). Quality reconstructions of objects or areas of interest depend on the acquisition of detailed images with comprehensive coverage of the target; however, expensive equipment is not required for generating viable 3D models. Best practices for data capture would include a DSLR camera with a fixed focal length lens shooting in RAW format, but results are also achievable with setups as simple as a cell phone camera or inexpensive point-and-shoot.

Whatever the camera arrangement, acquiring comprehensive overlapping coverage is the most important factor in generating a complete and detailed model.

Once the photos are taken, processing IBM models typically consists of three or more main steps. First, an algorithm identifies identical points across multiple images, triangulating their location as well as that of the camera when the photograph was taken in arbitrary space. This process results in the creation of a sparse point cloud. A dense point cloud, consisting of substantially more points, may be developed as a subsequent stage. In the second main step of IBM processing, the point cloud is used as the basis to form a mesh, a continuous 3D model constructed of polygons. In the last stage of model development, the images used to create the model are mosaicked or averaged onto the mesh to create a more-or-less photorealistic 3D model. IBM software packages contain one or all of these processing capabilities, with some programs also offering additional features such as the ability to edit models between stages or georeference the 3D model. IBM's advocates have highlighted the technology's cost-effectiveness, given that its application requires only a basic digital camera and software, and its efficiency in field recording (Olson et al. 2013; Lerma et al. 2010: 500). The simplicity of IBM's workflow (depending on the software used to implement it) has also been praised by its users (Kjellman 2012: 23). The technology, though not usually as precise or accurate as laser scanning, can rival laser scanning in these regards when precisely and carefully used (Doneus et al. 2011: 84–5). IBM—like laser scanning—can be applied terrestrially or aerially.

Review

Before considering the usefulness of these 3D technologies for addressing broader questions in archaeology, we must turn to how they are applied in the field today. Our discussion will begin with laser scanning, which had been more widely applied by archaeologists until very recently. Laser scanning, as mentioned, allows for both terrestrial and aerial approaches. Archaeological applications of terrestrial laser scanning have most frequently related to the recording, documentation, and preservation of monuments and ancient art (see De Reu et al. 2013 for examples). These uses often border on the related fields of cultural heritage and/or cultural resource management. Laser scanning has been less often applied to actively excavated archaeological sites, though these uses still occur (Doneus and Neubauer 2005; Forte 2014; Levy et al. 2010: 138–42; Neubauer 2004: 162–3; Schreiber et al. 2012). The length of time per laser scan (upwards of 1.5 h, according to Levy et al. [2010: 140]), the necessity of multiple scans for complete coverage (which then necessitates co-registration of point clouds), and the cost of laser scanners (potentially tens of thousands of dollars or more, prohibitively expensive for many projects) may explain why terrestrial laser scanning has not seen widespread adoption on active excavations, despite its widely touted accuracy.

Aerial laser scanning (or LiDAR), on the other hand, has become increasingly popular with archaeologists in recent years. LiDAR has been used primarily for two purposes: for the collection of high-resolution elevation data at an inter-site/inter-regional scale for background data or mapping and for investigative survey of heavily vegetated areas. Archaeologists have made use of LiDAR's resolution to identify and map archaeological features across the landscape through their identification in elevation differential as seen in the point cloud or a derived DEM (Fisher and Leisz 2013; Harmon et al. 2006; Štular et al. 2012). Archaeologists have also applied LiDAR in heavily vegetated areas in order to get a view of the ground below the canopy. By applying certain filters to the point cloud data acquired from aerial scans, archaeologists have been able to filter out points recorded on the vegetation, leaving only a subset of the points consisting of laser strikes on the ground (Devereux et al. 2005; Sithole and Vosselman 2004). The remaining points from this process enable the creation of a digital terrain model (DTM) consisting of only elevation data from ground level, as opposed to a digital surface model, which consists of the highest recorded elevation, i.e., including vegetation (Doneus et al. 2008; White 2013: 183–4). This application of LiDAR has become especially popular in regions where sites and the archaeological landscape are often obscured by dense vegetation, allowing researchers to identify features and sites under the canopy (e.g., Chase et al. 2013; Evans 2016; Fernandez-Diaz et al. 2014; Hare et al. 2014).

Image-based modeling—though sometimes applied in concert with laser scanning—is often used differently than its laser-based counterpart. Terrestrial applications of IBM often relate to the modeling of excavation units or specific contexts at archaeological sites (De Reu et al. 2013; De Reu et al. 2014) or to the lab-based recording of artifacts, which is beyond the scope of this chapter. Archaeologists have applied IBM for recording of excavation units because of the temporal efficiency of this approach and its benefits for accurate recording of archaeological features (Verhoeven et al. 2012; Olson et al. 2013). Scholars have applied the technique for the generation of orthophotographs for the purpose of digitization of features (Quartermaine et al. 2014: 115–7), updating the method of field recording by drawing directly on vertical imagery in GIS (Levy and Smith 2007: 53). These vertical images can also be captured by aerial photography platforms (such as UAVs or balloons), and archaeologists have applied these airborne systems to record excavation units as well (Howland et al. 2014; Quartermaine et al. 2014). However, aerial applications of IBM are more often performed at a sitewide scale, where researchers have used the technique to collect GIS-compatible datasets such as orthophotos and digital elevation models (DEMs) for site mapping (Howland et al. 2014; Verhoeven et al. 2012). Aerial IBM is gaining popularity as an archaeological field recording technique as the use of UAVs/drones becomes increasingly popular and effective (Remondino et al. 2011; Verhoeven et al. 2012). IBM does suffer from limitations related to lighting conditions, including an inability to function at night or in poor lighting conditions (Lercari 2016: 8). In general, however, IBM has seen widespread adoption over the past several years due to the cost-effectiveness and temporal efficiency of the technique in the field.

Evaluation

Techniques of 3D recording in archaeology have spread far and fast in recent years in what some have called a "3D revolution" (Guery and Hautefort 2014). The question of whether or not the contributions of these techniques will remain relevant after their novelty fades remains, however. Whether or not these approaches can contribute to outstanding archaeological research questions is also an outstanding issue. Each of the four techniques detailed above has been applied by archaeologists in differing ways, so it is important to continue to separate them when evaluating their effectiveness in contributing to grand narratives in archaeology.

Terrestrial laser scanning, providing the most precise and accurate data of any 3D field recording method applied to archaeology, is probably the least likely to achieve widespread adoption. The prohibitive cost of laser scanners as well as the time required to properly scan and process data from archaeological terrain means that laser scanners are unlikely to be applied regularly for the recording of active excavations in the near future. Thus, their effectiveness in answering archaeological research questions is necessarily limited. However, the recording of more static archaeological features is still a possibility, and laser scanning sees wide use in the related fields of cultural heritage and archaeological conservation, given that the technology's precision allows for the monitoring of monuments or structures for degradation over time or structural defects (Al-Kheder et al. 2009; Armesto-González et al. 2010; Fanti et al. 2013). This type of application of the technique is effective, as data acquired through terrestrial laser scanning is extremely precise and avoids much of the human error inherent to field measurements. In fact, the majority of uses of terrestrial laser scanning relate primarily to documentation for the sake of preserving the present form of a structure or site or guiding conservation efforts. Even proponents of TLS have highlighted its particular usefulness for "large-scale data capture of buildings and heritage sites" (Lercari 2016: 27). Despite the usefulness of terrestrial laser scanning for documenting static contexts, however, archaeologists do not often make use of the approach for the generation of new archaeological knowledge, thus missing the potential of terrestrial laser scanning for explaining or understanding the behavior of ancient people. In a few cases, archaeologists have found useful applications for terrestrial laser scanning in these ways, allowing them to conduct measurement-based analyses on archaeological features in the landscape. For example, recent investigations into construction techniques and uses of "desert kites" in the Negev using terrestrial laser scanning serve as an example of one particularly useful application of the technology, providing an insight into past labor, subsistence, and lifeways (Arav et al. 2014; Nadel et al. 2013). Yet this example is a rare case of archaeological fieldwork applying terrestrial laser scanning to gain a greater understanding of how and why a particular feature was used. It does, however, show the potential of the approach for understanding how and why ancient people modified and constructed their environments in the ways that they did. Thus, while terrestrial laser scanning clearly possesses the potential for facilitating complex archaeological analysis and interpretation, it is seldom used in such a way. The jury will remain out on the long-term viability for terrestrial laser scanning to significantly contribute to grander questions for many archaeological projects and depend on dedicated users of the technology to apply it to appropriate research questions. The restrictions of price and time of use will likely remain limitations on the approach going forward, however. As such, it seems that—for the time being, at least—terrestrial laser scanning is not an essential part of the toolkit of the archaeologist looking to investigate culture change or other grand questions in archaeology.

Aerial laser scanning, on the other hand, has already demonstrated substantial utility for archaeologists in a number of ways. This approach retains the characteristic accuracy and precision of terrestrial scanning while also remaining a cost-intensive technique. However, aerial laser scanning possesses an additional advantage over its competitors in remote sensing. Of primary importance is the ability of LiDAR to cut through foliage and allow archaeologists to see the ground level beneath vegetation. This is perhaps the most significant contribution of the technique (Opitz 2016). This capacity of the technology has allowed archaeologists to discover previously unknown sites in heavily forested areas, which may be too densely vegetated for traditional survey approaches (Chase et al. 2013; Fernandez-Diaz et al. 2014; Hare et al. 2014). LiDAR, in these cases, represents not only a methodological advance in terms of aerial survey but also a substantial step forward in our ability to discover sites and understand the spatial patterning of ancient societies. The use of LiDAR for regional data collection, while not as much of a revolutionary advance for the field, also improves archaeologists' ability to collect and use site-scale (e.g., Harmon et al. 2006) or landscape-scale (e.g., Werbrouck et al. 2011) spatial data. These types of data collection initiatives can supply archaeologists with high-resolution elevation data (DEMs on the order of a few meters spatial resolution), much higher than the (ca. 15–30 m) resolution typically available from satellite sources. This type of elevation data can allow for the identification and location of landscape features that may be difficult or impossible to see from the ground, at scales and resolution not achievable through other methods (Bewley et al. 2005; Štular et al. 2012). As such, LiDAR can be a very effective tool for landscape-level feature identification and mapping in both forested and nonforested areas. Given aerial laser scanning's effectiveness for survey across varying biomes, the approach clearly has the potential to be a powerful tool for archaeologists moving forward. The cost of applying this technique may be prohibitive in many cases, but this cost can often be justified, especially where the approach achieves results not possible through other methods, as is the case with survey through heavy vegetation. LiDAR can clearly be seen as a methodological advance for archaeologists interested in acquiring regional elevation and survey data. More important is the question of whether or not the technique can help archaeologists to address grander questions in archaeology, however. From the studies presented above and others, the answer would seem to be yes. As noted already, LiDAR can provide high-resolution dataset elevation in both forested and nonvegetated areas, which can result in the discovery of new sites or archaeological features at known sites. By enabling the expansion of knowledge of the settlement patterns of ancient people at a site or landscape level, aerial laser scanning can contribute new knowledge about the ways in which people lived in the past. Thus, despite the limitations of cost, LiDAR has great potential to substantially contribute to archaeological knowledge in many situations and will likely continue to remain of great use in the future.

Terrestrial IBM, as previously mentioned, has been primarily used for the documentation and recording of excavation units. The main characteristics of this approach that recommend its use are its time and cost efficiency, as well as the simplicity of its application. These characteristics make IBM very easy for archaeological projects to adopt and implement into their workflow. However, the usefulness of photographic-based 3D recording for archaeological research, rather than its ease of use, is the factor that will ultimately determine whether or not it achieves widespread adoption. As noted above, scholars have primarily applied terrestrial IBM for the purposes of documentation and recording of excavation units. Documentation of the process of investigation of a site on a regular basis (e.g., Olson et al. 2013: 252–5) can allow for the creation of photorealistic 3D models at every stage of excavation, made feasible by the temporal efficiency of IBM. Having a complete 3D record of a site as it is excavated facilitates the efforts of future researchers desiring to view loci in their original contexts or even make field measurements (De Reu et al. 2014: 260–1). IBM also has a second purpose for archaeologists in recording and digitization of features, as we have seen. IBM recording allows for the production of orthophotographs, which are an accurate basis for the GIS-based digitization of archaeological features. These images allow for an improvement in accuracy and precision of GIS-based digitization over other methods (De Reu et al. 2014: 260–1; Olson et al. 2013: 254–5). Taking these two aspects of terrestrial IBM recording in concert, we must attempt to determine the extent that their advantages translate to an improved ability to investigate larger issues in archaeology, such as social change and grand narratives in the field. What does seem clear is that terrestrial IBM provides some clear benefits in the documentation of sites, and would seem to greatly facilitate the work of researchers working on data from recorded sites after they are excavated. Bringing the standard of archaeological documentation closer to the high standard of cultural heritage projects must be seen as a significant step forward for archaeology in general. However, this benefit, in and of itself, does not directly contribute to archaeologists' ability to connect the dots of ancient material evidence into a line of broader issues. Similarly, an improvement in the specific accuracy of field recording could be advantageous to archaeologists desiring to attain the highest degree of accuracy possible, but would not necessarily provide any additional aid to archaeologists asking the big questions. Thus, while terrestrial IBM may very well be a useful tool for archaeologists—and one that is increasingly applied for these reasons—it remains a tool and not an approach for answering questions at scales beyond the minutiae of daily excavation.

Aerially applied IBM potentially has a broader utility to match the wider scale at which it is normally applied. Practitioners of aerial IBM have used the technique to record excavation areas, sites, and even larger areas, usually producing DEMs and/or orthophotos as GIS-compatible outputs in addition to 3D models approaching photorealism (Olson et al. 2013; Quartermaine et al. 2014; Verhoeven et al. 2012). These GIS datasets have a substantial resolution advantage over satellite data (by a factor of 10 or more in orthophotos in terms of horizontal resolution, and even more for elevation data), which often is the only readily available source of these types of datasets. IBM-based production of elevation data also provides an efficient alternative to its acquisition through traditional total station survey, which can take up valuable time in the field. These data enable archaeologists to augment their work in a few main ways. First, much like terrestrial IBM, aerial applications of this technique have the potential to improve the accuracy and precision of mapping archaeological features in comparison to the use of georeferenced vertical imagery for the same purpose. IBM recordings of entire sites can also provide a new, potentially invaluable perspective on sites. Combining site-wide scale with local levels of detail, aerial IBM potentially allows archaeologists to discover and investigate patterns at a site not immediately recognizable from the ground. Archaeologists have long recognized the potential for using aerial photography to identify certain types of features that may not be obvious from the ground but immediately stand out when seen from above, such as cropmarks (Bewley 2003). Aerial images can also be effective in identifying partially buried walls or disconnected continuations of walls when these features may be difficult to identify from a lower perspective. Aerial IBM, as a subset of aerial photography, shares these advantages and adds three-dimensional perspective that can help clarify features by viewing from different angles. The GIS datasets produced by aerial IBM also can serve as a basis for intra-site GIS analyses, which potentially require high-resolution GIS datasets not available through other means of acquisition.

The drawbacks of aerial IBM include its accuracy in recording and its applicability in certain environments. IBM, while in some cases reaching the level of accuracy attained by laser scanning, has been criticized for its failure to always do so (Boehler and Marbs 2004: 293). Because aerial IBM is practiced with a camera positioned much farther from the object of interest, pixels in the photographic datasets represent larger real-world areas. For example, while a terrestrial IBM model taken of a small excavation unit might consist of images with pixels representing 1 mm^2 or less, an aerial model of a site might contain images with pixels of 4 cm^2 or more. In other words, an image for a typical terrestrial IBM model might have a ground-sample distance (GSD) of <1 mm, while an aerial image could have a GSD of >2 cm, depending on camera resolution and elevation. In general, the sizes and distances involved in aerial IBM-oriented recording come along with a natural decrease in data resolution and a corresponding expansion in error margins. As such, aerial IBM practitioners would be well advised to take particular care in checking the accuracy of their datasets with other methods, especially if they are relying on their data for point elevations or precise location measurements. The nature of IBM as a line-of-sight technology also carries with it some potential issues. Sites obscured by vegetation may be difficult or impossible to record by aerial IBM, either because of the impracticality of flying balloons or kites among trees or because of the obscuring of features by leaves and branches. IBM also fails to accurately reconstruct scenery in motion, such as tree leaves shifting in the wind.

Aerial IBM also carries a greater risk of loss or breakage of equipment than other 3D field recording methods. Elevating camera equipment tens or hundreds of meters into the air is a risky proposition and can potentially result in its damage or destruction. These limitations and risks, while significant, have not seemed to slow the trend of enthusiastic adoption of aerial IBM approaches in archaeology, however.

Discussion

The approaches detailed above vary in cost and effectiveness, as we have seen. Cost, in particular, can be a prohibitive factor in adoption by archaeological projects. Laser scanning, aerial and terrestrial, is particularly affected by this issue, with aerial LiDAR scans running into the tens of thousands of dollars and terrestrial laser scanning units also in the five-figure range. IBM can provide archaeologists with a cheaper alternative to laser scanning, although potentially at the cost of a loss of accuracy and/or precision. However, one must account for the general downward trend in the prices of developing technology before ruling out the future use of currently expensive technologies. With time, we might expect the costs of pricier equipment, such as a terrestrial laser scanner, to fall into the range of affordability for smaller projects, though this remains to be seen.

We have also discussed the usefulness of these approaches for archaeological research, although this discussion warrants a summary. For regional projects, aerial laser scanning/LiDAR is probably the most useful approach. The scale of recording allowed by aerial laser scanning vastly outpaces other 3D methods. Thus, archaeologists can record large areas with LiDAR, making the approach a legitimate technique of regional site survey. This holds true even in areas covered with heavy vegetation, where LiDAR is still able to record the ground surface after points relating to vegetation are sorted out. This function of LiDAR has already demonstrated the potential to be a game changer for archaeology. Instead of hacking through dense vegetation for days or weeks, archaeologists can conduct vast surveys from their desk chair. Thus, LiDAR can allow for a fuller picture of ancient settlement patterns, shedding light on past lifeways and helping to address grander questions in archaeology. This technology's land-based cousin seems to lack the same capacity to drastically change the way in which archaeology is done. Terrestrial laser scanning does not have the same possibility of recording at broad scales due to problems of occlusion and perspective. These issues also mean that setting up the laser scanner and taking scans multiple times could be necessary. This process of slow yet precise and accurate documentation can be ideal for static monuments, though it is not efficient for the kind of constantly changing conditions found at an archaeological site under active excavation. In any case, the high-resolution documentation of archaeological sites can provide an excellent basis for digitization of features and later reinterpretation by scholars, though it does not necessarily contribute to archaeologists' ability to contribute to theoretical debates in archaeology. The same holds true for terrestrial IBM approaches, which are also effective for digitization of features and later reinterpretation by scholars. Terrestrial IBM is better suited to regular documentation of changing conditions than terrestrial laser scanning due to its rapidity and efficiency of data collection, though it may suffer from lower precision and accuracy in some cases. Again, terrestrial IBM can potentially be an important improvement for archaeologists' methodological toolbox in the field, although it is unlikely to inspire or answer grander questions of human behavior. Aerial IBM approaches allow for the collection of data at a broader scale (though not as broad as aerial LiDAR). The perspective of an aerial dataset can be valuable in its own right for identifying features, while the collection of orthophoto and elevation data at area, site, or even wider scales can be a powerful asset in comprehensive site mapping or conducting intra-site spatial analyses, as we have seen. These more complex approaches to the archaeological record can potentially facilitate the archaeologist's ability to move beyond simple interpretations of ancient material evidence and potentially investigate social and ideological structures of the past. In general, the usefulness of 3D recording of archaeological sites is a mixed bag, as some techniques will improve recording accuracy and precision at sites, while others may provide an avenue of insight into past societies and culture change. Ultimately, as long as 3D recording technologies are applied with caution, preparation, and within a theoretical framework, they can and will be useful to archaeologists going forward.

Conclusion

At the outset of this discussion, we envisioned three possible futures for 3D recording in archaeology: that 3D is flashy but ultimately a distraction from legitimate research, that it represents a methodological advance in field recording, and, most optimistically, that it has potential for helping archaeologists to understand ancient lifeways, society, and culture change. We have seen that in many cases, 3D recording represents a clear methodological advance over traditional recording techniques, demonstrating that there is likely a future for these techniques. Furthermore, some of the excellent work of archaeologists highlighted above demonstrates that, when properly conceived and applied, certain types of 3D recording do have the potential to revolutionize archaeological fieldwork and shed light on some of the driving questions of archaeology. However, the usefulness of 3D recording techniques for archaeological purposes clearly depends on the specific technology itself, as well as the method of its application. Any critical consideration of the appropriateness or usefulness of 3D technology must take this into account and not consider 3D recording approaches to be a monolithic field. To this end, the application of 3D approaches in the field should be tailored specifically to the project in question. Particularly important are the issues of the budget of the project and the clearly defined envisioned research goals of the project. 3D documentation and recording in general is not a cure-all any more than is GIS software, a total station, or even a trowel. One must apply tools to accomplish definite objectives, without which 3D approaches can quickly become a money sink. In general, three-dimensional recording techniques vary greatly in their ability to be effectively applied to active archaeological excavations, with some more applicable than others to facilitate archaeological research and inquiry. Perhaps most encouraging is the possibility of some techniques to raise the level of archaeological analysis. These approaches can—literally and figuratively—provide a new perspective on archaeological sites. As such, it seems reasonable to conclude with a cautiously optimistic view of 3D recording for archaeology. As with many other techniques widely used by archaeologists around the world, 3D recording technologies have the capacity to substantially contribute to our understanding of ancient societies when used judiciously. The utility of these approaches ultimately depends on the way they are used. As such, archaeologists interested in applying three-dimensional technologies to their field projects would be well advised to carefully consider the pros and cons of specific technologies and application strategies with regard to their specific research goals in order to best apply 3D recording.

References

Agisoft. (2017). Agisoft PhotoScan User Manual Professional Edition, Version 1.3.

Al-Kheder, S., Al-shawabke, Y., & Haala, N. (2009). Developing a documentation system for desert palaces in Jordan using 3D scanning and digital photogrammetry. *Journal of Archaeological Science, 36*, 537–546.

Arav, R., Filin, S., Avner, U., Bar-Oz, G., Nachmias, A., & Nadel, D. (2014). Use of terrestrial laser scans for high-resolution documentation and 3D modeling of "desert kites". *Near Eastern Archaeology, 17*(3), 219–222.

Armesto-González, J., Riveiro-Rodríguez, B., González-Aguilera, D., & Teresa Rivas-Brea, M. (2010). Terrestrial laser scanning intensity data applied to damage detection for historical buildings. *Journal of Archaeological Science, 37*(12), 3037–3047.

Bewley, R. H. (2003). Aerial survey for archaeology. *Photogrammetric Record, 18*(104), 273–292.

Bewley, R. H., Crutchley, S. P., & Shell, C. A. (2005). New light on an ancient landscape: Lidar survey in the Stonehenge world heritage site. *Antiquity, 79*(305), 636–647.

Boehler, W., & Marbs, A. (2002). 3D scanning instruments. In W. Böhler (Ed.), *Proceedings of the CIPA WG 6 international workshop on scanning for cultural heritage recording, September 1–2, 2002, Corfu, Greece* (pp. 9–18). Thessaloniki: ZITI.

Boehler, W., & Marbs, A. (2004). 3D scanning and photogrammetry for heritage recording: A comparison. In S. A. Brandt (Ed.), *Proceedings of 12th international conference on geoinformatics: Geospatial information research: Bridging the Pacific and Atlantic, University of Gävle, Sweden* (pp. 291–298). Gävle: Gävle University Press.

Bretzke, K., & Conard, N. J. (2012). Evaluating morphological variability in lithic assemblages using 3D models of stone artifacts. *Journal of Archaeological Science, 39*, 3741–3749.

Chase, A. F., Chase, D. Z., & Weishampel, J. F. (2013). The use of LiDAR at the Maya site of Caracol, Belize. In D. C. Comer & M. J. Harrower (Eds.), *Mapping archaeological landscapes from space* (pp. 199–212). New York: Springer.

Church, T., Brandon, R. J., & Burgett, G. R. (2000). GIS applications in archaeology: Method in search of theory. In K. L. Wescott & R. J. Brandon (Eds.), *Practical applications of GIS for archaeologists: A predictive modeling toolkit* (pp. 135–155). Philadelphia: Taylor & Francis.

De Reu, J., Plets, G., Verhoeven, G., De Smedt, P., Bats, M., Cherretté, B., De Maeyer, W., Deconynck, J., Herremans, D., Laloo, P., Van Meirvenne, M., & De Clercq, W. (2013).

Towards a three-dimensional cost-effective registration of the archaeological heritage. *Journal of Archaeological Science, 40*, 1108–1121.
De Reu, J., De Smedt, P., Herremans, D., Van Meirvenne, M., Laloo, P., & De Clercq, W. (2014). On introducing an image-based 3D reconstruction method in archaeological excavation practice. *Journal of Archaeological Science, 41*, 251–262.
Devereux, B. J., Amable, G. S., Crow, P., & Cliff, A. D. (2005). The potential of airborne lidar for detection of archaeological features under woodland canopies. *Antiquity, 79*, 648–660.
Doneus, M., & Neubauer, W. (2005). 3D laser scanners on archaeological excavations. In *Proceedings of the XXth international symposium CIPA, Torino* (pp. 226–231). Torino: ACTA.
Doneus, M., Briese, C., Fera, M., & Janner, M. (2008). Archaeological prospection of forested areas using full-waveform airborne laser scanning. *Journal of Archaeological Science, 35*(4), 882–893.
Doneus, M., Verhoeven, G., Fera, M., Briese, C., Kucera, M., & Neubauer, W. (2011). From deposit to point cloud—A study of low-cost computer vision approaches for the straightforward documentation of archaeological excavations. *Geoinformatics, 6*, 81–88.
Evans, D. (2016). Airborne laser scanning as a method for exploring long-term socio-ecological dynamics in Cambodia. *Journal of Archaeological Science, 74*, 164–175.
Fanti, R., Gigli, G., Lombardi, L., Tapete, D., & Canuti, P. (2013). Terrestrial laser scanning for rockfall stability analysis in the cultural heritage site of Pitigliano (Italy). *Landslides, 10*(4), 409–420.
Fernandez-Diaz, J. C., Carter, W. E., Shrestha, R. L., Leisz, S. J., Fisher, C. T., Gonzalez, A. M., Thompson, D., & Elkins, S. (2014). Archaeological prospection of north eastern Honduras with airborne mapping LiDAR. In *2014 IEEE international geoscience and remote sensing symposium (IGARSS)* (pp. 902–905). Piscataway: IEEE.
Fisher, C. T., & Leisz, S. (2013). New perspectives on Purépecha urbanism through the use of lidar at the site of Angamuco, Mexico. In D. C. Comer & M. J. Harrower (Eds.), *Mapping archaeological landscapes from space* (pp. 199–212). New York: Springer.
Fletcher, R., & Winter, R. (2008). Prospects and problems in applying GIS to the study of Chalcolithic archaeology in southern Israel. *Bulletin of the American Schools of Oriental Research, 352*, 1–28.
Forte, M. (2014). 3D archaeology: New perspectives and challenges — The example of Çatalhöyük. *Journal of Eastern Mediterranean Archaeology and Heritage Studies, 2*(1), 1–29.
Guery, J., & Hautefort, R. (2014). Perception and representation, the 3D revolution. *EVA Berlin, 2*, 1–7.
Hare, T., Masson, M., & Russell, B. (2014). High-density LiDAR mapping of the ancient city of Mayapán. *Remote Sensing, 6*, 9064–9085.
Harmon, J. M., Leone, M. P., Prince, S. D., & Snyder, M. (2006). LiDAR for archaeological landscape analysis: A case study of two eighteenth-century Maryland plantation sites. *American Antiquity, 71*(4), 649–670.
Howland, M. D., Kuester, F., & Levy, T. E. (2014). Photogrammetry in the field: Documenting, recording, and presenting archaeology. *Mediterranean Archaeology and Archaeometry, 14*(4), 101–108.
Jorayev, G., Wehr, K., Benito-Calvo, A., Njau, J., & de la Torre, I. (2016). Imaging and photogrammetry models of Olduvai Gorge (Tanzania) by unmanned aerial vehicles: A high-resolution digital database for research and conservation of early stone age sites. *Journal of Archaeological Science, 75*, 40–56.
Karasik, A., & Smilansky, U. (2008). 3D scanning technology as a standard archaeological tool for pottery analysis: Practice and theory. *Journal of Archaeological Science, 35*, 1148–1168.
Kjellman, E. (2012). *From 2D to 3D—A Photogrammetric Revolution in Archaeology?* Unpublished M.A. thesis, University of Tromsø.
Kvamme, K. L. (1999). Recent directions and developments in geographical information systems. *Journal of Archaeological Research, 7*(2), 153–201.
Lambers, K., Eisenbeiss, H., Sauerbier, M., Kupferschmidt, D., Gaisecker, T., Sotoodeh, S., & Hanusch, T. (2007). Combining photogrammetry and laser scanning for the recording and

modelling of the late intermediate period site of Pinchango alto, Palpa, Peru. *Journal of Archaeological Science, 34*(10), 1702–1712.

Lercari, N. (2016). Terrestrial laser scanning in the age of sensing. In M. Forte & S. Campana (Eds.), *Digital methods and remote sensing in archaeology* (pp. 3–33). Cham: Springer.

Lerma, J. L., Navarro, S., Cabrelles, M., & Villaverde, V. (2010). Terrestrial laser scanning and close range photogrammetry for 3D archaeological documentation: The upper Palaeolithic cave of Parpalló as a case study. *Journal of Archaeological Science, 37*(3), 499–507.

Levy, T. E., & Smith, N. G. (2007). On-site digital archaeology: GIS-based excavation recording in southern Jordan. In T. E. Levy, M. Daviau, R. Younker, & M. M. Shaer (Eds.), *Crossing Jordan – North American contributions to the archaeology of Jordan* (pp. 47–58). London: Equinox.

Levy, T. E., Petrovic, V., Wypych, T., Gidding, A., Knabb, K., Hernandez, D., Smith, N. G., Schulz, J. P., Savage, S. H., Kuester, F., Ben-Yosef, E., Buitenhuys, C., Barrett, C. J., Najjar, M., & DeFanti, T. (2010). On-site digital archaeology 3.0 and cyber-archaeology: Into the future of the past – New developments, delivery and the creation of a data avalanche. In M. Forte (Ed.), *Cyber-archaeology* (pp. 135–153). Oxford: Archaeopress.

Magnani, M., & Schroder, W. (2015). New approaches to modeling the volume of earthen archaeological features: A case-study from the Hopewell culture mounds. *Journal of Archaeological Science, 64*, 12–21.

McCoy, M. D., & Ladefoged, T. N. (2009). New developments in the use of spatial technology in archaeology. *Journal of Archaeological Research, 17*, 263–295.

Nadel, D., Bar-Oz, G., Avner, U., Malkinson, D., & Boaretto, E. (2013). Ramparts and walls: Building techniques of kites in the Negev Highland. *Quaternary International, 297*, 147–154.

Neubauer, W. (2004). GIS in archaeology—The interface between prospection and excavation. *Archaeological Prospection, 11*(3), 159–166.

Olson, B. R., & Placchetti, R. A. (2015). A discussion of the analytical benefits of image based modeling in archaeology. In B. R. Olson & W. R. Caraher (Eds.), *Visions of substance: 3D imaging in Mediterranean archaeology* (pp. 17–26). Grand Forks: The Digital Press at the University of North Dakota.

Olson, B. R., Placchetti, R., Quartermaine, J., & Killebrew, A. E. (2013). The Tel Akko total archaeology project (Akko, Israel): Assessing the suitability of multi-scale 3D field recording in archaeology. *Journal of Field Archaeology, 38*, 244–262.

Opitz, R. (2015). Three dimensional field recording in archaeology: An example from Gabii. In B. R. Olson & W. R. Caraher (Eds.), *Visions of substance: 3D imaging in Mediterranean archaeology* (pp. 73–86). Grand Forks: The Digital Press at the University of North Dakota.

Opitz, R. (2016). Airborne laserscanning in archaeology: Maturing methods and democratizing applications. In M. Forte & S. Campana (Eds.), *Digital methods and remote sensing in archaeology* (pp. 35–50). Cham: Springer.

Quartermaine, J., Olson, B. R., & Killebrew, A. E. (2014). Image-based modeling approaches to 2D and 3D digital drafting in archaeology at Tel Akko and Qasrin: Two case studies. *Journal of Eastern Mediterranean Archaeology and Heritage Studies, 2*(2), 110–127.

Remondino, F., Barazzetti, L., Nex, F., Scaioni, M., & Sarazzi, D. (2011). UAV photogrammetry for mapping and 3D modeling – Current status and future perspectives. *International Archives of the Photogrammetry, Remote Sensing and Spatial Information Sciences, 38*, 1–7.

Reshetyuk, Y., & Mårtensson, S. (2016). Generation of highly accurate digital elevation models with unmanned aerial vehicles. *Photogrammetric Record, 1*(154), 143–165.

Roosevelt, C. H. (2014). Mapping site-level microtopography with real-time kinematic global navigation satellite systems (RTK GNSS) and unmanned aerial vehicle photogrammetry (UAVP). *Open Archaeology, 1*, 29–53.

Sapirstein, P. (2016). Accurate measurement with photogrammetry at large sites. *Journal of Archaeological Science, 66*, 137–145.

Schreiber, S., Hinzen, K. G., Fleischer, C., & Schütte, S. (2012). Excavation-parallel laser scanning of a medieval cesspit in the archaeological zone, Cologne, Germany. *Journal on Computing and Cultural Heritage, 5*(3), 12.

Sithole, G., & Vosselman, G. (2004). Experimental comparison of filter algorithms for bare-earth extraction from airborne laser scanning point clouds. *ISPRS Journal of Photogrammetry and Remote Sensing, 59*(1–2), 85–101.

Štular, B., Kokalj, Ž., Oštir, K., & Nuninger, L. (2012). Visualization of lidar-derived relief models for detection of archaeological features. *Journal of Archaeological Science, 39*, 3354–3360.

Verhoeven, G. (2011). Taking computer vision aloft – Archaeological three-dimensional reconstructions from aerial photographs with photoscan. *Archaeological Prospection, 18*, 67–73.

Verhoeven, G., Doneus, M., Briese, C., & Vermeulen, F. (2012). Mapping by matching: A computer vision-based approach to fast and accurate georeferencing of archaeological aerial photographs. *Journal of Archaeological Science, 39*, 2060–2070.

Werbrouck, I., Antrop, M., Van Eetvelde, V., Stal, C., De Maeyer, P., Bats, M., Bourgeois, J., Court-Picon, M., Crombé, P., De Reu, J., De Smedt, P., Finke, P. A., Van Meirvenne, M., Verniers, J., & Zwertvaegher, A. (2011). Digital elevation model generation for historical landscape analysis based on LiDAR data, a case study in Flanders (Belgium). *Expert Systems with Applications, 38*, 8178–8185.

White, D. A. (2013). LIDAR, point clouds, and their archaeological applications. In D. C. Comer & M. J. Harrower (Eds.), *Mapping archaeological landscapes from space* (pp. 175–186). New York: Springer.

Yastikli, N. (2007). Documentation of cultural heritage using digital photogrammetry and laser scanning. *Journal of Cultural Heritage, 8*, 423–427.

Chapter 3
Integrating Micro- and Macro-Archaeology at a Multi-period Site: Insights and Outcomes from Tell es-Safi/Gath

Aren M. Maeir

Introduction

Excavations in the Middle East, and especially those conducted at large, multi-period tell sites, have substantially evolved over the last century and a half. If one compares the techniques used in such excavations—for sure in the early years, but even those that were conducted just a few decades ago—there is almost a feeling of a difference in technique and methods which is as stark as the difference between nineteenth- and twenty-first-century modern medicine. Just about every aspect of the archaeological project, from the actual excavation and documentation through the various types of analyses conducted—whether in the field or subsequently in the lab, the analytic and theoretical perspectives by which the finds are studied, and all the way through to the various modes of publication—indicates the leaps and bounds in which the field of archaeology has advanced.

I would like to thank the staff and team members of the Tell es-Safi/Gath Archaeological Project for their dedicated work in excavating, analyzing, and interpreting the finds from Tell es-Safi/Gath. In particular, I am particularly grateful to Prof. Steve Weiner, of the Weizmann Institute in Rehovot, for spearheading the implementation of the micro-archaeology program at the excavations. In addition, thanks to the area and square supervisors in charge of the various excavation areas discussed in this article: R. Avissar, J. Chadwick, A. Dagan, H. Greenfield, L. Hitchcock, J. Katz, S. Kissos, C. Shafer-Elliott, I. Shai, J. Uziel, E. Welch, and A. Zukerman. From the micro-archaeological side, I would like to thank Y. Asscher, E. Boaretto, S. Gur-Arieh, A. Eliyahu, D. Namdar, J. Regev, L. Regev, R. Shahack-Gross, M. Toffolo, C. Trueman, and N. Yahalom for the various micro-archaeological analyses conducted both on-site and off-site. This research was partially funded by grants from the Israel Science Foundation (#100/2013 to AMM), the Canadian Social Science and Humanities Research Council (#895-2011-1005 to H. Greenfield and AMM), and the Kushitzky Fund of Bar-Ilan University.

A.M. Maeir (✉)
The Tell es-Safi/Gath Archaeological Project, Bar-Ilan University, Ramat-Gan, 52900, Israel
e-mail: arenmaeir@gmail.com

T.E. Levy, I.W.N. Jones (eds.), *Cyber-Archaeology and Grand Narratives*, One World Archaeology, https://doi.org/10.1007/978-3-319-65693-9_3

As having had the honor, and pleasure, to direct a large-scale excavation for more than 20 years (e.g., Maeir 2012, 2013), I would like to briefly describe, in this short contribution, some of the developments that my colleagues and I have tried to implement into the excavations at Tell es-Safi/Gath (Fig. 3.1) over the last years and how these new perspectives, methods, and approaches, carried out in a multi- and interdisciplinary framework, have not only pushed the envelope on the methods used, but have contributed to a better understanding of the past societies—in the end, the aim of our work.

For close to 15 years, we have benefited at Tell es-Safi/Gath from a close collaboration with a large team of scientists from various disciplines, who have joined us in the field, creating a unique inter- and multidisciplinary research environment, rarely paralleled in current archaeological research.

Stephen Weiner of the Kimmel Center for Archaeological Science at the Weizmann Institute of Science in Rehovot has created and refined a field protocol (see Weiner 2010) in which "micro-archaeologists" from various fields (chemistry, physics, materials science, biology, geoscience, etc.) work together in the field *during* the actual excavation season, side-by-side and in close collaboration and cooperation with the so-called "plain vanilla" archaeologists, fully participating in the daily excavations. In addition to their wide range of expertise that they bring to the field, in-the-field laboratories are set up (Fig. 3.2), which enable select on-the-spot analyses of various types of sediments, finds, and materials. This creates a unique collaborative atmosphere, where researchers of diverse backgrounds and perspectives jointly study the finds and contexts as they are discovered, each contributing to the understanding of the work. This enables not only better understanding of the finds and their context, but also on-the-spot "tactical" decisions on the methods of excavation, sampling, documentation, and analysis of specific contexts. Thus, as opposed to what very often occurs in archaeological excavations, finds that need to be analyzed by specialists are not removed by a nonspecialist and then delivered after the excavation to the specialists' labs, but rather, the specialist participates in the retrieval of the specific find, often using very specific protocols, ensuring that the finds are sampled in the most appropriate manner, and retrieving information that might be relevant for the specific analyses from the environment of the finds. This way, already in the field, the maximum amount of information is retrieved so that the post-excavation analyses of the finds will be as complete as possible.

This has important implications for several reasons. First, it enables the retrieval and analyses of finds that in many other cases would not even be noticed. Second, as the specific finds are excavated by the specific specialist, it gives higher chances that the maximum amount of data, which will enable robust interpretation, will be available. Third, since an interdisciplinary team works on the finds in the field, this ensures that we do not limit ourselves to narrow analyses and/or interpretations, but enable a wide range of scientific viewpoints to be incorporated into our interpretative understanding. Finally, the very fact that new classes of finds and contexts are excavated, sampled, and analyzed opens up new windows on understanding many new issues—in our case relating to the daily life of the ancient inhabitants of the

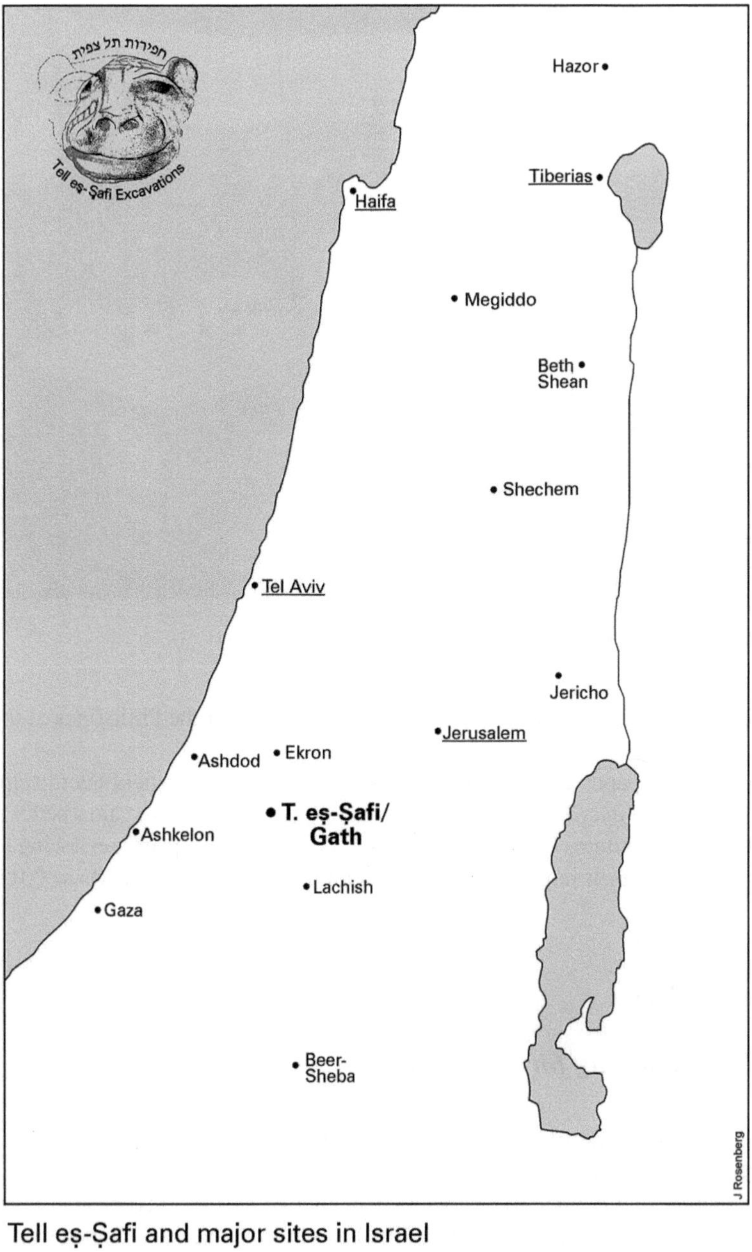

Fig. 3.1 Location of Tell es-Safi/Gath and other sites in the Southern Levant

Fig. 3.2 On-site micro-archaeology laboratory at Tell es-Safi/Gath

site, whether of the Canaanites of the Early Bronze Age or the Philistines of the Iron Age.

In this short paper, I would like to illustrate how this in-the-field interdisciplinary work, combining micro- and macro-perspectives, has enabled us to gain a better understanding of the cultures of the past at Tell es-Safi/Gath (for a paper reviewing similar perspectives and their ramifications for the Philistine household, see Maeir 2015).

Case Studies

On-Site Sampling for ^{14}C Dating

The importance and utility of ^{14}C dating has long been recognized in archaeology and has in fact contributed substantially to solving important issues (e.g., disproving the suggested connection between Stonehenge and the Mycenaean culture—Renfrew 1968). In the archaeology of the Levant, in the last two decades or so, ^{14}C dating has been of critical importance—and debate—particularly in relationship to the chronology of the Iron I-Iron IIA sequence (e.g., Ben-Yosef et al. 2010; Boaretto et al. 2005; Finkelstein and Piasetzky 2011; Levy et al. 2010; Mazar 2011). Clear-cut developments in the attention paid to the types of materials sampled (moving from generic charcoal to single-year cultigens) and the contexts from which the samples are taken (from "cherry-picking" samples for dating from general contexts to carefully choosing samples from good contexts) have substantially improved the "tightness" of much of the chronological discussions; nevertheless, problems still do exist. For example, time and time again, there have been cases in which dated samples from contexts which are seemingly robustly and clearly related to a specific chronological horizon, when dated by ^{14}C, give a much different date than one would assume from the relative chronological scheme. One of the issues at the basis of such discrepancies is problems relating to local "micro-stratigraphy." In other words, while an archaeological context may seem to be of "high quality," i.e., uniform material assemblage from a well-preserved, primary context, well defined between other clear stratigraphic contexts (such as material on a floor which is sealed between layers above and below), at times, at the micro-level, disturbances may occur. While from a macro point of view, a context may appear to represent a primary context of limited time, closer analysis of such a context may reveal otherwise.

To alleviate this problem, Elisabetta Boaretto and her colleagues, of the Weizmann Institute of Science, decided that the only way to truly insure high-quality samples for ^{14}C dating was to conduct micro-contextual sampling in the field. In other words, while in the past the field archaeologist retrieved the samples for ^{14}C dating and sent them to the ^{14}C laboratory, the idea here was for the ^{14}C specialists to be in the field and to be in charge of taking the samples while ensuring that the contexts were of the highest quality. This was done through careful excavation of the related contexts and their physical and micromorphological characterization to ensure that in fact these contexts were of a primary and well-sealed nature. This method of sample retrieval has been used on several occasions at Tell es-Safi/Gath (Fig. 3.3), in various contexts, providing very important and interesting results. Thus, samples for ^{14}C dating were taken from excellent primary contexts from Area E at Tell es-Safi/Gath dating to the EB III (Shai et al. 2014) and provided dates that agree fully with the new "high chronology" of the EB (e.g., Regev et al. 2012). Similarly, contexts of the terminal Late Bronze and early Iron Age from Areas A and F at Tell es-Safi/Gath were also sampled, and both provided evidence that the transition between the Late Bronze and Iron Ages may have commenced ca. the late thirteenth century BCE, earlier than often assumed (Asscher et al. 2015; Toffolo et al. 2012).[1]

[1] Finkelstein (2016) has recently questioned the early dates suggested by Asscher et al. (2015) for the beginning of the appearance of the Philistine culture in Canaan. While a more detailed joint response is in preparation, I would like to note that I do not believe that the full-blown appearance of the Philistine culture was in the thirteenth century BCE, but rather that the processes associated with the Philistines and "Sea Peoples" were long and drawn out processes (e.g., Yasur-Landau 2010: 315–325). Yasur-Landau (2010: 328) has suggested that from a stylistic point of view, some of the early Philistine pottery might even date to the late thirteenth century BCE. Similarly, early dates (first decade of the twelfth century BCE) for the LB/Iron I transition have been suggested already at Tell Tweini (Kaniewksi et al. 2011). In addition, there is no reason to assume that only after this or that historical event (such as Rameses III's battle against the Sea Peoples—if in fact this is a historical event—e.g., Ben-Dor Evian 2015) would the earliest material evidence of these processes appear. Thus, I believe that it may very well be possible that the initial phases of the Philistine phenomenon may have occurred in the late thirteenth century BCE, while the main, full-blown phases occurred later. As mentioned above, this will be discussed in further detail in another publication.

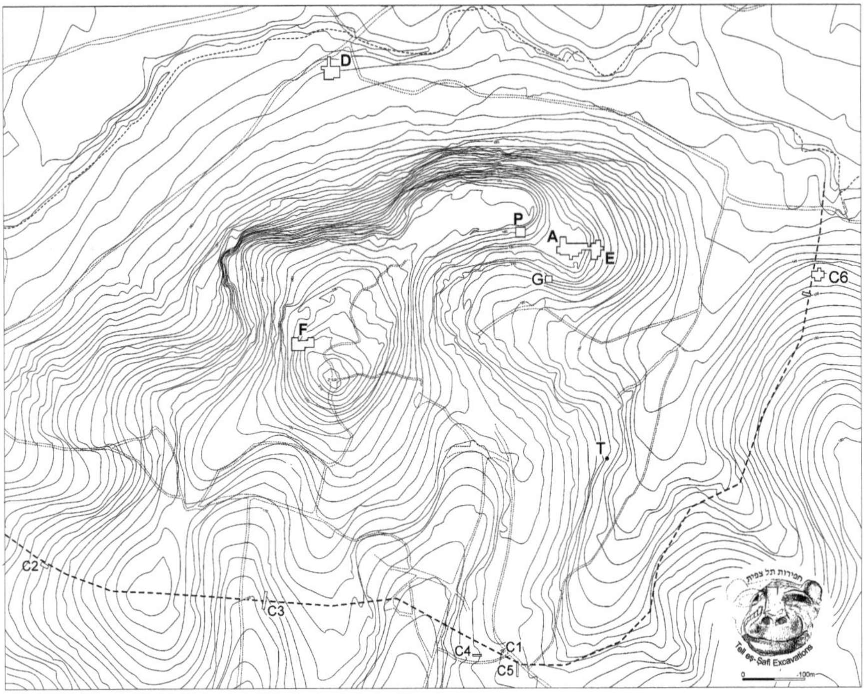

Fig. 3.3 Plan of Tell es-Safi/Gath with main excavation areas

Early Philistine Metallurgy

Up until quite recently, very little was known about Philistine metallurgical technology. Based on an understanding of the biblical narrative (I Sam 13:19), it was suggested that the Philistines had a monopoly on metal production during the early Iron Age. In fact, very little physical evidence for actual Philistine metallurgical abilities—and very few actual objects (see, e.g., Dothan 2002; see also Shalev 1988)—was known from early Iron Age Philistia.

Due to the close collaboration between macro- and micro-archaeology, we have been able to provide some concrete data regarding Philistine metallurgy in the early Iron Age (Eliyahu-Behar et al. 2012). During the 2010 season of excavations at Tell es-Safi/Gath, in the immediate vicinity of an early Iron Age temple in Area A, evidences of metallurgical-related activities were found (Fig. 3.4). This context, with evidence of both iron and bronze production dating to the early tenth century BCE, had two pitlike features, each considerably different from one another in color, texture, and content. Each pit was used for an activity related to iron production, as seen by the hammer scales, slag prills, and slag that were found in and around them. In addition, a crucible was found on top of one of the pits. Interestingly, analysis of

Fig. 3.4 Tell es-Safi/Gath, Area A—location of Iron Age I metallurgical activities

the crucible slag showed that it was used for bronze metallurgy. Within the pits, tuyères of specific types associated with both bronze and iron production were also found. The presence of bronze and iron industries at the same location is to be noted, as well as the location near the temple, perhaps indicating small-scale production of metal objects for use in the temple-related cult. While cult-related production is known from various ancient Near Eastern sites (e.g., Mierse 2012: 231–233; Stager and Wolff 1981), the archaeological context at Tell es-Safi/Gath provides evidence for this practice in Philistine culture as well. Needless to say, the scarcity of evidence of metal production in the Levantine early Iron Age makes this find quite important in general.

The discovery of this unique context may be very much due to the presence, on site, of an interdisciplinary team. C. Shafer-Elliott, the square supervisor, noticed a slight change in the texture and color of the sediments in the area and immediately called over the micro-archaeology team, which straightaway started examining these sediments. Their unique character was observed, and a meticulous and high-resolution excavation, specifically metallurgically oriented, was commenced in this area. Due to the limited size of this context (less than 2 sq. m, and only 10 cm deep), "standard" excavation procedures might very well have removed the evidence before their importance was noted, leaving only the unique objects themselves, but none of the associated sediments with important data. In fact, it may very well be that other such contexts have been excavated in the past at other early Iron Age sites in Philistia and elsewhere, but were not noticed by the excavators![2]

[2] In the 2014–2017 seasons of excavations at Tell es-Safi/Gath, an additional context with evidence of metallurgical activity was also discovered. This context, dating to the late ninth century BCE,

Hydraulic Plaster

In addition to the metallurgical context discussed above (found near a cultic context), various domestic contexts were excavated in Area A as well, dating to different stages of the Iron Age I, IIA, and IIB (ca. 1180–700 BCE). In what appears to be a courtyard of a house dating to ca. 1000 BCE, a plaster feature was discovered (Fig. 3.5); at first it was interpreted as a "standard" plaster floor. On-site analysis using Fourier transform infrared spectrometry (FTIR) told another story. As detailed in Regev et al. (2010), this plaster is of a unique type ("hydraulic plaster"), previously unreported from the pre-Classical Levant (except for a much earlier example from PPNB Yiftahel [Goren and Goldberg 1991]). Such plasters, or mortars, with the addition of silicate minerals, are rare prior to the Roman period, when they are used to enable the hardening of plaster, mortar, or cement in non-aerobic environments (such as underwater). Plasters from other pre-Classical sites in the Levant have not been known to contain these additives. Following the on-site FTIR analyses, in-depth characterization of the plasters was conducted, using a wide battery of analytic tools, including FTIR, acid dissolution, X-ray fluorescence (XRF), X-ray powder diffractometry (pXRD), heating experiments, and scanning electron microscopy (SEM) coupled with energy dispersive spectroscopy (SEMeEDS). These analyses demonstrated that specific, nonlocal silicate-containing minerals were added to this plaster. As this is a very specific technology, it is most likely that these surfaces were deliberately produced for specific functions (which unfortunately could not be identified, despite the fact that there was evidence of organic materials on the surfaces) or at least reflect a very specific technological tradition—and were not the result of a fortuitous addition of local silicate minerals.

While the production of hydraulic plasters is not known from the Bronze and Iron Age Levant, it is seen in both the Minoan and the Mycenaean cultures (see Regev et al. 2010: 3008). It may very well be that this plaster technology is another example of the nonlocal cultural facets found in the early Iron Age with the appearance of the Philistines' culture, brought by the non-Levantine population components of the early Philistines. While such nonlocal components were previously known, such as those relating to pottery, architecture, cooking (see below), and other facets, the micro-archaeological perspective on these plaster floors has enabled us to reveal yet another, previously unknown foreign facet of the early Philistine culture, hinting at the complex and multifaceted components of this fascinating "entangled" culture (e.g., Davis et al. 2015; Hitchcock and Maeir 2013).

---

was found in the lower city of Gath, in the vicinity of a temple. As the finds are still being analyzed, their character is not yet fully known, but in any case, the fact that both early Iron Age and Iron Age IIA metallurgical contexts are now known from Tell es-Safi/Gath may help us to better understand the development and character of the metal technology in Iron Age Philistia (for a preliminary overview, see Eliyahu-Behar et al. in press).

Fig. 3.5 Tell es-Safi/Gath, Area A—Iron Age I hydraulic plaster surfaces

Early Bronze Age Hearths

While many of the case studies described in this paper deal with Iron Age remains, the Tell es-Safi/Gath Project includes study of many periods and cultures. This includes extensive remains of the Early Bronze Age. In particular, the ongoing excavations in Area E, on the eastern side of the Upper City, have revealed an EB II–III domestic quarter (for a preliminary report, see Shai et al. 2014).[3]

During the excavations of the various EB III domestic structures in Area E, a specific type of installation was discerned (Fig. 3.6). These installations were constructed of small (2–5 cm, round or oval) limestone pebbles, often blackened from soot and cracked from heat, arranged surrounding (and occasionally lining) a small and shallow circular pit (diameter c. 40 cm and 20–30 cm deep). In some cases, the pebble arrangement extended beyond the pit's edge to create a slightly larger surface, up to c. 65 cm in diameter.

During the excavation, a particular focus was placed on collecting a broad spectrum of finds from these installations. This included macro finds from within the installations and their vicinity (e.g., pottery, bones, stones, etc.), extensive sediment samples, some of which were dry or wet sieved, while others were kept for a range of analytical methods. All told, both in the field and in subsequent laboratory analyses, we combined macro-perspectives (architecture, stratigraphy, pottery, chipped stone, fauna) and micro-perspectives (microfauna, archaeobotany, phytolith analysis,

[3]Excavation and research on the EB levels at Tell es-Safi/Gath was funded by a grant from the Canadian Social Science and Humanities Research Council to Haskel Greenfield (University of Manitoba) and Aren M. Maeir (Bar-Ilan University).

Fig. 3.6 Tell es-Safi/Gath, Area E—EB III pebble hearth (notice sediment sampling procedure)

materials analysis), in an attempt to understand the use and function of these installations (Eliyahu-Behar et al. 2017). This, as will be demonstrated below, enhanced our ability to clarify the use and function of these installations.

FTIR analysis of the stones and sediments demonstrated that the installations were the focus of a low-temperature fire (probably below 400 °C). All the installations contained ash, and analysis of the ash showed that the burned materials were both dung and various vegetal materials. From the various evidences, we suggested that these installations functioned as hearths for the cooking and preparation of food. When comparing the installations to those found at other EB sites in the Southern Levant (e.g., Beth Yerah, Tell Sakan; for references, see Eliyah-Behar et al. 2017), similar installations were excavated at other sites as well, although the exact function and use of these installations had previously not been clearly defined. Based on our recent interdisciplinary study, we can thus propose that these sunken hearths were a dominant method for the preparation of food in the EB Southern Levant and can be seen as an important component of daily domestic life. Interestingly, following the EB, the hearth becomes relatively rare in the Southern Levant, only to reappear during the early Iron Age, in the context of the Philistine culture (see below).

Philistine Hearths

Evidence from various Iron I sites in Philistia, such as Ashdod, Ekron, and Ashkelon, demonstrated the appearance of one of the unique attributes of the Philistine culture, a new type of cooking/heating installation: the hearth. While this type of installation is known from earlier periods in the Levant, it is not found in Late Bronze Age sites in Canaan and is not found in non-Philistine early Iron Age sites, where clay ovens (*tabun/tanur*) are common. The hearth is seen as one of the foreign elements brought from outside of the Levant by the foreign components among the early Philistines (see Maeir and Hitchcock 2011).

In the early Iron I levels at Tell es-Safi/Gath, several rounded, pebble-lined hearths were discovered (Fig. 3.7), similar to what is known from other sites in Iron I Philistia. Very little was known about the use and function of these hearths. What they were used for? What fuel was used? At what temperatures were they heated? What types of vessels, if at all, were placed on the hearths—and how they were placed?

As part of the ongoing work at Tell es-Safi/Gath, an interdisciplinary research program on these hearths was initiated, combining careful excavation, on-site micro-archaeological sampling, ethno-archaeology, and experimental archaeology, along with traditional stratigraphic-comparative studies, in an attempt to better understand these heaths (e.g., Gur-Arieh et al. 2011, 2012, 2013, 2014). From these studies, we can create a better, but far from complete, understanding of the use and function of these hearths. To start with, it appears that vessels were not placed directly on the hearths and were either placed near or on the periphery of the hearths (Gur-Arieh et al. 2011). Secondly, it appears that they were used both for heating/cooking with open fires and with embers (Gur-Arieh et al. 2012). And finally, diverse types of fuels were used (Gur-Arieh et al. 2013).

While much remains to be learned about the Philistine hearths, the application of micro-archaeological methods in the analysis of these installations opened new vistas and methods of interpretation for the ongoing study of both this specific feature and also related aspects of the Philistine culture. This is particularly important in

Fig. 3.7 Tell es-Safi/Gath, Area A—Iron Age I Philistine pebble hearth

relation to food production and consumption, which has been shown to be of critical importance in identifying and understanding, from the macro- and micro-perspectives, the new features that appear in early Iron Age Philistia and in attempts to differentiate between the Philistines and other Levantine cultures (e.g., Maeir et al. 2013; Maeir and Hitchcock 2017).

Destruction and Abandonment of Philistine Gath

Extensive evidence for the late ninth-century BCE (ca. 830 BCE) destruction of Philistine Gath by Hazael, king of Aram-Damascus, has been found at the site (Maeir 2004, 2012) and is connected to the monumental siege system surrounding the site (Maeir et al. 2006; 2012; Maeir and Gur-Arieh 2011). In light of the substantial evidence of buildings that had been destroyed, in which a large number of relatively well-preserved and undisturbed objects were found, for more than a decade, it was assumed that the process of destruction and abandonment during and immediately after the conquest of the town was relatively brief. It was understood that the houses in the city had been deliberately burnt down and immediately collapsed, burying within them the objects, and sometimes the inhabitants, of the city themselves, in a relatively brief amount of time.

This interpretation was challenged when a well-preserved section of this destruction level was carefully excavated and analyzed, using micro-archaeological protocols (Fig. 3.8).[4] The detailed analyses conducted on half a 5 × 5 m square produced rather unexpected results (see Namdar et al. 2011).

Clear evidence of a major fire was found, preserving and consolidating construction components, and we were able to differentiate between the roof, the walls, and the floor materials of the building. This facilitated a reconstruction of natural and man-made events which led to the formation and buildup of the ca. 80 cm thick accumulation associated with the destruction and its aftermath. The lowest layer overlying the original floor was comprised of ash sediment rich in thin charred organic material. As we soon saw, this ash was not evidence of a fire at this location, as the clays in this layer were not altered by heat and the ceramics found on this floor still have preserved organic residues. It seems that the ash on the floor formed elsewhere and was redistributed to this location. This is an important insight, as often, archaeologists assume that the presence of ash can be interpreted as evidence of a fire at that specific location. But as we see in this case, ash can be redeposited by the wind from another, nearby location. In other locations in the analyzed building, the analysis of the sediments showed heat-related alteration, there were few signs of ash, and the associated ceramics did have preserved organic residues. This reiterates that the presence or absence of ash is not necessarily a trustworthy criterion to define areas of conflagration. We also learned that the process of collapse of

[4] The micro-archaeological team was directed by Prof. Steve Weiner. Dr. Jill Katz was the archaeological supervisor of the relevant squares in the excavations.

Fig. 3.8 Tell es-Safi/Gath, Area A—house in Iron IIA destruction level

the structure was not a quick event, but rather something that may have occurred over years and even decades. This was shown, for example, by the fact that windblown sediments containing ash were redeposited while part of the structure was still standing, and only at a slightly later stage did the walls and roof collapse.

These insights are important for the understanding of the processes related to the destruction of the city by Hazael and its aftermath. While in the past it was assumed that the destruction of the city was total and all the buildings and objects within were quickly buried (thus supposedly explaining the excellent preservation), the results described above indicate that at least in some cases, the buildings may have been only partially destroyed, and nevertheless, many objects were left on the floors of the structures after the destruction, without having been buried immediately by the destruction debris. Only later, with time, did the buildings collapse and then bury the objects as well. This indicates that perhaps the entire population of the city, or at least the overall majority, did not survive the conquest, and very few, if any, came back after the destruction to salvage items from the destroyed houses.[5] This would indicate the enormity and severity of the destruction of Philistine Gath and fits in well with its demise as a city of any significant political status after this event (Maeir 2004).

[5] Additional, as yet unpublished, evidence that supports this was found in the analyses of some of the human skeletal remains found in the destruction, which indicates that skeletons were left unburied and exposed to the elements after the destruction and were not buried. Excavations in the Lower City (Area D) revealed that following the destruction, there was a brief attempt to return to the site (only discerned in this area); but this "squatters' phase" lasted for a very brief period and was quickly abandoned.

Summary

If one endeavors to combine micro- and macro-archaeological techniques and perspectives in a large-scale archaeological excavation, this can open up new windows and vistas for the interpretation and understanding of a complex, multi-period, and multidimensional site. Not only does the extensive use of micro-archaeological tools and methods enable us to retrieve classes of data that were previously unattainable (such as with the hydraulic plaster), but we can see, based on the examples noted above, that the integration of the macro- and micro-perspectives clearly expands our understanding of the past. The collaborative perspectives can correct previously unproven observations (such as with the understanding of the process of destruction) or broaden our understanding of various issues (such as with the hearths). The fact that all these vistas come to play *during* the excavation enables this integration of methods to have an immediate effect on the excavation methods and analytic results—as opposed to much of what was done in the past, where the macro-archaeologists excavated and only in the post-excavation analyses were the micro-perspectives taken into account. In the past, even if analytic results revealed new and surprising results which warranted further excavation of a specific context or find, if the analyses were done weeks, months, or years after the original excavations, this often would not be possible.

References

Asscher, Y., Cabanes, D., Hitchcock, L. A., Maeir, A. M., Weiner, S., & Boaretto, E. (2015). Radiocarbon dating shows an early appearance of philistine cultural material in Tell es-Safi/Gath, Philistia. *Radiocarbon, 57*(5), 825–850.

Ben-Dor Evian, S. (2015). The battles between Ramesses III and the sea-peoples. When, where and who? An iconic analysis of the Egyptian reliefs. *Zeitschrift für Ägyptische Sprache und Altertumskunde, 143*(2), 151–168.

Ben-Yosef, E., Levy, T. E., Higham, T., Najjar, M., & Tauxe, L. (2010). The beginning of Iron Age copper production in the southern Levant: New evidence from Khirbat al-Jariya, Faynan, Jordan. *Antiquity, 84*, 724–740.

Boaretto, E., Jull, A., Gilboa, A., & Sharon, I. (2005). Dating the Iron Age I/II transition in Israel: First intercomparison results. *Radiocarbon, 47*(1), 39–55.

Davis, B., Maeir, A. M., & Hitchcock, L. A. (2015). Disentangling entangled objects: Iron Age inscriptions from Philistia as a reflection of cultural processes. *Israel Exploration Journal, 65*(2), 140–165.

Dothan, T. (2002). Bronze and iron objects with cultic connotations from Philistine temple building 350 at Ekron. *Israel Exploration Journal, 52*(1), 1–27.

Eliyahu-Behar, A., Yahalom-Mack, N., Shilstein, S., Zukerman, A., Shafer-Elliott, C., Maeir, A. M., Boaretto, E., Finkelstein, I., & Weiner, S. (2012). Iron and bronze production in Iron Age IIA Philistia: New evidence from Tell es-Safi/Gath, Israel. *Journal of Archaeological Science, 39*(2), 255–267.

Eliyahu-Behar, A., Shai, I., Gur-Arieh, S., Frumin, S., Elbaz, S., Weiss, E., Manclossi, F., Rosen, S., Greenfield, T., Greenfield, H. J., & Maeir, A. M. (2017). Early Bronze Age pebble installations from Tell es-Safi/Gath, Israel: Evidence for their function and utility. *Levant, 49*(1), 46–63.

Eliyahu-Behar, A., Workman, V., & Dagan, A. (in press). Comparative metallurgy in the Iron Age Levant: Early Philistine iron production at Tell es-Safi/Gath vs. Canaanite (Israelite?) Megiddo. In A. Berlejung & A. M. Maeir (Eds.), *Researches on Israel and Aram: Autonomy, interdependence and related issues. Proceedings of the first annual RIAB center conference, Leipzig, June 2016*. Researches on Israel and Aram in Biblical Times [RIAB] (Vol. 1). Tübingen: Mohr Siebeck.

Finkelstein, I. (2016). To date or not to date: Radiocarbon and the arrival of the Philistines. *Ägypten und Levante, 26*, 275–284.

Finkelstein, I., & Piasetzky, E. (2011). The Iron Age chronology debate: Is the gap narrowing? *Near Eastern Archaeology, 74*(1), 50–54.

Goren, Y., & Goldberg, P. (1991). News and short contributions: Special studies. Petrographic thin sections and the development of Neolithic plaster production in Northern Israel. *Journal of Field Archaeology, 18*(1), 131–140.

Gur-Arieh, S., Maeir, A. M., & Shahack-Gross, R. (2011). Soot patterns on cooking vessels: A short note. In V. Karageorghis & O. Kouka (Eds.), *On cooking pots, drinking cups, loom weights and ethnicity in Bronze Age Cyprus and neigbouring regions. An international archaeological symposium held in Nicosia, November 6th–7th 2010* (pp. 349–355). Nicosia: A.G. Leventis Foundation.

Gur-Arieh, S., Boaretto, E., Maeir, A. M., & Shahack-Gross, R. (2012). Formation processes in Philistine hearths from Tell es-Safi/Gath (Israel): An experimental approach. *Journal of Field Archaeology, 37*(2), 121–131.

Gur-Arieh, S., Mintz, E., Boaretto, E., & Shahack-Gross, R. (2013). An ethnoarchaeological study of cooking installations in rural Uzbekistan: Development of a new method for identification of fuel sources. *Journal of Archaeological Science, 40*(12), 4331–4347.

Gur-Arieh, S., Shahack-Gross, R., Maeir, A. M., Lehmann, G., Hitchcock, L. A., & Boaretto, E. (2014). The taphonomy and preservation of wood and dung ashes found in archaeological cooking installations: Case studies from Iron Age Israel. *Journal of Archaeological Science, 46*(1), 50–67.

Hitchcock, L. A., & Maeir, A. M. (2013). Beyond Creolization and hybridity: Entangled and transcultural identities in Philistia. *Archaeological Review from Cambridge, 28*(1), 51–74.

Kaniewski, D., Van Campo, E., Van Lerberghe, K., Boiy, T., Vansteenhuyse, K., Jans, G., Guiot, J., Nys, K., Weiss, H., Morhange, M., Otto, T., & Bretschneider, J. (2011). The sea peoples, from cuneiform tablets to carbon dating. *PloS One, 6*(6), e20232. doi:10.1371/journal.pone.0020232.

Levy, T. E., Najjar, M., & Higham, T. (2010). Ancient texts and archaeology revisited – radiocarbon and biblical dating in the Southern Levant. *Antiquity, 84*, 834–847.

Maeir, A. M. (Ed.). (2012). *Tell es-Safi/Gath I: Report on the 1996–2005 seasons*. (Ägypten und Altes Testament, Vol. 69). Wiesbaden: Harrassowitz.

Maeir, A. M. (2004). The historical background and dating of Amos VI 2: An archaeological perspective from tell es-Safi/Gath. *Vetus Testamentum, 54*(3), 319–334.

Maeir, A. M. (2013). Gath. In D. M. Master (Ed.), *The Oxford encyclopedia of the bible and archaeology* (pp. 443–451). New York: Oxford.

Maeir, A. M. (2015). Micro-archaeological perspectives on the Philistine household throughout the Iron Age and their implications. In M. Muller (Ed.), *Household studies in complex societies. (Micro) Archaeological and textual approaches* (Oriental Institute Seminars, Vol. 10, pp. 307–319). Chicago: Oriental Institute of the University of Chicago.

Maeir, A. M., Ackermann, O., & Bruins, H. J. (2006). The ecological consequences of a siege: A marginal note on Deuteronomy 20: 19-20. In S. Gitin, J. Wright, & J. Dessel (Eds.), *Confronting the past: Archaeological and historical essays on Ancient Israel in honor of W.G. Dever* (pp. 239–243). Winona Lake: Eisenbrauns.

Maeir, A. M., & Hitchcock, L. (2011). Absence makes the hearth grow fonder: Searching for the origins of the Philistine hearth. *Eretz Israel (A. Ben-Tor volume), 30*, 46*–64*.

Maeir, A. M., & Gur-Arieh, S. (2011). Comparative aspects of the Aramean Siege System at Tell eş-Şāfi/Gath. In I. Finkelstein & N. Na'aman (Eds.), *The fire signals of Lachish: Studies in the archaeology and history of Israel in the late Bronze Age, Iron Age and Persian period in honor of David Ussishkin* (pp. 227–244). Winona Lake: Eisenbrauns.

Maeir, A. M., Hitchcock, L. A., & Horwitz, L. K. (2013). On the constitution and transformation of Philistine identity. *Oxford Journal of Archaeology, 32*(1), 1–38.

Maeir, A. M., & Hitchcock, L. A. (2017). The appearance, formation and transformation of Philistine culture: New perspectives and new finds. In P. Fischer & T. Bürge (Eds.), *The sea peoples up-to-date: New research on the migration of peoples in the 12th century BCE. Contributions to the Chronology of the Eastern Mediterranean* (Vol. 35, pp. 149–162). Vienna: Austrian Academy of Sciences.

Mazar, A. (2011). The Iron Age chronology debate: Is the gap narrowing? Another viewpoint. *Near Eastern Archaeologist, 74*, 105–110.

Mierse, W. (2012). *Temples and sanctuaries from the early Iron Age Levant: Recovery after collapse*. (History, Archaeology, and Culture of the Levant, Vol. 4). Winona Lake: Eisenbrauns.

Namdar, D., Zukerman, A., Maeir, A. M., Katz, J. C., Cabanes, D., Trueman, C., Shahack-Gross, R., & Weiner, S. (2011). The 9th century BCE destruction layer at Tell es-Safi/Gath, Israel: Integrating macro- and microarchaeology. *Journal of Archaeological Science, 38*(12), 3471–3482.

Regev, J., de Miroschedji, P., Greenberg, R., Braun, E., Greenhut, Z., & Boaretto, E. (2012). Chronology of the early Bronze Age in the Southern Levant: New analysis for a high chronology. *Radiocarbon, 54*(3–4), 525–566.

Regev, L., Zukerman, A., Hitchcock, L., Maeir, A. M., Weiner, S., & Boaretto, E. (2010). Iron Age hydraulic plaster from Tell es-Safi/Gath, Israel. *Journal of Archaeological Science, 37*(12), 3000–3009.

Renfrew, C. (1968). Wessex without Mycenae. *The Annual of the British School at Athens, 63*, 277–285.

Shai, I., Greenfield, H. J., Eliyahu-Behar, A., Regev, J., Boaretto, E., & Maeir, A. M. (2014). The early Bronze Age remains at Tell eş-Şāfi/Gath, Israel: An interim report. *Tel Aviv, 41*(1), 20–49.

Shalev, S. (1988). Redating the 'Philistine sword' at the British Museum: A case study in typology and technology. *Oxford Journal of Archaeology, 7*(3), 303–311.

Stager, L., & Wolff, S. (1981). Production and commerce in temple courtyards: An olive press in the sacred precinct at Tel Dan. *Bulletin of the American Schools of Oriental Research, 243*, 95–102.

Toffolo, M., Maeir, A. M., Chadwick, J. R., & Boaretto, E. (2012). Characterization of contexts for radiocarbon dating: Results from the early Iron Age at Tell es-Safi/Gath, Israel. *Radiocarbon, 54*(3–4), 371–390.

Weiner, S. (2010). *Microarchaeology: Beyond the visible archaeological record*. Cambridge: Cambridge University Press.

Yasur-Landau, A. (2010). *The Philistines and Aegean migration at the end of the late Bronze Age*. Cambridge: Cambridge University Press.

Chapter 4
Using Tools in Ways in Which They Were Not Intended: A Test Case of the Use of PlanGrid for Field Registration at Tel Burna

Chris McKinny and Itzhaq Shai

Introduction

Archaeologists of the modern era have attempted to successfully implement the large and expanding amount of digital tools into their archaeological work, in both documentation and research. This implementation can be divided into two basic categories. First, archaeologists have attempted to create[1] specific technological tools for the specific needs of their archaeological projects. Second, archaeologists have adapted existing well-established digital tools to the needs of their archaeological research interests. The first category seems to be the more common of the two with many archaeological projects attempting "trial" implementations of these technologies with various levels of success (e.g., Gay et al. 2010; Prins et al. 2014; Smith and Levy 2012, 2014). The topic of this paper falls within the second category of implementation, namely, using PlanGrid (created through the funding of Y Combinator), the construction tablet and smartphone app, as a platform for archaeological field data collection/registration and post-excavation analysis.

[1] We do not mean to suggest that all of these archaeological tools are built "from scratch," since many of these tools are built to various degrees using existing technologies.

C. McKinny (✉)
Texas A&M University Corpus Christi, Corpus Christi, Texas, United States
e-mail: chrismckinny@gmail.com

I. Shai
Israel Heritage Department, Ariel University, P.O.B. 3, Ariel 40700, Israel
e-mail: shai.itzick@gmail.com

T.E. Levy, I.W.N. Jones (eds.), *Cyber-Archaeology and Grand Narratives*, One World Archaeology, https://doi.org/10.1007/978-3-319-65693-9_4

The Tel Burna Archaeological Project

Before we discuss the implementation of PlanGrid at Tel Burna, a few general words on the project and the context of Area B, where the system was first implemented, are in order.

Tel Burna is situated in the lowland hills of Israel, or Shephelah, along the northern banks of the Nahal Guvrin. Sites in its immediate vicinity include Lachish, Mareshah, Tel Goded, and Tel Zayit, with Tell es-Safi/Gath and Azekah not too far off (Fig. 4.1). Six seasons of fieldwork at the site including a survey season and five excavation seasons have presented us with a coherent picture of the site's past settlement history.

The excavations have thus far focused on three areas (Fig. 4.2). The first area (A2) is located on the center of the summit of the tell, where a fortification system has created a flat, almost square area of 70 × 70 m. The second area (A1) was placed along the eastern slopes of the summit, forming a section of the upper tell. The third area, Area B, sits on a long platform to the west of the upper tell between the rise of the presumed Iron Age II fortifications on the east and the slope of the natural hill to the west (Fig. 4.3). This area yielded the earliest levels excavated to date, and below we will present our experience with PlanGrid in this area.[2]

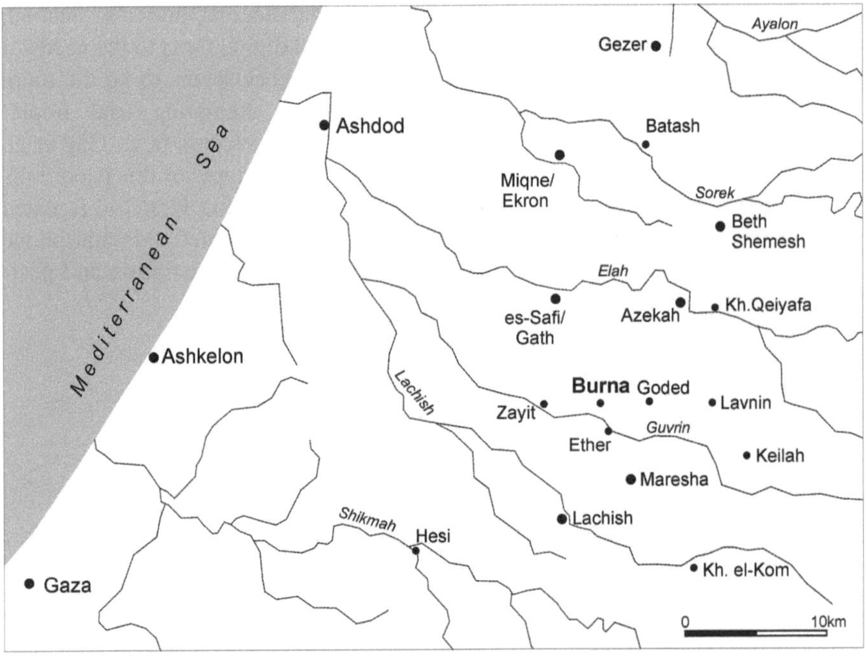

Fig. 4.1 Map of area around Tel Burna

[2] In Area B we used PlanGrid in the 2013 season as a study case. Since 2014 we use it in the other areas as well.

Fig. 4.2 Aerial view of Tel Burna looking north showing excavation areas

Area B

The area was opened in 2011 and has undergone three seasons of excavation in which eleven 5 × 5 m excavation squares have been opened.

Our rationale for beginning to work in Area B came from the results of the 2009 surface survey of the entire tell and its surrounding slopes and shovel test pits (Shai and Uziel 2014; Uziel and Shai 2010). The analysis of the ceramic materials from the survey strongly suggested that Tel Burna's western platform contained occupational debris from only one period, the Late Bronze Age. This is significant when it is compared to our survey results from the summit of the tell, which revealed mostly Late Bronze, Iron Age I, and Iron Age II,[3] with the vast majority of the indicative sherds (77%) dating to the Iron Age II (Shai and Uziel 2014; Uziel and Shai 2010: 238).

The excavation of Area B has revealed several peculiarities that can be defined as follows: First, the area, as the survey indicated, is made up of only the Late Bronze Age IIB (thirteenth century BCE). Second, this period is manifested in an archaeological deposit that sits directly on the bedrock on the one hand and only a few centimeters below the surface on the other hand. Third, the finds and the associated architecture in Area B have a clear cultic context. These finds (Fig. 4.4) include

[3] The Iron Age II fortifications (Shai et al. 2012:141–157) are visible directly on the surface and have been noticed by explorers as far back as the mid-nineteenth century CE (McKinny and Dagan 2013: 294–305).

Fig. 4.3 Aerial view of Area B after 2014 season

many local cultic objects such as masks, chalices, goblets, cup-and-saucers,[4] and figurines, as well as a vast array of imported artifacts from Cyprus and Mycenae (e.g., base ring "bilbil" juglets, white slip "milk bowls," and large "wavy-band" pithoi). Most of these finds were located in a large public building (Building 29305), which taken together with the finds indicated that cultic activity was probably carried out on regular basis inside of this building. Specifically, our excavation revealed that the above mentioned building is much larger than we had previously thought and apparently included a huge courtyard with dimensions around 16 × 16 m. Inside of this bedrock courtyard, we found two ovens and a large amount of restorable vessels. While the exact dimensions and layout of this building are still unclear (Fig. 4.5), 15 m of a well-built, wide (1.40–1.75 m) wall have been uncovered with many cultic finds on the eastern side of the structure, which we have interpreted as a large bedrock courtyard.

[4] For a discussion on the relationship between cup-and-saucer and cult, see Uziel and Gadot (2010: 41–57).

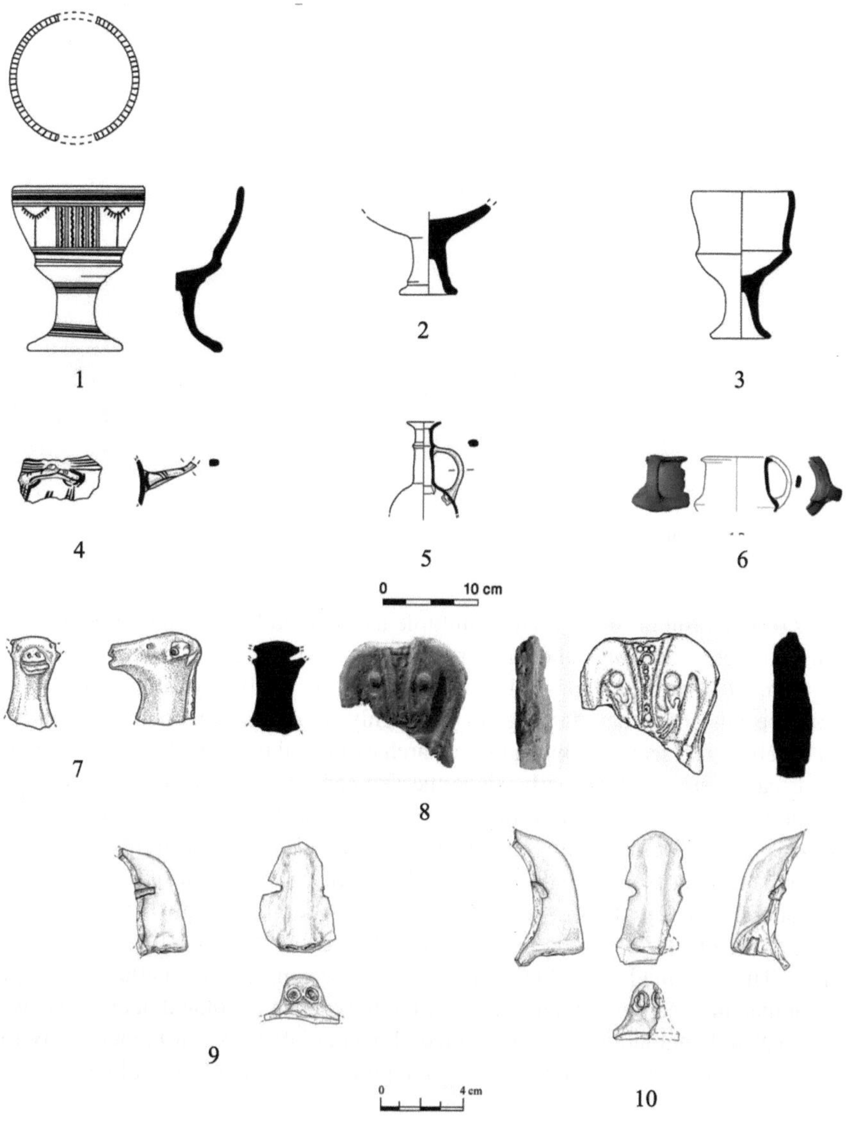

Fig. 4.4 Late Bronze Age finds from Building 29305

Using PlanGrid as a Field Tool

In 2013, the first author became acquainted with PlanGrid through a friend who was in charge of managing a large commercial construction project. He was informed that the iPad/iPhone[5] app PlanGrid allowed him to organize and annotate high quan-

[5] Since then PlanGrid has also developed an Android version of the app (http://www.plangrid.com/en/android).

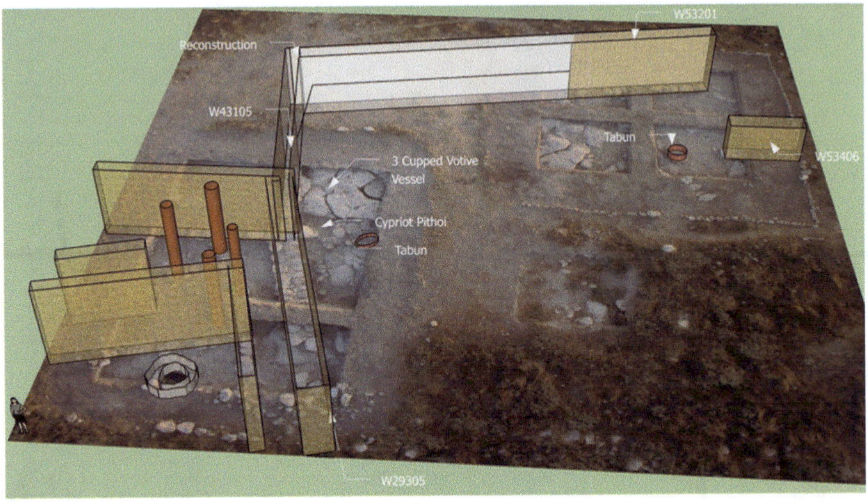

Fig. 4.5 Area B with a 3D reconstruction of Building 29305

tities of blueprint drawings, while multiple users could have cloud-based access to the same set of drawings and store their work in the cloud. After only a short time experimenting with the app and dialoguing with the accommodating app developers, it became clear that the program was highly adjustable and could potentially be an excellent replacement for traditional archaeological paper forms (e.g., top plans, locus cards, etc.). Additionally, since the app came with many stock features that would be beneficial for field forms, we believed that it would be a good alternative to other developed or developing archaeological registration programs.

In the 2013 season at Tel Burna, we successfully used PlanGrid as a replacement for hand-drawn top plans in Area B. For the 2014 season, we made the decision to implement PlanGrid as our primary field data collection tool for all excavation areas. This was made possible after making some simple modifications to the program that allowed our team to record different types of annotated data by means of personalized annotation buttons (termed "Punches" or Issues in PlanGrid). Below, we shall detail these modifications and the processes for field use of PlanGrid.

General Description

PlanGrid allows users to upload plan drawings (in PDF format only) and arrange them into projects that can be tagged and hyperlinked to other plans in the project. An administrator can assign these projects to multiple users, so that they can each have access to the same set of drawings. The basic version of the program ("Hammer") is free and allows for up to 50 sheets of storage. There are also 3 paid subscription plans, which offer storage of between 550 and an unlimited number of sheets.[6] Each plan includes free storage of images taken within PlanGrid. Depending on the size and duration of a project, it is entirely possible for a project to use a single free subscription, as was the case for our team. If there is a need to have more plans than the 50 that comes with the base package, then one can either pay for a subscription or simply have a separate free account for each excavation area.[7]

Over the course of two years' experience with the app, the app has added major features (e.g., the ability to add and edit notations via the web browser), fixed problematic aspects of the software, and rapidly returned inquiries regarding software issues and adaptability. The level of professionalism that this product has reached is clearly due to the fact that the program is operating on a daily basis in the high-pressure world of commercial and residential construction. This reality ensures that PlanGrid will be in use for a long time and constantly be updated with new features. In our opinion, this dynamic permanence is one of the major advantages that PlanGrid has over archaeological-specific programs, which are often created by people who move on to other careers and other projects and funded by scientific grants that always run out.[8]

In our experience with the app, the most powerful means of operating the program was with an iPad; however, the app also works with full functionality on other mobile devices (including Android). One of the main advantages of the iPad is the larger screen, which allows users to easily use the program even in the harsh environment of an archaeological excavation.[9] The long battery life of the iPad is also a major advantage over smartphones and computers. In our experience with PlanGrid on an iPad, the battery would last 2–3 excavation days before needing to be recharged. Besides, even if the iPad runs out of battery in the field, a user can easily recharge the device using a car charger or powerbank.

Beyond using PlanGrid on a tablet or smartphone, users can also access the plans, notes, and annotations via a web browser, but this access is somewhat limited in its navigation tools and ability to integrate pictures directly from the device and draw stratigraphic features.[10] On the other hand, this web browser access is an extremely powerful tool for accessing, editing, and searching annotations once

[6] https://app.plangrid.com/en/pricing

[7] If a project decides to pay for a subscription, then one of the immediate advantages is the ability to simply import personalized "Issues" between projects.

[8] That is not to say that there is not a use for this software, as there are clear success stories (e.g., Karasik et al. 2014; Karasik and Smilansky 2008; Smith and Levy 2012) that have greatly furthered the interaction between archaeology and technology.

[9] It should be noted that our excavation uses 90% UV reduction 12 × 12 m shades throughout the excavation area. These shades aid in keeping the iPad below its maximum operating temperature (45 °C/113 °F) and reducing the sun's glare on the screen.

[10] Although it should be noted that PlanGrid has greatly revamped this aspect of their program (Lunden 2012). On account of this, it seems likely that the web version of the application will continue to become more robust due to the popularity of the program in the construction community (Lawler 2013).

they have been recorded in the field. In this regard, PlanGrid on the web acts as a searchable database with spatially referenced field annotations that can be exported in CSV format for imputation into an existing database or an itemized PDF report with linked pictures, plans, and data. These features are extremely helpful for being able to readily access and disperse data in an intuitive and simple way.[11]

Implementation

After downloading the app to the device and registering with PlanGrid, specific modifications were made in order to adapt the "Issues" from the default setting of construction categories (e.g., "AC" acoustical ceiling, "D" door, etc.) to archaeological categories (e.g., "L" locus, "W" wall, "01 Sherds only", etc.) The Issue or "Punch" feature is the primary basis for using PlanGrid in the field, as it allows a user to categorize specific types that may be selected and entered directly onto the excavation plan. These modifications allowed users to record the data from our forms for spatially defined contexts (loci) and finds (baskets) directly on the top plan. These "Punches" are spatially linked, time stamped, and may be tagged with images taken with the iPad (see screenshot) or imported into PlanGrid.

The next step is to create a "project" and then to upload a set of architectural drawings (again, PDF only) into the project. This step can only be done via web browser access from plangrid.com. Once a plan has been uploaded to your project, you can begin adding annotations to it. This step should be repeated for each day of excavation, since you need a fresh "blank sheet" uploaded for the daily top plan drawing (Fig. 4.6). For this process, it is advisable to make architectural changes to the excavation plan on a fresh copy of the "blank sheet" in a program such as Adobe Photoshop, although it is also possible to do these drawings by hand after scanning and uploading it to PlanGrid as a PDF. This step is an integral part of the process, as it allows users to create a new set of drawings for each day of work based upon an accurate updated drawing from the previous day. By using a "blank sheet" template in Adobe Photoshop (or similar program), one can easily update the architectural elements of the top plan for use in the field the following day. Assuming that the original set is accurate, then this process helps ensure that each subsequent plan is both accurate and easily modifiable for continuing fieldwork.

The number of devices using PlanGrid will change depending on the specific needs of an excavation. In our excavation, we worked with three iPads, which were synced to two different projects, Areas A2 and B. In Area B, the supervisor (C.M.) worked with one iPad synced to the "Area B" project in PlanGrid. However, in Area A2 we had two iPads working in the same excavation area that were synced to "Area A2." The work process in Area B was simple. Everything that was entered into a single iPad was uploaded to the PlanGrid cloud once we returned to the Wi-Fi at the excavation

[11] PlanGrid is not and cannot be a full archaeological database. However, the excellent export CSV tool allows for easy import into an existing database (e.g., Microsoft Access or FileMaker).

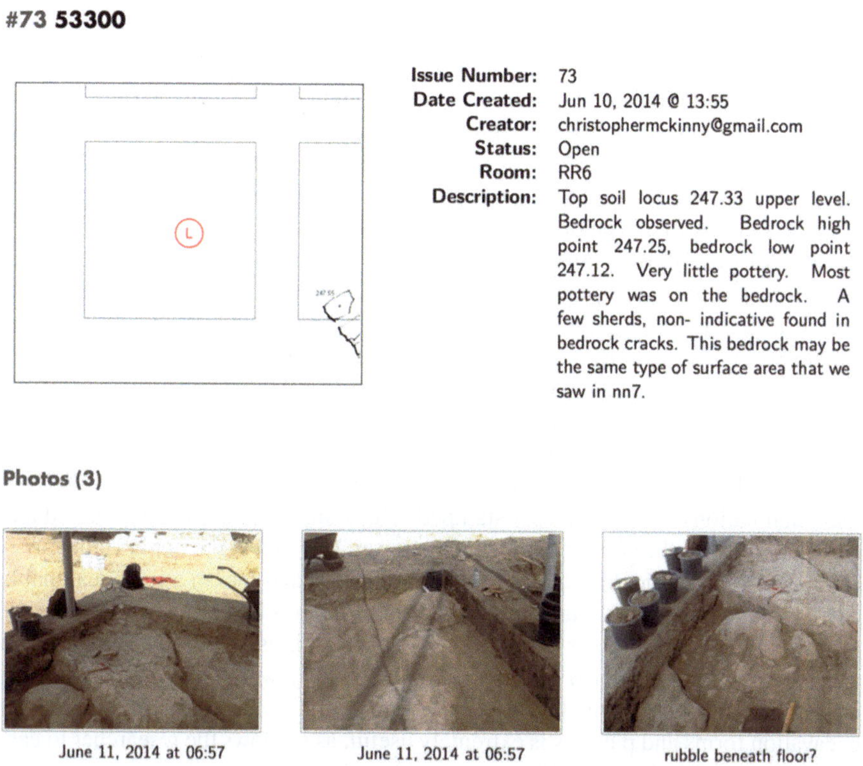

Fig. 4.6 Screenshot of Area B showing an example of a PDF report for a locus annotation

camp. But for Area A2, the process differed in that we entered data independently from different excavation squares within Area A2 and then synced their annotations and data at excavation camp. Once the data was uploaded, both Area A2 iPads were identically synchronized to the most up-to-date version.

This procedure worked throughout the season with minimal difficulty.[12] For the needs of our small excavation staff, this registration procedure worked quite well. But how would this process work in a larger excavation with a more complicated and tiered structure of supervision and field registration, for example, multiple areas each with an area supervisor with several square/trench supervisors? Without testing out the program on a similar scale, it is difficult to speak with certainty. However, given the program's success in the construction industry with its demanding work environment, it seems that the program could function with equal efficiency in a larger excavation setting. In our estimation, it seems feasible that square supervisors could run/register their subareas with an iPad, while an area supervisor concurrently follows their progress and adds his/her own notes and annotations on an iPad or laptop.

[12] The greatest hurdle to working with a cloud-based platform is reliable Wi-Fi.

Annotations and Pictures

PlanGrid's annotation tools are very intuitive and reliable. All of the tools are located on the tool palette on the right side of the app. The most basic tools are the drawing and text features, which allow users to label and draw features in the field. For drawing, it is advisable to use a good stylus. The drawing feature does not have a lot of settings or adaptability (basic colors and either a pen or a highlighter). Because of this, all drawings done in PlanGrid should be corrected in the "blank plan" for subsequent top plans. As a general rule, when creating any type of annotation, it is best to zoom in as much as possible, as the app automatically sizes the annotation to the depth of the plan at the time of your entry. In our excavation, we used the text tool as a title for our locus forms[13] (issues/punching glove symbol), which we place right next to the title. Within these forms, users have the ability to record locus and basket information (levels, stratigraphic description, etc.), as well as take field photographs of the artifacts and architecture in their context. Each of these annotations is time and user stamped. These annotations can be accessed and edited directly on the plan or in the "issue drawer," located in the upper right corner of the app. The "issue drawer" lists all of the baskets and loci in a fully searchable list.[14] Beyond these tools, PlanGrid also has built-in tools that allow one to measure distance and calculate areas directly on the plan. This is especially helpful in an excavation area like Area B where the context is very well defined with multiple artifacts uncovered in situ (Fig. 4.7). The integration of this measuring tool with excavation forms and pictures is extremely useful, as it allows the researcher to easily and accurately plot these finds using a single data-entry source.

It should be noted that all of the above annotations can be copied and pasted from one day's drawing to the next day's drawing (top button in the palette). This final feature is the biggest time saver, as it allows the user to carry over all of the relevant annotations to subsequent top plans.[15] Traditionally, this has been achieved by hand-tracing the previous day's plans and annotations, a process that can take several hours. Using these features in PlanGrid greatly reduces this preparation time, while increasing the accuracy of the architectural drawings since each drawing is based on the same set of plans and not a traced-over iteration.

Pictures can either be taken inside an issue or punch annotation or they can be their own picture annotation (camera tool button on the bottom of the tool

---

[13] The basket form is identical, but we did not give the basket a text label, as it would crowd the plan with too much information.

[14] When you are in a specific plan, then the issue drawer will only show you issues related to that plan; however, if you are looking at all of the plans in the "tiled view," you can search all of the issues (loci, baskets, etc.) for the entire project.

[15] Given that the top plans are of the same size. Since this process is quite simple, it should be emphasized that a user should double check all pasted annotations; otherwise you will end up with irrelevant annotations on the next day's top plan.

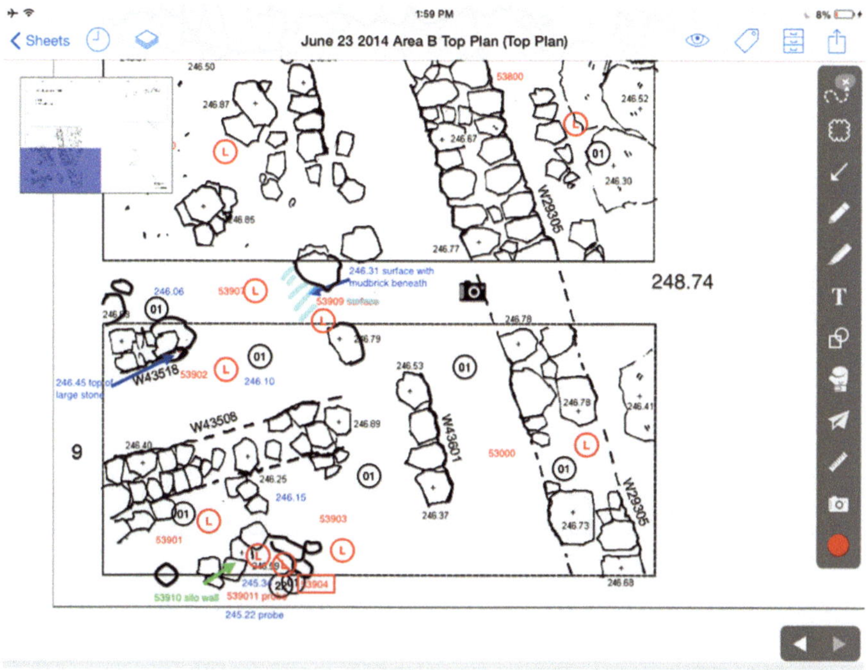

Fig. 4.7 PlanGrid app screenshot of 2014 Tel Burna Area B—*Red* (L) punch/issue annotation = Locus, *Black* (01) punch/issue annotation = pottery. Notice the tool palette on the right side

palette (Fig. 4.8]).[16] The suitability of the iPad for archaeological field registration is obvious (Fee et al. 2013: 50–55). It allows an archaeologist to easily take pictures and record notes (either through dictation or typing) anywhere in the excavation area. This ability is heightened by PlanGrid's picture annotation tool, which allows one to write or dictate their thoughts on the title of a photograph, thereby removing the need for a separate journaling app. Other apps have features such as this (e.g., Microsoft OneNote), but they are not integrated into a larger application that is suitable for archaeological field registration.

One of the few limitations of the app is the inability to modify data fields within the Punches/Annotations forms. Currently, users must use the set data fields of Issue Number (auto-created),[17] Stamp (loci or basket type), Title (alternately used as Locus or Basket number), Description (measurements, description, etc.), Date (auto-filled), Status, Sheet (auto-filled), Room (alternately used for Locus or Square Number), Created by (auto-filled), Assigned to (auto-filled), Company (auto-filled), Number of Photos (auto-counted), Color (chosen based on our parameters), and

[16] Additionally, pictures taken with a different camera (e.g., for a higher resolution) can be uploaded and inserted in either the issue annotation or the picture annotation.

[17] Our adaption in parenthesis

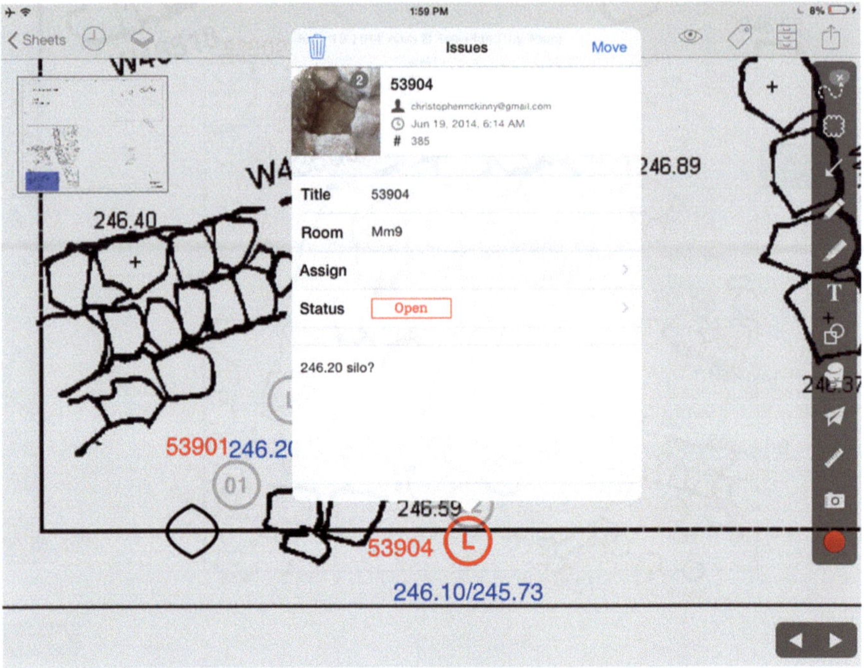

Fig. 4.8 Screenshot showing a Locus punch annotation with attached field pictures

Archived (static drop-down menu). As stated above, our inquiries and questions to the PlanGrid support staff have been swiftly and helpfully responded to. However, as of yet, they have decided to not make the "Issue" data fields modifiable. If this change were to be implemented in the future, it would greatly streamline the process of importing data from PlanGrid into a database and streamline the process of data entry. We hope in the future, PlanGrid will add the ability to make these modifications, which would make the application an even greater archaeological field tool.

Analysis

After the data has been recorded in the field, artifacts need to undergo further analyses, such as pottery reading/dating. PlanGrid is very helpful in this regard, as the program allows researchers to rapidly search and retrieve artifact details by using the "issue drawer." Once a user has found the artifact in question, they can easily navigate between the data within the form, the physical location of the artifact in the top plan, and the photos and notes attached to the artifact or locus. This is a clear advantage to traditional paper forms and binders, which are cumbersome and easily damaged, destroyed, or lost during the rigors of fieldwork.

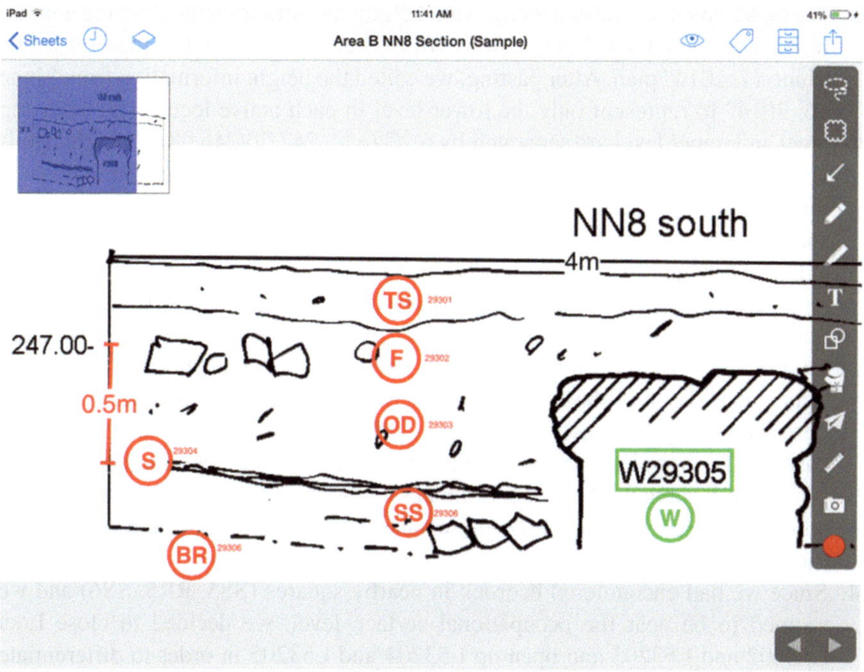

Fig. 4.9 Sample Section, *TS* Top Soil, *F* Fill, *OD* Occupational Debris, *S* Surface, *SS* Subsurface, *BR* Bedrock, *W* Wall. Notice the measuring tool

These same field excavation features can easily be adapted for use as a post-excavation analysis tool. Specifically, PlanGrid can be used as a tool for plotting finds for spatial analysis within a structure. Similarly, we have also used PlanGrid as a tool for illustrating and plotting stratigraphy on an excavated balk section (Fig. 4.9).

Case Study of PlanGrid in Area B at Tel Burna

Now that we have described the nature of Area B and defined how to implement PlanGrid in the field, we shall briefly detail how we used PlanGrid in Area B on a typical day of excavation. For this case study, we will use square SS5 of Area B on June 17, 2014. Our desire is that this case study will be useful as a reference guide; as such, we have formatted our description of the case study in outline form:

1. On June 16, 2014, we uploaded a "blank sheet" (PDF) named "June 17, 2014" with our implemented architectural changes (Adobe Photoshop) from that day's excavation work.

2. We then copied and pasted locus, wall, height, and stratigraphic drawing annotations (note: not Basket annotations) from the "June 16, 2014" plan on to the "June 17, 2014" plan. After pasting, we edited the height information from "June 16, 2014" to represent only the lower level in each active locus. The day's top level and upper level are separated by a "/" (e.g., 247.20/246.98). This change is simply made by touching the height annotation (blue font) and removing the upper level from "June 16, 2014," which leaves the lower level as the upper level for the "June 17, 2014" plan.
3. When we began excavating the next morning, we opened up several Basket annotations for pottery (01), a complete storage vessel ((05) – B532029), and material for flotation ((22) – B532030) from around the storage vessel and related them to the applicable loci. This was accomplished by using the "Punchlist." Each of these baskets was given an upper and lower level and was described using the "description" data field within the basket annotation. In the case of the complete storage vessel, we measured the vessel's placement in Square SS5 using the known coordinates of the steel pegs on the northwest and southwest corners. Once we had these measurements, we plotted the vessel using the "measuring tool."
4. Since we had encountered bedrock in nearby squares (SS5, RR5, SS6) and we seemed to be near the occupational surface level, we decided to close Loci L53202 and L53203 and open up L53204 and L53205 in order to differentiate between surface and subsurface remains. In order to close the former loci, we selected the locus tag or title and enclosed it with a box and then selected the Locus punch/issue button (L) and selected "closed" from the drop-down menu in the issue annotation form. This last step automatically adds a diagonal line slashed through the (L) button. We then selected two new punch/issue buttons (L) and red titles for L53204 and L53205. Lastly, we provided a description of why we opened these loci and took photos with titles to document them within the locus annotation form.
5. At the end of the excavation day, we measured the vertical extent of our work and then added the lower level to the plan.
6. Since each day's plan is editable, we exported and emailed[18] a PDF of "June 17, 2014" as a permanent, unchangeable record of our work from that day. This export can be emailed as a CSV file (annotations, but no top plan), a packet (includes annotations and plan), a snapshot, or as a full-size PDF. This last option is our preference, because it provides the highest resolution of the top plan. It is advisable to export a CSV file from each day, in addition to the full-size PDF of the plan.
7. After returning to the excavation camp, we processed ceramic finds from the previous day by adding the pottery reading to the applicable basket annotations. We then repeated the process of adding a blank sheet for June 18, 2014 in the PlanGrid Tel Burna Area B project library (Fig. 4.10).

[18] This process can also be synced to an online cloud storage service such as Box.

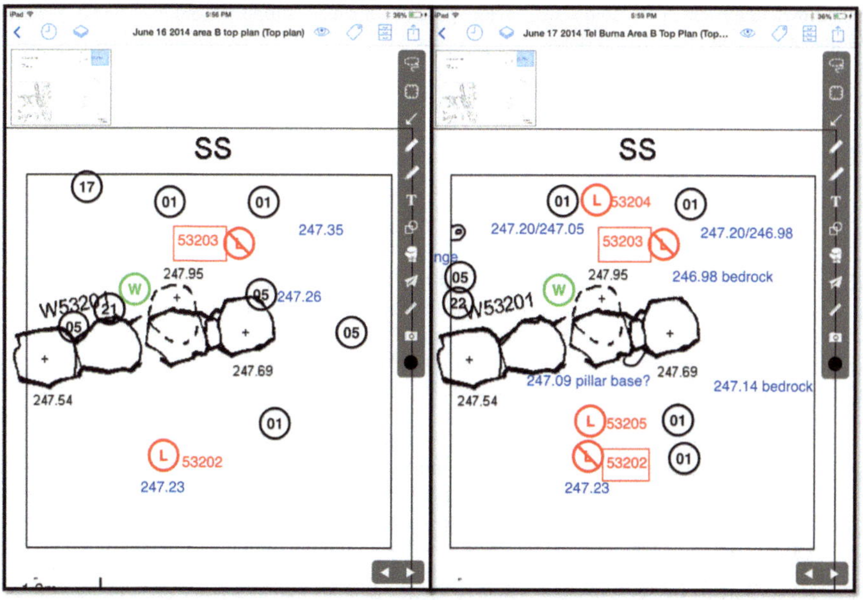

Fig. 4.10 Comparison of June 16, 2014 and June 17, 2014 Top Plans

Conclusion

In sum, our experiences with PlanGrid over the last two seasons indicate that the program has a high degree of adaptability that allows an archaeologist to concisely and accurately collect many types of data in an organized and intuitive manner. The key feature of PlanGrid is the integration of graphics (top plan drawings and photos) with locus and basket field documentation. We look forward to PlanGrid's continued use in the excavation at Tel Burna and future updates and features that will even further enhance its usability. We hope that our experience with PlanGrid at Tel Burna serves as a good example for the usefulness of adapting an existing technological tool for use in an archaeological field excavation.

As shown above, the one main drawback to using PlanGrid as an archaeological digital recording tool is the lack of a built-in relational database. However, in this upcoming season, we plan to integrate our adaption of PlanGrid with the newly developed system of Ninox. Using Ninox as our relational database (from 2017) and PlanGrid as our mobile top plan and data collection tool, it will allow us to have a connected set of excavation forms and data.

Acknowledgement This study was made possible through support from the Israel Science Foundation Grant No. 522/16 (I.S.).

References

Fee, S. B., Pettegrew, D. K., & Caraher, W. R. (2013). Taking mobile computing to the field. *Near Eastern Archaeology, 76*(1), 50–55.

Gay, E., Cooper, D., Kimia, B., Taubin, G., Cabrini, D., Karumuri, S., Doutre, W., Liu, S., Galor, K., & Sanders, D. (2010). Reveal intermediate report. In *2010 IEEE computer society conference on computer vision and pattern recognition – workshops, San Francisco, CA, 2010* (pp. 1–6). Piscataway: IEEE. doi:10.1109/CVPRW.2010.5543548.

Karasik, A., Greenhut, Z., Uziel, J., Szanton, N., Grosman, L., Zandbank, I., & Smilansky, U. (2014). Documentation and analyses on the National Scale at the Israel Antiquities Authority: The story of one (broken) Sherd. *Near Eastern Archaeology, 77*(3), 209–213.

Karasik, A., & Smilansky, U. (2008). 3D scanning technology as a standard archaeological tool for pottery analysis: Practice and theory. *Journal of Archaeological Science, 35*(5), 1148–1168.

Lawler, R. (2013). PlanGrid's Blueprint App Adds Automatic Hyperlinking and Web-Based Markup. TechCrunch. http://techcrunch.com/2013/06/03/plangrids-blueprint-app-adds-automatic-hyperlinking-and-web-based-markup. Accessed 27 Oct 2014.

Lunden, I. (2012). YC Alum/Construction Disruptor PlanGrid Nails $1.1M Seed Funding From Box, 500 Startups, And More. TechCrunch. http://techcrunch.com/2012/05/29/plangrid-ipad-construction-seed-funding-bo. Accessed 27 Oct 2014.

McKinny, C., & Dagan, A. (2013). The explorations of Tel Burna. *Palestine Exploration Quarterly, 145*(4), 294–305.

Prins, A. B., Adams, M. J., Homsher, R. S., & Ashley, M. (2014). Digital archaeological fieldwork and the Jezreel Valley regional project, Israel. *Near Eastern Archaeology, 77*(3), 192–197.

Shai, I., Cassuto, D., Dagan, A., & Uziel, J. (2012). The fortifications at Tel Burna: Date, function and meaning. *Israel Exploration Journal, 62*(2), 141–157.

Shai, I., & Uziel, J. (2014). Addressing survey methodology in the southern Levant: Applying different methods for the survey of Tel Burna, Israel. *Israel Exploration Journal, 64*(2), 172–190.

Smith, N. G., & Levy, T. E. (2012). Real-time 3D archaeological field recording: ArchField, an open-source GIS system pioneered in southern Jordan. *Antiquity Project Gallery, 86*(331). http://antiquity.ac.uk/projgall/smith331. Accessed 27 Oct 2014.

Smith, N. G., & Levy, T. E. (2014). ArchField in Jordan: Real-Time GIS data recording for archaeological excavations. *Near Eastern Archaeology, 77*(3), 166–170.

Uziel, J., & Gadot, Y. (2010). The "cup-and-saucer" vessel: Function, chronology, distribution and symbolism. *Israel Exploration Journal, 60*(1), 41–57.

Uziel, J., & Shai, I. (2010). The settlement history of Tel Burna: Results of the surface survey. *Tel Aviv, 37*(2), 227–245.

Chapter 5
From Multispectral 3D Recording and Documentation to Development of Mobile Apps for Dissemination of Cultural Heritage

Miriam Cabrelles, Silvia Blanco-Pons, Berta Carrión-Ruiz, and José Luis Lerma

Introduction

As pointed out by Letellier et al. (2007), heritage recording, meaning the graphic or photographic capturing of information describing the physical configuration, evolution, and condition of heritage at known points in time, and documentation, the systematic collection and archiving of records in order to preserve them for future reference, are of special importance to describe in detail the physical and dimensional configuration of heritage at a given point in time. There are a large number of tools or techniques that can be used for base recording, condition assessment, data management, investigation and monitoring (Eppich and Chabbi 2007). Special attention will be given herein to metric and imagery techniques such as photogrammetry, terrestrial laser scanning, multispectral photography, and thermography to build up scientific knowledge of a monument, object, or site previous to conservation, preservation, monitoring, research, and dissemination endeavors.

The combination of image-based photogrammetry and laser scanning is very common in cultural heritage recording and surveying. Terrestrial laser scanning and photogrammetry can be used either stand-alone or together to complement each other (Biosca Taronger et al. 2007; Lerma et al. 2010), for instance, to improve the overall/partial resolution of the eventually built up 3D model. Additionally, both techniques can be integrated to deliver highly accurate 3D objects, improve the definition of complex geometries, and enhance the color information. Thermal infrared (TIR) images provide users additional non-visible information about surface details and can be used to provide information about the condition of a

M. Cabrelles • S. Blanco-Pons • B. Carrión-Ruiz • J.L. Lerma (✉)
Department of Cartographic Engineering, Geodesy and Photogrammetry, Photogrammetry & Laser Scanning Research Group (GIFLE),
Universitat Politècnica de València, C° de Vera, s/n. Building 7i, 46022 Valencia, Spain
e-mail: micablo@doctor.upv.es; silblapo@doctor.upv.es; bercarru@doctor.upv.es; jllerma@cgf.upv.es

T.E. Levy, I.W.N. Jones (eds.), *Cyber-Archaeology and Grand Narratives*, One World Archaeology, https://doi.org/10.1007/978-3-319-65693-9_5

monument (Lerma et al. 2011). According to Cabrelles et al. (2009), the addition of thermographic data is recommended to identify alterations and damages.

The application of multispectral photography to document cultural heritage is still a challenge and not a common practice for large outdoor features. Nevertheless, this solution offers great benefits to automate and enhance thematic mapping outdoors, not only for architectural facades but also archaeological features independently of the image scale (Lerma 2001; Lerma et al. 2011). Furthermore, false color composition with ultraviolet, visible, and infrared information also helps to detect the damage and the material variations not visible to the human eye.

Besides the scientific documentation and conservation, dissemination is considered as a vital part of any survey to raise awareness to the society about its wellness (even if the object is very much deteriorated). Nowadays, museums and sites dealing with cultural content are analyzing and exploring different ways of dissemination that rely on the usage of new technologies to engage a higher number of visitors, making visits more interesting and enjoyable and increasing the satisfaction of participants. This new concept of dissemination based on multimedia applications allows users, on the one hand, to enrich their experiences, facilitating the understanding of the cultural heritage object and, on the other, increasing the pleasure of enjoying our legacy. Both facts in the end allow indirectly the achievement of two facts: participants come back more often, and participants share their experiences with their colleagues and friends. Thus, more participants are willing to visit the museum or site. All these ways of multimedia solutions are considered as supplemental dissemination methods to traditional ones such as conventional visits to archaeological sites with or without audio/guides.

There is no doubt that the chance to carry out a remote virtual experience from anywhere at any time is an advantage. In these experiences, you can manipulate exact virtual copies, visit places that do not exist at present, or even learn relevant information through games, augmented reality, videos, and animations.

The use of smartphones and mobile applications (apps) is becoming more prevalent in daily life, and the number of devices is exponentially increasing year after year. Due to the portability of a smartphone, the integration of these devices as tools supporting the visit of museums has increased enormously. Shaw and Challis (2013) discuss the development and testing of a smartphone application (app) for iOS in which users can explore archaeological information relating to the Stonehenge World Heritage Site. Similarly, the authors assess ways to improve the landscape study, analysis, and interpretation. Charlotte (2011) presents a practical research project based at the Curzon Community Cinema and develops an app for iOS that complements the Curzon's new Heritage Lottery funded exhibition, enabling users to gain further insight into the building history.

Mobile apps are an effective approach for data dissemination and understanding (Shaw et al. 2013). Currently, there are apps focused on games as learning tools in museums. This is the case of MuseUS (Coenen et al. 2013), where players are invited to create their own exposition and are guided by the app. Mortara et al. (2014) discuss the current situation of the game industry in the field of cultural heritage and present numerous examples of available games. Another example of game app created for a visit to a museum is provided by Rubino et al. (2015). This game joins two objectives, entertainment and learning cultural content through storytelling. Furthermore, the authors describe the possible differences between participants who played the game and those who used a multimedia guide to know how these different approaches affected the visitors.

Augmented reality (AR) is a technology that allows users the integration of digital information such as images, text, video, or 3D models within a real (physical, true) environment. The virtual elements are blended with the real environment in real time through, for example, a device with a camera. By contrast, virtual reality (VR) creates a complete virtual environment, while AR does not replace the physical reality. AR is very useful to add additional information in real scenarios such as museums or archaeological sites. An example of this approach is described by Gutierrez et al. (2015), who have designed and developed an AR application to help visitors to locate graffiti in the Temple of Debod more easily and to know the history of each engraving.

Throughout AR applications, either a user or multiple users can visualize 3D reconstructions (Han et al. 2013) or information associated with paintings. In any case, it is necessary in order to launch the AR application to have a medium that will activate it, which could be the image of a painting or just a black and white code.

AR can be applied to teaching and learning. Bustillo et al. (2015) present a different way to teach the cultural heritage using light 3D models of sufficient visual quality. Novotný et al. (2013) propose a multi-touch AR system, which uses two displays, and shows two contexts of the same object. Within this system, historical maps and 3D representation of historical buildings are shown; consequently, the user can see both the changes in the 3D buildings and the changes in the historical maps. In addition, the visualization of a historical object in 3D allows a better historical understanding of the object.

The visualization of a virtual reconstruction provides the users the possibility to visit extinct sites. Valtolina et al. (2005) describe a way to integrate traditional concepts of cultural heritage with virtual reality technology. A virtual reconstruction allows users to understand the history of the site. Besides, through an interactive digital narrative and a real-time visualization, the users are able to learn and enjoy (Valtolina et al. 2005).

The technologies explained so far are mainly applied in smartphones but they can be applied in web platforms too. Guarnieri et al. (2010) present a web-based application for interactive exploration of 3D models using open source tools and segmented sub-models. The use of sub-models reduces both the file size and the downloading time (Guarnieri et al. 2010). Another example of a web viewer for 3D models is described by Potenziani et al. (2015) and Scopigno et al. (2017). The authors present an open-source software package for the creation of interactive web presentations of high-resolution 3D models oriented to the cultural heritage field. Meyer et al. (2007) propose a web information system hosting different types of documentation, for example, graphs, photos, scanned drawings, line plans, 3D models, and virtual images. Finally, Caro and Hansen (2015) propose the usage of game engines to incorporate realistically 3D models for the case study of the Menga Dolmen.

All processes described above could be unified with the name of cyber-archaeology. Stanish and Levy (2013) define a workflow model for cyber-archaeology, considering acquisition (archaeology research design, digital data collection tools, and diagnostic imaging), curation (data storage, geospatial mapping, and AR), analysis (modeling and simulation, 3D visualization), and dissemination of data. Besides, the authors argue that cyber-archaeology harnesses the benefits of computer science and engineering to tackle the needs of world cultural heritage research and conservation. Forte (2011) presents cyber-archaeology as a cybernetic simulation process and describes this process as the relations produced by the interaction between users, environment, and behaviors.

This paper describes the techniques carried out for recording, documentation, analysis, and dissemination of Djinn Block No. 9 inside the Petra Archaeological Park in Jordan. Furthermore, the development of a smartphone app for Android devices is described. The description includes the design and development of the application, the way users can interact with the app, and how the app can be used to increase the dissemination of cultural heritage. This application is focused on disclosing relevant information to the visitors in a way that allows them to appreciate more the significant value of the architectural monument in the Petra Archaeological Park.

The rest of the chapter is structured as follows: section "Djinn Block No. 9 in the Petra Archaeological Park" introduces the case study selected. Section "Recording and Documentation Techniques" presents four main recording techniques considered to record and document Djinn Block No. 9. Section "Mobile Apps for Dissemination: Djinn Block No. 9 as a Case Study" describes the app specifically created for dissemination of Djinn Block No. 9, including its functions, design, and possible improvements. Section "Discussion" presents a discussion of the methods carried out and different ways to disseminate cultural heritage. Finally, section "Conclusion" draws some conclusions.

Djinn Block No. 9 in the Petra Archaeological Park

Petra (Jordan) is one of the world's most famous archaeological sites, where ancient Eastern traditions blend with Hellenistic architecture (UNESCO 1985). Petra was declared a World Heritage Site in 1985. The Petra Archaeological Park is characterized by its beautiful multicolored mineralogical formations. Relevant monuments were carved from the Cambrian or Ordovician rock. The city has a Nabataean architectural style. The Nabataeans were creative builders and carved great altars, temples, tombs, theatres, and even a vast network of cisterns and reservoirs, which controlled and conserved seasonal rains.

Djinn blocks are one of the park's archaeological monuments and they are characterized for their peculiar styles: large rock-cut monuments, unique in antiquity. Djinn blocks are free-standing (fully 3D) monuments against Petra's typically 2D rock-cut monuments. They are large stone-carved funerary structures that resemble towers and lie in the upper Ordovician sandstone formations along the open streambed (Outer Siq) that forms the main entrance leading to the famous gorge conduit (the Siq) that leads into the city (Akasheh et al. 2005). Djinn blocks can be easily identified in the Park due to their morphology. In particular, Djinn Block No. 9 (5.5 m long × 5.5 m wide × 9.8 m high) is one of the best-preserved samples (Fig. 5.1). The four façades of Djinn Block No. 9 are similarly carved, while the roof

Fig. 5.1 View of the complex of Djinn blocks along the entrance to the Siq (gorge) in Petra Archaeological Park, Jordan: (**a**) View of Djinn Block No. 9 (background) and Djinn Block No. 8 (foreground), (**b**) *Top view* of Djinn Block No. 9 from the northern side depicting the grave

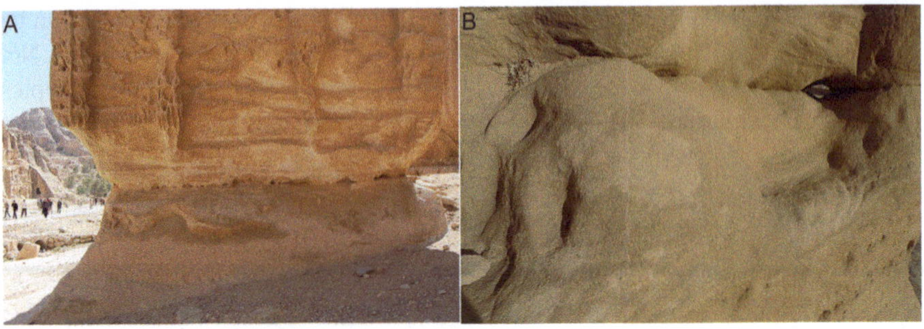

Fig. 5.2 Alveolar weathering and erosion effects. Close-up views of Djinn Block No. 9: (**a**) Eastern side, (**b**) Western side

is flat and hollowed out, probably serving as a grave. A row of inset stones forms a cornice that runs all around the block (Lerma et al. 2011). Figure 5.1 displays Djinn Block No. 9 placed along the open streambed near the entrance to the Park.

The causes of weathering are many and not simple. Several factors cooperatively act on the monuments, slowly damaging the structural strength of the rock (Akasheh 2000). The weathering and deterioration effects are clearly visible nowadays. Most of its outer decoration is inevitably lost. Similar to the rest of the features inside the Park, Djinn Block No. 9 is subject to ongoing alveolar weathering and erosion effects due to wind, rain, temperature cycles, capillary rise at the base, and salt depositions due to evaporation of water (Fig. 5.2). More concrete details about the weathering effects can be found in Akasheh (2000), Akasheh et al. (2005), and Heinrichs (2008).

The monument under study is peculiar and still allows visitors to infer the stylistic and building study of Nabateans. That is why the preservation and conservation of the significant heritage of the Djinn blocks requires the adoption of right measures carefully specified on risk management and conservation plans (Haddad et al. 2015).

Recording and Documentation Techniques

Recording and documentation techniques to improve the level of understanding of cultural heritage are of great importance. A plethora of 3D digitization systems are available to achieve a complete recording and documentation of cultural heritage. The suitability and the applicability of any approach depend basically on three issues as pointed out by Pavlidis et al. (2007): (a) complexity of the object in size and shape; (b) morphological complexity; and (c) diversity of raw materials.

Techniques such as photogrammetry, terrestrial laser scanning, multispectral photography, and thermography provide scientific knowledge of the monument and help to undertake conservation and preservation measures. The results of the aforementioned techniques are presented next. However, other sources of data are noteworthy to enrich a comprehensive database (Akasheh 2000): maps, old photographs, environmental data, and satellite images.

Photogrammetry

Photogrammetry is the science that enables accurate measurements and 2D and 3D reconstructions of all types of existing objects using images at different scales. Nowadays, there are different low-cost photogrammetric techniques to obtain a 3D model of archaeological sites from the ground (Barazzetti et al. 2010a, b; Kersten and Lindstaedt 2012; Lerma et al. 2013), from the air (Remondino et al. 2011; Rinaudo et al. 2012), and under water (Skarlatos et al. 2012). The choice of single-image photogrammetry, stereo-based photogrammetry or multi-image convergent photogrammetry, manual or fully automatic approaches, depends, in addition to the issues pointed out by Pavlidis et al. (2007), on the end use of the recording, the availability of solutions (i.e. high-end, low-end), the urgency to achieve the final solution, and last but not least, the level of expertise of the users. This latter aspect should not be underestimated.

A 3D model is a very important tool for visualizing and understanding a real cultural heritage object, archaeological monument, or site. Nowadays, a 3D model has many different uses from the analysis and documentation to dissemination and reconstruction through virtual scenarios. Highly detailed 3D models are generated in order to achieve exact replicas of an object or asset. In the dissemination field, high-quality 3D models are not so important. The aim is to show users a reliable reconstruction of an object that might be scientifically right from an interpretative point of view, but not always necessarily accurate in geometry.

Nowadays, it is possible to obtain accurate 3D models quickly and easily using structure from motion (SfM) algorithms. This is a low-cost technique that obtains dense 3D reconstructions from 2D images. As in traditional photogrammetry, SfM makes use of overlapping images obtained from multiple perspectives, but without requiring the knowledge beforehand of the interior and exterior orientation parameters of the camera nor control points (visible points usually targeted in which the spatial coordinates are accurate enough to either geo-reference or orient the output products). More information about SfM versus photogrammetric and SfM photogrammetric performance can be found in Barazzetti et al. (2010a, b), Lerma and Muir (2014), and Westoby et al. (2012).

The photogrammetric SfM approach to obtain point clouds based on imagery is fully automatic. A significant maturity is reached due to the capability of processing a vast number of images. After loading the images, corresponding (matching) features (either points, lines, curves, or blobs) between multiple images are detected with detectors and descriptors such as scale invariant feature transform (SIFT), speeded up robust features (SURF), smallest univalue segment assimilating nucleus (SUSAN), features from accelerated segment test (FAST), etc. (Jazayeri and Fraser 2010; Moreels and Perona 2007). Then, the precision of the image coordinates can be improved with a least squares matching (Barazzetti et al. 2010a, b; Lerma et al. 2013). SfM algorithms use these correspondences to estimate the orientation (camera pose) and sparse bundle adjustment is used to achieve better orientation estimates, determining also the 3D points of the corresponding image features. The final step is dense 3D reconstruction, also known as dense matching. Multi-view stereo (MVS) methods take the image orientation as input and produce dense 3D point clouds with accuracy nearly on par with laser scanners (Furukawa et al. 2010), although this depends on the image scale, number of images, image network, and, last but not least, the object's texture. More details on how the two most well-known MVS methods, CMVS (clustering view for multi-view stereo) and PMVS2 (patch-based multi-view stereo), perform can be found in Furukawa and Ponce (2010), Furukawa et al. (2010), and Westoby et al. (2012). With these MVS methods, very high-resolution models are generated in a few minutes. The process to obtain a dense point cloud and the workflow for the application of SfM photogrammetry is presented by Micheletti et al. (2015).

This low-cost and automatic method has many advantages, including minimum user interaction and no special instrument being needed due to the fact that any camera in the market can be used (usually conventional off-the-shelf cameras, such as DSLR, compact, video, or smartphone cameras). In theory, there are no restrictions on the object's geometry, in case there is enough texture. In practice, strong image network geometry is mandatory to achieve satisfying results. This latter statement requires experience and should not be underestimated by the users to achieve both metric and successful deliverables.

Terrestrial Laser Scanning

Laser scanning is an efficient, high-precision, and ultrafast active remote sensing technique used to acquire dense 3D point clouds (with reflectivity values). These instruments can generate vast amounts of 3D data (millions of points) in a few minutes. The usage of laser scanners is justified for objects, monuments, and sites with complex geometry, a lack of texture, and a lack of light. The quality of the results depends largely on the object's reflectivity. In-depth information about laser scanning systems can be found in Shan and Toth (2008) and Vosselman and Maas (2010), and more specific hands-on information on terrestrial laser scanners can be found in Lerma García et al. (2008). Böhler (2006) sets the advantages and disadvantages of laser scanners for the documentation of cultural heritage and compares laser scanning with other 3D measurement techniques.

Terrestrial laser scanning is used a priori to determine with maximum reliability the shape and volume of an architectural monument. Depending on the purpose, it might not be necessary to deal with high resolution, for instance, for applications oriented to dissemination activities and serious games.

Some terrestrial laser scanning systems are designed to acquire complementary color information through either internal or external cameras, while some devices do not. For cultural heritage documentation, this is a clear disadvantage. The easiest way to overcome the color issue is to integrate efficiently laser scanning and photogrammetry. The trend is to integrate different techniques based on range-based and image-based approaches to achieve successful surveying and modeling (Fiorillo et al. 2013; Lerma et al. 2010). Furthermore, the integration should be beyond geometrical 3D issues and tacking more the identification and recognition of materials and damages not only using photogrammetry and laser scanning but multispectral sensors and thermography (Cabrelles et al. 2009; Lerma et al. 2012; Haddad et al. 2015). The next section presents how the integration of multi-sensors was carried out to target the documentation of Djinn Block No. 9.

Multispectral 3D Recording and Documentation Pipeline

The recording and documentation can be undertaken with a wide range of metric and multispectral techniques such as photogrammetry, terrestrial laser scanning, multispectral photography, and thermography (Fig. 5.3) to build up scientific

Fig. 5.3 Data acquisition on site with thermal infrared sensor (*left*), and visible/near-infrared camera

knowledge of a monument, object, or site previous to conservation, preservation, monitoring, research, and dissemination endeavors.

The 2D/3D documentation with multispectral recording is presented in Fig. 5.4. It is a general documentation pipeline where specific recording tasks are particularized. The basic idea of the presented pipeline is that a proper and exhaustive recording and documentation satisfies the four essential reasons for recording outlined by ICOMOS (1996): (a) to acquire knowledge in order to advance the understanding; (b) to promote the interest and involvement of the people in the preservation of heritage through the dissemination of recorded information; (c) to permit informed management and control of construction works; and (d) to ensure maintenance and conservation.

In particular, three out of four steps presented in Fig. 5.4 are emphasized next to integrate multi-source data sets:

1. Data acquisition from multiple sensors, namely, total station, terrestrial laser scanner, digital camera, and thermal camera. A subset of the acquired data is presented in Fig. 5.5.
2. Generation of 3D models from laser scanning point clouds (Fig. 5.6); alternatively, from SfM or stereoscopic photogrammetric solutions. It is supposed that the 3D model is eventually free of errors and ready to be used after registration, filtering, decimation, smoothing, and hole filling.
3. Warping of imagery to register multispectral bands. From the multispectral bands, the false color compositions will be determined after choosing three bands (Fig. 5.7). In addition, digital image processing will be used to enhance image features.
4. Photorealistic 3D model generation for each of the composite images (visible, near-infrared [NIR], thermal infrared [TIR], and false color images). Figure 5.8 displays some snapshots of the output 3D models. More details can be found in Cabrelles et al. (2010) and Lerma et al. (2012).
5. Thermographic analysis undertaken from the multiple thermograms acquired at different periods (day–night, spring–autumn) in order to monitor the behavior of the monument over time (Lerma et al. 2011).

The software used to integrate the multi-source (laser scanning, photogrammetry, surveying, and imagery) data was FOTOGiFLE; 3DVEM – 3D Viewer, Editor & Meter; and 3DVEM – Register GEO, developed by GIFLE (2010).

Mobile Apps for Dissemination: Djinn Block No. 9 as a Case Study

In the last decade, mobile technology has experienced exponential growth. Nowadays, a smartphone is a little personal computer and portable computer and everyone carries one. These small computers are evolving quickly. Smartphones are fully equipped with a variety of devices such as global navigation satellite system

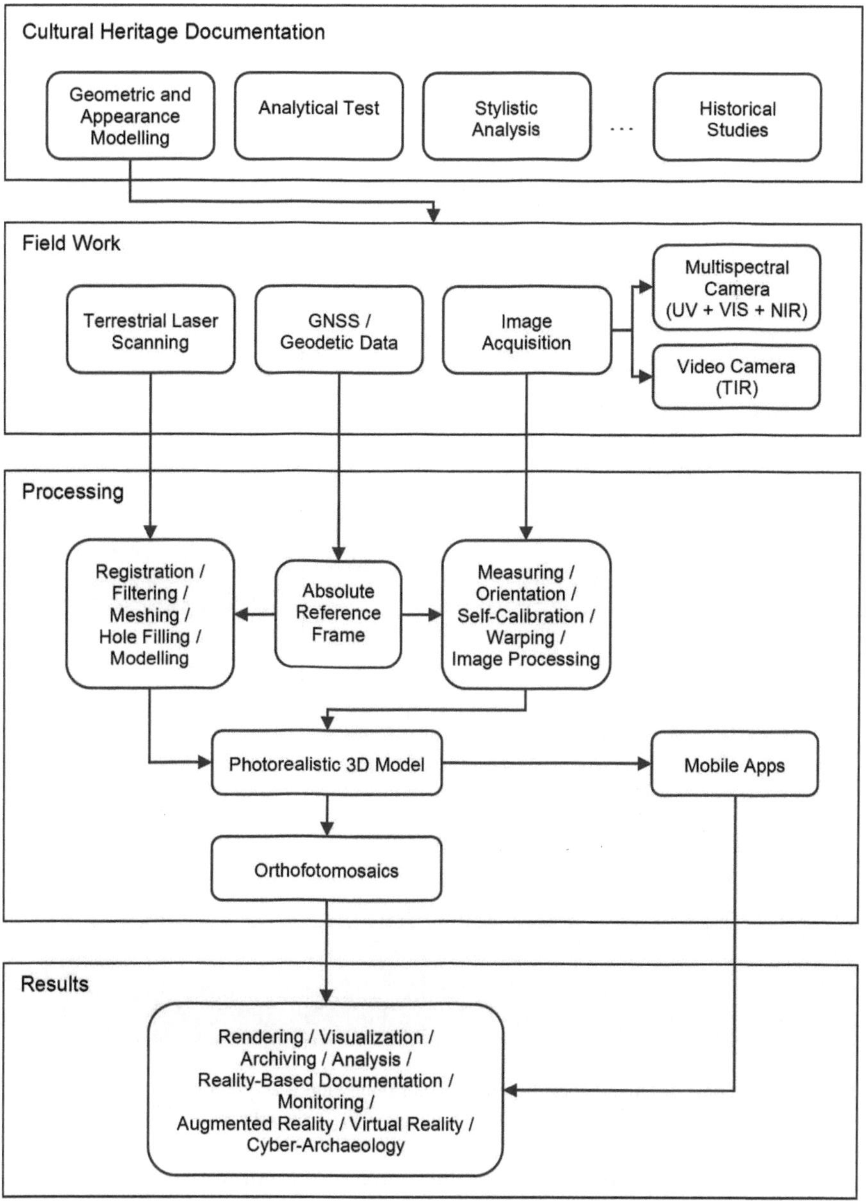

Fig. 5.4 Cultural heritage documentation and dissemination pipeline with emphases on multispectral recording and mobile applications

(GNSS), wireless internet for frequent interface (WIFI), Bluetooth, small and high resolution color video or still camera, image stabilization, capacity (touch) sensors, accelerometers, gyroscopes, digital compass, barometer and proximity sensors, and so on. On the one hand, this set of devices together with advanced chips, i.e. faster

Fig. 5.5 Input data of Djinn Block No. 9: (**a**) Color point clouds acquired from the laser scanner, (**b**) Visible image, (**c**) NIR image, (**d**) Thermal image taken in the afternoon. Western side

central processing unit (CPU) and graphics processing unit (GPU), allow information technology and communication (ITC) users to create powerful mobile apps. On the other hand, each generation of mobile phones is changing the way people experience with technology.

A mobile app is a software application developed to run on mobile devices such as smartphones and tablets. The mobile apps can be used to provide users with many services for entertainment or communication as well as specific applications, too. The scientific applications can also benefit from the powerful mobile devices and create powerful apps for dissemination.

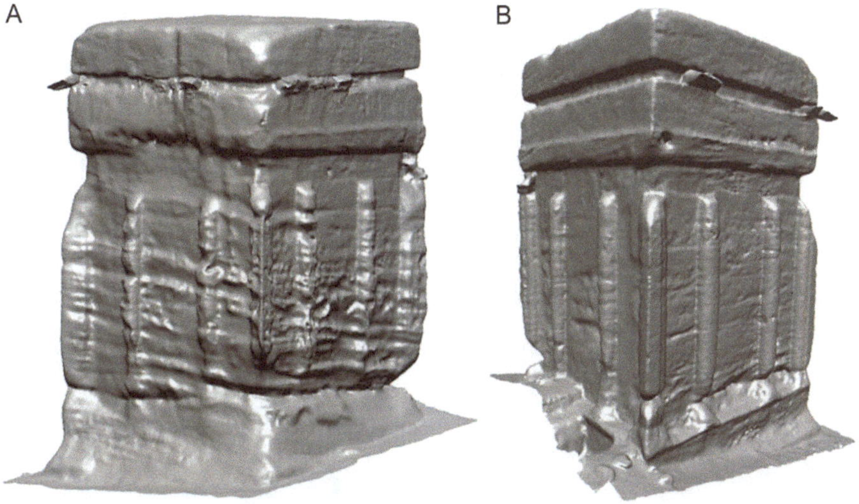

Fig. 5.6 Djinn Block No. 9 perspective views of the 3D model: (**a**) southern and eastern sides, (**b**) northern and western sides

Fig. 5.7 Western elevation of Djinn Block No. 9: (**a**) BW visible image, (**b**) near-infrared image, (**c**) false color composition with the NIR, green and red bands

The final goal of the developed mobile app is to create a service that can be used to improve the level of understanding of one of the monuments featured in the Petra Archaeological Park. It can also be used to disseminate the studies and research carried out on the Djinn Block No. 9.

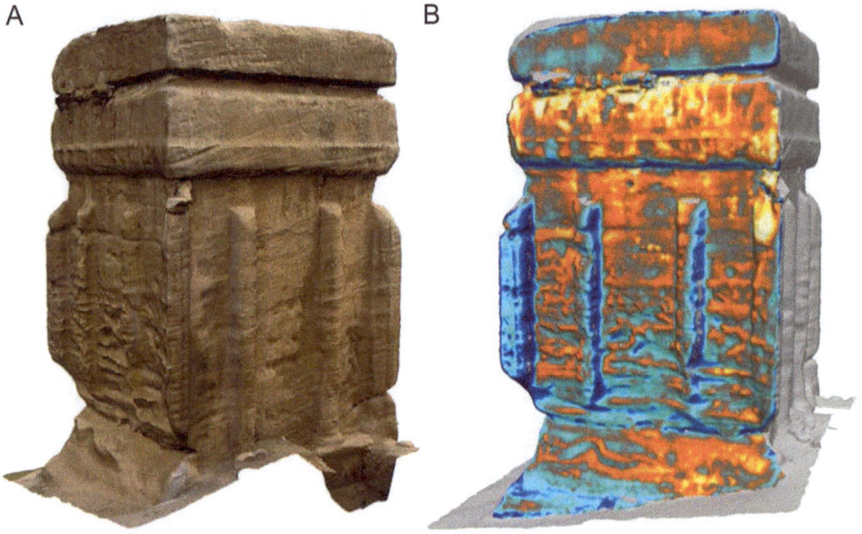

Fig. 5.8 Overall photorealistic model of Djinn Block No. 9: (**a**) photorealistic model of the eastern and northern sides, (**b**) thermorealistic model of the eastern side

There are several operating systems: Google Android, Apple iOS, Windows Phone, BlackBerry OS, among others. The two most important ones are Apple iOS and Android. Since 2009, Android mobile sales have grown steadily. Nowadays, Android dominates the smartphone market with a share of 82.8%, followed by iOS that shares 13.9% (IDC 2015).

Android is a mobile operating system (OS) currently developed by Google. It was designed principally for smartphones but now can be found in many devices like tablets, computers, watches, televisions, and cars. This OS is installed in many phones so it is definitely one of the main platforms for the development of apps.

Google's Android OS is based on the open Linux kernel and is open source. Android programs are written in Java and run Google's Davlik virtual machine, which is optimized for mobile devices. Java is an object-oriented computer programming language and is one of the most popular programming languages in use.

Through the Google Play store, users can download Android apps. There are thousands of apps published. This store helps the developer to distribute their applications easily. The Play Store is a great tool to disseminate services but it is difficult to position your app on top.

The app that is presented herein is thought to disseminate heritage features found inside the Petra Archaeological Park. The app is focused on the Djinn Block No. 9, but the Djinn9 app can be expanded to any other monuments in the Park. Furthermore, it can be used as an interactive guide to the Petra Archaeological Park.

Fig. 5.9 Picture of the home screen

Functions

The implemented Djinn9 app (Fig. 5.9) is composed of various views that allow users to interact. The views are the elements that develop the user interface of an application. The views can be either icons or texts. Our Djinn9 app has six functions that allow us to know in detail the features of Djinn Block No. 9.

The first function (Fig. 5.10) of the app allows users to show a Google map with the location of the monument and the approximate distance from the user to it. Following this way, the user can get a global positioning of the monument. Google's hybrid style map is adopted to display aerial imagery with additional information on top. This mapping style enhances the user's experience.

This function is developed with the Google Maps API. It offers several features such as the chance to add marks, calculate routes, or display the current location of the device. It can be used free of charge but with limitations; an application cannot request more than 15,000 geographical encodings per day. This API is very useful to show both specific locations and places worth visiting (map displaying points of interest). In addition, the user can compare between the device's location and the position of the points of interest.

The second function contains a map with points of interest in Petra Archaeological Park. This map provides information with the approximate location of monuments and facilities such as restaurants, toilets, and shops (Fig. 5.11). The developed infor-

Fig. 5.10 Localization screen

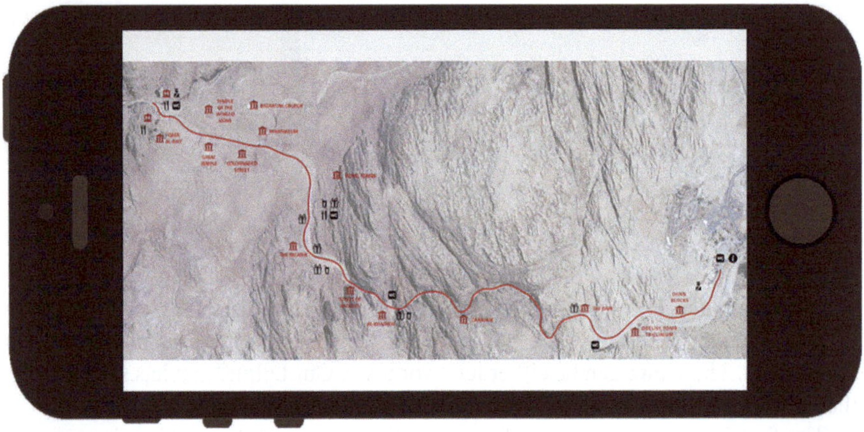

Fig. 5.11 Map of interest points screen

mation is based on the Petra Archaeological Park's guide presented in Viñals et al. (2007).

Third, the content of a photorealistic 3D model of Djinn Block No. 9 is presented (Fig. 5.12). The user is free to move around it and zoom in/out. The homemade function is developed with the Min3D library. This library is an open source 3D framework that is based on OpenGL ES v. 1.0/1.1 for Android devices. This framework provides tools to load a 3D model and to add functions. Min3D allows users to visualize 3D models, translate, rotate and scale, and add lights into the 3D model. Android's Min3D library supports the following 3D file formats: OBJ, MD2, and 3DS, as long as the files are small.

A smartphone cannot visualize and interact with large point clouds and 3D meshes over one million points. Ideal meshes must contain less than 10,000 points,

Fig. 5.12 Home screen 3D model

due to hardware limitations. As a result, it is necessary to create low-resolution 3D models of the monument. As the 3D model generated for Djinn Block No. 9 had over 600,000 points, it was downsized to be used in the mobile app. It is possible to get in the market 3D modeling software packages that allow decimation, filtering, and smoothing of the final 3D model. The one used by the authors to carry out this task was MeshLab (2014). MeshLab is open source software for processing and editing unstructured 3D irregular meshes. Furthermore, it provides a set of tools for editing, cleaning, inspecting, rendering, and converting different meshes.

The simplification process in MeshLab requires the usage of the quadric edge collapse decimation algorithm which managed to reduce the mesh over 10,000 points, achieving an OBJ file size of around 3 MB. The simplified model has fewer details.

In the case of creation of semi-immersive environments, the suitability of the different techniques will be restricted to 3D models and real-time rendering applications (Bustillo et al. 2015). The 3D models used for these applications cannot be too large.

The fourth function of the app contains a gallery of images taken in situ (Fig. 5.13). Initially thumbnail images are displayed in a grid view. After the user selects the thumbnail, the selected image is displayed in full size. After selecting one image, the rest can be displayed after swiping them to the right or left to continue viewing the rest of the image gallery.

The fifth function provides a historical context of the location of the monument. Relevant information is displayed to inform the user about details and curiosities of the monument. Information is shown in a scroll view. The user can scroll up and down the screen in order to read all the related information.

The last function contains a summary of the technical analysis undertaken on the monument, not only to improve the knowledge about the monument but also to safeguard its state of conservation. In this way, it can be used to inform users about the importance of preserving cultural heritage. Furthermore, the application contains an information button at the top right that displays the developers and people that have contributed to the successful development of the project.

Fig. 5.13 Images gallery screen

Design

The design of the user interface is a critical part in the development of any application. Therefore, enough resources should be devoted to the graphical design of the visual elements. This step is usually undertaken in the design stage of the mobile app. For the Djinn9 app, the following elements were designed:

- The launcher icon, also known as the application launcher. This icon emulates the outline of the monument (foreground) on a gradient background to give a sense of volume (Fig. 5.14).
- On top of the Home screen, another image was created that contains the application name, "Djinn9," in 3D letters. This image occupies the entire screen width. Below, six buttons were added and centered on the screen (Fig. 5.9).
- Color range is similar throughout the application and buttons are flat white icons that indicate what each function represents.

There are different types of devices and applications that can be developed with the Android OS. Because of this, the designer must adjust the design of the app to all types of screens.

Fig. 5.14 Icon application launcher

Discussion

There are different ways to record, present, and disseminate cultural heritage. There is still a gap between high-end recording and documentation with photogrammetric and laser scanning techniques and mobile apps. Mobile and web applications can include videos, explanatory texts, 3D models, images of different wavelength, level of detail and purpose, geo-localization, the history of the site, etc. In short, any type of information can be disseminated if the technological innovations are exploited. Nowadays, the latest high-end technologies allow information providers to disseminate cultural heritage through learning games, AR apps, and virtual environments. These technologies are becoming very popular to show particularized cultural content to different audience.

Our application is focused on Djinn Block No. 9 as example of a VR mobile app for the dissemination of cultural sites. The application can be extended to the rest of the monuments inside the Petra Archaeological Park. Generating 3D models of the rest of the monuments might allow the app to present information altogether in a 3D viewer. The drawback of displaying 3D models in great detail is that large mesh files need to be processed because most smartphones are not as powerful as personal computers. Whether more 3D models need to be added to the app, it is necessary to find optimization algorithms that are able to reduce significantly the point cloud resolution without losing much detail. Besides, using segmented sub-models reduces both the file size and the downloading time (Guarnieri et al. 2010).

Improving the visualization of 3D models into the app is possible after creating a virtual environment for the 3D model. This would bring more realism to the display model. There is software developed specifically to create virtual scenarios such as Unreal Engine or Unity. Despite being mainly developed for the videogames industry, they can be useful for this purpose.

Actually, VR applications are very popular and Google has created the virtual reality glasses, Google Cardboard. Google Cardboard converts an Android smartphone into a VR viewer. Based on this, a virtual visit could be created to visualize the virtual environment of the Petra Archaeological Park.

On the other hand, through current AR libraries such as Vuforia or ARToolkit, it is possible to enrich Petra app with AR tools and create semi-immersive environments. Therefore, it would be possible to recreate the past performing immersive or semi-immersive environments and would be an excellent way to visit, explore, and disseminate virtually the wonders of Petra.

Conclusion

This paper presented an extensive review of the recording and documentation activities undertaken by the authors inside the Petra Archaeological Park targeting Djinn Block No. 9, among other monuments. In particular, a variety of multispectral image-based and range-based approaches were tested, and fruitful results were delivered and foreseen. Beyond recording and documentation, dissemination was introduced through the creation of a VR mobile app, "Djinn9," developed initially for Android OS.

Within the development of the presented Djinn9 app, unforeseen problems deriving from high-end 3D modeling came up. In fact, mobile phone technology is not ready to handle large file sizes. It meant that decimation, filtering, and smoothing tasks were requested to simplify the originally derived 3D mesh of Djinn Block No. 9. Nevertheless, the performance of the simplified 3D model on the Djinn9 app is unaffected.

The usage of these new mobile app technologies such as Djinn9 opens the door to new dissemination strategies of our cultural heritage and demonstrates its potential as an effective self-learning method specially designed for virtual (on-site and off-site) visits and actual tourists on-site. These types of mobile and web-based applications enrich the user experience, foster knowledge, and encourage people to exploit more our historical legacy.

Finally, the development of our mobile Djinn9 app is still an ongoing project. Future activities are foreseen such as analyzing user feedback to strengthen the weak points of the app, and adding new functionalities (functions) to extend the app services. In order to achieve them, the Djinn 9 app will be published in Google's Play Store and the user experience will be evaluated.

Acknowledgments The authors would like to express their gratitude for the fruitful collaboration with the Jordan partners, namely, Prof. Talal Akasheh and Prof. Naif Haddad. This work was supported by the *Agencia Española de Cooperación Internacional para el Desarrollo* (AECID) under Project Number A/025999/09, the authorities of the Petra Archaeological Park, and the Spanish *Ministerio de Economía y Competitividad* under Project Number HAR2014–59873–R.

References

Akasheh, T. (2000). Eine Datenbank für Petra. A Database for Petra. In M. Kühlenthal & H. Fischer (Eds.), *PETRA die Restaurierung der Grabfassaden/the restoration of the Rockcut Tomb Façades* (pp. 230–240). Munich: Landesamt fur Denkmalpflege.

Akasheh, T., Shaer, M., Khrisat, B., Naes, M., & Sarayrah, R. (2005). A Conservation Study of Djin Block No. 9 in Petra. Report presented to Prodomea, an EC funded project under INCO-Med program FP5, contract number ICA3-CT-2002–10021. doi:10.1017/CBO9781107415324.004.

Barazzetti, L., Remondino, F., & Scaioni, M. (2010a). Extraction of accurate tie points for automated pose estimation of close-range blocks. *The International Archives of Photogrammetry and Remote Sensing, 37*(3A), 151–156.

Barazzetti, L., Scaioni, M., & Remondino, F. (2010b). Orientation and 3D modelling from markerless terrestrial images: Combining accuracy with automation. *The Photogrammetric Record, 25*(132), 356–381. doi:10.1111/j.1477-9730.2010.00599.x.

Biosca Taronger, J. M., Navarro Tarín, S., & Lerma García, J. L. (2007). Modelado tridimensional de una bóveda barroca mediante la combinación de láser escáner y fotogrametría. Proceedings of the 7 Setmana Geomàtica, pp. 1–9.

Böhler, W. (2006). Comparison of 3D laser scanning and other 3D measurement techniques. In M. Baltsavias, A. Gruen, L. Van Gool, & M. Pateraki (Eds.), *Recording, modeling and visualization of cultural heritage* (pp. 89–100). London: Taylor & Francis Group.

Bustillo, A., Alaguero, M., Miguel, I., Saiz, J. M., & Iglesias, L. S. (2015). A flexible platform for the creation of 3D semi-immersive environments to teach cultural heritage. *Digital Applications in Archaeology and Cultural Heritage, 2*(4), 248–259. doi:10.1016/j.daach.2015.11.002.

Cabrelles, M., Galcerá, S., Navarro, S., Lerma, J. L., Akasheh, T., & Haddad, N. (2009). Integration of 3D laser scanning, photogrammetry and thermography to record architectural monuments. In *Proc. of the 22nd CIPA symposium* (p. 6). Kyoto. http://cipa.icomos.org/fileadmin/template/doc/KYOTO/74.pdf.

Cabrelles, M., Seguí, A. E., Navarro, S., Galcerá, S., Portalés, C., & Lerma, J. L. (2010). 3D photo-realistic modelling of stone monuments by dense image matching. *The International Archives of Photogrammetry, Remote Sensing and Spatial Information Sciences, XXXVIII*(5), 121–124.

Caro, J. L., & Hansen, S. (2015). De la fotogrametría a la difusión del patrimonio arqueológico mediante game engines: Menga un caso de estudio. *Virtual Archaeology Review, 6*(12), 58–68. doi:10.4995/var.2015.4159.

Charlotte, C. (2011). Technologies of seeing the past: The Curzon Memories App. In *EVA London 2011: Electronic visualization and the arts* (pp. 163–170). Publisher: BCS, The Chartered Institute for IT. Location: London, UK.

Coenen, T., Mostmans, L., & Naessens, K. (2013). MuseUs: Case study of a pervasive cultural heritage serious game. *Journal on Computing and Cultural Heritage, 6*(2), 1–19. doi:10.1145/2460376.2460379.

Eppich, R., & Chabbi, A. (2007). Recording, documentation, and information management for the conservation of heritage places: Illustrated examples. *Getty Conservation Institute, 2*, 1–163.

Fiorillo, F., Jiménez Fernández-Palacios, B., Remondino, F., & Barba, S. (2013). 3d surveying and modelling of the archaeological area of Paestum, Italy. *Virtual Archaeology Review, 4*(8), 55–60. doi:10.4995/var.2013.4306.

Forte, M. (2011). Cyber-Archaeology: Notes on the simulation of the past. *Virtual Archaeology Review, 2*(4), 7–18. doi:10.4995/var.2011.4543.

Furukawa, Y., Curless, B., Seitz, S. M., & Szeliski, R. (2010). Towards internet-scale multi-view stereo. In *2010 IEEE computer society conference on computer vision and pattern recognition* (pp. 1434–1441). Piscataway: IEEE. doi:10.1109/CVPR.2010.5539802.

Furukawa, Y., & Ponce, J. (2010). Accurate, dense, and robust multiview stereopsis. *IEEE Transactions on Pattern Analysis and Machine Intelligence, 32*(8), 1362–1376. doi:10.1109/TPAMI.2009.161.

GIFLE. (2010). Photogrammetry & laser scanning research group, Department of Cartographic Engineering, Geodesy and Photogrammetry, Universitat Politècnica de València. http://gifle.webs.upv.es/. Accessed 20 Sept 2015.

Guarnieri, A., Pirotti, F., & Vettore, A. (2010). Cultural heritage interactive 3D models on the web: An approach using open source and free software. *Journal of Cultural Heritage, 11*(3), 350–353. doi:10.1016/j.culher.2009.11.011.

Gutierrez, J. M., Molinero, M. A., Soto-Martín, O., & Medina, C. R. (2015). Augmented reality technology spreads information about historical graffiti in temple of Debod. *Procedia Computer Science, 75(Vare)*, 390–397. http://dx.doi.org/10.1016/j.procs.2015.12.262.

Haddad, N. A., Akasheh, T. S., Lerma, J. L., & Khresat, B. R. (2015). Towards a risk management and conservation plan for the Djin blocks at the world heritage site of Petra, Jordan: The case of Djin block no. 9. *Conservation and Management of Archaeological Sites, 17*(2), 175–191. doi:10.1080/13505033.2015.1124182.

Han, J.-G., Park, K.-W., Ban, K.-J., & Kim, E.-K. (2013). Cultural heritage sites visualization system based on outdoor augmented reality. *AASRI Procedia, 4*, 64–71. doi:10.1016/j.aasri.2013.10.011.

Heinrichs, K. (2008). Diagnosis of weathering damage on rock-cut monuments in Petra, Jordan. *Environmental Geology, 56*, 643–675. doi:10.1007/s00254-008-1358-1.

ICOMOS. (1996). Principles for the recording of monuments, groups of buildings and sites. International Council on Monuments and Sites. http://www.icomos.org/charters/archives-e.pdf.

IDC. (2015). Smartphone OS market share, 2015 Q2. International Data Corporation. http://www.idc.com/prodserv/smartphone-os-market-share.jsp#. Accessed 1 Feb 2016.

Jazayeri, I., & Fraser, C. S. (2010). Interest operators for feature-based matching in close range photogrammetry. *Photogrammetric Record, 25*(129), 24–41. doi:10.1111/j.1477-9730.2009.00559.x.

Kersten, T., & Lindstaedt, M. (2012). Image-based low-cost Systems for Automatic 3D recording and modelling of archaeological finds and objects. *Progress in Cultural Heritage Preservation, 7616*, 1–10. doi:10.1007/978-3-642-34234-9_1.

Lerma García, J. L., Santana Quintero, M., Heine, E., & Van Genechten, B. (Eds.). (2008). *Theory and practice on terrestrial laser scanning. Training material bases on practical applications.* Valencia: Editorial Universitat Politècnica de València.

Lerma, J. L. (2001). Multiband versus multispectral supervised classification of architectural images. *Photogrammetric Record, 17*(97), 89–101. doi:10.1111/0031-868X.00169.

Lerma, J. L., Akasheh, T., Haddad, N., & Cabrelles, M. (2011). Multispectral sensors in combination with recording tools for cultural heritage documentation. *Change Over Time, 1*(2), 236–250. https://muse.jhu.edu/journals/change_over_time/v001/1.2.lerma.html. Accessed 28 Jan 2016.

Lerma, J. L., Cabrelles, M., Akasheh, T. S., & Haddad, N. A. (2012). Documentation of weathered architectural heritage with visible, near infrared, thermal and laser scanning data. *International Journal of Heritage in the Digital Era, 1*(2), 251–276. doi:10.1260/2047-4970.1.2.251.

Lerma, J. L., & Muir, C. (2014). Evaluating the 3D documentation of an early Christian upright stone with carvings from Scotland with multiples images. *Journal of Archaeological Science, 46*, 311–318. doi:10.1016/j.jas.2014.02.026.

Lerma, J. L., Navarro, S., Cabrelles, M., Seguí, A. E., & Hernández-López, D. (2013). Automatic orientation and 3D modelling from markerless rock art imagery. *ISPRS Journal of Photogrammetry and Remote Sensing, 76*, 64–75. doi:10.1016/j.isprsjprs.2012.08.002.

Lerma, J. L., Navarro, S., Cabrelles, M., & Villaverde, V. (2010). Terrestrial laser scanning and close range photogrammetry for 3D archaeological documentation: The upper Palaeolithic Cave of Parpallo as a case study. *Journal of Archaeological Science, 37*(3), 499–507. doi:10.1016/j.jas.2009.10.011.

Letellier, R., Schmid, W., & LeBlanc, F. (2007). *Recording, documentation, and information Management for the Conservation of heritage places: Guiding principles* (Vol. 1). Los Angeles: The Getty Conservation Institute.

MeshLab. (2014). Visual computing lab, ISTI - CNR. Pisa. http://meshlab.sourceforge.net/. Accessed 3 Feb 2016.

Meyer, É., Grussenmeyer, P., Perrin, J. P., Durand, A., & Drap, P. (2007). A web information system for the management and the dissemination of cultural heritage data. *Journal of Cultural Heritage, 8*(4), 396–411. doi:10.1016/j.culher.2007.07.003.

Micheletti, N., Chandler, J. H., & Lane, S. N. (2015). Structure from Motion (SfM) photogrammetry. *Geomorphological Techniques, 2*, 1–12.

Moreels, P., & Perona, P. (2007). Evaluation of feature detectors and descriptors based on 3D objects. *International Journal of Computer Vision, 73*(3), 263–284. doi:10.1007/s11263-006-9967-1.

Mortara, M., Catalano, C. E., Bellotti, F., Fiucci, G., Houry-Panchetti, M., & Petridis, P. (2014). Learning cultural heritage by serious games. *Journal of Cultural Heritage, 15*(3), 318–325. doi:10.1016/j.culher.2013.04.004.

Novotný, M., Lacko, J., & Samuelčík, M. (2013). Applications of multi-touch augmented reality system in education and presentation of virtual heritage. *Procedia Computer Science, 25*, 231–235. doi:10.1016/j.procs.2013.11.028.

Pavlidis, G., Koutsoudis, A., Arnaoutoglou, F., Tsioukas, V., & Chamzas, C. (2007). Methods for 3D digitization of cultural heritage. *Journal of Cultural Heritage, 8*(1), 93–98. http://dx.doi.org/10.1016/j.culher.2006.10.007.

Potenziani, M., Callieri, M., Dellepiane, M., Corsini, M., Ponchio, F., & Scopigno, R. (2015). 3DHOP: 3D Heritage Online Presenter. *Computers & Graphics, 52*(April 2014), 129–141. doi:10.1016/j.cag.2015.07.001.

Remondino, F., Barazzetti, L., Nex, F., Scaioni, M., & Sarazzi, D. (2011). UAV photogrammetry for mapping and 3d modeling–current status and future perspectives. *The International Archives of the Photogrammetry Remote Sensing and Spatial Information Sciences, 38-1*(C22), 25–31.

Rinaudo, F., Chiabrando, F., Lingua, A. M., & Spanò, A. T. (2012). Archaeological site monitoring: UAV photogrammetry can be an answer. *The International Archives of the Photogrammetry, Remote Sensing and Spatial Information Sciences, 39*(B5), 583–588.

Rubino, I., Barberis, C., Xhembulla, J., & Malnati, G. (2015). Integrating a location-based mobile game in the museum visit: Evaluating visitors' behaviour and learning. *Journal on Computing and Cultural Heritage, 8*(3), 15:1–15:18. doi:10.1145/2724723.

Scopigno, R., Callieri, M., Dellepiane, M., Ponchio, F., & Potenziani, M. (2017). Delivering and using 3D models on the web: are we ready? *Virtual Archaeology Review, 8*(17), 1–9. doi:10.4995/var.2017.6405.

Shan, J., & Toth, C. K. (2008). *Topographic laser ranging and scanning: Principles and processing*. Boca Raton: CRC Press.

Shaw, L., & Challis, K. (2013). "There's an app for that": Building smartphone applications to improve the ergonomics of landscape study, analysis and interpretation. In E. Ch'ng, V. Gaffney, & H. Chapman (Eds.), *Visual heritage in the digital age* (pp. 297–307). London: Springer. doi:10.1007/978-1-4471-5535-5_15.

Skarlatos, D., Demestiha, S., & Kiparissi, S. (2012). An "open" method for 3D modelling and mapping in underwater archaeological sites. *International Journal of Heritage in the Digital Era, 1*(1), 1–24. doi:10.1260/2047-4970.1.1.1.

Stanish, C. S., & Levy, T. E. (2013). Cyber-archaeology and world cultural heritage: Insights from the holy land. *Bulletin of the American Academy of Arts and Sciences, 66*, 26–33. https://www.amacad.org/multimedia/pdfs/publications/bulletin/spring2013/bulletin_spring2013.pdf.

UNESCO. (1985). Petra. World heritage list. http://whc.unesco.org/en/list/326. Accessed 28 Jan 2016.

Valtolina, S., Franzoni, S., Mazzoleni, P., & Bertino, E. (2005). Dissemination of cultural heritage content through virtual reality and multimedia techniques: A case study. 11th international multimedia modelling conference, pp. 214–221. doi:10.1109/MMMC.2005.36. Conference Location: Melbourne, Australia. Date of Conference: 12–14 Jan. 2005.

Viñals, M. J., Farajat, S., & Alonso-Monasterio, P. (2007). Petra archaeological park. Self-guided Visit Map. Universitat Politècnica de Valènica / Agencia Española de Cooperación Internacional y Desarrollo / Petra Archaeological Park.

Vosselman, G., & Maas, H. G. (2010). *Airborne and terrestrial laser scanning*. Dunbeath: Whittles Publishing.

Westoby, M. J., Brasington, J., Glasser, N. F., Hambrey, M. J., & Reynolds, J. M. (2012). "Structure-from-motion" photogrammetry: A low-cost, effective tool for geoscience applications. *Geomorphology, 179*, 300–314. doi:10.1016/j.geomorph.2012.08.021.

Chapter 6
Toward a Grand Narrative of Bronze Age Vegetation Change and Social Dynamics in the Southern Levant

Patricia L. Fall, Mariela Soto-Berelov, Elizabeth Ridder, and Steven E. Falconer

Introduction

Archaeological narratives may be made "grand" through the analysis of big data to address broadly applicable themes, span lengthy time frames or cover extensive space. Current archaeological narratives applied on a regional scale (e.g., to the southern Levant) tend to derive from interpretive methods and lines of evidence that shift through time, making long-term linkages challenging. Paleoenvironmental narratives benefit from more consistent forms of data and analytical methods (e.g., palynological analysis of sediment cores), but often are more specific to a locality and correspondingly challenging to extrapolate over larger regions. This study, in contrast, strives toward a grand narrative for the development of Bronze Age civilization centered on digital paleovegetation modeling through multiple millennia in the mid-Holocene across the southern Levant. Our modeling integrates multiple

P.L. Fall (✉)
Department of Geography & Earth Sciences, University of North Carolina Charlotte, Charlotte, NC 28223, USA
e-mail: pfall@uncc.edu

M. Soto-Berelov
School of Mathematical and Geospatial Sciences, RMIT University, GPO Box 2476, Melbourne, VIC 3001, Australia
e-mail: mariela.soto-berelov@rmit.edu.au

E. Ridder
Department of Liberal Studies, California State University San Marcos, San Marcos, CA 92096, USA
e-mail: eridder@csusm.edu

S.E. Falconer
Department of Anthropology, University of North Carolina Charlotte, Charlotte, NC 28223, USA
e-mail: sfalcon1@uncc.edu

T.E. Levy, I.W.N. Jones (eds.), *Cyber-Archaeology and Grand Narratives*, One World Archaeology, https://doi.org/10.1007/978-3-319-65693-9_6

geographical and paleoclimatic variables, coordinates temporally or geographically separate narratives, and links those narratives with the modern world. We highlight specific localities as they illustrate details of vegetation change, and provide counterpoints for comparative discussion. Ultimately, our grand narrative allows us to infer new linkages and discontinuities between more time- or space-specific narratives.

Levantine Narratives

Levantine archaeology is populated by multiple narratives that tend to be specific to time periods, methods, or historical traditions. For the Bronze Age, these narratives have been linked sequentially to form a longer interpretive chain with prime emphasis shifting at various junctures to social dynamics, historical relations, or climatic change. The social foundations for Levantine complex society that led to the formation of towns and localized polities, as well as the development of metallurgy, are ascribed commonly to the Chalcolithic Period (e.g., Bourke 2001; Golden 2010; Levy 1995, 2014; Rowan and Golden 2009). Building from this basis, current narratives for the Bronze Age then begin with the axiom that "urbanism, and the route taken by different societies towards it, is the primary story of the Early Bronze Age Levant ..." (Greenberg 2014: 269; cf. Chesson 2003; Chesson and Philip 2003; Richard 2014). Extending this perspective to the "longue duree of the history of Palestine," the Early Bronze Age provides "a kind of rehearsal before the golden age of Canaanite civilization in the Middle Bronze Age" (de Miroschedji 2014: 322).

In orthodox terms, the intervening Intermediate Bronze Age (or Early Bronze IV) bifurcates these periods with evidence of pronounced settlement discontinuity, including the abandonment of Early Bronze towns (Dever 1995; Palumbo 1990), tempered by possible cultural and demographic continuity between Early and Middle Bronze populations (Cohen 2009; Prag 2014). The Intermediate Bronze Age has been cited as "an alluring Holocene example of societal responses to abrupt climate change across the eastern Mediterranean and west Asian landscapes" prompted by sudden cooling and aridification and followed a few centuries later by a rebound in precipitation (Weiss 2014: 367).

The subsequent "reurbanization" of the Middle Bronze Age ushered in "the first age of regular interregional contact and trade, and large-scale international conflict" (Bourke 2014: 465; see also Cohen 2014; Greenberg 2002), which continued in the Late Bronze Age with the establishment of Canaanite polities (Savage and Falconer 2003; Strange 2000) and Levantine involvement in the economic and cultural world system of the eastern Mediterranean and Near East (Bunimovitz 1995; Panitz-Cohen 2014). According to some archaeological scenarios, the end of the Late Bronze Age ushers in a "Dark Age" (e.g., Cline 2014; Herr 2014) triggered by the appearance of multiple linguistic/historical groups (most notably the "Sea Peoples") ca. 1200 BC (Killebrew and Lehmann 2013; Liverani 2014: Table 1.1; Oren 2000). The emergence of these distinct ethnic groups may be seen as a "text-generated historical punctuation mark" (Sherratt 2014: 498) marked by widespread collapse of the highly interdependent economic systems of the eastern Mediterranean (Liverani 1987; Sherratt 2003; Singer 2012). This perspective harkens back to Braudel's emphasis on Mediterranean cultural interconnectedness (e.g., 2001: 114). Indeed, the collapse of civilization has been proposed as the singular narrative for the Late Bronze Age, based on a "perfect storm of calamities" including "climate change (drought), seismic events, internal rebellions and 'systems collapse'" (Cline 2014: 11; see Drake 2012 on climate change), which disarticulated the eastern Mediterranean world.

Thus, the prevailing interpretive narrative for Levantine civilization stitches together archaeological patterns of settlement nucleation and disintegration, junctures of climatic stress, and historically documented social and political disruptions. This amalgamated perspective holds the implicit expectation of long-term elaboration of Levantine social complexity prior to its catastrophic demise at the end of the Late Bronze Age. This viewpoint implicitly directs archaeological explanation to the seemingly anomalous discontinuities and downturns that punctuate and ultimately truncate Bronze Age social development. In contrast, this paper initiates a grand narrative based on analytical methods applied uniformly across the Jordan Rift and through the Bronze Age, which permits more cohesive regional and temporal interpretation, reexamination of more specific narratives, and redefinition of phenomena meriting attention and explanation.

Study Area

The development of complex societies in the Southern Levant featured discontinuous trends of aggregation and dispersal among the populations of Bronze Age towns, villages, and pastoral encampments. Limited water sources and rainfall, as well as considerable topographic relief, made the success of agrarian society particularly susceptible to the influences of environmental fluctuations. These circumstances were particularly acute along the fertile, but arid low elevation bottom lands of the Jordan Rift (descending to −410 masl). Pronounced topographic contrasts between the arable lands below sea level along the Rift, and the high elevation (rising to 1200 masl) Levantine Central Hills to the west and Transjordanian Plateau to the east help illustrate ancient vegetation dynamics particularly well. These changes also emerge along the major wadis draining into the Jordan Rift, particularly from the east. Accordingly, this narrative unfolds along the Jordan Rift from the Sea of Galilee to the Dead Sea Basin, in the Hill Country west to Megiddo and Hebron, and on the Plateau east to Amman (Fig. 6.1).

The climate along the Jordan Rift incorporates wet, cool winters and long, dry, and hot summers. The coolest temperatures accord with higher elevations in the Levantine Hill Country and Transjordanian Plateau, while the highest temperatures (up to 50 °C) occur in the lowest reaches of the Rift around the Dead Sea (Al-Eisawi 1996). Annual precipitation, received mostly in winter and spring, decreases from

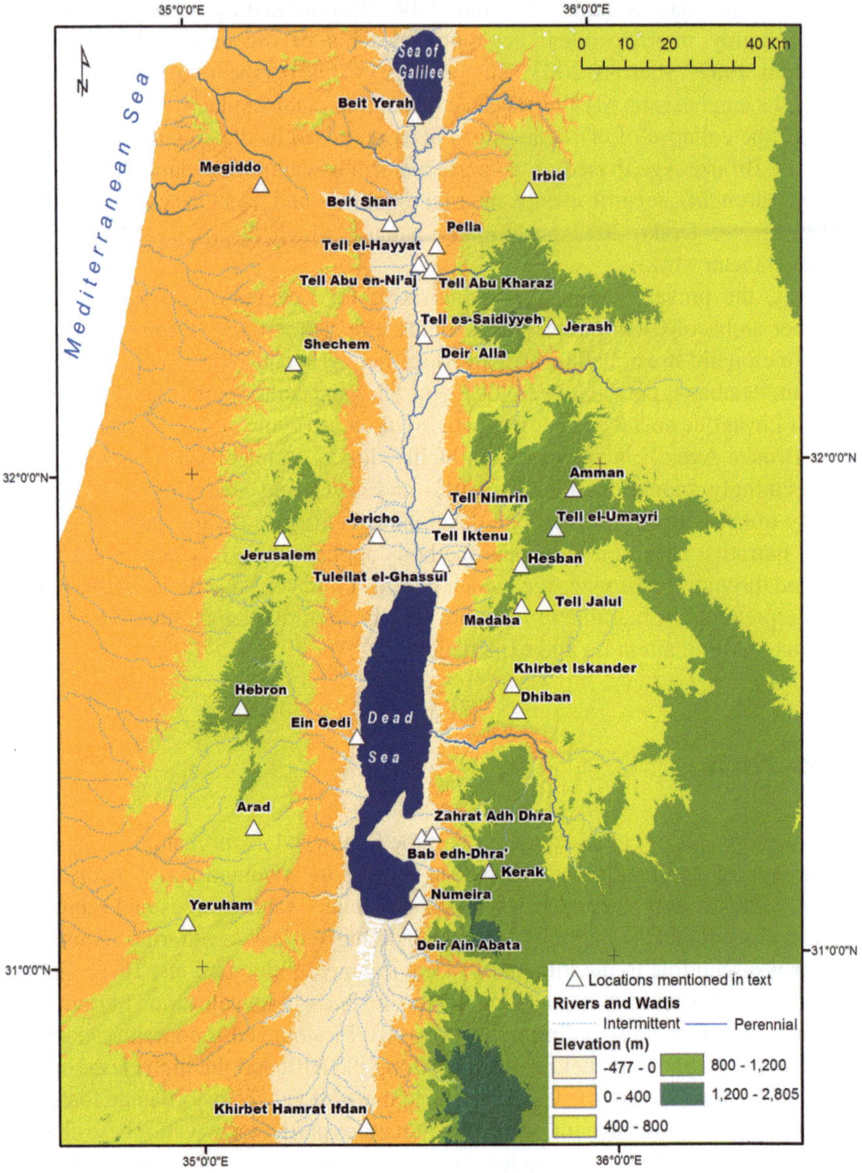

Fig. 6.1 Map of the southern Levant showing major topographical features and Bronze Age archaeological sites along the Jordan Rift and its surrounding uplands

west to east with increasing distance from the Mediterranean Sea, and from north to south with declining influence of cyclonic storms. Topography also influences rainfall, leading to particularly low precipitation in the lowest reaches of the Jordan Rift.

This study models Levantine vegetation according to Sudanian, Saharo-Arabian, Irano-Turanian and Mediterranean "plant geographical regions" (following Zohary 1973). We also model three transitional zones: Sudanian/Saharo-Arabian, Saharo-Arabian/Irano-Turanian, and Irano-Turanian/Mediterranean. In general terms, these zones consist of varying suites of woody plant species that range from desert Sudanian and Saharo-Arabian vegetation to Irano-Turanian steppe and Mediterranean woodlands (see Soto-Berelov et al. 2015: Table 1). This complex vegetation regime has evolved through the Holocene as a product of climate change, plant and animal domestication, and a series of ever-shifting anthropogenic impacts (e.g., Butzer 2012; Cordova 2007; Cordova et al. 2013; Fall et al. 2002, 2004; Rollefson and Kohler-Rollefson 1992; Rosen 2007).

Methods

Our study integrates multiple environmental variables to produce a series of time-specific maps of potential vegetation modeled without the effects of human intervention along the Jordan Rift and its adjacent highlands (see detailed methods in Soto-Berelov et al. 2015). This modeling builds from observations of woody plant species at nearly 1700 locations surveyed across the southern Levant in a series of studies conducted over the past century (see Soto-Berelov et al. 2015: Fig. 2), which we augmented with data from the Israel Biodiversity Information System database (BioGIS 2000, 2002). Observed plant species locations were linked with geographical data from 2002 Terra ASTER satellite imagery (http://asterweb.jpl.nasa.gov) and substrate data from geological maps (Bartov 1994; Sneh et al. 1998) to create a digital elevation model (DEM) with 1 km spatial resolution, which conforms to the spatial resolution of our climate modeling (see below).

Climatic values for our vegetation modeling were generated from a macrophysical climate model (MCM; Bryson and Bryson 2000; Bryson et al. 2006; Bryson and DeWall 2007). Our application of this model incorporates recent historical temperature and precipitation data from 40 weather stations across the southern Levant (see Soto-Berelov et al. 2015: Fig. 3). The chronology for this climate modeling is based on calibrated radiocarbon dates (expressed as cal BP) for volcanic dust events (Bryson & DeWall 2007). After removal of some variables due to spatial autocorrelation, our modeling uses four environmental parameters: mean annual temperature, mean annual precipitation, elevation, and geological substrate (see Soto-Berelov et al. 2015: Table 3). Our application of this MCM generates past mean temperature and precipitation values for each 1 km^2 grid cell between 6500 and 2800 cal BP, on a centennial interval.

We use MAXENT (version 3.3.3e; http://www.cs.princeton.edu/~schapire/MaxEnt), a probabilistic species modeling program, to model past and present potential vegetation according to plant geographical regions (see discussions in Galletti et al. 2013; Soto-Berelov et al. 2015). Our modeling begins by correlating the modern locations at which species are observed with the environmental values for those locations. MAXENT calculates relationships between variables and generates functions to estimate the probable occurrence of a species in each 1 km^2 cell. This method accommodates presence-only datasets and produces a continuous surface in which each cell has a value indicating the probability of species occurrence. The predicted distributions of indicator species (Soto-Berelov et al. 2015: supplementary materials S1) are combined across our study area to model modern plant geographical regions. Areas in which two regions overlap are classified as transitional. For instance, the *transitional Irano-Turanian/Mediterranean* region indicates the presence of key indicator species of both these regions, suggesting a transition zone between steppe and woodland vegetation.

We model past potential vegetation at 100-year intervals through the Bronze Age between 5500 and 3000 cal BP. In each model, the distributions of plant geographical regions are predicted and mapped on the basis of 1 km^2 grids of climatic values generated by the MCM for each modeled date. To illustrate a narrative of Bronze Age vegetation change along the Jordan Rift, in this work we present a 3-D visualization of plant geographical regions along the Jordan Rift at a series of critical junctures.

Results

Our results reveal paleoclimatic values and potential vegetation distributions with which we synthesize the environmental dynamics that underlay the course of Bronze Age civilization in the southern Levant. Among major climatic trends, as exemplified at Jerusalem, modeled annual precipitation shows a clear gradual decrease from 6500 to 2800 cal BP (Fig. 6.2a). Modeled average annual temperature shows a very different pattern of relatively steady values, punctuated by two dramatic drops: 5400–5300 cal BP and 4000–3900 cal BP (Fig. 6.2b). Thus, the climatic backdrop of this study features a long-term drying trend beginning at least as early as the Chalcolithic and continuing through the entire Bronze Age. This precipitation decline is coupled with relatively steady temperatures that are punctuated by two pronounced intervals of cooler temperatures at the beginnings of the Early and Middle Bronze ages, eras of population aggregation and the development of complex societies marked by fortified towns and geographically defined polities.

Potential vegetation modeling provides more nuanced perspectives on the effects of these climatic trends. Environmental conditions at 5400 cal BP could have supported steppe vegetation over large areas south of the Sea of Galilee, into the Jezreel Valley, and in the Jordan Valley south to Tell es-Saidiyyeh (Fig. 6.3). Farther south, while our modeling suggests that the Jordan Rift bottomlands could only have supported desert vegetation, settlements along the flanks of the valley (e.g., Deir Alla, Tell Nimrin, Jericho, Bab edh-Dhra) would have been situated near potential steppe or Mediterranean vegetation (Fig. 6.4). During this time period, wadi slopes to the east of the Rift could have supported steppe vegetation. Upland settlements, from

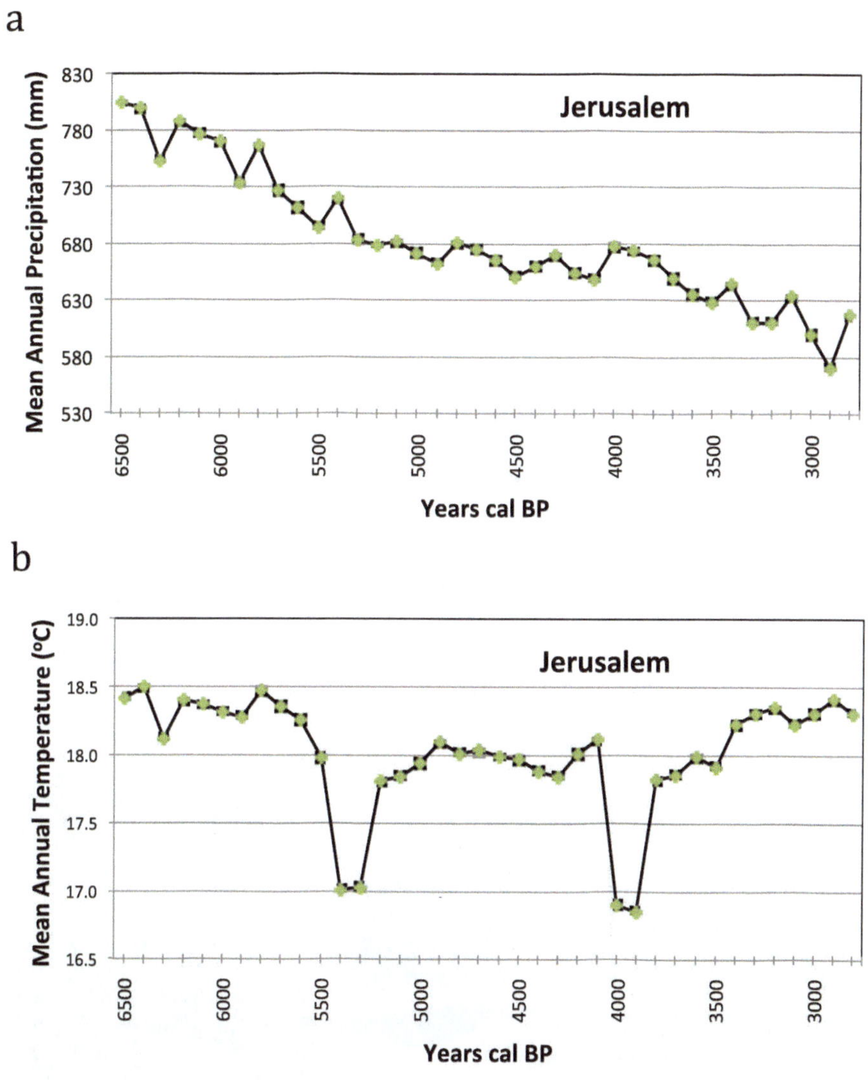

Fig. 6.2 Modeled mean annual precipitation (**a**) and mean annual temperature (**b**) for Jerusalem, 6500–2800 calibrated years BP (at 100-year intervals)

Irbid to Madaba, and from Megiddo to Hebron enjoyed environmental conditions conducive to Mediterranean woodlands (Figs. 6.3 and 6.4).

By 4200 cal BP, following the abandonment of Early Bronze towns and more than two millennia of declining precipitation, drier environmental conditions would have shifted the potential vegetation along the Northern Rift toward desert species (Fig. 6.5), with steppe vegetation modeled only for the fringes just south of the Sea of Galilee, near Beit Shan and around settlements in the eastern foothills of the Rift (e.g., Pella, Tell Abu Kharaz). Towns farther south (e.g., Saidiyyeh, Deir Alla,

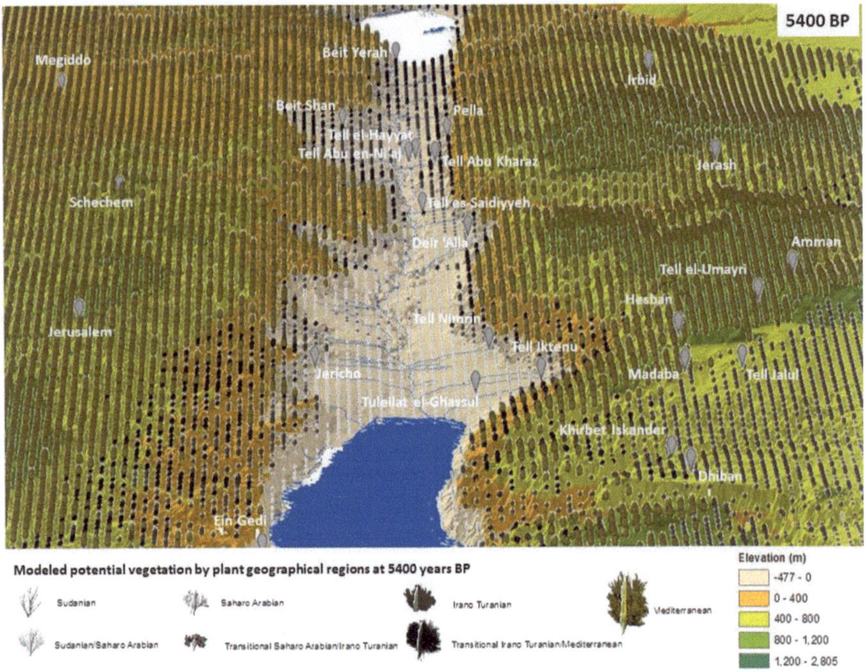

Fig. 6.3 3-D model of potential vegetation in the Northern Rift by plant geographical regions at 5400 calibrated years BP

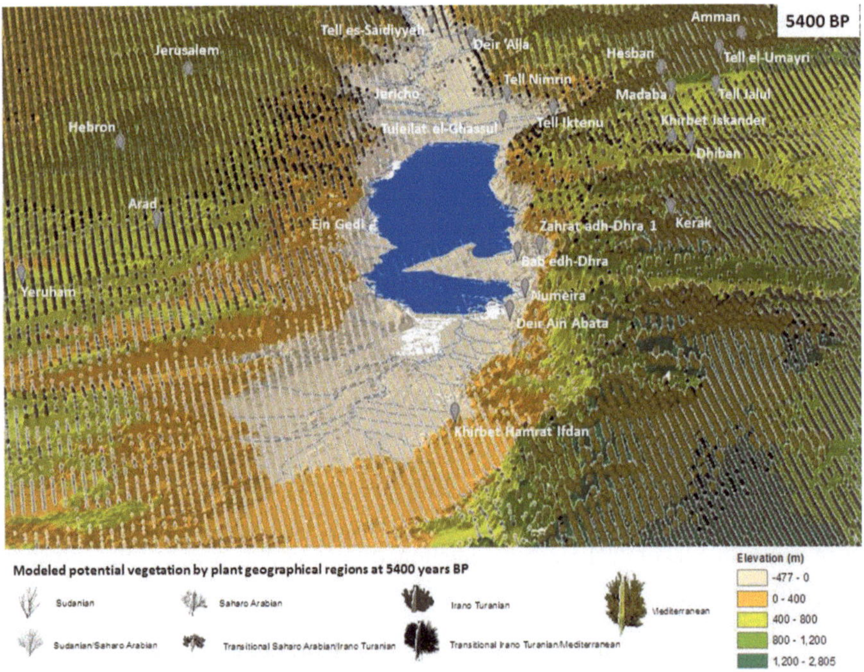

Fig. 6.4 3-D model of potential vegetation in the Southern Rift by plant geographical regions at 5400 calibrated years BP

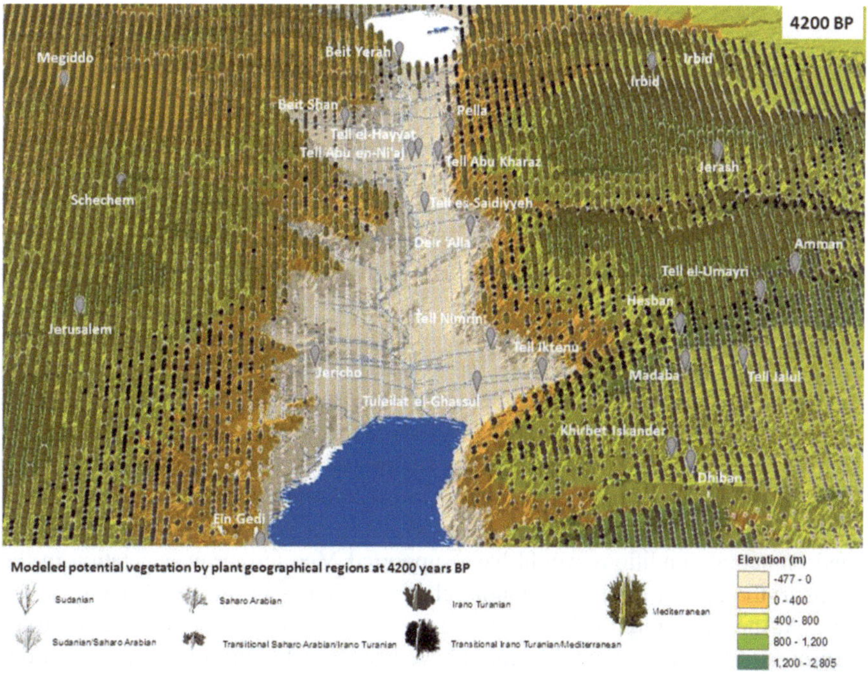

Fig. 6.5 3-D model of potential vegetation in the Northern Rift by plant geographical regions at 4200 calibrated years BP

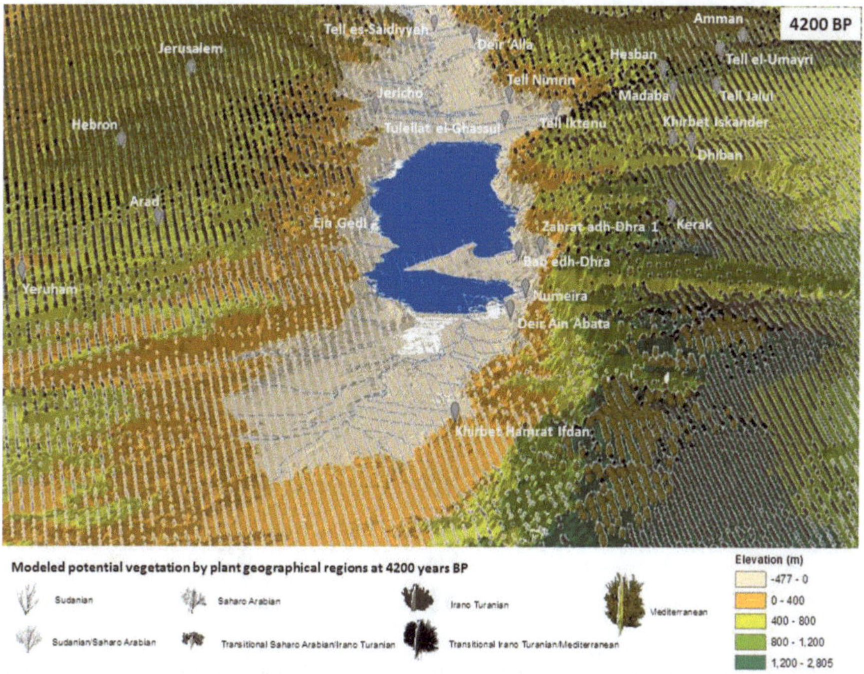

Fig. 6.6 3-D model of potential vegetation in the Southern Rift by plant geographical regions at 4200 calibrated years BP

Nimrin, Jericho) now lie amid potential desert vegetation. Settlements in the Southern Rift (Fig. 6.6) continue to be modeled in desert, but are now clearly disconnected from areas of potential Mediterranean woodlands or steppe vegetation. Vegetation along the upland settlements to the west of the Rift remain modeled as Mediterranean woodlands, while woodland areas east of the Rift have contracted and no longer form a continuous forested region. Likewise, the wadis that traverse these upland areas now support steppe rather than woodland vegetation (Figs. 6.5 and 6.6).

The brief interval between 4200 and 4000 cal BP represents a rapid resurgence in steppe and Mediterranean potential vegetation coincident with a pronounced drop in annual temperature and slight increase in yearly precipitation. By 4000 cal BP, settlements along the Jordan Valley south of the Sea of Galilee and in the lower Jezreel Valley once again are modeled as steppe and located close to Mediterranean woodlands (Fig. 6.7). While the valley bottom continues to be modeled as desert, settlements north of the Dead Sea are modeled in or very near steppe vegetation. Environmental conditions would have supported Mediterranean vegetation in the wadis to the east of the Rift and along the lower flanks of the Hill Country to the west. At the beginning of the Middle Bronze Age, all upland settlements north of Hebron and Madaba potentially could have been situated in Mediterranean woodlands. In the Southern Rift ca. 4000 cal BP, however, environmental conditions did

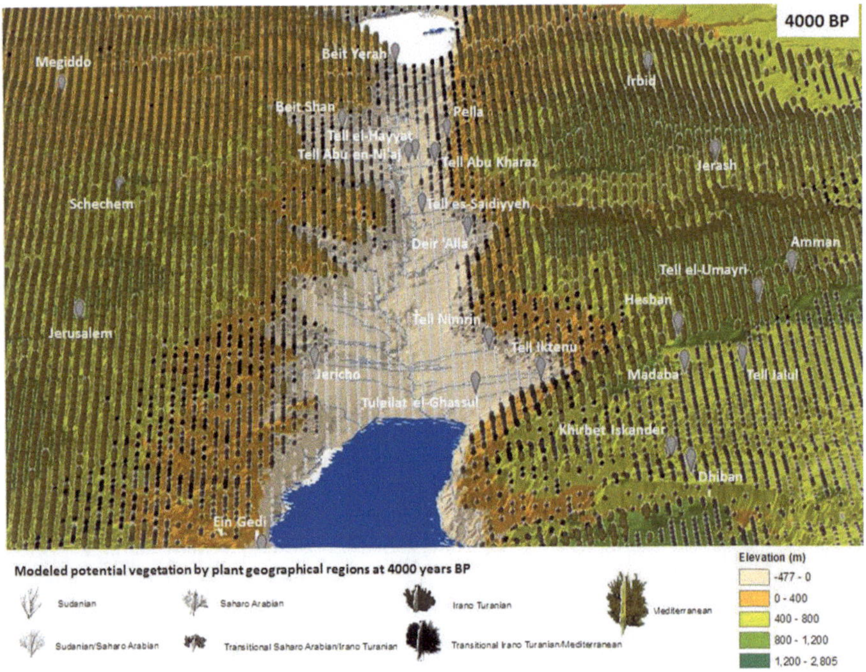

Fig. 6.7 3-D model of potential vegetation in the Northern Rift by plant geographical regions at 4000 calibrated years BP

not rebound sufficiently to support revegetation to the same extent as in the north (Fig. 6.8). Potential Mediterranean woodlands were more limited, wadis are modeled with steppe vegetation and settlements along the Southern Rift clearly were subject to desert conditions. Thus, the regional cooling ca. 4000 cal BP seems to have favored greater expansion of Mediterranean vegetation along the Northern, rather than the Southern Rift.

The millennium between 4000 and 3000 cal BP features a variety of systematic shifts in modeled vegetation, which are most pronounced along the Northern Rift and in the southern Transjordanian highlands (e.g., east of Khirbet Hamrat Ifdan). Steppe vegetation near the Sea of Galilee and in the Jezreel Valley (e.g., around Beit Shan) is progressively replaced by desert, and Mediterranean woodlands are supplanted by steppe in the wadis along the Northern Rift by 3500 cal BP (Figs. 6.9 and 6.10). In the south, steppe vegetation is replaced by desert in the wadis east of the Rift (Figs. 6.11 and 6.12). Steppe retreats along the margins of the Rift, which is now modeled as desert virtually everywhere below sea level. While Mediterranean woodlands remain spread over much of the Central Hills west of the Rift, steppe now appears in some upland areas (e.g., near Megiddo, Fig. 6.10). Mediterranean woodlands are modeled only for the highest elevation enclaves in the east and are virtually absent south of Amman (Fig. 6.12), producing a distinctly fragmented vegetation landscape, with highly variable local environmental conditions, especially

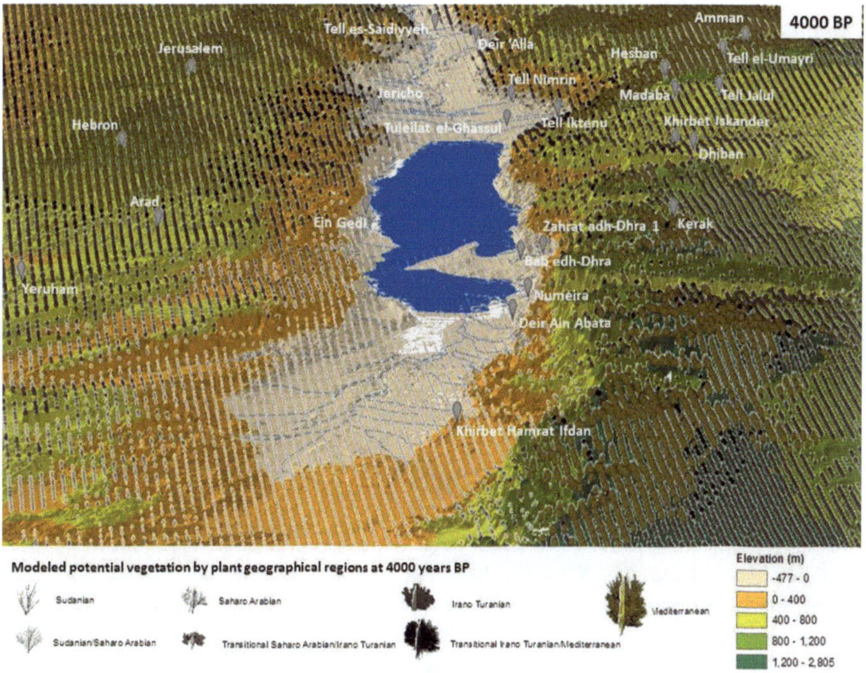

Fig. 6.8 3-D model of potential vegetation in the Southern Rift by plant geographical regions at 4000 calibrated years BP

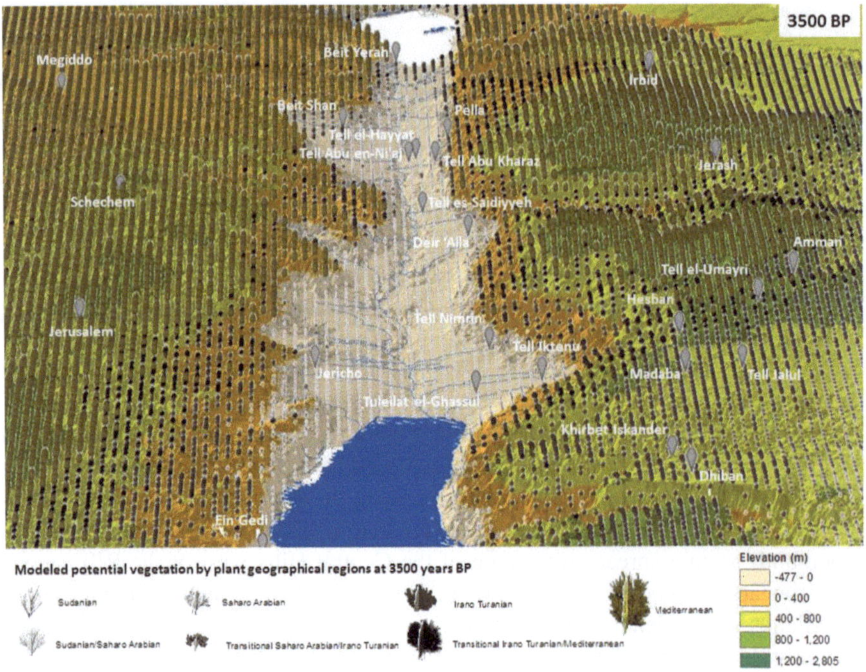

Fig. 6.9 3-D model of potential vegetation in the Northern Rift by plant geographical regions at 3500 calibrated years BP

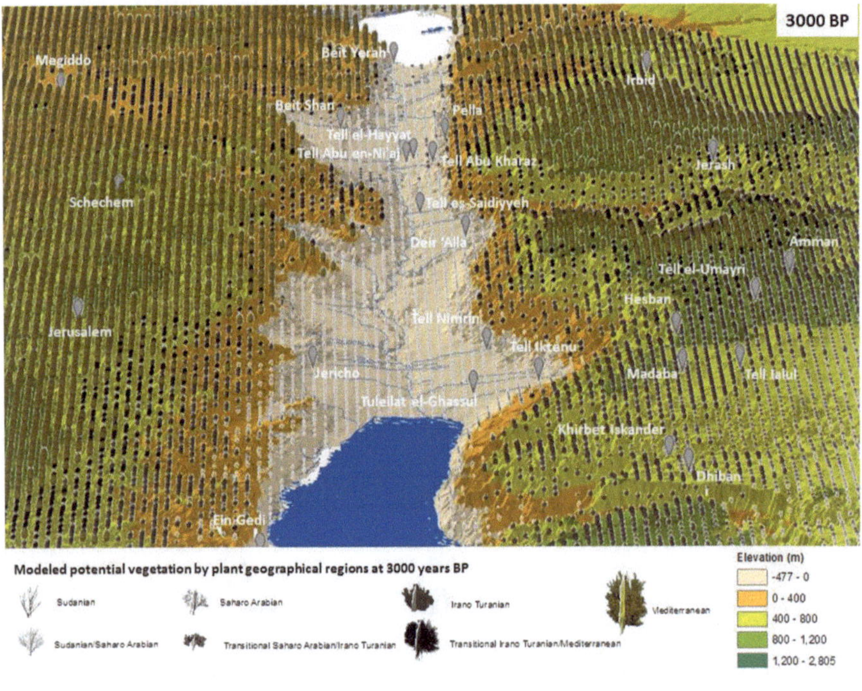

Fig. 6.10 3-D model of potential vegetation in the Northern Rift by plant geographical regions at 3000 calibrated years BP

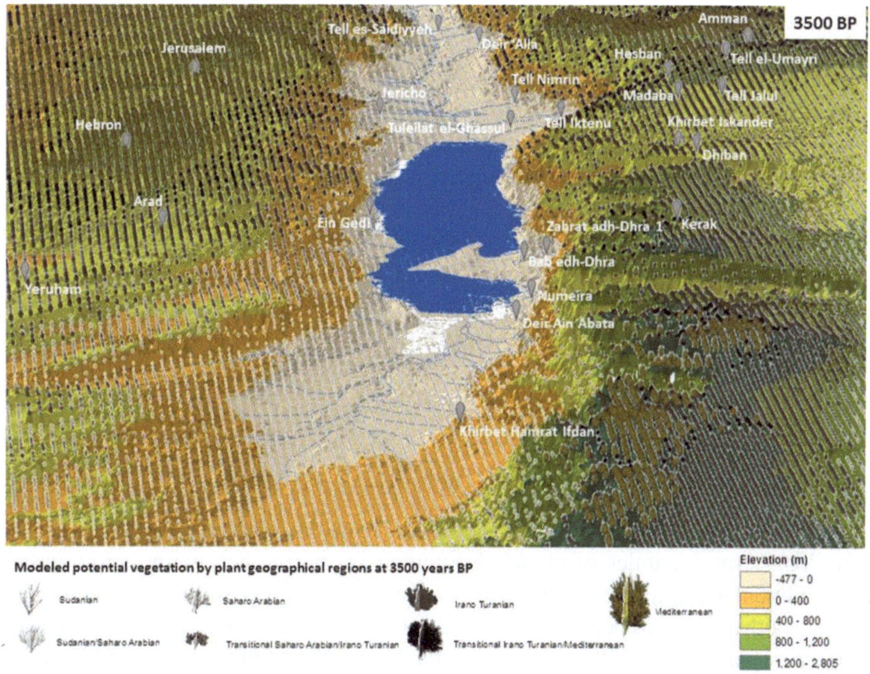

Fig. 6.11 3-D model of potential vegetation in the Southern Rift by plant geographical regions at 3500 calibrated years BP

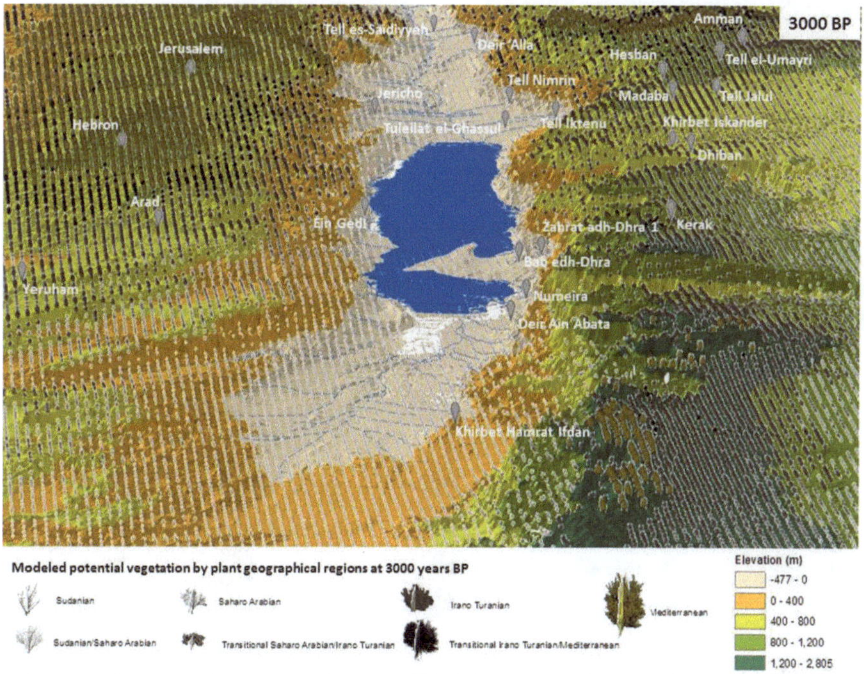

Fig. 6.12 3-D model of potential vegetation in the Southern Rift by plant geographical regions at 3000 calibrated years BP

east of the Rift. The remaining forest enclaves are surrounded by encroaching steppe and desert vegetation.

Over the past 3000 years, environmental conditions have ameliorated sufficiently to support a less disjunct potential vegetation landscape (Fig. 6.13). Notable characteristics of modeled modern vegetation include a return of Mediterranean vegetation along some northern wadi systems, and the replacement of desert by steppe south of the Sea of Galilee, along the margins of the Northern Rift, and in southern wadi systems (Fig. 6.14). These shifts, however, do not approach the more favorable conditions for steppe and Mediterranean vegetation seen at the outset of the Bronze Age ca. 5400 cal BP.

Discussion

The long-term dynamics of modeled potential vegetation bear witness to a grand environmental narrative underlying the course of Bronze Age settlement and society in the southern Levant between 5500 and 3000 cal BP. This narrative includes very different spatial expressions of vegetation change. Most notably, modeled shifts in potential vegetation are most acute in the more northerly portions of the study area,

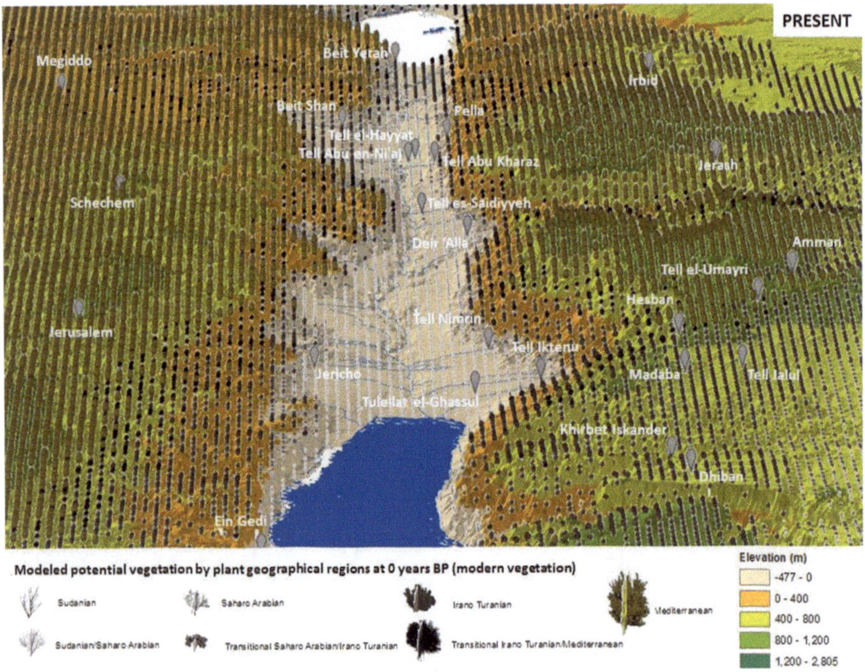

Fig. 6.13 3-D model of potential vegetation in the Northern Rift by plant geographical regions at 0 calibrated years BP (modern vegetation)

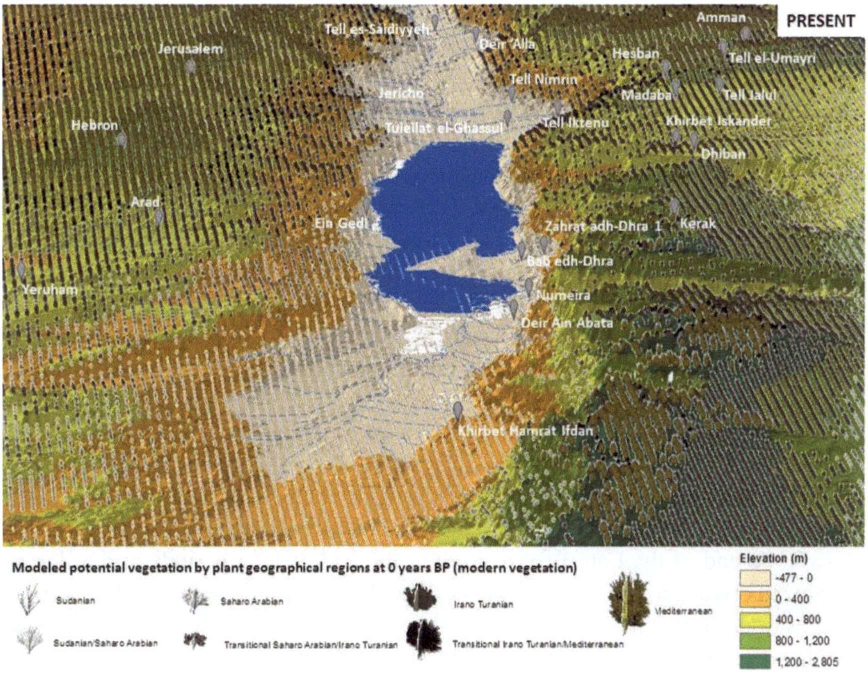

Fig. 6.14 3-D model of potential vegetation in the Southern Rift by plant geographical regions at 0 calibrated years BP (modern vegetation)

along the margins of the Jordan Rift and into the wadi systems east of the Rift. Particularly dramatic shifts unfold across the arable landscapes of the northern Jordan Valley and Jezreel Valley. In this setting, numerous Bronze Age towns (e.g., Beit Yerah, Pella, Beit Shan, Tell Abu Kharaz, Tell es-Saidiyyeh, Deir Alla) and villages (e.g., Tell el-Hayyat, Tell Abu en-Ni'aj) would have enjoyed conditions characteristic of Mediterranean woodlands or steppe vegetation at some junctures (e.g., 5400 and 4000 cal BP), but only supportive of desert vegetation at others (e.g., 4200 and 3000 cal BP) (see van der Kooij 2012).

Based on new radiocarbon chronologies (e.g., Bourke et al. 2009; Bruins and van der Plicht 1995; Golani and Segal 2002; Regev et al. 2012), the Early Bronze Age and each of its constituent sub-periods began earlier than assumed previously, thereby portraying an increasingly lengthy era of long-term drying bracketed by sharp temperature declines. The last of these sub-periods, known variously as Early Bronze IV or the Intermediate Bronze Age, formerly marked a roughly two-century abandonment of towns possibly sparked by sharp drying. Detailed radiocarbon evidence from the northern Jordan Valley now stretches Early Bronze IV over at least a half millennium (4500–4000 cal BP; Falconer and Fall 2016), implicating this period as a lengthy era of town-less society with correspondingly depleted woodland potential vegetation along the Rift.

Middle Bronze Age towns developed earlier and more abundantly along the Northern Rift and its tributary wadis than in the more southerly reaches of the Levant (Bourke 2014; Cohen 2014; Falconer 2008). Accordingly, the more pronounced vegetation shifts in the north represent particularly important environmental influences on the oscillating success of Levantine town life and agrarian economy. In particular, the diminished potential for woodland vegetation just after 4000 cal BP in southern Jordan helps explain the relative dearth of Middle Bronze Age settlement in this region compared to the countryside west of the Jordan Rift (Bourke 2014; Falconer 2008). In general terms, our modeling portrays the Middle Bronze Age, which may end in the Jordan Valley by about 3650 cal BP (Falconer and Fall 2017), as a short-lived urban resurgence in the longer-term context of diminishing potential woodlands associated with resumed desiccation and increasing temperatures.

Archaeological and historical narratives surrounding Bronze Age civilization commonly adopt a temporal perspective predicated on pronounced and relatively sudden deleterious events (e.g., desiccation and collapse at the end of the Early Bronze Age; political and economic upheaval with the arrival of the Sea Peoples toward the end of the Late Bronze Age) at the end of long periods of developing urbanized civilization (e.g., Cline 2014; Greenberg 2002; de Miroschedji 2009). In contrast, our landscape-based narrative depicts vegetation changes associated with a long steady trend of environmental drying, which is punctuated most noticeably by two short-term but pronounced drops in temperature (coupled with slight increases in precipitation) at 5400 cal BP and 4000 cal BP, coincident with the beginnings of Early and Middle Bronze town life. These two shifts appear related to "abrupt climate change events" ca. 5200 and 4200 cal BP (a.k.a. the "4.2" and "5.2" events) proposed by other studies (e.g., Kaniewski et al. 2012; Weiss et al. 2012; Weiss 2014). While environmental change seems increasingly apparent at these approximate junctures, our narrative reveals a slightly different facet, which emphasizes the rapid spread of potential Mediterranean vegetation and changes in the climatic variables that would have supported these woodlands.

Thus, our grand narrative features dramatic temporal vegetation shifts, which often articulate with regional trends of settlement and social development, while offering unorthodox interpretive perspectives on them. In general, vegetation modeling reveals substantial decline in potential Mediterranean woodlands, redistribution of steppe vegetation, and expansion of deserts over the course of the Bronze Age (see also Soto-Berelov et al. 2015). More specifically, the beginning of Early Bronze town life coincides with moderately high regional precipitation, cooler temperatures, and potentially widespread Mediterranean woodlands. The gradual decline of Early Bronze towns may have resulted, in part, from diminishing precipitation as reflected by shrinking woodlands between 5400 and 4200 cal BP. From this perspective, however, the pervasive town abandonment of the Intermediate Bronze Age clearly follows a decidedly long-term environmental trend, rather than a sudden climatic catastrophe. Rapid change instead characterizes the southern Levant's landscape at the beginning of the Middle Bronze Age, as signaled by the sudden expansion of Mediterranean and steppe vegetation coincident with a marked drop in temperature and slight precipitation increase at 4000 cal BP. Subsequently, the coupled trends of declining Mediterranean woodlands and expanding desert vegetation resume during the Middle and Late Bronze ages between 4000 and 3000 cal BP. The gradual trends in potential vegetation change through this millennium suggest that the transition from the Middle Bronze urban heyday to Late Bronze internationalism ca. 3500 cal BP does not correlate with a juncture of sudden environmental change. This aspect of our grand narrative accords instead with historically inferred political changes between Egypt and the Levant that mark the end of Middle Bronze Age urbanism (Bourke 2014; Cohen 2002; Greenberg 2002). Subsequently, our narrative reveals continued contraction of Mediterranean and steppe vegetation through the Late Bronze Age, leading to greatly expanded deserts by ca. 3000 cal BP. Thus, the Levantine vegetation landscape at the end of the Bronze Age emerges as the product of multi-faceted environmental dynamics that feature more than three millennia of long-term drying. In a manner similar to the end of Early Bronze Age towns, our narrative suggests that a major factor in the systemic collapse of the Late Bronze Age world (see Liverani 1987; Sherratt 2003; Singer 2012) was a long ebbing of Mediterranean vegetation and the environmental conditions that supported it, rather than a calamitous perfect storm.

Conclusion

Digital potential vegetation modeling provides a broadly applicable means of initiating and interpreting a grand narrative of Levantine Bronze Age civilization. When applied over 2500 years in the mid-Holocene, this approach provides a broadly applicable analytical method with which we may span and coordinate the pivotal environmental, historical, and social changes running between the region's late prehistory and early history. In this initial formulation of the narrative, long-term diminishing Mediterranean woodland, expanding desert, and the environmental changes underlying them emerge as a fundamental narrative theme. This primary narrative trend is tempered by sudden shifts in vegetation that correlate with the coalescence of towns and localized polities, first at the beginning of the Early Bronze Age and second at the outset of the Middle Bronze Age. Conversely, the dramatic abandonment of Early Bronze town life during the Intermediate Bronze Age prior to ca. 4000 cal BP and the collapse of Late Bronze Age internationalism ca. 3000 cal BP do not correlate with sudden downturns, but represent the culminations of multiple deleterious environmental trends whose coordinated effects are synthesized in our modeling of regional potential vegetation along the Jordan Rift.

References

Al-Eisawi, D. (1996). *Vegetation of Jordan*. Cairo: UNESCO.

Bartov, Y. (1994). *The geology of the Arava Valley*. Israeli Geological Survey Report GSI/4/94, 16.

BioGIS. (2000). A. Danin's grid database. Israel Biodiversity Information System. http://www.biogis.huji.ac.il. Accessed 18 Mar 2015.

BioGIS. (2002). Israel Nature and Parks Authority database. Israel Biodiversity Information System. http://www.biogis.huji.ac.il. Accessed 18 Mar 2015.

Bourke, S. J. (2001). The Chalcolithic period. In B. MacDonald, R. Adams, & P. Bienkowski (Eds.), *The archaeology of Jordan* (pp. 107–162). Sheffield: Sheffield Academic Press.

Bourke, S. J. (2014). The southern Levant (Transjordan) during the Middle Bronze Age. In M. L. Steiner & A. E. Killebrew (Eds.), *The archaeology of the Levant c. 8000–332 BCE* (pp. 463–481). Oxford: Oxford University Press.

Bourke, S. J., Zoppi, U., Hua, Q., Meadows, J., & Gibbins, S. (2009). The beginning of the early Bronze Age in the north Jordan Valley: New 14C determinations from Pella in Jordan. *Radiocarbon, 51*(3), 905–913.

Braudel, F. (2001). *The Mediterranean in the ancient world.* London: Allen Lane, Penguin Books.

Bruins, H., & van der Plicht, J. (1995). Tell es-Sultan (Jericho): Radiocarbon results of the short-lived cereal and multiyear charcoal samples from the end of the Middle Bronze Age. *Radiocarbon, 37*, 213–220.

Bryson, R. A., & Bryson, R. U. (2000). Site-specific high-resolution models of the monsoon for Africa and Asia. *Global and Planetary Change, 26*, 77–84.

Bryson, R. U., Bryson, R. A., & Ruter, A. H. (2006). A calibrated radiocarbon database of Late Quaternary volcanic eruptions. *eEarth Discuss, 1*, 123–134. http://www.electronic-earth-discuss.net/1/123/2006/eed-1-123-2006.pdf.

Bryson, R. A., & DeWall, K. M. (2007). *A paleoclimatology workbook: High resolution, site-specific, macrophysical climate modeling*. Hot Springs: The Mammoth Site.

Bunimovitz, S. (1995). On the edge of empires – Late Bronze Age (1500–1200 BCE). In T. E. Levy (Ed.), *The archaeology of society in the Holy Land* (pp. 320–331). New York: Facts on File.

Butzer, K. W. (2012). Collapse, environment and society. *Proceedings of the National Academy of Sciences, 109*, 3628–3631.

Chesson, M. S. (2003). Households, houses, neighborhoods and corporate villages: Modeling the Early Bronze Age as a house society. *Journal of Mediterranean Archaeology, 6*, 79–102.

Chesson, M. S., & Philip, G. (2003). Tales of the city? 'Urbanism' in the Early Bronze Age Levant from Mediterranean and Levantine perspectives. *Journal of Mediterranean Archaeology, 16*, 3–16.

Cline, E. H. (2014). *1177 B.C.: The year civilization collapsed.* Princeton: Princeton University Press.

Cohen, S. L. (2002). *Canaanites, chronology and connections: The relationship of Middle Bronze Age IIA Canaan to Middle Kingdom Egypt.* Winona Lake: Eisenbrauns.

Cohen, S. L. (2009). Continuities and discontinuities: A re-examination of the Intermediate Bronze Age—Middle Bronze Age transition in Canaan. *Bulletin of the American Schools of Oriental Research, 354*, 1–13.

Cohen, S. L. (2014). The southern Levant (Cisjordan) during the Middle Bronze Age. In M. L. Steiner & A. E. Killebrew (Eds.), *The archaeology of the Levant c. 8000–332 BCE* (pp. 451–464). Oxford: Oxford University Press.

Cordova, C. E. (2007). *Millenial landscape change in Jordan: Geoarchaeology and cultural ecology*. Tucson: The University of Arizona Press.

Cordova, C. E., Nowell, A., Bisson, M., Ames, C. J. H., Pokines, J., Chang, M., & al-Nahar, M. (2013). Interglacial and glacial desert refugia and the Middle Paleolithic of the Azraq Oasis, Jordan. *Quaternary International, 300*, 94–110.

Dever, W. G. (1995). Social structure in the Early Bronze IV Period in Palestine. In T. E. Levy (Ed.), *The archaeology of society in the Holy Land* (pp. 282–296). New York: Facts on File.

Drake, B. L. (2012). The influence of climatic change on the Late Bronze Age collapse and the Greek Dark Ages. *Journal of Archaeological Science, 39*, 1862–1870.

Falconer, S. E. (2008). The Middle Bronze Age. In R. Adams (Ed.), *Jordan: An archaeological reader* (pp. 263–280). London: Equinox.

Falconer, S. E., & Fall, P. L. (2016). A radiocarbon sequence from Tell Abu en-Ni'aj, Jordan and its implications for Early Bronze IV chronology in the Southern Levant. *Radiocarbon, 58*(3), 615–647.

Falconer, S. E., & Fall, P. L. (2017). Radiocarbon evidence from Tell Abu en-Ni'aj and Tell el-Hayyat, Jordan and its implications for Bronze Age Levantine and Egyptian chronologies. *Journal of Ancient Egyptian Interconnections, 13*, 7–19.

Fall, P. L., Falconer, S. E., & Lines, L. (2002). Agricultural intensification and the secondary products revolution along the Jordan Rift. *Human Ecology, 30*, 445–482.

Fall, P. L., Falconer, S. E., Lines, L., & Metzger, M. (2004). Environmental impacts of the rise of civilization in the southern Levant. In C. L. Redman, P. R. Fish, S. R. James, & J. D. Rogers (Eds.), *Prehistoric human impact: Global perspectives on environmental degradation* (pp. 261–291). Washington, DC: Smithsonian Institution Press.

Galletti, C. S., Ridder, E., Falconer, S. E., & Fall, P. L. (2013). Maxent modeling of ancient and modern agricultural terraces in the Troodos foothills, Cyprus. *Applied Geography, 39*, 46–56.

Golani, A., & Segal, D. (2002). Redefining the onset of the Early Bronze Age in Southern Canaan: New ^{14}C evidence from Ashqelon Afridar. In E. van den Brink & E. Yannai (Eds.), *In quest of ancient settlements and landscapes* (pp. 135–154). Tel Aviv: Ramot Publishing.

Golden, J. M. (2010). *Dawn of the Metal Age: Technology and society during the Levantine Chalcolithic*. London: Equinox.

Greenberg, R. (2002). *Early urbanizations in the Levant: A regional narrative*. London: Leicester University Press.

Greenberg, R. (2014). Introduction to the Levant during the Early Bronze Age. In M. L. Steiner & A. E. Killebrew (Eds.), *The archaeology of the Levant c. 8000–332 BCE* (pp. 269–277). Oxford: Oxford University Press.

Herr, L. G. (2014). The southern Levant (Transjordan) during the Iron Age I period. In M. L. Steiner & A. E. Killebrew (Eds.), *The archaeology of the Levant c. 8000–332 BCE* (pp. 649–659). Oxford: Oxford University Press.

Kaniewski, D., Van Campo, E., & Weiss, H. (2012). Drought is a recurring challenge in the Middle East. *Proceedings of the National Academy of Science, 109*(10), 3862–3867.

Killebrew, A. E., & Lehmann, G. (Eds.). (2013). *The Philistines and other "sea peoples" in text and archaeology*. Atlanta: Society for Biblical Literature.

van der Kooij, G. (2012). Chapter 3: Tell Deir 'Alla: The Middle and Late Bronze Age chronology. In P. M. Fischer (Ed.), *The chronology of the Jordan Valley during the Middle and Late Bronze Ages: Pella, Tell Abu al-Kharaz and Tell Deir 'Alla* (pp. 199–226). Vienna: Verlag der Österreichischen Akademie der Wissenschaften.

Levy, T. E. (1995). Cult, metallurgy and rank societies—Chalcolithic period (ca. 4500–3500 BCE). In T. E. Levy (Ed.), *The archaeology of society in the Holy Land* (pp. 226–244). New York: Facts on File.

Levy, T. E. (2014). Introduction to the Levant during the Chalcolithic Period: Regional perspectives. In M. L. Steiner & A. E. Killebrew (Eds.), *The Oxford handbook of the archaeology of the Levant c. 8000–332 BCE* (pp. 203–211). Oxford: Oxford University Press.

Liverani, M. (1987). The collapse of the Near Eastern regional system at the end of the Bronze Age: The case of Syria. In M. J. Rowlands, M. T. Larsen, & K. Kristiansen (Eds.), *Centre and periphery in the ancient world* (pp. 66–73). Cambridge: Cambridge University Press.

Liverani, M. (2014). *The Ancient Near East. History, society and economy*. New York: Routledge.

de Miroschedji, P. (2009). Rise and collapse in the southern Levant in the Early Bronze Age. In A. Cardarelli, A. Cazzella, M. Frangipane, & R. Peroni (Eds.), *Reasons for change: Birth, decline and collapse of societies from the end of the fourth to the beginning of the first millennium BC* (pp. 101–129). Rome: Universita degli Studi di Roma 'La Sapienza'.

de Miroschedji, P. (2014). The southern Levant (Cisjordan) during the Early Bronze Age. In M. L. Steiner & A. E. Killebrew (Eds.), *The Oxford handbook of the archaeology of the Levant c. 8000–332 BCE* (pp. 307–329). Oxford: Oxford University Press.

Oren, E. D. (Ed.). (2000). *The sea peoples and their world: A reassessment*. Philadelphia: University of Pennsylvania.

Palumbo, G. (1990). *The Early Bronze Age IV in the Southern Levant: Settlement patterns, economy and material culture of a 'Dark Age'*. Rome: Universita di Roma 'La Sapienza.'.

Panitz-Cohen, N. (2014). The southern Levant (Cisjordan) during the Late Bronze Age. In M. L. Steiner & A. E. Killebrew (Eds.), *The archaeology of the Levant c. 8000–332 BCE* (pp. 541–560). Oxford: Oxford University Press.

Prag, K. (2014). The southern Levant during the Intermediate Bronze Age. In M. L. Steiner & A. E. Killebrew (Eds.), *The archaeology of the Levant c. 8000–332 BCE* (pp. 388–400). Oxford: Oxford University Press.

Regev, J., de Miroschedji, P., Greenberg, R., Braun, E., Greenhut, Z., & Boaretto, E. (2012). Chronology of the Early Bronze Age in the Southern Levant: New analysis for a high chronology. *Radiocarbon, 54*(3–4), 525–566.

Richard, S. (2014). The southern Levant (Transjordan) during the Early Bronze Age. In M. L. Steiner & A. E. Killebrew (Eds.), *The archaeology of the Levant c. 8000–332 BCE* (pp. 330–352). Oxford: Oxford University Press.

Rollefson, G., & Kohler-Rollefson, I. (1992). Early Neolithic exploitation patterns in the Levant: Cultural impact on the environment. *Population and Environment, 13*, 243–254.

Rosen, A. M. (2007). *Civilizing climate: Social responses to climate change in the ancient near East*. New York: AltaMira Press.

Rowan, Y. M., & Golden, J. M. (2009). The Chalcolithic period of the southern Levant: A synthetic review. *Journal of World Prehistory, 22*, 1–92.

Savage, S. H., & Falconer, S. E. (2003). Spatial and statistical inference of Late Bronze Age polities in the Southern Levant. *Bulletin of the American Schools of Oriental Research, 330*, 31–45.

Sherratt, E. S. (2003). The Mediterranean economy: "Globalization" at the end of the second millennium B.C.E. In W. G. Dever & S. Gitin (Eds.), *Symbiosis, symbolism, and the power of the past: Canaan, ancient Israel, and their neighbors from the Late Bronze Age through Roman Palaestina. Proceedings of the Centennial Symposium, W.F. Albright Institute of Archaeological Research and American Schools of Oriental Research, Jerusalem, May 29–31, 2000* (pp. 37–54). Eisenbrauns: Winona Lake.

Sherratt, E. S. (2014). Introduction to the Levant during the Late Bronze Age. In M. L. Steiner & A. E. Killebrew (Eds.), *The archaeology of the Levant c. 8000–332 BCE* (pp. 463–481). Oxford: Oxford University Press.

Singer, I. (2012). The Philistines in the north and the Kingdom of Taita. In G. Galil, A. Gilboa, A. M. Maeir, & D. Kahn (Eds.), *The Ancient Near East in the 12th–10th centuries BCE: Culture and history. Proceedings of the international conference held at the University of Haifa, 2–5 May, 2010* (Vol. 392, pp. 451–472, Alter Orient und Altes Testament). Munster: Ugarit-Verlag.

Sneh, A., Bartov, Y., Weissbrod, T., & Rosensaft, M. (1998). *Geological map of Israel*. Geological Survey of Israel, scale 1:200,000.

Soto-Berelov, M., Fall, P. L., Falconer, S. E., & Ridder, E. (2015). Modeling vegetation dynamics in the southern Levant through the Bronze Age. *Journal of Archaeological Science, 53*, 94–109. http://dx.doi.org/10.1016/j.jas.2014.09.015.

Strange, J. (2000). The Palestinian city-states of the Bronze Age. In M. H. Hansen (Ed.), *A comparative study of thirty city-state cultures: An investigation* (pp. 67–76). Copenhagen: Kongelige Danske Videnskabernes Selskab.

Weiss, H. (2014). The southern Levant during the Intermediate Bronze Age: Altered trajectories. In M. L. Steiner & A. E. Killebrew (Eds.), *The archaeology of the Levant c. 8000–332 BCE* (pp. 367–387). Oxford: Oxford University Press.

Weiss, H., Manning, S. W., & Ristvet, L. (2012). Tell Leilan Akkadian imperialization, collapse and short-lived reoccupation defined by high-resolution radiocarbon dating. In H. Weiss (Ed.), *Seven generations since the fall of Akkad* (Vol. 3, pp. 193–217, Studia Chaburensia). Wiesbaden: Harrassowitz.

Zohary, M. (1973). *Geobotanical foundations of the Middle East*. (Geobotanica Selecta (Vol. 3). Stuttgart: Gustav Fischer.

Chapter 7
The Challenge of Digitized Survey Data

Moti Haiman

Introduction

The use of Geographic Information System (GIS)/Global Positioning System (GPS) in the digitized mapping project provided a tool that enabled massive documentation of all components comprising the sites. This transition of site display, from points to scatter of features, poses two different direction challenges: one is the integration of such a digitized map in multidisciplinary environmental studies, and the other is the possibility of identifying political and cultural upheavals, for example, identifying the special role of the Byzantine Church in the agricultural settlement, due to an unusually large number of churches and monasteries directly connected to the agricultural systems. Another discovery was the possible location of the northern border of the Byzantine province of *Palaestina Tertia*, ca. 50 km north of Be'er Sheva, based on the changes in the agricultural systems.

History of Site Presentation

About 30,000 archaeological sites have been documented in Israel since the British Survey of Western Palestine in the nineteenth century CE. A quick look at the history of surveys shows two general directions in data collection and analysis.

One direction, before the introduction of pottery analysis, characterizes the late nineteenth and early twentieth centuries CE. Despite technological and conceptual restrictions, some of those early surveys intended to display sites from a high-resolution perspective, focusing on the variety of features that comprise the sites

M. Haiman (✉)
Israel Antiquities Authority, Jerusalem, Israel
e-mail: Haiman_or@bezeqint.net

T.E. Levy, I.W.N. Jones (eds.), *Cyber-Archaeology and Grand Narratives*, One World Archaeology, https://doi.org/10.1007/978-3-319-65693-9_7

and on their morphological and functional aspects. This was the case for Palmer, and despite the lack of chronological tools, he was able to correlate between a specific type of sites (Early Bronze Age II [EBII] sites) and cairn fields (Palmer 1871: 344–346, 351, 359). Woolley and Lawrence, likewise, stressed the idea of features that specify the desert landscape, rather than centralized sites (Woolley and Lawrence 1915: 20–23).

The second direction, influenced by the introduction of pottery analysis during the first half of the twentieth century, neglected the morphological aspects of the sites, and the archaeological site turned to be a centralized point presenting a place where pottery has been collected mainly for historical and chronological enquiry. This is the case of Glueck (1959) and the basic concept of the Archaeological Survey of Israel begun in 1964 (Cohen 1981, 1986). The high-resolution approach, based on the analysis of all components that comprise sites for further studies, such as environmental relationships, was practiced, if at all, only to a limited extent (Aharoni et al. 1960; Rothenberg 1967: 71–79).

In the frame of the Negev Emergency Survey, conducted in 1978–1989 (Cohen 1983), 5000 km^2 was surveyed and ca. 10,000 archaeological sites were documented (Avni 1992; Baumgarten 2004; Govrin 1991; Haiman 1986, 1989; Lender 1990; Rosen 1994). The mass of data of the Negev Emergency Survey enabled a large variety of spatial, environmental, and methodological studies that still yield research and survey for survey studies that manipulates mainly its own findings and not survey as a secondary source that supports historical studies (Fig. 7.1). The following

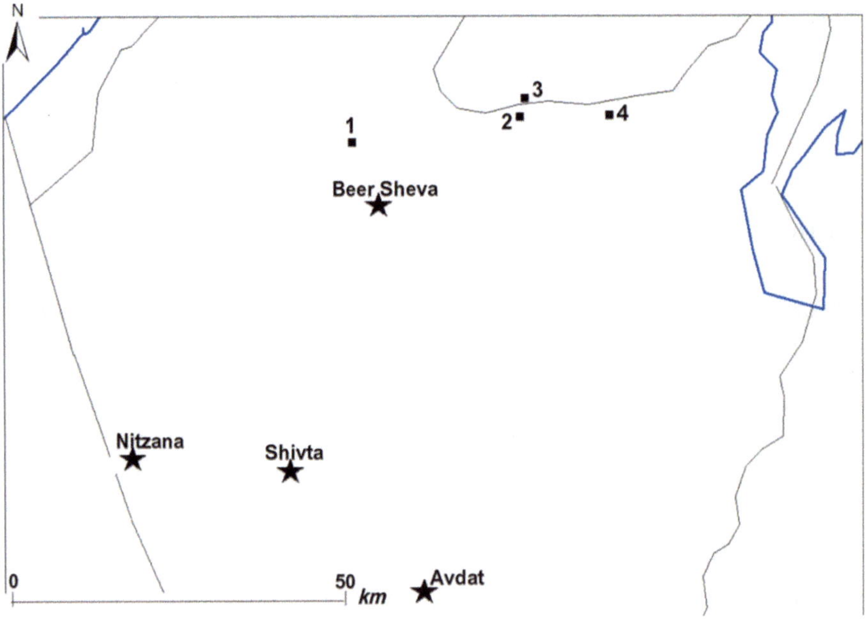

Fig. 7.1 Map of the Northern Negev desert showing location of sites mentioned in this paper: (1) Khirbat Karkor/Horvat Karkur ‘Illit; (2) Khirbat Anim; (3) Khirbat Ghoyane el-Fauqa; (4) Nahal Adasha

is the methodological concept of this author, of a high-resolution approach to survey (Haiman 1989).

The desert is characterized by an unusual density of well-preserved dwelling sites of all sizes and features such as farmhouses, fortresses, threshing floors, winepresses, cult installations, burial cairns, and more that pose a challenge for how to define a site. Owing to this dense scatter, the ruins overlap one another; in many cases, an installation belonging to a certain dwelling site was found closer to another dwelling site of a different period.

The method to approach this data after the process of documentation was to sort the features and correlate them to the relevant dwelling sites, in order to create maps of periods or cultures. For example, the silos of Site 249 are adjacent to a Byzantine campsite comprised of a pottery scatter and a few stone foundations, and both were recorded as one Byzantine site (Fig. 7.2b). The silos are actually part of an Iron Age II site, Site 247, located on a hilltop 150 m northwest. This definition is based on the recurring pattern in which Iron Age structures were built on elevated areas, while associated silos and threshing floors were built near the *wadi*. Byzantine campsites do not include silos. Similar is the conclusion that the watchtower of Site 246 is part of the farmhouse of Site 243, although it was found closer to the Iron Age II site. Other elements of Site 243 are the winepress and the terraced *wadi*s that dominate the entire area. These features were found consistently near Byzantine and early Islamic farmhouses only. Another combination of features is the cairns of Site 241 and the EBII Site 244, located 150 m away.

Figure 7.2 shows the discrepancy between the conventional method of presenting sites as points (Fig. 7.2a) and the fact that the same sites are made up of scattered features (Fig. 7.2b). I believe that only this alternative display provides a basis for a spatial analysis, exploiting efficiently the full potential of the rich data such as site size, number of structures, number and size of rooms, the volume of water cisterns, the size of agricultural plots, etc. Although the Negev Emergency Survey still possessed centralized points, the high-resolution approach to features rather than to centralized "sites" made it possible to exploit the data for a variety of spatial calculations (Haiman 2002).

Introduction of Digital Facilities

The introduction of the GPS/GIS system to the Israel Antiquities Authority (IAA) in 1995 provided a tool that enabled massive documentation of survey findings and to move from a display of sites as points to a display that encompasses all of the visible features. In this transition of site display, from a centralized point to scatter of features, I would like to identify the essence of the revolution that the GIS system, for instance, is effecting in spatial archaeology. This also marks a distinction in the way GPS/GIS system is used in organizations for administrative and scientific goals.

The GPS/GIS system in the Israel Antiquities Authority, for example, was aimed mainly at the purpose of site recording and display, as well as a variety of spatial manipulations in accordance with the tasks of the IAA. This is the creation of a raw

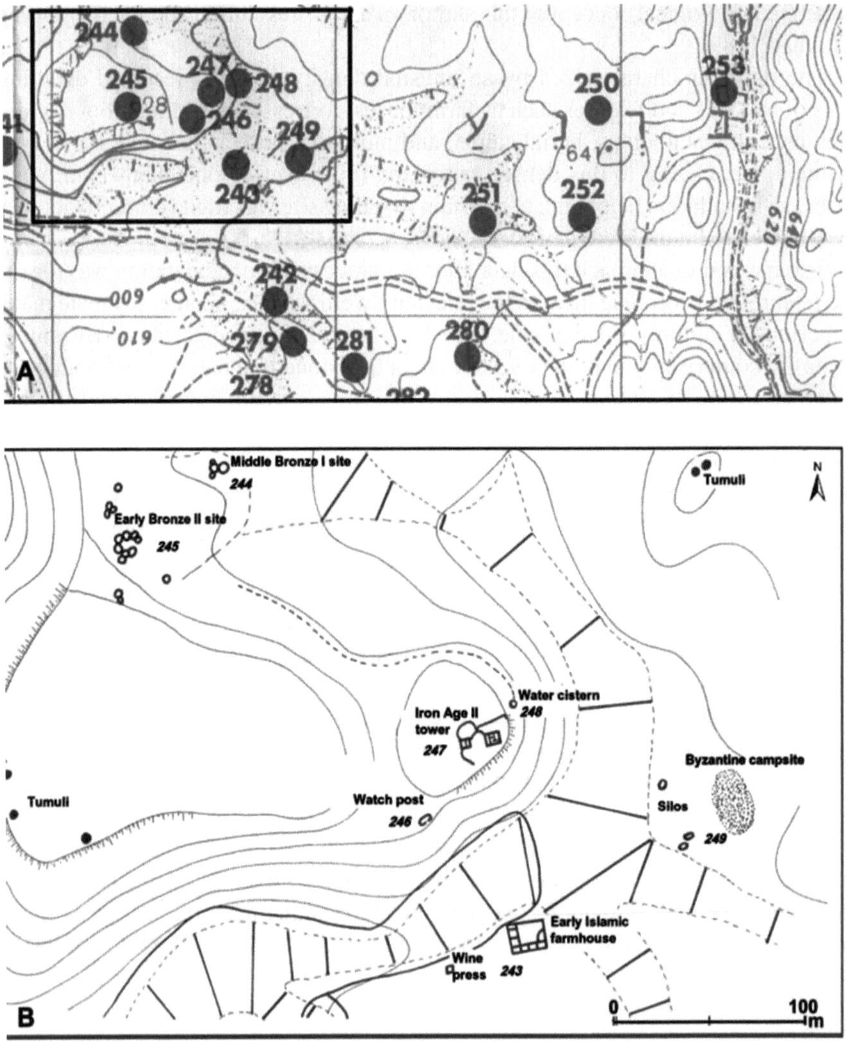

Fig. 7.2 Two ways to define sites. The *upper part* (**a**) shows the conventional way to present a site as a point in the Survey of Israel (Haiman 1986). The *lower part* (**b**) shows a full detailed map of the same sites

database that enables efficient access to all the known sites for administrative needs. One of the administrative tools to bridge the gap between the centralized points that mark the site and the scattered features is the Development Survey, a hyperintensive mapping of features supported by the GPS/GIS system. The weakness of this method is that the survey is limited to a specific turf and not directed by research questions.

The scientific aspect of possessing digital facilities poses two challenges concerning data acquisition. One is that despite the large number of sites known in Israel, almost all the data is still "metadata," which means that it is impossible to manipulate the formal data without involvement of experienced surveyors with expertise in specific arenas. The second challenge is the necessity of large-scale conversion of points to features directed by research questions.

The Mapping Agricultural Systems Project

Manipulating high-resolution survey findings, assisted by remote sensing facilities, was the goal of establishing the Ancient Desert Agriculture Systems Revived project (ADASR; Ancient Desert Agriculture System Revived 2015), later followed by the Mapping Agricultural Systems Project (Haiman 2012). These research programs were located at Bar Ilan University, with collaboration from the Israel Antiquities Authority. Noteworthy is that the project, possessing GPS and other facilities, adopted the old methods of high-resolution feature manipulation, practiced already more than a century ago. The fieldwork carried out in the frame of the ADASR project is a mapping project with a GPS, mainly in sites that were known before and, however, presented as points (see Figs. 7.3, 7.4, and 7.5).

According to the concept presented here, the goal of the work with GPS is to create a spatial archaeological GIS layer of features that enables further multidisciplinary analysis.

The issue of desert runoff agriculture facilities may demonstrate well one of the project's goals (see Figs. 7.6, 7.7, 7.8, and 7.9). The runoff agriculture facilities constitute the main characteristic of the desert landscape. Their distribution covers large areas; however, most of them cannot be recorded in the frame of a conventional survey of "points" because they are not "sites." Systems of hundreds of kilometers of terraced *wadis*, as well as the large areas covered by the enigmatic *tuleilat al-'anab* (Arabic for "mounds of grapes"), yielded no pottery. It was impossible to define their location as a point, and they were not present in any chronological discussion based on pottery analysis.

The ADASR and Mapping Agricultural Systems Project attempt to create a layer of Byzantine and early Islamic sites in the encounter theater between the desert and the sown. The projects combine five elements:

1. Analog data: sorting about 70 known ruins (larger than 40 dunams) from the Byzantine and early Islamic periods, presented as points.
2. Converting a selected group to high-resolution display with GPS, including features that cannot be recorded in a conventional survey. For example, Fig. 7.4 shows a detailed map of Khirbat Karkor/Horvat Karkur 'Illit (Figueras 2004), which includes a 150 dunam settlement ruin surrounded by characteristic features of desert runoff agriculture systems from the Byzantine and early Islamic periods. Noteworthy is the fact that the same site was represented in an old survey by two points and dated to the Byzantine period.
3. Sorting the finds on the basis of morphology and typology and then correlating the right features one to the other on the basis of recurring patterns. The results enabled distinguishing between two types of agricultural strategies, which in the conventional method would be all defined as Byzantine "sites." Type one is the

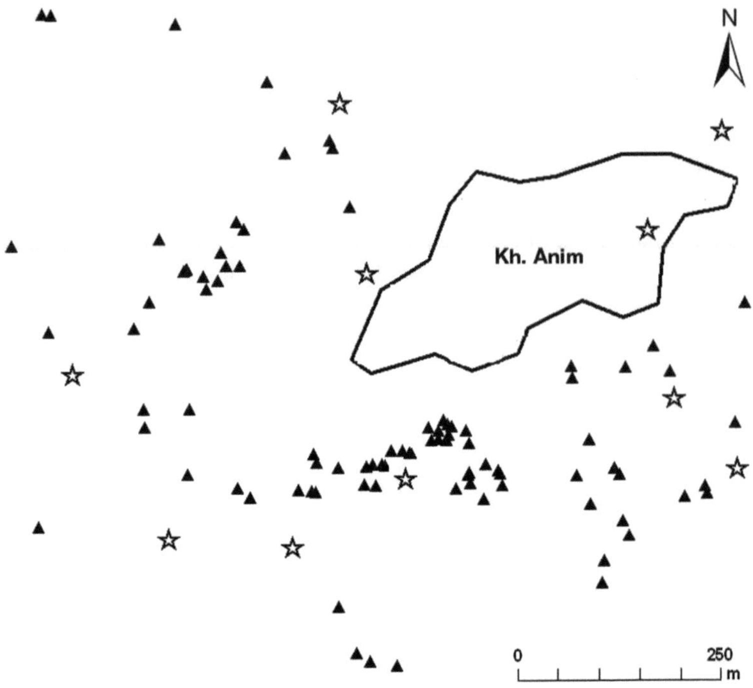

Fig. 7.3 A GPS map of Khirbat Anim. The triangles represent the scatter of burial caves and agricultural installations around a Roman and Byzantine period village. The stars represent an old survey location of the ancient village and some of the features around it (Unpublished survey, data courtesy of the Israel Antiquities Authority)

traditional agriculture of the sown (see Fig. 7.3). Findings associated with this type include small wine presses, oil presses, and burial caves distributed densely around the close periphery of the villages. This periphery includes also a substantial natural agricultural land (Fig. 7.5). Type two is desert runoff agriculture. In contrast to the limited distribution of the sown agricultural and other features around villages, evidence of desert runoff agriculture is scattered throughout the entire area (see Figs. 7.4, and 7.5). This includes industrial wine presses, square watchtowers, farmhouses, churches, and all sizes of settlement. The agricultural infrastructure includes an enormous system of terraced *wadi*s, which are a sophisticated water management facility that enables agriculture in the desert based on runoff surplus, and enigmatic slope facilities consisting of stone piles and trips built on rock surfaces. These look like shallow terraces, always in correspondence with industrial wine presses. The possibility that these are a sort of *tuleilat al-'anab* known in the extreme desert, e.g., around Shivta, Nitzana, and Avdat (Evenari et al. 1971: 104–112), is based on the gradual changing of the stone strips to stone piles as moving southward (Fig. 7.10).

4. Adding high-resolution remote sensing data, for example, GPR and satellite imagery.

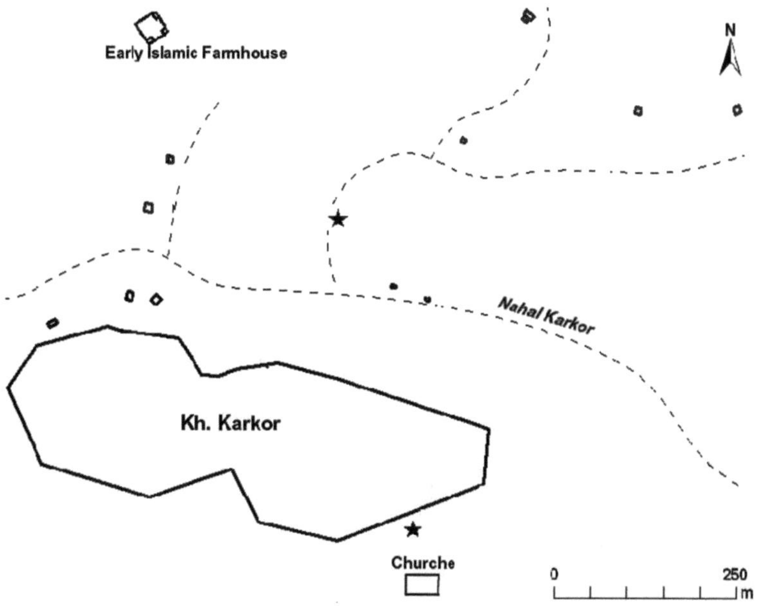

Fig. 7.4 A GPS map of Khirbat Karkor/Horvat Karkur 'Illit, including the ruins of a 150 dunam Byzantine and early Islamic village and a church (Figueras 2004). The site is surrounded by Byzantine period square watchtowers. The stars represent the site's location in an old survey (Unpublished survey, data courtesy of the Israel Antiquities Authority)

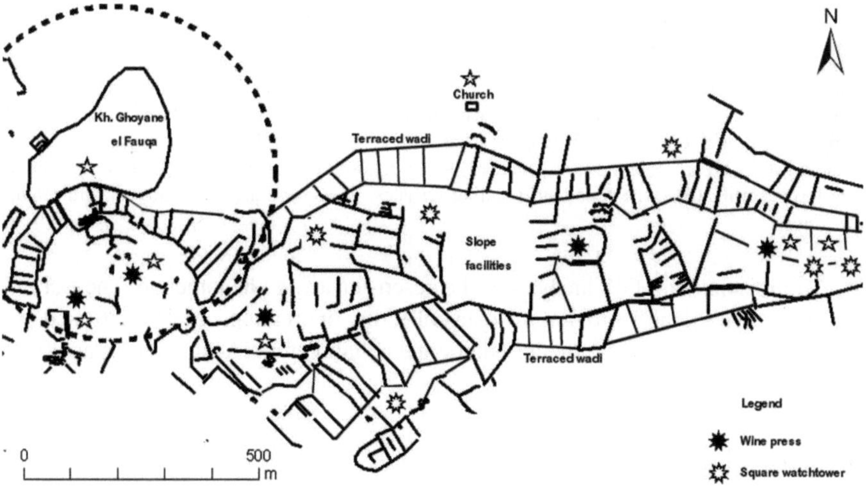

Fig. 7.5 A GPS map of a typical desert agricultural landscape encountered in the sown area in the Northern Negev. The dotted circle represents the distribution boundary of burial caves and agricultural installations directly connected to a Roman and Byzantine period village of the sown area. The stars represent an old survey location of the "main" elements in the same area (Unpublished survey, data courtesy of the Israel Antiquities Authority)

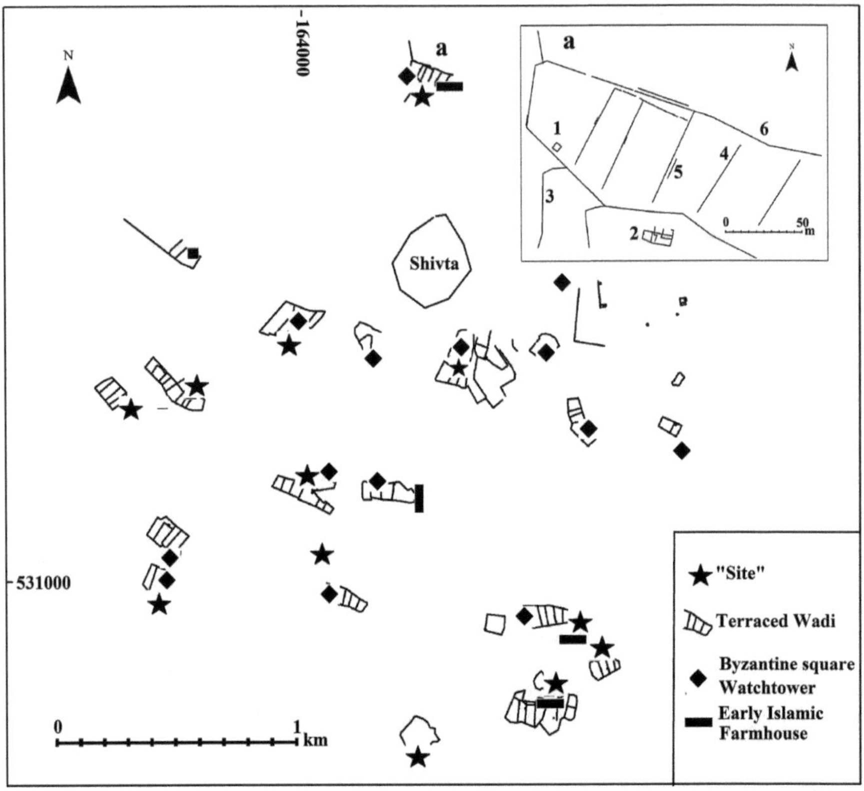

Fig. 7.6 Mapping Agricultural Systems Project (Haiman 2012): the periphery of Shivta. Notice the discrepancy between defining the farm (marked "a") as a Byzantine "site" (Baumgarten 2004: Site 133) and mapping the features of a farm defined as a "runoff collecting farm." The terminology of features 3–6 is based on Evenari et al. (1971: 95–119, 179–182): (1) Byzantine square watchtower; (2) early Islamic farmhouse; (3) water conduit; (4) terrace wall; (5) drop structure in the terrace wall; (6) stone fence surrounding terraces. The entire area is scattered with *tuleilat al-'anab*

5. Multidisciplinary GIS analysis of the desert-terracing phenomenon. The last two points, the scientific goal of the data collecting or creating, are demonstrated in a recent published article by this author and collaborators (Ackermann et al. 2008).

Conclusions

Creating the infrastructure of GPS archaeological layers in the frame of ADASR and Mapping Agricultural Systems Project for further spatial studies yielded some principles:

1. Mapping rather than surveying. The area was previously surveyed, and the main components of the ancient landscape were known before, but as points. Points do

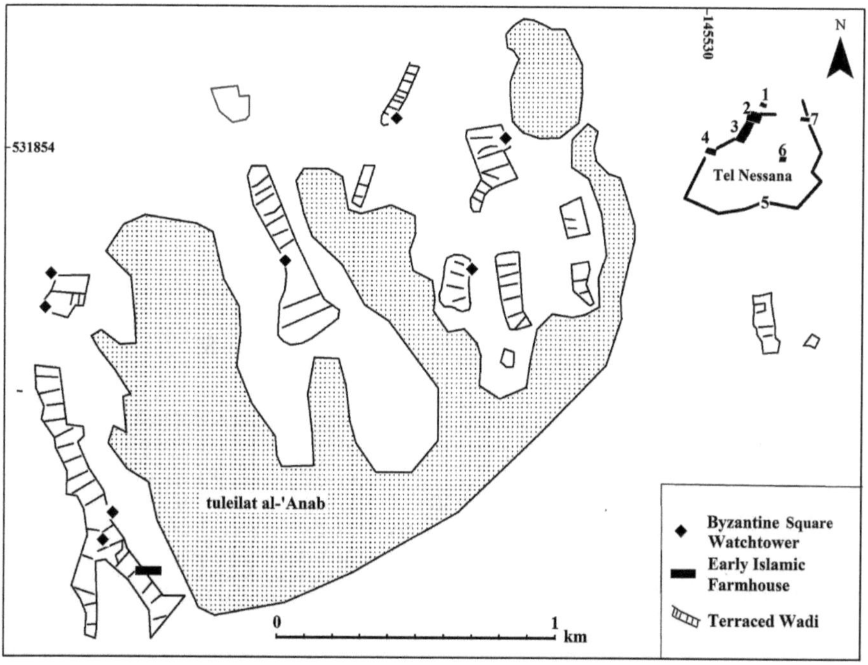

Fig. 7.7 Mapping Agricultural Systems Project: the periphery of Nessana. The Tel includes (1, 2, 4, 6, and 7) Churches and monasteries, (3) the acropolis, and (5) the town's wall (Based on Urman 2004)

not allow an appropriate record and analysis of the network of terraced *wadis* and slope facilities. These are not "sites" in terms of conventional survey, dominated by centralizing the site to a point and manipulating the historical background of the periods identified in the pottery. However, those desert agriculture facilities that are not "sites" pave the entire desert, constituting the dominant element of the landscape and the only factor that enables desert cultivation.

2. Feature correlation and synchronization rather than dating. Excavations conducted in the past, in the Byzantine and early Islamic sites and agricultural features, save the necessity to pursue dating issues based on surface pottery collections. The real challenge is to correlate, based on typology and excavation results, between certain elements that according to the surveyor's concept comprise a certain period's spatial picture.
3. The search for multidisciplinary study. There is a high potential of such a GPS infrastructure layer as a foundation for further spatial studies (Ackermann et al., 2008; Ancient Desert Agriculture Systems Revived 2015; Haiman 2006). In the age of GIS, viewing the archaeological site as a point is not relevant and does not allow the full exploitation of the GIS potential. The rise of geotechnologies calls for an equal rise in archaeological data manipulating methodologies. Achieving this goal depends on the capability of potential collaborators to create high-resolution data based on the specialization of the partners and not only on acquiring existing layers of data.

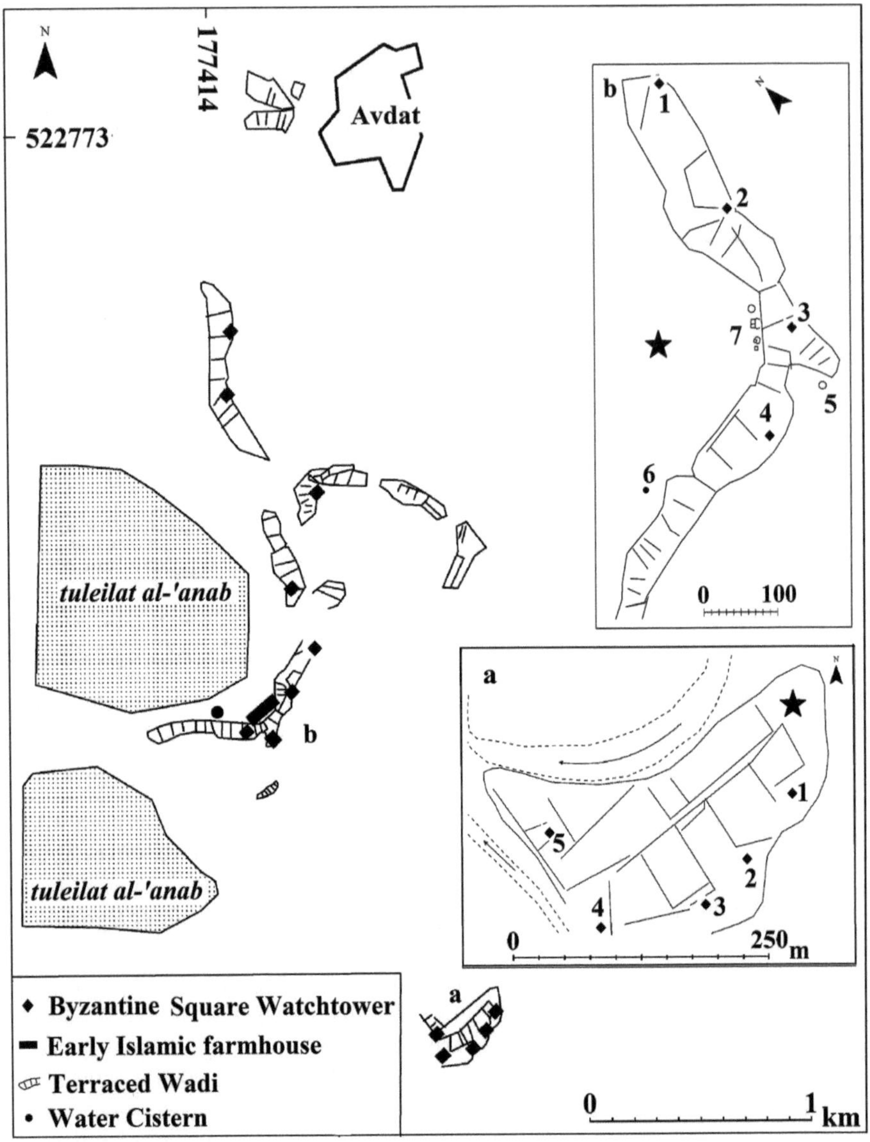

Fig. 7.8 Mapping Agricultural Systems Project: the periphery of Avdat. Farm "a" is a "diversion system" farm (Evenari et al. 1971: 110–119). Features 1–5 on inset map "a" are Byzantine square watchtowers. Farm "b" (partly excavated, Nevo 1991) includes (1–4) Byzantine square watchtowers, (5) threshing floor, (6) water cistern, and (7) early Islamic farmhouse complex consisting of three structures and a threshing floor. The stars in both farms represent "a Byzantine site" as defined in the past

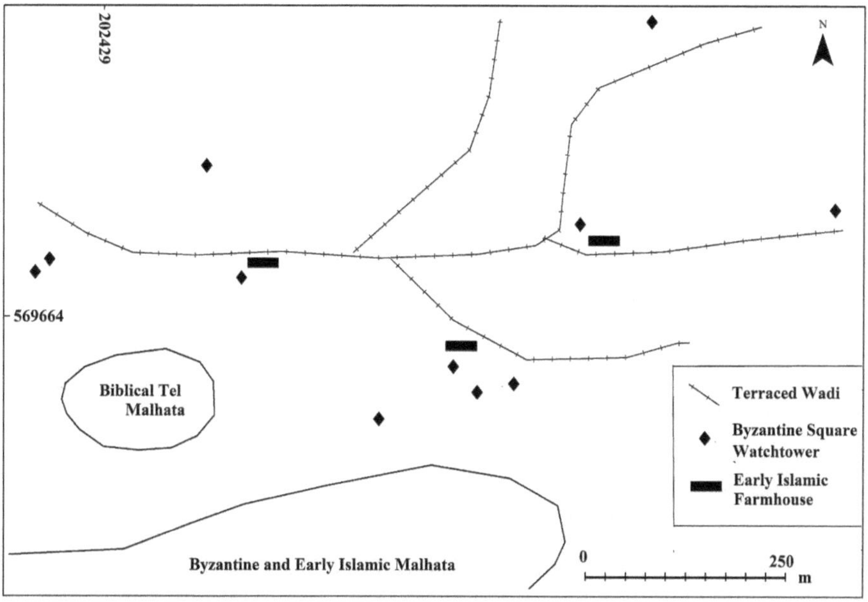

Fig. 7.9 Mapping Agricultural Systems Project: the periphery of Malhata

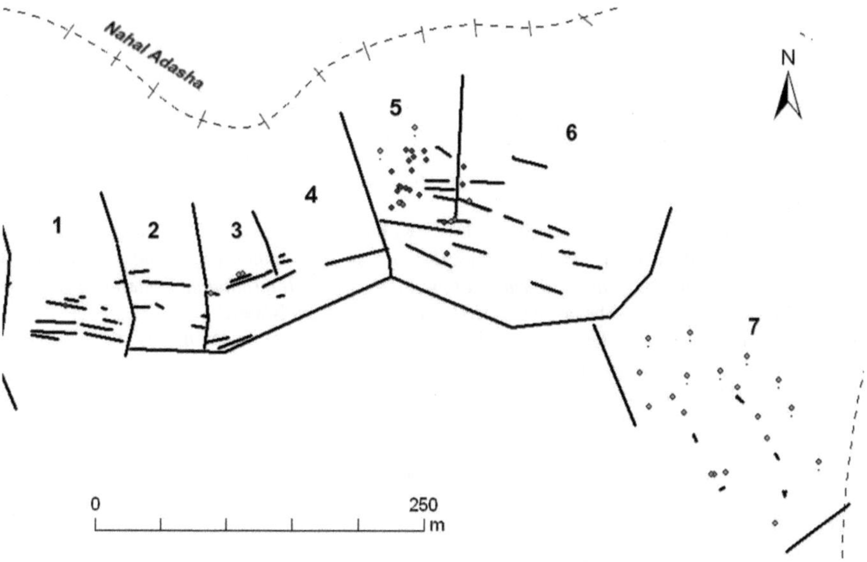

Fig. 7.10 A GPS map of a cluster of slope facilities at Nahal Adasha. Fields 1–4 and 6 contain stone strips. Fields 5 and 7 contain piles of stones (1 m diameter, 0.5 m high) resembling the *tuleilat al-ʻanab* of the extreme desert. The entire cluster is located 1 km from an industrial wine press at Khirbat Merkaz (Data courtesy of the Israel Antiquities Authority)

References

Ackermann, O., Savoray, T., & Haiman, M. (2008). Nari (calcrete) outcrop contribution to ancient agricultural terraces in the Southern Shephelah, Israel: Insights from digital terrain analysis and geoarchaeological field survey. *Journal of Archaeological Science, 35*, 930–941.

Aharoni, Y., Evenari, M., Shanan, L., & Tadmor, N. H. (1960). Ancient desert agriculture of the Negev. *Israel Exploration Journal, 10*, 23–36.

Ancient Desert Agriculture Systems Revived. (2015). GeoArchaeology GIS Support. http://www.mnemotrix.com/adasr/map.html. Accessed 30 Jan 2015.

Avni, G. (1992). *Map of Har Saggi northwest (225)*. Jerusalem: Israel Antiquities Authority.

Baumgarten, Y. (2004). *Map of Shivta (166)*. Jerusalem: Israel Antiquities Authority.

Cohen, R. (1981). *Map of Sede Boqer east (168)*. Jerusalem: Archaeological Survey of Israel.

Cohen, R. (1983). The Negev emergency survey. In D. R. Keller & D. W. Rupp (Eds.), *Archaeological survey in the Mediterranean area, BAR international series* (Vol. 155, p. 367). Oxford: British Archaeological Reports.

Cohen, R. (1986). *Map of Sede Boqer west (167)*. Jerusalem: Department of Antiquities.

Evenari, M., Shanan, L., & Tadmor, N. (1971). *The Negev: The challenge of a desert*. Cambridge, MA: Harvard University Press.

Figueras, P. (2004). *Horvat Karkur 'Illit: A Byzantine cemetery church in the Northern Negev (final report of the excavations 1989–1995), Beer-Sheva archaeological monographs, Beer-Sheva archaeological monographs* (Vol. 1). Beer-Sheva: Ben-Gurion University of the Negev Press.

Glueck, N. (1959). *Rivers in the desert: A history of the Negev*. New York: Farrar, Straus and Cudahy.

Govrin, Y. (1991). *Map of Nahal Yattir (139)*. Jerusalem: Israel Antiquities Authority.

Haiman, M. (1986). *Map of Har Hamran southeast (198)*. Jerusalem: Department of Antiquities.

Haiman, M. (1989). Preliminary report of the western Negev highlands emergency survey. *Israel Exploration Journal, 39*, 174–191.

Haiman, M. (2002). Water sources and the Iron Age II settlement pattern in the Negev desert. In C. Ohlig, Y. Peleg, & T. Tsuk (Eds.), *Cura Aquarum in Israel* (pp. 13–31). Sieburg: Deutsche Wasserhistorische Gesellschaft.

Haiman, M. (2006). The archaeological surveys in the Arabah reconsidered: Data and metadata. In P. Bienkowski & K. Galor (Eds.), *Crossing the rift: Resources, routes, settlement patterns and interaction in the Wadi Arabah*, (Levant supplementary series, Vol. 3, pp. 45–49). Oxford: Oxbow Books.

Haiman, M. (2008). Creating archaeological data with GPS – Results from the Negev desert survey. In I. Gilead, R. Winter, & R. Fletcher (Eds.), *New approaches for computer applications in the archaeology and cultural heritage of the south Levant, International conference program book* (pp. 36–40). Beer-Sheva: Ben-Gurion University of the Negev.

Haiman, M. (2012). Dating the agricultural terraces in the southern Levantine deserts, the spatial-contextual argument. *Journal of Arid Environments, 86*, 43–49.

Lender, Y. (1990). *Map of Har Nafha (196)*. Jerusalem: Israel Antiquities Authority.

Nevo, Y. D. (1991). *Pagans and herders: A re-examination of the Negev runoff cultivation systems in the Byzantine and early Arab periods* (New sources for the history of the Byzantine and early Arab periods: The Negev, fourth to eighth centuries AD, Vol. 1). Midreshet Ben Gurion: IPS Ltd.

Palmer, E. H. (1871). *The desert of the exodus: Journeys on foot in the wilderness of the forty years' wanderings*. Cambridge: Deighton, Bell, &.

Rosen, S. (1994). *Map of Makhtesh Ramon (204)*. Jerusalem: Israel Antiquities Authority.

Rothenberg, B. (1967). *Tzfunot Negev*. Tel Aviv: Masada (Hebrew).

Urman, D. 2004. Nessana excavations 1987–1995. In D. Urman (Ed.), *Nessana: Excavations and studies, Vol. 1* (Beer-Sheva studies by the department of Bible and Ancient Near East, Vol. 17, pp. 1*–118*). Beer-Sheva: Ben-Gurion University of the Negev Press.

Woolley, C. L., & Lawrence, T. E. (1915). *The wilderness of Zin (archaeological report)*, (Palestine exploration fund annual, Vol. III). London: Harrison and Sons.

Chapter 8
The West Bank and East Jerusalem Archaeological Database: Narratives of Archaeology and Archaeological Practices

Adi Keinan-Schoonbaert

Introduction

The central hill country of the Holy Land, encompassed by the modern political boundaries of the West Bank and East Jerusalem, has long attracted the interest and curiosity of archaeologists and scholars. Starting in the late nineteenth century and during the decades that followed, researchers studied some of the key pieces in the historical and archaeological mosaic of the Holy Land found here. The most extensive work, however, has occurred in the years since June 1967. During this time, the areas occupied by Israel have been subject to intensive archaeological survey, salvage excavations, and research projects conducted mainly by Israeli government and academic institutions and to a limited extent by American and European institutions often cooperating with Israeli authorities. Currently, the Archaeology Department of the Civil Administration (ADCA, formerly known as the Staff Officer for Archaeology in Judea and Samaria; see Civil Administration 2011), working under the Israeli Ministry of Education and funded by the military authorities, administers the archaeology of the occupied West Bank. East Jerusalem, officially annexed to Israel after its occupation, is under the jurisdiction of the Israel Antiquities Authority (IAA); as the Green Line (armistice line of 1967) is not legally recognized inside Jerusalem, the municipality of Jerusalem as a whole, including outlying Palestinian villages, is treated as one unit. The parts of the West Bank controlled by the Palestinian National Authority (Areas A and B) are under the jurisdiction of the Palestinian Department of Antiquities and Cultural Heritage (Taha 2002, 2005, 2010).

The first Israeli archaeological initiative in the West Bank was the large-scale "Emergency Survey," which began just a few months after the end of the 1967 war and included the entire area of the West Bank and the Golan Heights (Kochavi 1972a). This survey, which was intended to record mainly known sites located on

A. Keinan-Schoonbaert (✉)
University College London, London, UK
e-mail: adi.keinan.09@ucl.ac.uk

T.E. Levy, I.W.N. Jones (eds.), *Cyber-Archaeology and Grand Narratives*,
One World Archaeology, https://doi.org/10.1007/978-3-319-65693-9_8

British Mandate maps, was followed by many others: regional surveys, such as the survey of Samaria (Finkelstein and Lederman 1997a; Zertal 2004, 2005, 2008; Zertal and Mirkam 2000) or the survey of Judah (Ofer 1993), topical surveys such as "Operation Scroll" (Wexler 2002), academic surveys in the framework of PhD dissertations such the works of Bar (2008) and Ben-Yosef (2007) in the Jordan Valley, and the 10 × 10 km map surveys, such as the Map of Herodium (Hirschfeld 1985) and the Map of Deir Mar Saba (Patrich 1994). Planned excavations of sites—from single elements to large, multilayered tells—started to take place, alongside salvage work conducted prior to construction or maintenance. The diverse Israeli archaeological activity in these territories has yielded substantial information: new sites, new finds, new data, and new interpretations—in other words, new knowledge.

In 2005, a joint working group dealing with archaeology in the Israeli-Palestinian conflict was formed by Lynn Swartz Dodd (USC) and Ran Boytner (UCLA). The Israeli-Palestinian Archaeology Working Group, which included Palestinian, Israeli, and American archaeologists and cultural heritage specialists, discussed topics of shared cultural heritage, public opinion, the status of Jerusalem, and the fate of archaeological sites and artifacts in event of the implementation of a two-state solution (IPAWG 2007; Much 2007; Swartz Dodd and Boytner 2010, 9–13; Yahya 2010). During the deliberations of this joint working group, the need for a coherent summary of the Israeli activity in the occupied territories became obvious—a database of all surveys and excavations. The West Bank and East Jerusalem Archaeological Database Project (WBEJAD), conducted in Tel Aviv University between 2005 and 2009 by Prof. Raphael Greenberg and the author, was developed and constructed to fulfill this need (Greenberg and Keinan 2007, 2009; Keinan 2010).

Constructing the Database

The main aim of this database was the construction of one source of information for the archaeological and administrative data deriving from Israeli archaeological activity in the occupied territories. Since this information is not provided on a regular, organized basis by the authorities and since the database crosses important lines of jurisdiction, this information had to be collated from many different sources, some of which were not easily accessible. The archaeological data (basically site location, finds, periods of existence, etc.) was generally found in published surveys, preliminary and final excavation reports, articles in periodicals or books, unpublished PhD or MA dissertations, etc. The administrative data (excavation license numbers or permits, names of excavators and excavating institutions) had to be obtained directly from the ADCA, the IAA, and the major universities in Israel. These institutions provided lists of sites excavated by the ADCA, sites excavated by universities, license numbers issued by the ADCA for excavations in the West Bank, permits issued by the IAA for excavations in Jerusalem, and lists of scheduled sites in Judea and Samaria. The combination of all the relevant information is presented in our database—a synthesis of the available administrative and archaeological information produced by Israeli sources.

As noted above, prior to the database construction the information was scattered in many different places. A meticulous process of cross-checking filled in many gaps and permitted the correction of numerous errors. The data integration was not a simple task. Database construction involved combining all sources of information and thoroughly cross-checking the data, taking into account missing data (often site coordinates), inaccuracies, and contradictory data. The compilation of all available information resulted in one dataset with many different parameters for each archaeological site, covering archaeological activity in the West Bank and East Jerusalem from 1967 to 2007. Its potential users can search for information regarding all surveyed and excavated archaeological sites: their exact location, their major finds and periods of existence, their excavators, a list of bibliographic references, and more. This database is innovative by being a synthesis of available data in specific fields regarding the archaeological sites in the occupied territories and a combination of archaeological and administrative information and by including information which is now published and thus available for the first time.

One of the first decisions we made was to create the database in English, in order to maximize its accessibility. This required translation of large portions of the information that were in Hebrew, especially older survey publications, many site reports, and almost all administrative lists. The Survey of Western Palestine (Palestine Exploration Fund) maps and British Mandate maps were used as an aid in the transliteration of site names.

Because the West Bank has been surveyed repeatedly—the topical and grid surveys overlap the 1968 Emergency Survey, and some overlap each other—identical sites appear in different publications. The data entry carefully avoided the creation of double entries of these identical sites, taking into consideration the possible deviation in site coordinates and different site names for the same site. The opposite phenomenon—identical site names for different sites—also posed a challenge while inserting data. In addition, the fact that some surveyors (e.g., Kloner for Jerusalem, Zertal for Samaria) did not recognize the Green Line as a separator between Israel proper and the occupied territories posed a challenge of its own, requiring first the reinsertion of the line onto a base map, then the careful division of archaeological sites between Israel and the West Bank according to their grid reference and exact location in relation to the resurrected Green Line, and eventually the insertion in the database of only those located inside the occupied West Bank and East Jerusalem.

Upon completion, the database stores the following data:

- More than 6000 sites surveyed in the West Bank after 1967, out of which about a thousand are in East Jerusalem
- Approximately 1000 sites excavated in the West Bank, one-third of them in East Jerusalem

- One thousand one hundred forty-eight excavation licenses issued by the ADCA as of the end of 2007
- About 450 excavation permits issued by the IAA for excavations in East Jerusalem

The database is organized in three tables: a list of surveyed sites, a list of excavated sites, and a list of licenses issued by the ADCA for excavations in the West Bank. The tabular fields of the excavations and surveys tables include grid reference (old Israel grid), site name and additional names, IAA site number, survey site number, survey reference, primary and secondary periods, site components, excavator and excavating institution, license or permit numbers, abbreviated bibliography, and comments. Some fields were added to the database tables in order to facilitate GIS search (see below): surveyed (yes/no), in Jerusalem (yes/no), and a table divided into time periods, in which each period receives the value "0," "1," or "2" ("0" stands for no presence, "1" for possible presence or transitional period, and "2" for certain presence of that period in the site).

Linking the Database to GIS

During the construction of the database, as we realized its tremendous potential, it was decided to link it to a GIS platform. The original tabular lists are indeed very useful in their own right: they can be searched and data can be easily retrieved from them. The integration of the text-based database with the GIS ArcView-generated maps has, however, far greater possibilities: the presentation of data on a map allows a broad picture and many research options, particularly by means of the combination of archaeological data retrieved from the database with other GIS layers. These include geographic, topographic, and demographic layers: precise and updated layers of the Green Line and the Separation Barrier, Jewish and Palestinian localities (including Jerusalem's neighborhoods) marked as polygons, a topographic map, roads, water courses, precipitation isohyets, soil types, and altitudes. It is possible to choose any combination of one or more of these layers with a variety of query-made archaeological layers, in order to create the desirable map.

There are many different ways to search and query the database in order to retrieve information and create statistical data on a variety of subjects. Both tabular and cartographic information can be easily retrieved from the GIS system. After importing the database tables into the GIS as new layers, the first way to retrieve data is through the *Definition Query > Query Builder* option in the *Layer Properties*. The *Query Builder* allows the user to view the database fields on the left side (*[Site_Name]*, *[Major_Periods]*, *[Site_Components]*, etc.), some sample values on the right side (*Tell Shiloh*, *MB2b*, *Fortified site*, etc.), and the operators, which are used to specify the query, in between (=, *LIKE*, *NOT*, etc.) (Fig. 8.1). I will give a few examples for this type of database search.

Example 1 Retrieval of a list of sites excavated by a certain excavator.

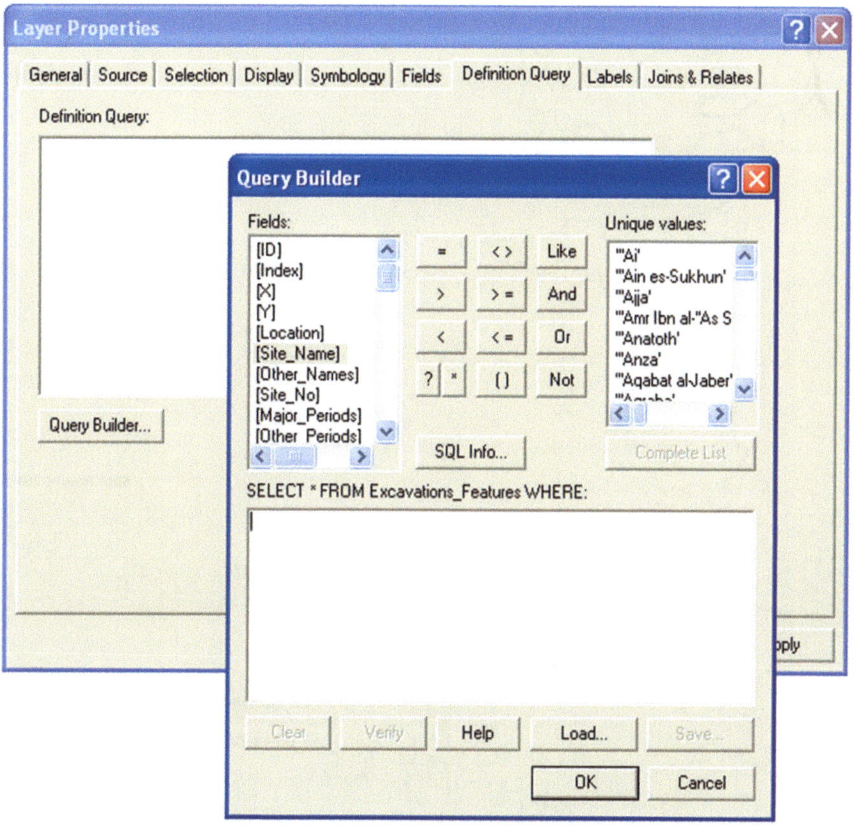

Fig. 8.1 ArcView screenshot of the *Query Builder* option

The query would be as follows: *[Excavator] LIKE '*Yizhar Hirschfeld*'*. The *[Excavator]* refers to the field in the database containing excavators' names; the operator *LIKE* is used to search the excavator's name within each cell of data. Since there is often other information besides the name of the excavator (such as year of excavation in parenthesis or additional excavators), it is always recommended to use the operator "*LIKE*" instead of the operator "=," which means "equals to"; *'*Yizhar Hirschfeld*'* gives the desirable result—the excavator's name, with optional characters before or after his name. The result will be shown on the GIS map as the distribution of Hirschfeld's excavations in the West Bank, represented by dots (Fig. 8.2). Clicking on each dot using the "Information" icon will open a dialogue box, which details all the data relevant to that excavated site. The *Attribute Table* of this layer will be a table of all sites excavated by Hirschfeld. It is possible to export this table to an external file, which could be used and manipulated outside the GIS software. The excavator's name could be searched with one or more conditions, for example, the query *([Excavator] LIKE '*Yizhar Hirschfeld*') AND ([Site_Components] LIKE '*onast*')* would produce a list of monasteries excavated by Hirschfeld, taking into

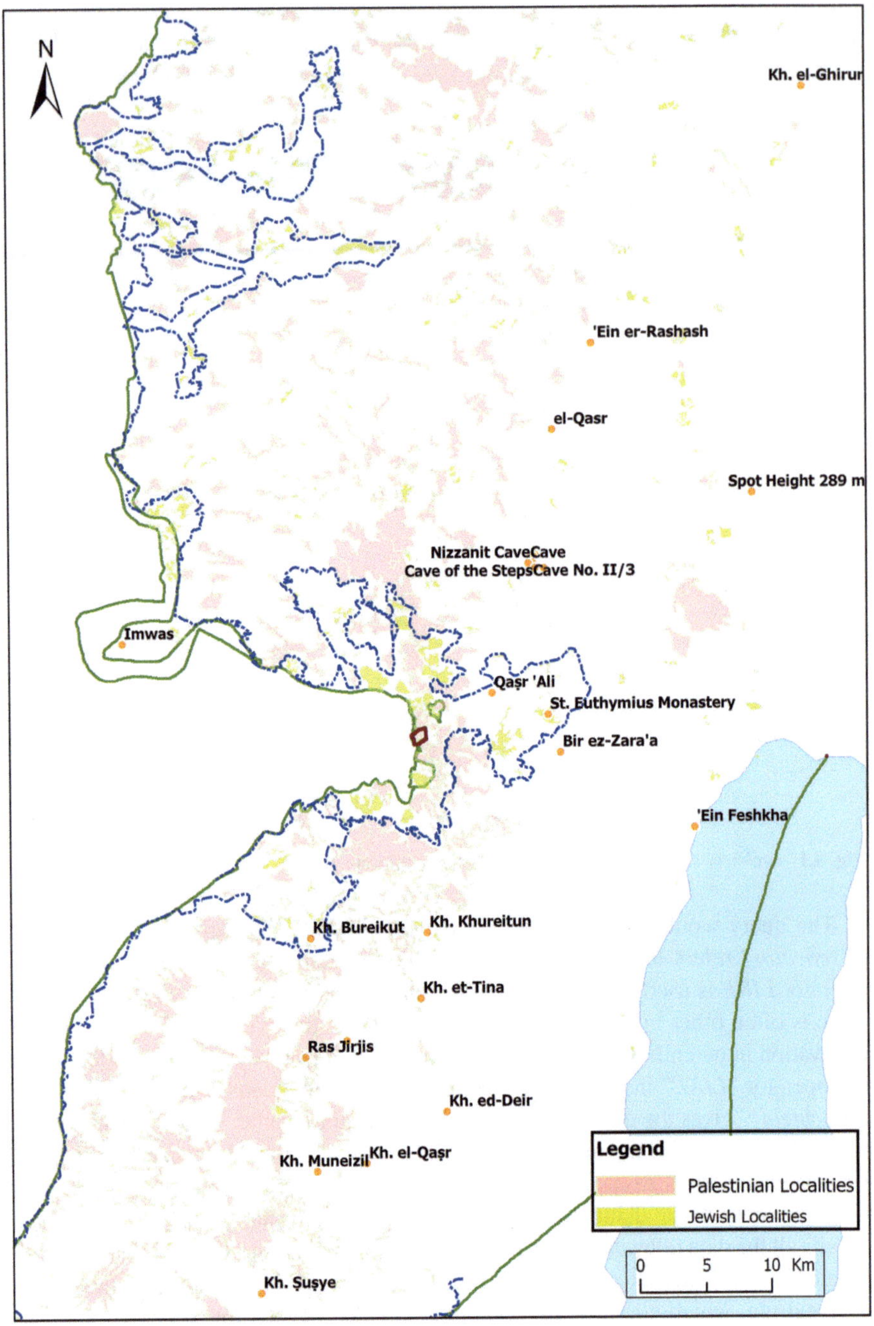

Fig. 8.2 Sites excavated by Yizhar Hirschfeld in the West Bank

account the variations of *Monastery*, *monastery*, *Monasteries*, *monasteries*, *Monastic*, and *monastic*.

Example 2 Retrieval of all sites surveyed in Jerusalem.

The query would be as follows: *[Surveys] LIKE '*Kloner 200*'*. This query would cover all sites surveyed in Jerusalem and published in Kloner (2000, 2001, 2003). If there is an interest in a very specific area within Jerusalem, the added condition could be all sites surveyed in Jerusalem, which are located west of the coordinate 173,000 and south of coordinate 135,000. In this case, the query would be *([Surveys] LIKE '*Kloner 200*') AND ([X] > = 173,000) AND ([Y] < = 135,000)* (Fig. 8.3).

Example 3 Retrieval of excavated sites of a certain period or a few periods.

This search option was designed to provide very exact results for a search of periods. If one is interested in the Byzantine period, for instance, a few search options are available: every period in the database receives the value of "0," "1," and "2," where "0" stands for "no presence," "1" stands for "possible presence or transitional period," and "2" stands for "certain presence." So, a search of all excavated sites that have a clear presence of the Byzantine period would use the query *[Byz] = 2*; a search of sites that have any presence of the Byzantine period, including transitional periods (e.g., Roman–Byzantine), or uncertain presence (i.e., Roman/Byzantine) would use the query *[Byz] <> 0* (where the operator "<>" stands for "not equal to"; and, by the same token, to retrieve sites that have no Byzantine presence, the query would then be *[Byz] = 0*). It is also possible to search a period of existence by a textual query, e.g., *([Major_Periods] LIKE '*Byz*' OR [Other_Periods] LIKE '*Byz*')*. Here there is a distinction between *Major* and *Secondary* periods existing at the site; therefore, it is also optional to search for sites in which the Byzantine period is a prominent period at the site, or the other way around. The textual query is especially efficient for search of very specific periods, such as Crusader or Ayyubid (both of which are included under Medieval *[Med]* field) or Umayyad or Abbasid (which are included under Early Islamic *[EIs]* field). In these cases, a query of *[Med] <> 0* (searching for all Medieval sites) is not accurate enough; a more precise query, searching for Crusader sites, would be *([Major_Periods] LIKE '*Cru*') OR ([Other_Periods] LIKE '*Cru*')*.

These basic queries could, of course, lead to more complex data retrieval and statistical analysis. For example, it is possible to compare the archaeological activity of the various excavating institutions—the ADCA, the IAA, and universities—through the years: number of excavations, areas of excavations, periods, etc. To look for trends in the excavations of the Hebrew University of Jerusalem at 10-year intervals, the query for the 1970s would be *([Excavation_Institution] LIKE '*HUJ*') AND ([License_No] LIKE '*/197*')*.

As mentioned above, the query results are obtained both as textual results, in the form of a table, and visual results, on the GIS map. The addition of thematic layers to the query results viewed on the map is even more informative, since the archaeological sites are viewed in the context of their current natural or urban surroundings. Information can be obtained regarding the proximity of the site to the Green Line/

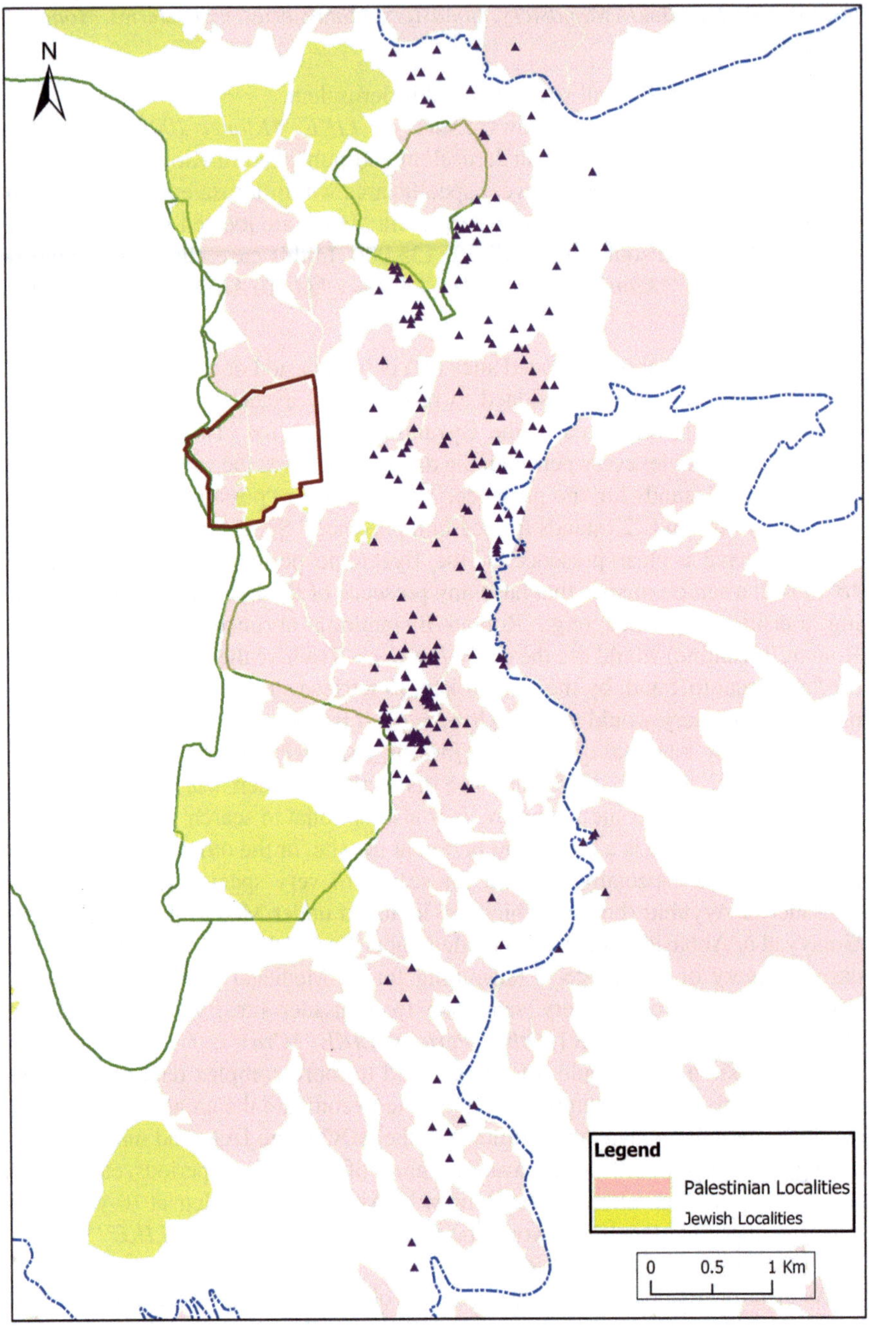

Fig. 8.3 Surveyed sites in a specific area inside Jerusalem

Separation Barrier/modern road/water course, the location of the site in relation to Palestinian or Jewish localities, the topography of the site, etc.

The GIS software allows even more options of site search and selection. For example, it is possible to request sites that are at a distance of maximum 1 km away from the Separation Barrier, using the *Selection > Select by Location* option in the main menu. The *Select by Location* dialogue box in this example would look like this:

I want to: *Select features from*
the following layers: *Surveyed Sites*
that: *are within a distance of*
the features in this layer: *Separation Barrier*
Apply a buffer to the features in *Separation Barrier*
of: *1000 meters*

The sites appearing on the map under that condition (Fig. 8.4) can be saved to a separate layer by right-clicking on the *Surveyed Site* layer and then choosing *Selection > Create Layer from Selected Features*. To view a list of these sites, one should open the *Attribute Table* of the newly made layer. Using the *Selection* tool of the GIS software, in this sense, allows the database users to create new data.

Another way of creating new data from existing information using GIS is the creation of polygons. This indicates the definition of a new area on the map, based on certain features or distribution of sites. For example, it is possible to add an aerial photo of East Jerusalem and the West Bank as a raster layer to the existing GIS layers, upon which the user is able to mark by polygons areas of interest: different neighborhoods in Jerusalem, agricultural plots close to settlements, etc. This way, the user can conduct research by examining the newly defined polygons in relation to archaeological sites. The creation of new polygons can also be based on the distribution of sites. For example, if a researcher is interested in defining clusters of Iron Age I sites, the relevant sites can be viewed on a map using a query and site clusters marked by polygons. This way, it is possible to define settlement patterns using information from the database.

Limitation of the Database and Data Trends

Clearly the database as it stands is a powerful and flexible research tool. Its limitations, however, which may be attributed to different factors, should not be overlooked. First, the fact that the data derives from Israeli sources alone must be emphasized. The database stores information and knowledge created by Israelis or by overseas institutions cooperating with the Israeli government and not by Palestinians or by third parties.[1] Several Israeli archaeological surveys digitized for the creation of the WBEJAD had shared a similar motivation—the collection of data

[1] For an elaborate overview of Israeli and Palestinian inventories, see Keinan (2013).

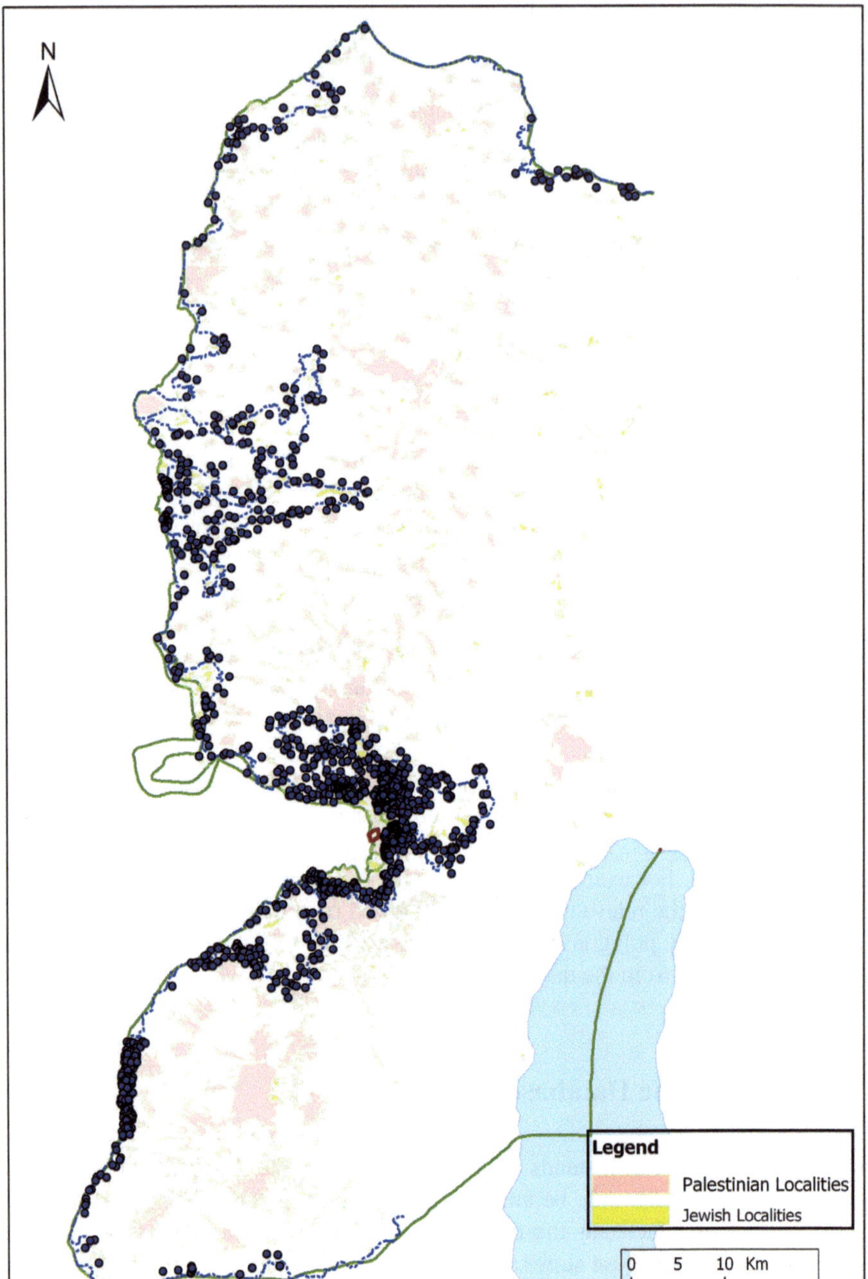

Fig. 8.4 Surveyed sites in the distance of 1 km away from the Separation Barrier

on biblical period sites, namely, from the Bronze and Iron Ages. For example, the aim of Avi Ofer's survey of Judah, in the framework of his PhD dissertation, was to provide a settlement distribution for the Judean Mountain region in biblical eras (Ofer 1993: A:26). The emphasis of his research was thus on the Iron Age period; however, the survey he conducted for the research was executed in a unified way for all periods of existence (Ofer 1993: A:27). Ofer was conscious of potential bias due to his very specific research interest and tried avoiding it by restricting himself to "a synthesis of the settlement processes, keeping the appropriate scientific distance" (Ofer 1993: 1*). However, as will be demonstrated below, his survey methodology did in fact have an impact on the final results of the survey.

Concurrent surveys of the northern regions of the West Bank (often referred to as the "Hill Country") also had the objective of learning more about the distribution of Bronze and Iron Age sites (Finkelstein and Lederman 1997a; Finkelstein and Magen 1993; Zertal 2004, 2005, 2008; Zertal and Mirkam 2000). Similar to the geographic designations of Ofer's survey and different regions of the Emergency Survey (the first Israeli survey conducted in the West Bank; see Kochavi 1972a), the naming of these surveys' regions according to their equivalent Israelite tribes clearly reflects their biblical framework: the Hill countries of Manasseh and Benjamin, the Land of Ephraim,[2] and the Highland of Judah. These surveys were sponsored by the Institute of Archaeology at Tel Aviv University and the Scandinavian Organization for Israel and the Bible (Zertal 2004: 7, 2005: 11); it is possible that their motivations are, at least to some extent, reflected by the inclinations and agendas of their funding institutions.

Similar to Ofer of Tel Aviv University, the archaeologist Adam Zertal was also drawn to his survey area while seeking a topic for his master's dissertation. He chose the region of Samaria since he viewed it as the "arena of the events which occupied the Biblical editor" (Zertal 2004: 1), an area "so crucial for the understanding of Biblical narratives and other texts" (Zertal 2004: 6). Zertal also indicated that his survey area was chosen according to the "Biblical tribal boundaries" as well as geomorphological units and not according to the arbitrary 10 km^2 surveyed according to the Israel Survey methodology (Zertal 2004: 13). This choice of survey method is in accordance with the "special needs of archaeological survey in the land of the Bible" and has its origins in the British surveys (Zertal 2004: 2). In the latest published volume of Zertal's survey, the biblical motivation is clearly inferred by his focus on two issues: "the relations with Transjordan and the archaeological experience of the Iron Age 1 Period" (Zertal 2005: 10, own translation).

It was not only Zertal's personal interest in the biblical history of the region of Samaria that led him to survey this region; he also aimed at "repairing" what he perceived as a bias or distortion in the Israeli archaeological research. According to him, the results of the Emergency Survey did not reflect the biblical archaeological picture in its entirety since it was not a full survey. This survey's results, in turn,

[2]The name of the Land of Ephraim Survey was later changed to the Southern Samaria Survey in order to "adhere to geographical features and avoid historical bias" (Finkelstein and Lederman 1997b: 1 no. 1).

encouraged the creation of "minimalist" schools of thought in the Israeli academia, which cast doubt on the historicity of the Bible. The main purpose of the Manasseh Hill Country Survey was, then, to provide scholars with as complete a picture as possible of the biblical region. Zertal regarded this mission as successful: "while many researchers reduce the historical reliability of the earlier part of the Bible, we pointed at a series of discoveries which contributed to the reliability of the Bible" (Zertal and Mirkam 2000: 11, own translation). Nevertheless, he does not regard his surveys to be political—only scientific (Hasson 2012).

The survey of the Hill Country of Benjamin also reflects its surveyors' motivations and personal interests; these were clearly manifested in the very first paragraph of the survey's publication:

> The hill country of Benjamin, the subject of this survey, is of major importance to the history of Eretz-Israel. Here were the roots of the Israelite monarchy, here the returning [Jewish] exiles settled in the Persian period and here the religious, political, and military infrastructure of the Hasmonean monarchy was consolidated. (Magen in Finkelstein and Magen 1993: 5*).

In addition to this description of the perceived significance of the region, it was stated that, in spite of its being surveyed "with the aim of maximal documentation of all archaeological remains," aspiring for objectiveness and use of scientific methods, the survey teams "worked independently and concentrated on topics of special interest" (Magen in Finkelstein and Magen 1993: 6*). This last quote from Finkelstein and Magen's Benjamin survey demonstrates the problematic aspect of approaching archaeological fieldwork with distinct interests. While taking interest in certain cultures or time periods is not in itself an issue, it may become one when methodology of data collection, analysis, and interpretation are affected. Surveyors of the "Emergency Survey," which took place immediately after the occupation, had to make some methodological decisions due to time and funding restrictions. Because of these constraints, the surveyors could not have achieved a full coverage of the West Bank; therefore, they had to make decisions on coverage priorities. Reviewing the methodological notes of one of this survey's regions, the Land of Judah, survey priorities were defined as follows:

> A. Archaeological examination of the sites to which historical identifications were proposed.
> B. Examination of sites that are marked on maps as antiquity sites.
> C. Continuous coverage of the entire survey square [survey area].

With the time allocated for its work, the survey group completed ca. 80% of the first priority, ca. 50% of the second priority, and very little of the third priority (Kochavi 1972b: 19, own translation).

The first priority of Kochavi's survey, priority "A," aimed to examine sites that were suggested historical identifications by previous scholars. Historical sources in this context are usually books of the Bible (e.g., Books of Joshua, Samuel or Chronicles) or the Iron Age-dated Samaria Ostraca but could also be Hellenistic or Byzantine historical accounts such as the Book of Maccabees and Eusebius' *Onomasticon*. Such Judeo-Christian sources focus mostly on biblical period or New

Testament sites—thus, the surveys placing their examination as a first priority inevitably favor biblical, Jewish, and Christian sites. Surveyors of other regions covered by this survey had to prioritize their levels of coverage as well (Bar-Adon 1972, 92; Kallai 1972: 153). To some extent, it seems that this survey—the first to be conducted by Israeli archaeologists in the region—followed the objectives of preceding Western surveys: to identify archaeological sites with places mentioned in the Bible.

Other types of methodological choices reflecting surveyors' priorities were made while planning the strategies of Israeli surveys. One notable example of such choice is the degrees of documentation of this period or another. It is evident that some specific periods were better documented than others, while, at times, some periods were not documented at all. For instance, the treatment of prehistoric periods during surveys was occasionally partially addressed, while at other times completely ignored. Most Israeli surveyors working in the West Bank were not accompanied by lithic experts, and their emphasis was set on pottery collection. This adopted practice resulted in a serious under-representation of Palaeolithic to early Neolithic sites in most surveys and in turn in the final WBEJAD inventory that had digitized them.

The noninclusion of prehistorians and subsequent impact on the final result of surveys' data collection were referred to in some survey publications. For example, in the survey of Benjamin, it was mentioned that "prehistorians did not participate in the survey teams, and therefore prehistoric finds are virtually absent from the survey" (Finkelstein in Finkelstein and Magen 1993: 11*; see also Goldfus and Golani 1993: 268). The survey of Judah excluded prehistory as well: "The Pre-Pottery periods are not discussed in this research" (Ofer 1993: 28*); and such was the case in the Southern Samaria survey as well (Finkelstein 1997: 13). Prehistoric sites were not recorded in the Map of Mar Saba survey either (Patrich 1994: 13), where the surveyor did not consider it necessary to conduct a prehistoric survey since "sites from the Paleolithic, Epipaleolithic and Neolithic periods were recorded within the area of neighboring Map of Herodium" (Patrich 1994: 12*). But, in fact, only 4% of the area of the Map of Herodium underwent a prehistoric survey—and even then it was not an exhaustive one (Gopher in Hirschfeld 1985: 17*). Figure 8.5 demonstrates how the distribution of prehistoric sites, dating from the Lower Paleolithic to the Pre-Pottery Neolithic period, is determined by the areas that were surveyed by prehistorians.

Later periods, notably from the Early Islamic period onwards, were frequently neglected too; this is especially true for the Ottoman period, which is the latest historical period recorded in archaeological surveys in this region. Some survey publications mentioned this inadequacy of the recording of late periods. In the Emergency Survey, for example, it was stated that "little attention has been given to these periods [Early Islamic period onwards] in this stage of the survey, and one should not draw historic-settlement related conclusions from the collected data" (Kochavi 1972b: 24, own translation). The sharp decline of surveyors' interest in post-Byzantine periods and lack of archaeological knowledge of later periods are also exemplified in the survey of Judah ("it was not possible to divide these long periods (1,300 years in total), or to detect internal processes" (Ofer 1993: 31*)) and in the

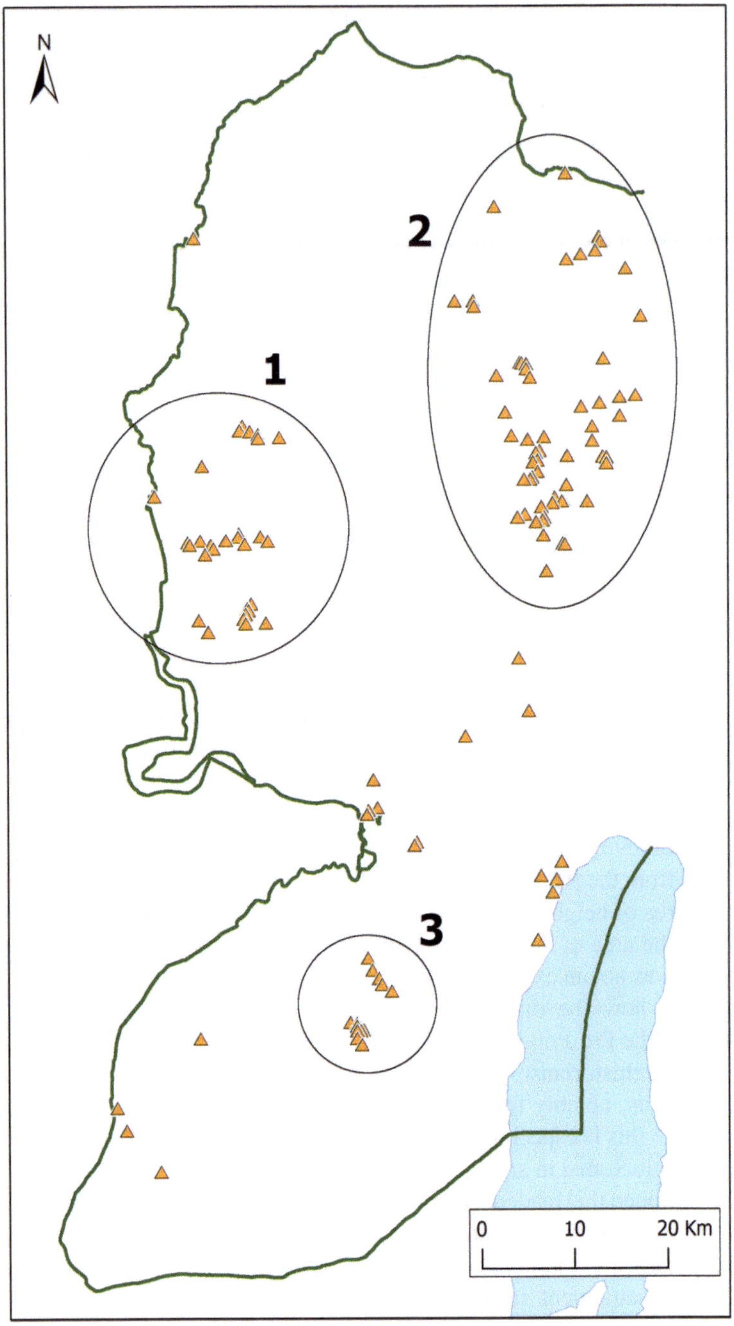

Fig. 8.5 The distribution of prehistoric sites digitized for the WBEJAD. The three main clusters of prehistoric sites represent the following surveys: *1* Barkai et al. (1997), *2* Zertal (2005, 2008), *3* Hirschfeld (1985)

survey of the Manasseh region ("These periods have been the most 'neglected' from the ceramic point of view, and it seems to us that their internal division is insufficient" (Zertal 2008: 55)). This compromise in data collection of the late periods is probably most distinct when it comes to the Ottoman period. The survey of Benjamin indicated that "it is possible that in some areas the collection of the Ottoman ware was somewhat insufficient" (Finkelstein in Finkelstein and Magen 1993: 11*) and "obviously, the relative portion of pottery sherds from the Ottoman period in Arab villages does not represent the real quantity of pottery sherds at the site" (Finkelstein 1993: 22, own translation).

These issues of period prioritization and neglect in archaeological surveys have a significant impact on generated maps illustrating site distribution in the region (for an on-the-ground assessment of the WBEJAD and other databases, see Keinan-Schoonbaert 2016). However, these are not the only types of methodological choices made by surveyors, affecting the nature of the final WBEJAD database. In the process of survey digitization and database construction, it became evident that different surveyors used different site definitions in their fieldwork and publication. Generally speaking, researchers depend on the good judgment of the surveyor who decides whether a few adjacent archaeological elements are to be considered together as one archaeological site or whether each element represents a site on its own. The outcome of this decision is evident in each survey's list of sites, where it is clear that while some surveyors list single elements such as structures, caves, tombs, and agricultural installations as independent sites, others group them as one complex site or attach them to the nearest major site. The different definitions of sites lead to different site densities, a phenomenon very evident when generating GIS maps from the database.

This brings us to another issue of survey coverage. While the surveys mentioned above aimed at a "full coverage" of their respective regions, other West Bank surveys aimed, by definition, at a partial coverage of specific areas. These include surveys covering only known sites indicated on older maps (e.g., Kochavi 1972a), surveys conducted for academic purposes, therefore focusing on specific periods or aspects of the archaeological remains, or other topical surveys. A good example of the latter would be Operation Scroll (Wexler 2002), a hurried survey of caves in the Judean Desert conducted immediately after the signing of the Oslo Accords (in September 1993) in search of hidden scrolls. The timing of this survey is of no coincidence, neither is the sense of urgency arising from the name given to this survey, "Operation" (Silberman 1996). As clearly indicated by its name, the goal of this survey, and focused excavations that took place during its execution, was to recover any scrolls still hidden in the caves of the Quruntul and Qumran mountain ranges, where most of the Dead Sea Scrolls had been discovered (Wexler 2002: v). The awkwardness of its timing and political context was best described by Silberman:

> On November 14, a month before Israeli forces would have begun a staged withdrawal from the Gaza Strip and the Jericho region, the IAA launched an ambitious survey and excavation project dubbed "Operation Scroll." At the very moment when Israeli and Palestinian negotiators were working out the details of the Israel-Palestine Liberation Organization understanding signed in Washington in September, 20 teams of Israeli archaeologists

> assisted by some 200 hired workers began searching for, and removing, ancient coins, pottery, manuscript fragments, and other archaeological finds from the caves and ravines of a 60 mile stretch of the lower Jordan Valley and the Western shore of the Dead Sea. (Silberman 1996: 132).

The IAA had to face Palestinian, Israeli, and international harsh criticism regarding the timing, scale, and opportunistic nature of this project. In response, the IAA's spokeswoman denied "any political implications" (Silberman 1996: 133), and the IAA's director at the time claimed that these accusations were groundless (Drori in Wexler 2002: i). As Operation Scroll aimed specifically at uncovering Hebrew and Aramaic scrolls, considered by many Israeli Jews as one of the most important types of tangible heritage, only caves were examined—thus, the survey's methodology was dictated by its motivation and agenda. Another example of the same objective is evident in one of the Benjamin survey areas, the Wadi el-Makukh region: "The aim of the Wadi el-Makukh caves survey was not archaeological; therefore we have ceramic finds from looted or excavated caves only" (Goldfus and Golani 1993: 268, own translation). In these two cases, as in other examples discussed above, survey motivations determined their methodology.

It is important to note here that even if all surveyors strove for objectivity, one cannot expect complete neutrality in fieldwork. As the WBEJAD is a synthesis of many surveys, conducted by different surveyors with different interests and agendas, different qualifications, and at different times, its final form portrays the diverse nature of its sources. Additional constraints in source data had contributed to the final result of database construction. For example, some archaeological surveys were never published, a fact that results in archaeological "dead zones" on GIS maps of the West Bank generated from the database. This is also the case with some excavations, especially in more recent years. Because of the contested nature of the area, and the fact that much of the work has been carried out in the context of a military occupation, many details regarding archaeological activity remain unknown or only partly published. We also had to take into account different scales of quality of information when handling administrative lists provided by the ADCA, the IAA, and academic institutions. Inaccuracies, contradictory information, missing data, and errors had to be dealt with during the database construction but could be coped with only to a certain extent. Therefore, it should be emphasized that due to gaps in information and the abovementioned limitations, the database is not definitive; however, it does represent the best approximation that could be reached based on available resources.

Summary

Israeli archaeologists have been working in the occupied territories for the last 50 years. Official published and unpublished records of their work exist in libraries, archives, and computer systems of the Israel Antiquities Authority, the Archaeology Department of the Civil Administration, and universities in Israel. Now there is one single source of information for all surveys and excavations in the West Bank and East Jerusalem, which includes both administrative and archaeological data. This database is a synthesis of information deriving from available sources; it provides as full an account as possible, within present limitations, of the extent of archaeological knowledge accumulated by Israeli research between 1967 and 2007 and comprises the most comprehensive summary of the Israeli activity in the occupied territories.

This detailed database is a very useful tool that can be employed by a wide variety of end users: the general public, archaeologists, cultural heritage specialists, educators, political decision-makers, and more. Developed on the most common platforms—MS Excel, MS Access, and ESRI ArcView—and in English, it is designed to be accessible and easy to use for as large an audience as possible. The tabular data can be searched, manipulated, or viewed on a GIS map, so that end users can produce limitless permutations of the data. It can also be used as a platform for further research, development, and upgrade, by adding more textual data, GIS layers, photographs, sketches, etc.

However, the WBEJAD is not devoid of problems and limitations. The analysis of most sources used to construct it reflects some clear patterns—mainly a special interest in biblical-period and Judeo-Christian archaeological sites, coupled with a systematic neglect of the earliest and latest archaeological periods. These research priorities had a crucial impact on the final form of the WBEJAD, being a digitized compilation of all of these Israeli surveys and excavations. The final WBEJAD inventory, therefore, clearly represents some types of archaeological sites better than others—and in this way it embodies Israeli research interests, priorities, and preferences. Nonetheless, we hope that the existence of this research tool will be beneficial for those who are interested in the different aspects of archaeology in the West Bank and East Jerusalem and will raise awareness of the importance of archaeology and cultural heritage in this contested area of the Middle East.

References

Bar, S. (2008). *The pattern of settlement in the Lower Jordan Valley and the desert fringes of Samaria during the Late Chalcolithic Period and Early Bronze Age I.* PhD dissertation, The University of Haifa. (Hebrew).

Bar-Adon, P. (1972). The Judaean Desert and plain of Jericho. In M. Kochavi (Ed.), *Judaea Samaria and the Golan: Archaeological survey 1967-1968* (pp. 92–149). Jerusalem: The Archaeological Survey of Israel. (Hebrew).

Barkai, R., Gopher, A., & Friedmann, E. (1997). Prehistoric occurrences in Western Samaria: The 1967-1968 survey. In I. Finkelstein & Z. Lederman (Eds.), *Highlands of many cultures: The Southern Samaria survey* (pp. 857–881). Tel Aviv: Tel Aviv University, Institute of Archaeology.

Ben-Yosef, D. (2007). *The Jordan Valley during the Iron Age I.* PhD dissertation, The University of Haifa (Hebrew).

Civil Administration. (2011). *Archaeology in the West Bank: Inside the Archaeology Department of the Civil Administration.* Bet El: Civil Administration of Judea and Samaria. http://www.cogat.idf.il/Sip_Storage/FILES/7/3097.pdf. Accessed 5 Nov 2014.

Finkelstein, I. (1993). Northern part of the Maps of Beit Sira, Ramallah and el-Bireh. In I. Finkelstein, & Y. Magen (Eds.), *Archaeological survey of the hill country of Benjamin* (pp. 17–131). Jerusalem: Israel Antiquities Authority Publications (Hebrew).
Finkelstein, I. (1997). Method of field survey and data recording. In I. Finkelstein & Z. Lederman (Eds.), *Highlands of many cultures: The Southern Samaria survey: The sites* (pp. 11–24). Tel Aviv: Tel Aviv University, Institute of Archaeology.
Finkelstein, I., & Lederman, Z. (1997a). *Highlands of many cultures: The Southern Samaria survey: The sites*. Tel Aviv: Tel Aviv University, Institute of Archaeology.
Finkelstein, I., & Lederman, Z. (1997b). Introduction. In I. Finkelstein & Z. Lederman (Eds.), *Highlands of many cultures: The Southern Samaria survey: The sites* (pp. 1–8). Tel Aviv: Tel Aviv University, Institute of Archaeology.
Finkelstein, I., & Magen, Y. (Eds.). (1993). *Archaeological survey of the hill country of Benjamin*. Jerusalem: Israel Antiquities Authority Publications.
Goldfus, H., & Golani, A. (1993). Map of Wadi el-Makukh. In I. Finkelstein, & Y. Magen (Eds.), *Archaeological survey of the hill country of Benjamin* (pp. 265–338). Jerusalem: Israel Antiquities Authority Publications (Hebrew).
Greenberg, R., & Keinan, A. (2007). *The present past of the Israeli-Palestinian conflict: Israeli archaeology in the West Bank and East Jerusalem since 1967*. Tel Aviv: The S. Daniel Abraham Center for International and Regional Studies, Tel Aviv University.
Greenberg, R., & Keinan, A. (2009). *Israeli archaeological activity in the West Bank 1967-2007: A sourcebook*. Jerusalem: Ostracon.
Hasson, N. (2012, September 30). Mapping Israel one foot at a time. *Ha'aretz*. http://www.haaretz.co.il/news/education/1.1832962. Accessed 5 Nov 2014 (Hebrew).
Hirschfeld, Y. (1985). *Map of Herodium (108/2) 17-11*. Jerusalem: The Department of Antiquities and Museums – The Archaeological Survey of Israel.
IPAWG. (2007). *Israeli-Palestinian Archaeology Working Group Website*. http://crcc.usc.edu/initiatives/shi/ipawg.html. Accessed 5 Nov 2014.
Kallai, Z. (1972). The land of Benjamin and Mt. Ephraim. In M. Kochavi (Ed.), *Judaea Samaria and the Golan: Archaeological survey 1967-1968* (pp. 153–193). Jerusalem: The Archaeological Survey of Israel (Hebrew).
Keinan, A. (2010). Archaeological inventories and cultural heritage management in the occupied Palestinian territories. *Forum Archaeologiae, 55*(VI/2010). http://homepage.univie.ac.at/elisabeth.trinkl/forum/forum0610/forum55keinan.pdf. Accessed 5 Nov 2014.
Keinan, A. (2013). *Israeli and Palestinian archaeological inventories, GIS and conflicting cultures in the occupied West Bank*. PhD dissertation, University College London.
Keinan-Schoonbaert, A. (2016). Multiple inventories and divided archaeology in the West Bank: An assessment of databases in the Etzion Bloc. *Journal of Field Archaeology, 41*(6), 645–659.
Kloner, A. (2000). *Survey of Jerusalem, the Southern sector*. Jerusalem: The Israel Antiquities Authority – The Archaeological Survey of Israel.
Kloner, A. (2001). *Survey of Jerusalem, the Northeastern sector*. Jerusalem: The Israel Antiquities Authority – The Archaeological Survey of Israel.
Kloner, A. (2003). *Survey of Jerusalem, the Northwestern sector: Introduction and indices*. Jerusalem: The Israel Antiquities Authority – The Archaeological Survey of Israel.
Kochavi, M. (Ed.). (1972a). *Judaea Samaria and the Golan: Archaeological survey 1967-1968*. Jerusalem: The Archaeological Survey of Israel (Hebrew).
Kochavi, M. (1972b). The land of Judah. In M. Kochavi (Ed.), *Judaea Samaria and the Golan: Archaeological survey 1967-1968* (pp. 19–89). Jerusalem: The Archaeological Survey of Israel (Hebrew).
Much, I. (2007). *Israeli Palestinian "track two" diplomacy. Negotiating identity in intractable conflicts: The Israeli Palestinian Archaeology Working Group*. MA dissertation, Fakultät für Sozialwissenschaften Studienrichtung Politikwissenschaft der Universität Wien.
Ofer, A. (1993). *The highland of Judah during the biblical period*. PhD dissertation, Tel-Aviv university (Hebrew).

Patrich, J. (1994). *Map of Deir Mar Saba (109/7)*. Jerusalem: The Israel Antiquities Authority – The Archaeological Survey of Israel.

Silberman, N. A. (1996). Operation scroll. In K. D. Vitelli (Ed.), *Archaeological ethics* (pp. 132–136). Walnut Creek: AltaMira Press.

Swartz Dodd, L., & Boytner, R. (2010). Filtering the past: Archaeology, politics, and change. In R. Boytner, L. Swartz Dodd, & B. J. Parker (Eds.), *Controlling the past, owning the future: The political uses of archaeology in the Middle East* (pp. 1–26). Tucson: The University of Arizona Press.

Taha, H. (2002). Protection of cultural heritage in Palestine. In F. Maniscalco (Ed.), *La tutela del patrimonio culturale in caso di conflitto* (pp. 265–270, Mediterraneum: Tutela e valorizzazione dei beni culturali ed ambientali, Vol. 2). Naples: Massa Editore.

Taha, H. (2005). A decade of archaeology in Palestine. In F. Maniscalco (Ed.), *Tutela, conservazione e valorizzazione del patrimonio culturale della Palestina* (pp. 63–71, Mediterraneum: Tutela e valorizzazione dei beni culturali ed ambientali, Vol. 5). Naples: Massa Editore.

Taha, H. (2010). The current state of archaeology in Palestine. *Present Pasts, 2*(1), 16–25.

Wexler, L. (Ed.). (2002). *Surveys and excavations of caves in the Northern Judean Desert (CNJD) – 1993, part 2. 'Atiqot, 41*. Jerusalem: Israel Antiquities Authority.

Yahya, A. H. (2010). The Palestinian-Israeli draft agreement on archaeological heritage. *Present Pasts, 2*(1), 72–74.

Zertal, A. (2004). *The Manasseh hill country survey, Vol. I – The Shechem Syncline* (Culture and history of the ancient Near East). Leiden/Boston: Brill.

Zertal, A. (2005). *The Manasseh hill country survey, Vol. IV – From Nahal Bezeq to the Sartaba*. Tel Aviv: IDF Publishing House and Haifa University (Hebrew).

Zertal, A. (2008). *The Manasseh hill country survey, Vol. II – The Eastern valleys and the fringes of the desert*, (Culture and history of the ancient Near East). Leiden/Boston: Brill.

Zertal, A., & Mirkam, N. (2000). *The Manasseh hill country survey, Vol. III – From Nahal 'Iron to Nahal Shechem*. Tel Aviv: IDF Publishing House and Haifa University (Hebrew).

Chapter 9
At-Risk World Heritage, Cyber, and Marine Archaeology: The Kastrouli–Antikyra Bay Land and Sea Project, Phokis, Greece

Thomas E. Levy, T. Sideris, M. Howland, B. Liss, G. Tsokas, A. Stambolidis, E. Fikos, G. Vargemezis, P. Tsourlos, A. Georgopoulos, G. Papatheodorou, M. Garaga, D. Christodoulou, R. Norris, I. Rivera-Collazo, and I. Liritzis

Introduction to the Land and Sea Project

The Kastrouli–Antikyra Bay Land and Sea Project near Greece's Gulf of Corinth was inspired by a number of interwoven research goals including: (a) applying a range of cyber-archaeology and geophysical tools to address the issue of at-risk cultural heritage in the eastern Mediterranean; (b) using this study to help develop a marine archaeology methodology suitable for studying human coastal adaption during the late Holocene across time and space; (c) focusing on the end of the Late Bronze Age in the eastern Mediterranean to address the problem of the collapse of Mycenaean, Hittite, and New Kingdom Egypt civilizations to investigate the role that

T.E. Levy (✉) • M. Howland • B. Liss • I. Rivera-Collazo
University of California, San Diego, Department of Anthropology, Center for Cyber-Archaeology and Sustainability, Scripps Center for Marine Archaeology, La Jolla, CA, USA
e-mail: tlevy@ucsd.edu

T. Sideris • I. Liritzis
University of the Aegean, Department of Mediterranean Studies, Lab of Archaeometry and Lab of Environmental Archaeology, Rhodes, Greece

G. Tsokas • A. Stambolidis • E. Fikos • G. Vargemezis • P. Tsourlos
Aristotle University of Thessaloniki, Exploration Geophysics Lab, School of Geology, Thessaloniki, Greece

A. Georgopoulos
National Technical University of Athens, Laboratory of Photogrammetry, School of Rural & Surveying Engineering, Athens, Greece

G. Papatheodorou • M. Garaga • D. Christodoulou
University of Patras, Department of Geology, Lab of Marine Geology and Physical Oceanography, Patras, Greece

R. Norris
University of California, San Diego; Scripps Center for Marine Archaeology, Scripps Institution of Oceanography, La Jolla, CA, USA

T.E. Levy, I.W.N. Jones (eds.), *Cyber-Archaeology and Grand Narratives*,
One World Archaeology, https://doi.org/10.1007/978-3-319-65693-9_9

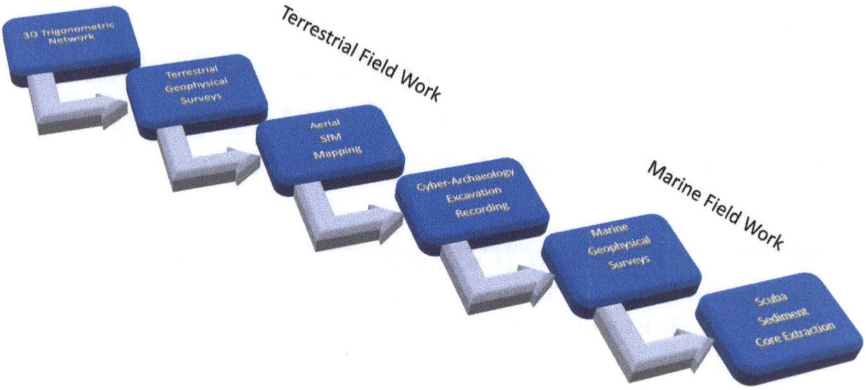

Fig. 9.1 The transdisciplinary workflow for the 2016 Kastrouli–Antikyra Bay, Greece, Land and Sea Project

climate, environmental, and social factors may have played in this process; and (d) finally to engage in the more local problem of understanding the nature of Mycenaean coastal worlds.

This integrated approach takes a transdisciplinary approach to research opening new understandings of issues concerning climate change, human adaptation, and culture change in sensitive coastal environments. The workflow for the 2016 land and sea expedition is shown in Fig. 9.1.

In the study presented here, we focus on describing the workflow and methods used in the Kastrouli–Antikyra Bay Project, which integrates recent developments in terrestrial cyber-archaeology (Levy 2013) and marine archaeology with the aim of developing a more effective field methodology for studying human adaptation to coastal environments during the Holocene around the world. As the focus of our research is on the archaeology of the eastern Mediterranean, issues concerning connectivity between societies and local cultural evolution from the Aegean region to the southern Levant are of great interest. A number of pan-eastern Mediterranean problems are of interest to the Kastrouli–Antikyra Bay project (Figs. 9.2 and 9.3): 1) the collapse of Late Bronze Age (LBA) civilizations ca. 1200–1100 BCE that brought the end of palatial culture of Mycenaean Greece, the Hittite Empire, and the Egyptian New Kingdom (Cline 2014); the nature of climate change during the Late Bronze–Iron Age based on proxy paleoenvironmental data including pollen, marine resources, geomorphology, and other datasets (Cramer et al. 2017; Langgut et al. 2013, 2014); and how the power vacuum that resulted from the LBA collapse opened up new economic, ideological, and trade opportunities for small-scale societies in the region such as the Israelites, Edomites, Sea Peoples, and others to evolve (cf. Ben-Shlomo et al. 2008; Killebrew 2005; Levy et al. 2014; Lipschitz and Maeir 2017). As suggested by Weiner (n.d.), some of the responses to climate and environmental deterioration at the end of the Late Bronze Age included famine, pandemics, and warfare.

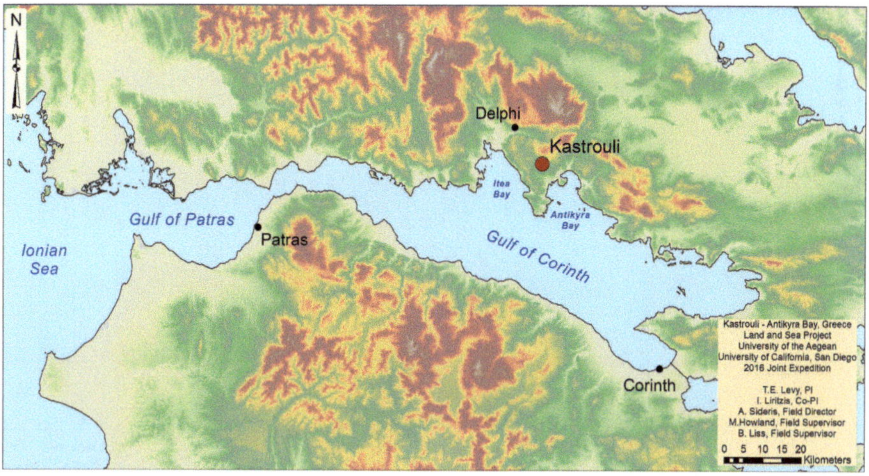

Fig. 9.2 Map of Gulf of Corinth region and location of Kastrouli in relation to major sites and towns on the mainland of Greece (Map by M. Howland, Center for Cyber-Archaeology and Sustainability, UC San Diego)

On the local scale, the Kastrouli–Antikyra Project aims to investigate what Thomas Tartaron (2013:7–11) defines as Mycenaean coast worlds, in particular at the end of the Late Bronze Age or Late Helladic (LH) period, which coincides the period leading up to and after the LBA collapse. There are no sharp chronological boundaries with archaeological periods. The LH begins ca. 1600 BCE and ends ca. 1050 BCE when it reached an apex, or *koine*, in the high palatial period of LH IIIA2 to early LH IIIB (ca. 1370 – 1250 BCE) with a "complex sociopolitical system based on the palaces and recorded using a syllabic script (Linear B) that represents an archaic form of the Greek language, and sometimes even an ethnicity..." (2013:7). Scholars debate whether there was a sharp end to the Mycenaean period. However, as Marina Thomatos (2006) points out, there was a kind of revival in LH IIIC of the Mycenaean culture. For the purposes of this paper, the end of the LH IIIC is 1190–1070 BCE (Tartaron 2013:3). It seems everything is debated in Mycenaean archaeology, including the notion of a "core area" of settlement. For this study, we assume that the Peloponnese and central Greece, which include Kastrouli and the Gulf of Corinth, are indeed part of the Mycenaean core area of settlement making this project a significant data source for examining the LBA issues noted above. The Kastrouli and Antiykra Bay coastlines were and still are tightly linked as a locus for economic and social intercourse making them an ideal setting for investigating a Mycenaean coastal world.

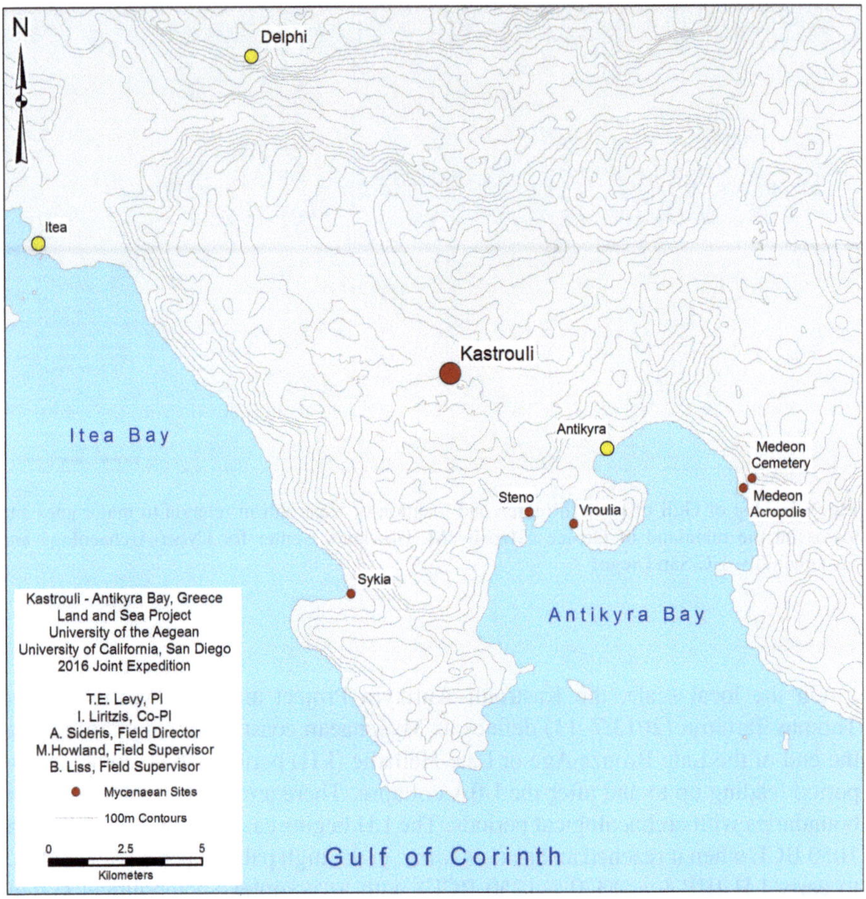

Fig. 9.3 Map of the area of Kastrouli. Red dots represent Mycenaean sites (After A. Sideris 2014:17; map by M. Howland)

Terrestrial Excavation at Kastrouli

Kastrouli (E375419.559, N4250792.352), a small fortified site in the Phokis region of central Greece (near the modern village of Desfina), was the focus of excavations in the summer of 2016 (July 20–August 3; Fig. 9.2) in the context of an at-risk cultural heritage site. An ancient fortification wall encompassing an area of 1.67 ha defines the size of the site where both archaeological features and ceramic sherds are found in abundance. The project aimed to fully and systematically excavate the exposed tomb on the site's surface and to section its fortification wall. The site was previously excavated in 2005, but this short project (lasting several days) performed little systematic excavation (primarily cleaning) to evaluate the condition of tombs at the site that were previously looted as evidenced by their disturbed nature (Raptopoulos 2012: 1074). Based on the brief excavations, the tomb was determined from the architecture to be a small Mycenaean Tholos tomb and was dated to the Late Helladic IIIB2 based on the ceramic typology. These were the only excavations at the site to date. The 2016 excavation season was directed by Thomas E. Levy (PI, University of California, San Diego), Athanasios Sideris (Excavation Director, University of the Aegean), and Ioannis Liritzis (Co-PI, University of the Aegean). Graduate students Matthew D. Howland and Brady Liss (University of California, San Diego) functioned as field supervisors, and a team of undergraduate students from the University of California, San Diego, were the primary excavators along with three local workers. In addition, three computer programmers (Rose Smith, Carolyn Breeze, and Taylor Harman) developing the web-based *ArchaeoSTOR* artifact database joined the team to manage and organize all excavated artifacts. Before the excavation started, the site was georeferenced, mapped, and surveyed using an array of state-of-the-art photogrammetric and geophysical methods described below (Sideris et al. 2017).

Transdisciplinary Methodologies

3D Network of Trigonometric Points for Georeferencing Archaeological Fieldwork

To facilitate high spatial accuracy for all recorded finds, the 2016 excavation season at Kastrouli began by establishing reliable control points throughout the site. Andreas Georgopoulos and Panagiotis Agrafiotis (National Technical University of Athens) headed the project to create a network of nine control points (numbered T1-T9, see Fig. 9.4), which were referenced to the Greek (Hellenic) Geodetic Reference System (GGRS'87–ΕΓΣΑ'87; see below). The locations for control points were selected based on the need to avoid any perceivable interventions at the Kastrouli site and to ensure the permanence of their position not only during the measurements but also for the future needs of the work. The nine points were permanently marked with concrete pillars, 0.1 m diameter and 10–15 cm height, equipped with steel marks to enable centering of the instruments (total stations, GPS, etc.). The coordinates of these locations were collected using a Topcon GPT 3003 total station.

Unfortunately, the control points were not established before the first day of excavation. As such, recording of loci and artifact finds during the excavation were based on two control points established by GPS provided by Grigoris Tsokas (University of Thessaloniki) (Table 9.1). These points provided the base control points for the total station/*ArchField* recording for the entire excavation to maintain consistency. However, in checking the accuracy of the coordinates of the GPS control points from the established control points described above, it was discovered that the GPS points were inaccurate by roughly 22 centimeters in the southeast direction. To correct this error, test points were recorded both from the GPS control

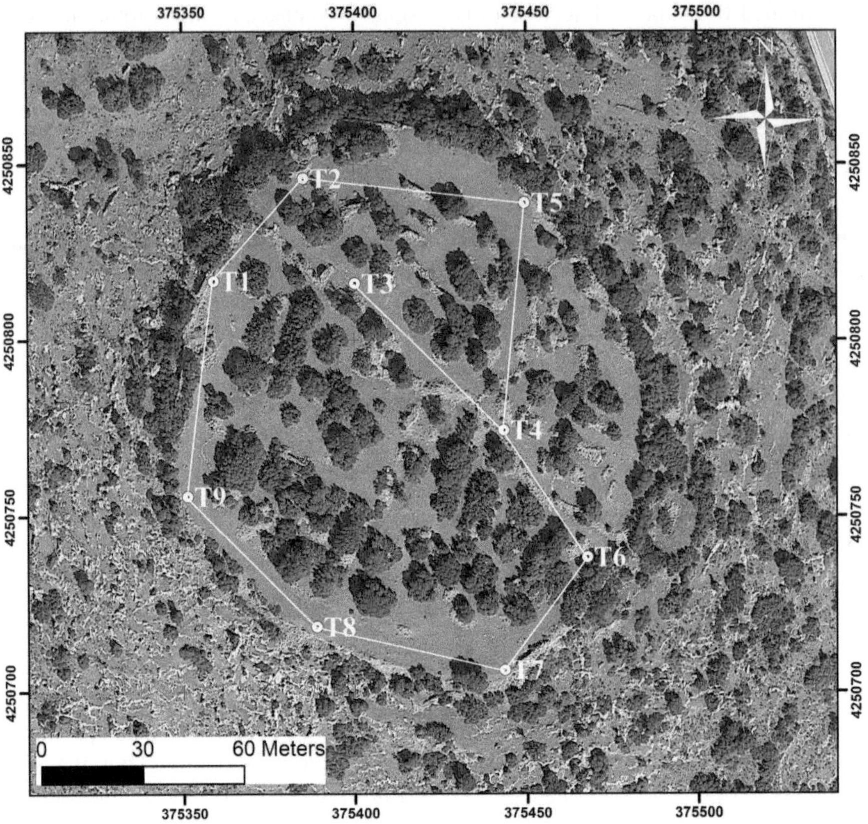

Fig. 9.4 The 3D trigonometric network at Kastrouli, Phokis, Greece. A total of nine points were established, each labeled with the letter "T" (Image: Courtesy A. Georgopoulos, Google Earth)

Table 9.1 Table of GPS points provided by Grigoris Tsokas used for recording artifact and loci locations

Kastrouli GPS point coordinates (m)			
Point name	Easting	Northing	Elevation
d1	375364.1344	4250804.235	547.87001
d2	375372.1963	4250809.271	548.24936

point and from T1 by total station. By having the same point recorded from both positions, all points and polygons recorded based on the GPS control point could subsequently be shifted in GIS based on the apparent difference. The accuracy of the points after correction became +/− 2 cm, in line with the levels of accuracy obtained by total station survey across the site.

Selection of Positions

In consultation with the excavation team, careful examination of the site surface was made that led to the decision to establish a network composed of nine points (Fig. 9.4) numbered T1, T2, ..., T9. These positions were selected in order to:

- Avoid any perceivable interventions at the archaeological site
- Ensure the permanence of their position not only during the measurements but also for the future needs of the work

The Greek Geodetic Reference System

In accordance with Greek antiquities laws, it was required that the Kastrouli network be referenced to the Greek (Hellenic) Geodetic Reference System (GGRS'87–ΕΓΣΑ'87). The Greek Geodetic Reference System 1987 or GGRS87 (ΕΓΣΑ'87) is a geodetic system commonly used in Greece. The system specifies a local geodetic datum and a projection system. GGRS87 specifies a non-geocentric datum that is tied to the coordinates of the key geodetic station at the Dionysos Satellite Observatory (DSO) northeast of Athens (38.078400°N 23.932939°E). The central pedestal (CP) at this location has by definition GGRS87 coordinates 38° 4′ 33.8000″ N - 23° 55′ 51.0000″ E, N = +7 m. Although HGRS87 uses the GRS80 ellipsoid, the origin is shifted relative to the GRS80 geocenter, so that the ellipsoidal surface is best for Greece. The specified offsets relative to WGS84 are $\Delta x = -199.87$ m, $\Delta y = 74.79$ m, and $\Delta z = 246.62$ m. The GGRS87 datum is implemented by a first-order geodetic network, which consists of approximately 30 triangulation stations throughout Greece and is maintained by the Hellenic Military Geographical Service. The initial uncertainty was estimated as 0.1 ppm. However, there are considerable tectonic movements that move parts of Greece toward different directions causing incompatibilities between surveys taking place at different times.

HGRS87 also specifies a transverse Mercator cartographic projection (TM) with m0 = 0.9996, covering six degrees of longitude either side of 24 degrees east (18–30 degrees east). This way all Greek territory (stretching to approximately 9° of longitude) is projected in one zone. References are in meters. Northings are counted from the equator. A false easting of 500,000 m is assigned to the central meridian (24° east), so eastings are always positive.

Accurate Geodetic Measurements

The established network at Kastrouli was connected and related to the Greek Geodetic Reference System '87 (GGRS '87) by using static GPS measurements. The elevation heights are orthometric and refer to the mean sea level. The nine points were permanently marked with concrete pillars, 0.1 m diameter and 10–15 cm

Fig. 9.5 For geodetic measurements, a TopCon GPT 3003 total station was employed. For daily excavation recording, a Leica TS02 Reflectorless Total Station was used

height, equipped with steel marks to enable centering of the instruments (total stations, GPS, etc.). Global Navigation Satellite System (GNSS) and classic geodetic measurements were used for two reasons: firstly, to adjust the network in the Greek Reference System and, secondly, to make sure that this reference is done with minimum constraints, thus maintaining its internal accuracy.

The geodetic measurements for the network constituted of vertical and horizontal angles and slope distances between the various vertices. These measurements were performed using the Topcon GPT 3003 Total Station (Figs. 9.5 and 9.6), which ensures accuracy of $\pm 3''$(1 mgon) for the angle measurements and $\pm$ (3 mm +2 ppm $\times$ D) (D: measuring distance (mm)) for the distances to a prism. For the GNSS measurements, a Spectra Precision receiver was used to perform static determination of selected points of the network.

For the geodetic measurements apart from the total station, the following ancillary equipment were used:

- Tripods for the total station and reflector setting
- Tribrachs for the reflector placement
- Reflector supporting bases
- Reflectors

Fig. 9.6 Tribrach, supporting base and reflector (Image: Courtesy A. Georgopoulos)

Table 9.2 The coordinates X, Y, the orthometric heights H, and their respective residuals for control points used at Kastrouli

	Point coordinates in EGSA '87 geodetic system (m)			Standard error σ_o (m)		
Point name	X	Y	H	X	Υ	H
T1	375359.215	4250817	547.578	0.002	0.003	0.008
T2	375385.464	4250846	548.052	0.003	0.003	0.008
T3	375400.279	4250816	549.36	0.004	0.003	0.013
T4	375443.318	4250774	547.775	0.002	0.002	0.007
T5	375449.559	4250839	547.394	0.003	0.003	0.008
T6	375467.651	4250738	544.375	0.003	0.002	0.006
T7	375443.609	4250706	542.125	0.003	0.001	0.006
T8	375389.142	4250718	542.08	0.002	0.001	0.006
T9	375351.359	4250756	543.048	0.002	0.002	0.007

Adjustment and Results

The measurements were adjusted as a network and not a simple traverse, and the adjusted coordinates (Table 9.2) were referenced with the minimum constraints to GGRS'87 based on T1 and T9. The determination of the coordinates of the points was performed with an accuracy of 0.9mm. In Table 9.2, the coordinates X, Y and the orthometric heights H are presented. For archaeoastronomical purposes at the site, we use the following coordinates -

Latitude: 38.399° N (38 23' 58" N)
Longitude: 22.574° E (22 34' 28" E)

Geophysical Investigations at Kastrouli: Introduction

A variety of geophysical methods (resistivity mapping, total field or differential magnetometry, electrical tomography, and ground-penetrating radar (GPR)) are usually employed to explore the subsurface with the aim of detecting and mapping concealed antiquities. However, the setting of each site dictates the particular methods to be employed. The decision of which methods to use is a collaborative one between the geophysicist responsible for the survey and the archaeologist who is in charge of the excavation. The most critical factor for the selection of suitable methods is the magnitude of the contrast in the physical properties between the targets and the hosting medium at the site.

As shown below, almost all the available geophysical methods were applied, a kind of "shotgun" approach (cf. Witten 2006) for the investigation of relatively small areas at the Mycenaean site of Kastrouli in Desfina in the region of continental Greece (central Greece). In fact, magnetic gradiometry, GPR, and electrical resistivity tomographies (ERTs) were carried out during the summer of 2016 (11, 12, 20, and 21 of August). Grids were established on the ground surface for carrying out the geophysical measurements which were referenced to the Hellenic Geodetic Reference System 1987 (ΕΓΣΑ 1987) described above. Processing and interpretation of the data took place in the installations of the Laboratory of Exploration Geophysics in Thessaloniki, immediately after the fieldwork. Below we present short descriptions of the principles of the methods used, followed by a discussion of the surveys, the data processing, and results.

The Resistivity Tomography Method

General

Resistivity techniques are well-established and widely used to solve a variety of geotechnical, geological, and environmental subsurface detection problems (Ward 1990) (i.e., foundation and integrity of dams, cavity detection, planning of infrastructure, assessing the hydraulic and anisotropical properties of the subsurface, location of man-made structures, etc.).

The goal of the resistivity method is to measure the potential differences on the surface due to the current flow within the ground. The measured drop of potential reflects the difficulty with which the electrical current can be made to flow through the earth, giving an indication of the earth's electrical resistivity, which is directly dependent on the way the current is being conducted within the earth. Since current conduction is related to the composition and the groundwater of the subsurface, a knowledge of resistivity can be the basis for distinguishing existing earth features (layering, voids, man-made structures, etc.).

Since the factors deciding the electrical current conduction into the soil (porosity, water distribution, chemical composition, etc.) are quite variable, it is often observed that similar formations at different sites can appear to have entirely different variations in resistivity. This fact renders resistivity as a property quite unstable and hence sometimes inadequate for extracting exact lithological conclusions for the subsurface. Therefore, it should be kept in mind while interpreting resistivity data that the measured resistivity values are not absolute but relative, and therefore only relative conclusions about the area's lithology can be made.

For instance, by observing the data, it can be said that there is a formation which is less resistive than the surrounding formations, but it will not be safe to determine its identity just by its resistivity value. Erroneous interpretations can be made when this fact is not taken into account. Conversely, this resistivity disadvantage (which is common in every geophysical technique) does not prohibit successful interpretations, but in order to achieve good results, prior information concerning the studied area should be considered. This prior information could include geological maps of the area, results from possible drilling and excavation, or in general any kind of information that could enhance the knowledge of what is possible to be found beneath the soil. This information is used to calibrate the interpretation and should be collected before the measuring procedure to allow the optimum resistivity array and survey strategy to be chosen.

Resistivity Tomography

In the resistivity technique, two current electrodes (a source and a sink) are inserted into the ground, and at the same time two different probes are used to measure the drop of electrical potential; thus, every measurement involves four electrodes in total. The depth that each measurement can "view" into the ground can be controlled by adjusting the electrode separation: the penetration depth increases as the distance between the electrodes gets bigger. Based on these principles, it is possible to obtain a series of measurement profiles with increased electrode spacing in order to get an indication of the earth resistivity variation of the studied area in both lateral and vertical directions. As in any geophysical technique, these measurements (called apparent resistivity measurements) do not provide a direct "image" of the subsurface but simply constitute the integrated effect of the subsurface property which could be (in cases of complex subsurface property distribution) far away from reality.

Traditionally the interpretation of these measured datasets is being made by the use of the pseudosection method (Edwards 1977; Griffiths et al. 1990). It is based on the fact that the larger the electrode separation, the more the measured apparent resistivity is related to greater depths. Hence, each measured resistivity value is arbitrarily placed under the center of the particular four-electrode arrangement at a depth proportional to the overall electrode separation. By doing this for every measurement, a trapezoidal pseudo-image of the subsurface can be obtained. Various arrays (e.g., dipole–dipole, Wenner, pole–dipole) can be used for the production of pseudosections. The term ERT includes the traditional geoelectrical method but can be considered more general as it also involves measurements obtained with no

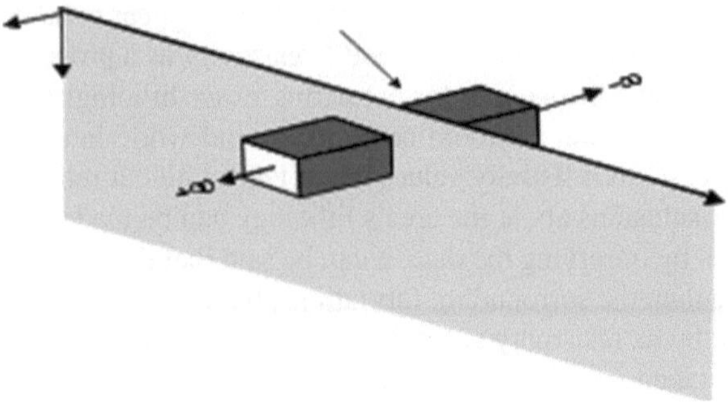

Fig. 9.7 Geoelectrical parameter of three dimensions. A section of the block is considered as 2D parameter (After Tsourlos 1995)

conventional arrays, while electrodes can be also positioned into boreholes (Shima 1990). Interpretation of the pseudosection images involves a great amount of "expertise," and yet for cases of complex resistivity, accurate interpretation is not possible. The advent of fast computers allowed the development of fully automated algorithms known as inversion algorithms which can produce "accurate" subsurface resistivity images. The term "inversion" in the resistivity method describes the (usually fully computerized) procedure of constructing an image of the "real" subsurface's resistivity distribution given the respective observed datasets. Such algorithms are mathematically complicated and allow the processing of any measured dataset independent of the electrode arrangement. Furthermore the advent of resistivity measuring instruments allowed the automation of the measuring procedure, and in that sense any type of measurements (even cross borehole) can be obtained easily.

The combination of the automated measuring systems with the new interpretation (inversion) schemes is described with the term resistivity tomography: the term is due to the similarities of the procedure to medical imaging techniques (X-ray tomography).

The techniques aiming to solve the inverse geoelectric problem use either approximation methods (e.g., Method of Zhody–Barker; Barker 1992; Tsourlos et al. 1993) or employment of fully nonlinear inversion schemes (e.g., Tripp et al. 1984; Shima 1990; Tsourlos et al. 1995).

During the 2D resistivity inversion procedure, the subsurface is considered as a set of individual blocks (parameters) that are allowed to vary their resistivity independently (Fig. 9.7). The aim is to calculate a subsurface resistivity estimate x for which the difference dy between the observed data dobs and the modeled data dcalc (calculated using the forward modeling technique) is minimized.

Since we are dealing with a nonlinear problem, this procedure has to be iterative: in every iteration an improved resistivity estimate is sought, and eventually the procedure stops until certain convergence criteria are met (i.e., until the RMS error is practically stable).

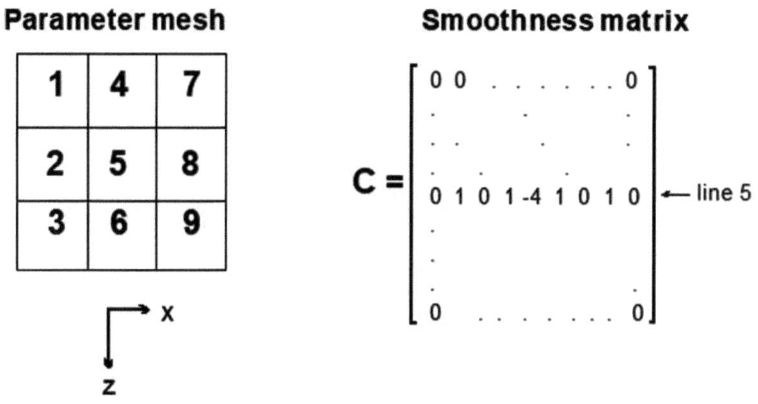

Fig. 9.8 Formation of the smoothness matrix for the case of nine parameters (After Tsourlos 1995)

Assuming a 2D case, a nonlinear smoothness-constrained inversion algorithm was used (Tsourlos 1995). The inversion is iterative, and the resistivity **xk**+1 at the k+1th iteration is given by:

$$\mathbf{xk}+1=\mathbf{xk}+\mathbf{dxk}=\mathbf{xk}+[(\mathbf{Jk}^{\mathrm{T}}\mathbf{Jk}+\mu\kappa\left(\mathbf{Cx}^{\mathrm{T}}\mathbf{Cx}+\mathbf{Cz}^{\mathrm{T}}\mathbf{Cz}\right)]^{-1}\mathbf{Jk}^{\mathrm{T}}\mathbf{dyk} \quad (9.1)$$

where **C**x and **C**z are matrices which describe the smoothness pattern (Fig. 9.8) of the model in the x and z axes, respectively (Degroot-Hedlin and Constable 1990), **dy**k is the vector of differences between the observed data dobs and the modeled data dkcalc (calculated using the forward modeling technique), and **J**k and μκ are the Jacobian matrix estimate and the Lagrangian multiplier, respectively, for the kth iteration.

A proven 2.5D finite element method (FEM) scheme is used as the platform for the forward resistivity calculations (Tsourlos et al. 1999). In 2.5D modeling the resistivity is allowed to vary only in two dimensions, but the sources are 3D which allows us to obtain values, which are realistic. The adjoint equation approach was incorporated into the FEM scheme in order to calculate the Jacobian matrix J (Tsourlos 1995). A flowchart of the algorithm is shown in Fig. 9.9.

Short Description of the Magnetic Prospecting Method

The magnetic prospecting method aims to detect variations of subsurface magnetization that reflect the presence of subsurface inhomogeneities. It is consisted in measuring the spatial distribution of the total magnetic field on the Earth's surface. Small changes of this field (anomalies) are caused by the subsurface variation of

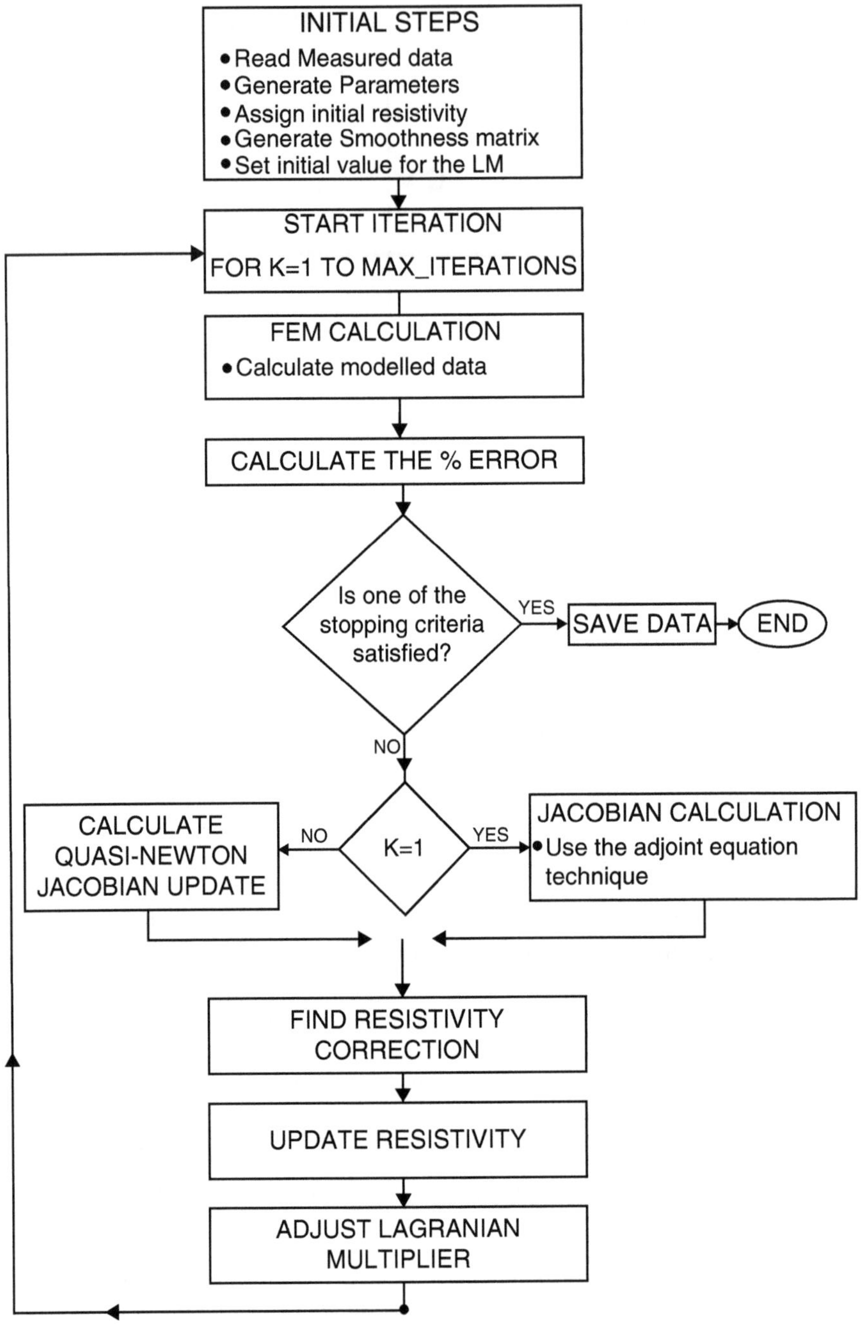

Fig. 9.9 A simplified flowchart of the algorithm (After Tsourlos 1995)

magnetization. Therefore, the location of the anomalies leads to the detection of the subsurface targets. The characteristics of the anomaly can be then analyzed and yield quantified parameters of the targets, such as its dimensions, its burial depth and susceptibility contrast with respect to the hosting medium. The method has been used successfully to study concealed natural and man-made structures. Its use in archaeology was introduced in the decade of 1950 (Aitken 1974). Suppose that we have a buried structure who poses a susceptibility contrast $\Delta\kappa$ with respect to the medium where it is hosted. If the Earth's magnetic field has a strength H at that particular location, then it creates induced magnetization in the structure having the magnitude of:

$$M = \Delta\kappa \, X \, H.$$

Consequently, a new field is produced whose intensity is H' and it is added locally to the inducing Earth's field. The vector addition of these two fields is called magnetic induction, and this parameter is recorded by the geophysical instruments. The magnitude of the induced magnetization and therefore the magnitude of the induced field are generally small with respect to the Earth's field. This is because most of the rocks found on Earth are paramagnetic (Parasnis 1997).

In case of prospecting for buried antiquities, the structures concealed in the subsurface are generally of small dimensions, usually having one or two orders of magnitude difference in their magnetic susceptibility with respect to the surrounding environment. Therefore, they create anomalies of small wavelength and usually of small amplitude in comparison to other applications of magnetic prospecting (e.g., mineral exploration). Consequently, dense spatial sampling of the total magnetic field (magnetic induction) is necessary to record the anomalies created by buried remnants of the past human activity.

Subsurface areas of increased magnetization will cause positive anomalies, while those of decreased magnetization will cause negative. Generally, buried ancient ditches, ruins of kilns, ruins of walls made by bricks, destruction phases, buried collapsed tiled roofs, etc. are expected to show positive anomalies. On the other hand, ruins of walls, whether made by hewn or raw stones, will show either negative or positive anomalies depending on the magnetic properties of the rock from which they were extracted. Limestone shows usually negligible magnetic susceptibility. On the contrary, the soils appear magnetized if the site was occupied by human activity in the past (Aitken 1974). Further, the soils that have been exposed to heating show also enhanced magnetic susceptibility (Le Borge 1955; Tite and Mullins 1971; Aitken 1974). Heating is most likely to have occurred in cultivated fields due to the practice of burning vegetation to clear the land. However, modern views (Linford 2006; Fassbinder 2015) on the mechanisms responsible for the enhancement of magnetic susceptibility of the topsoil and the lands occupied by humans indicate that the processes forming maghemite and magnetite are different and more complex than described in the early studies mentioned above.

Fig. 9.10 The gradiometer used for the Kastrouli geophysical survey described here

Magnetic Gradiometry

If two magnetic sensors are used to record the Earth's field at two different height levels, their difference is an approximation of the vertical gradient of the field (Parasnis 1997). In strict physics terms, it is an approximation of the first vertical difference, and divided by the height, difference yields the approximation of the gradient. This mode of measuring the Earth's field is operationally advantageous since no correction is needed for the diurnal variation of the Earth's field. This is why it has become very popular in archaeological prospection where large numbers of measurements are necessary to sample densely the spatial variation of the field.

For the Kastrouli study, the FM256 *Fluxgate* gradiometer from *Geoscan Research* was used. This is shown in Fig. 9.10. More precisely, the particular instrument measures the first vertical difference of the vertical component of the magnetic field.

Ground-Penetrating Radar (GPR)

Ground-penetrating radar (GPR) is the general term applied to techniques which employ radio waves, typically in the frequency range from 1 to 2000 MHz, for mapping features buried in the ground or beneath floors and inside walls.

The operating principle (Annan 1992) is that an electromagnetic pulse (energy) is emitted by an antenna called transmitter. This pulse travels into the subsurface and is partly reflected when it encounters media with different electrical properties

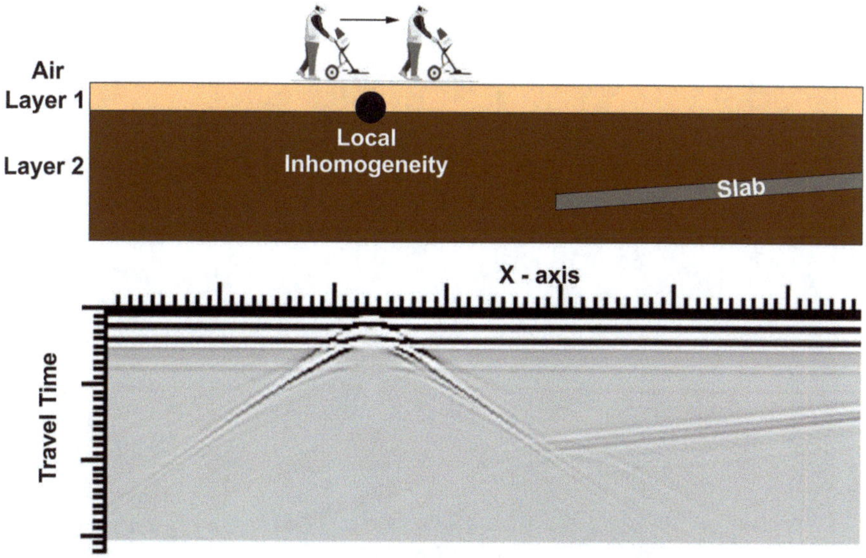

Fig. 9.11 Schematic view of a reflection mode GPR survey. A GPR unit is moved along a survey line (*top*) acquiring responses at regular intervals and creating a cross-sectional image of the subsurface (*bottom*)

and partly propagated into deeper layers. The reflected energy is recorded by an antenna called receiver, which is either in a separate antenna box or in the same antenna box as the transmitter. The GPR unit measures how long it takes for a reflected signal to return to the receiving antenna as well as its strength. Hence, measuring this time interval and estimating the velocity of pulse propagation in the subsurface, it is possible to determine the location of underground reflectors.

As the GPR antennas are moved on the ground surface, a two-dimensional (2D) radargram is built up by time-domain traces when collecting data in the field, in real time (Fig. 9.11). This is the typical way of GPR data display. The horizontal axis of the cross-sectional view is the horizontal distance along the survey line, while the vertical axis is the two-way travel time of signals. If the electromagnetic velocity of pulse propagation in the subsurface is known, the time scale can be converted in a depth scale.

After data acquisition, a number of processing techniques are applied to GPR datasets in order to produce a clearer image for data interpretation and evaluation. When GPR data have been collected in a grid, along parallel profiles, one closely next to the other, it is possible to produce three-dimensional (3D) images and/or depth slices (i.e., horizontal sections of the subsurface along the depth axis). Seeing these images, it is straightforward to determine the location, depth, form, and size of subsurface anomalies (Goodman et al. 1995; Goodman and Piro 2013). The depth of penetration of GPR is mainly controlled by the dielectric properties of the ground. The limiting factor for the application of GPR is the presence of materials

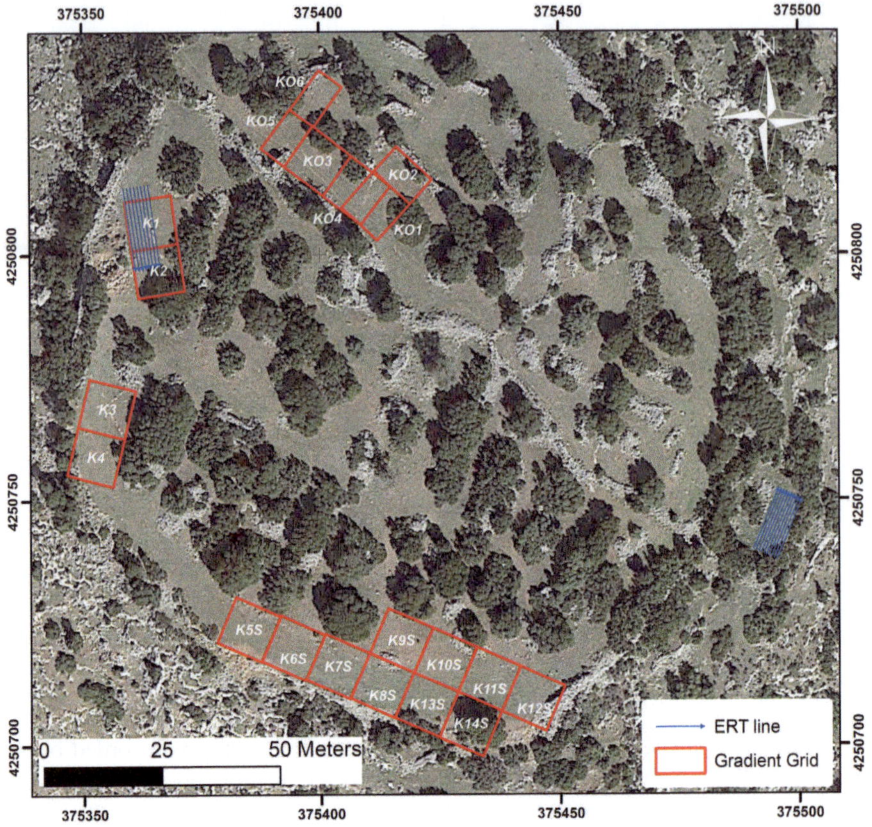

Fig. 9.12 Layout of the cells (red color) established on the ground surface for the needs of the magnetic gradiometry and the GPR survey. The blue lines mark the tomographic transects (A Google Earth satellite image is used as background)

with high electrical conductivity at the area of prospection. In a highly conductive environment (e.g., clays, saline soils), electromagnetic waves attenuate rapidly, which results in poor penetration. Moreover, the GPR pulse depth of penetration and its resolution (i.e., the smallest object that can be detected) are dependent on the transmitting antenna central frequency. A high antenna frequency gives shallower depth of signal penetration but better resolution. On the other hand, a lower frequency antenna provides poorer resolution but deeper penetration.

Survey Layout

Several meshes of grids (square cells) were established on the ground surface as shown in Fig. 9.12 to cope with the rather uneven topography. The cells denoted by red color were used for the magnetic gradiometry and the GPR survey, whereas the

ERTs carried out are depicted by blue lines. The resistivity tomography method was preferred wherever we were investigating for underground tombs, and thus the burial depth was expected to be big. On the other hand, wherever we were trying to image the buried remnants of walls, the classical magnetic gradiometry mapping method was used. The ground-penetrating radar (GPR) was also tested by carrying out parallel profiles in the cells K1 and K7S.

The ERT method was not extensively used during the first phase of the geophysical investigations which is reported in these pages. This is because ERT requires considerably more effort to set up. Thus, it was decided that it is better to use our resources to cover as large area as possible in order to get an idea of the urban complex inside the ancient walls. The survey was carried out during the highly dry period of the year, and thus the soil condition was rather optimum for the GPR survey. On the other hand, the dryness of the topsoil created some problems at the ERT survey since high contact resistances were encountered, and they had to be lowered by pouring water at the electrodes. Thus, good electrical coupling with the ground was established. It is clear that more than one method was applied in some cells. The subsurface of the cells K1 and K2 was explored with all the methods employed (gradiometry, GPR, and ERT). Also, both magnetic and GPR methods were used for the cell K7S.

The Resistivity Tomography Survey

The resistivity tomography survey at Kastrouli aimed to image the subsurface at two particular portions of the site in both 2D and 3D contexts. The area eastward of the already excavated tombs and that in the so-called eastern circle was investigated. The first area is referred to as the “western tomb area” and includes Tomb A. The layout of the profiles along which the ERTs were performed is shown in Fig. 9.12. In fact, eight two-dimensional tomography surveys were carried out in the western tomb area and ten in the eastern circle on the other side of the site.

The dipole–dipole array (Parasnis 1997) was used in both cases because it is very sensitive to lateral inhomogeneities of resistivity (Ward 1990). Since relatively shallow depths were investigated and antique structures were expected to be buried in the particular locations, the resistivity should vary laterally in an intense manner. The inter-probe spacing, as well as the separation between the traverses, was set accordingly for each case. The SYSCAL pro resistivity meter of IRIS instruments was used. The instrument is equipped with an automated switch and supported by custom built connectors. The instrument is capable of maximum ten simultaneously receiving channels. The multicore cables used are custom built by the Laboratory of Exploration Geophysics of the Aristotle University of Thessaloniki. Figures 9.13 and 9.14 show components of the instrumentation used for the resistivity tomography survey at Kastrouli and several tomographic transects established on the ground surface.

Each individual tomography section was inverted using the algorithm of Tsourlos (1995). This procedure resulted into 2D images. However, the set of the tomographic

Fig. 9.13 Parts of the instrumentation used and members of the field crew at the "eastern circle"

data of each sector were subjected to 3D inversion according to the scheme published by Tsourlos and Ogilvy (1999). Although the data acquisition cannot be considered as full 3D in our case, Papadopoulos et al. (2006) have proved that negligible imaging detail is lost provided that the inversion is performed by a full 3D algorithms. Also, the data have to be collected along dense parallel traverses, which should be ideally spaced at intervals equal to the spacing of the electrodes along the traverse. Both these constraints are fulfilled in our case.

The 3D inversion scheme performs an iterative optimization based on a 3D finite element modeling scheme. The algorithm is fully automated and self-correcting and performs smoothness-constrained inversion (Constable et al. 1987). The inversion procedure is accelerated by the use of a quasi-Newton technique for updating the Jacobian matrix. All inversions produced a low RMS error (less than 3%), indicative of the high data quality and of the high credibility of the results. The inversion results shown in the following pages of this report effectively depict the "real" subsurface resistivity.

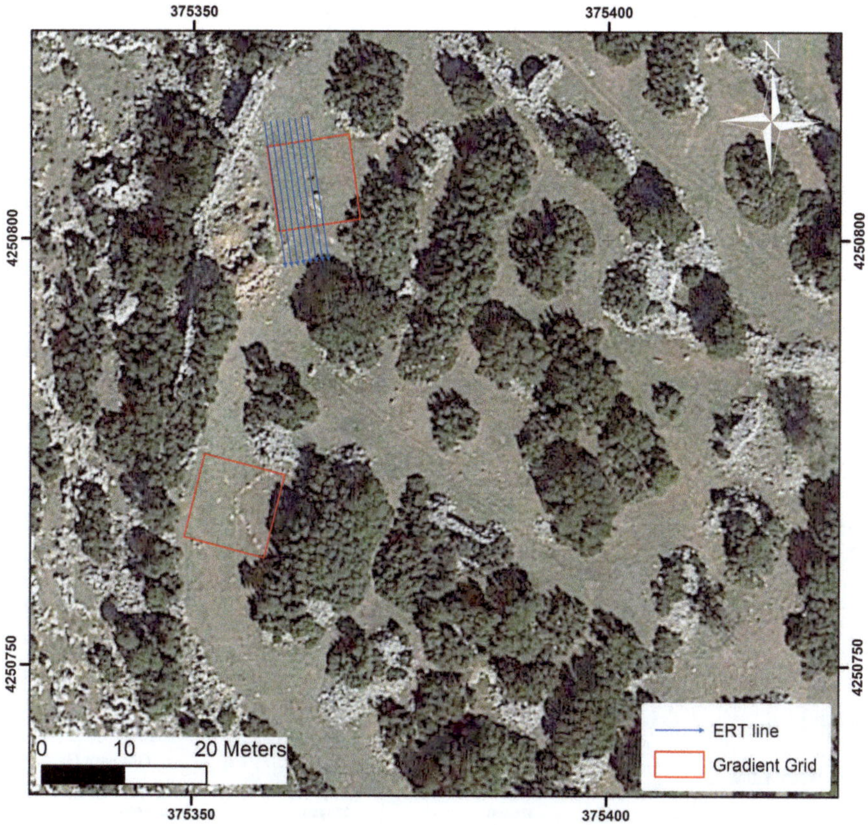

Fig. 9.14 The blue lines show the tomographies conducted in July 2016 at the location having the conventional name "western tomb area." The sketch is referenced to the Hellenic Geodetic System (ΕΓΣΑ 1987). A Google Earth satellite image is used as background

Western Tomb Area

Eight (8) parallel tomographies were carried out in area where the Myceanean tombs had been disturbed in the past (Tomb A and associated features). The layout is seen in Figs. 9.12, 9.14, and 9.15. The inter-probe spacing was set to 0.75 m ($a = 0.75$ m), while 24 channels were used. Thus, the length of each tomography was 17.25 m. The maximum dipole separation was set to $n = 8$. The length of the measuring dipole was then doubled (2a), and nmax was set to 6. Similarly, the length of the dipole increased up to 5a (3.75 m). The tomographies were established 0.75 m apart each from the other.

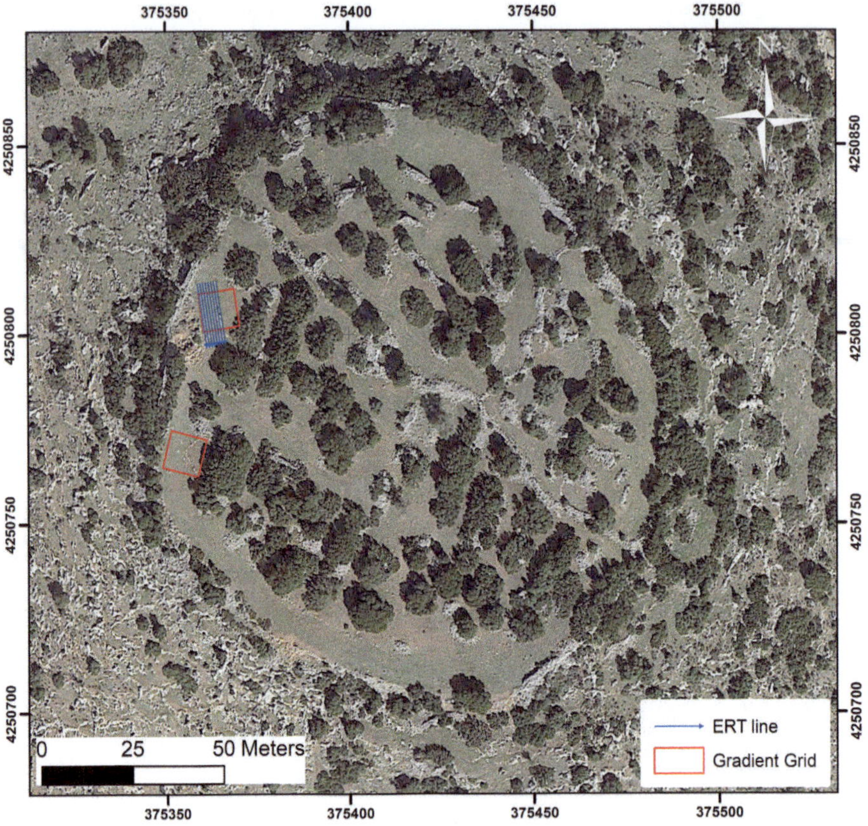

Fig. 9.15 Another view of the layout of the tomographies at the "western tomb area." The sketch is referenced to the Hellenic Geodetic System (ΕΓΣΑ 1987). A Google Earth satellite image is used as background

Eastern Circle

Situated on the eastern edge of the Kastrouli village site, the circular feature selected for detailed geophysical investigation could be another Mycenaean mortuary feature. Ten (10) parallel tomographies were carried out inside the circle, each one having 24 channels and being 0.6 m apart one from the other. Thus, a very good 3D mesh was formed. The inter-probe spacing was set to 0.60 m (a = 0.60 m), and therefore the length of each tomography was 13.8 m. The maximum dipole separation was set to $n = 8$. The length of the measuring dipole was then doubled (2a), and nmax was set to 7. Similarly, the length of the dipole increased up to 5a (3.00 m) (Fig. 9.16).

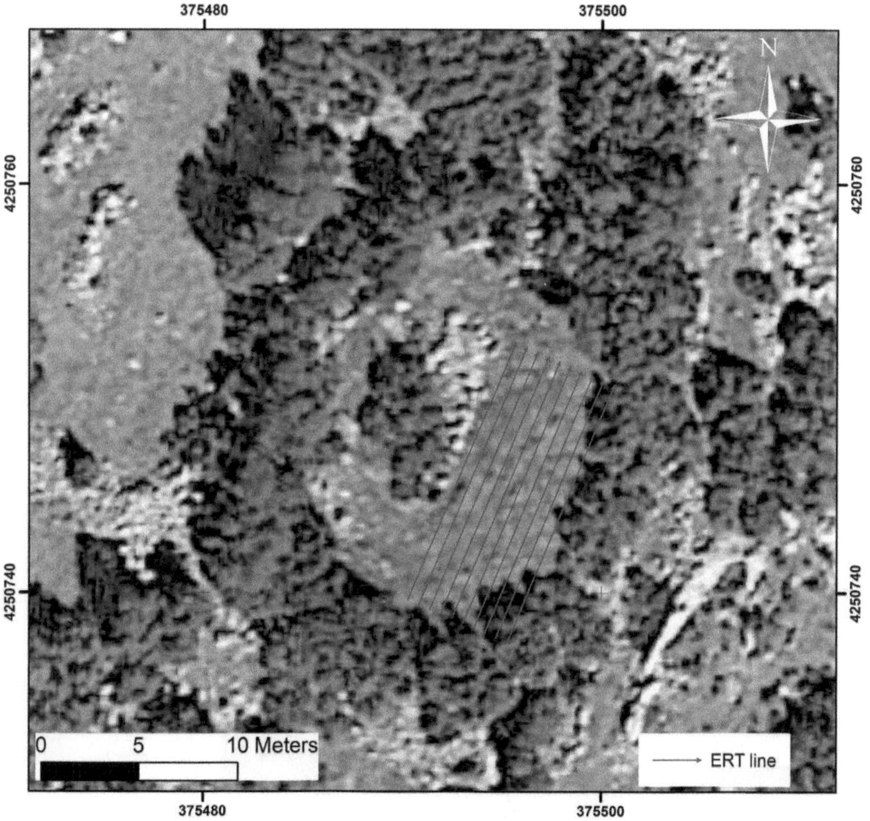

Fig. 9.16 Layout of the tomographies conducted at the eastern circle is in July 2016. A Google Earth satellite image is used as background

ERT Interpretation

Western Tomb Area

Figure 9.17 shows the distribution of the resistivity in the subsurface of the "western tomb area" at 1.70 m depth. The distribution was inferred from the 3D inversion of the data. Note that the color scale of the variation of the resistivity values is logarithmic. The high resistivities form a very clear pattern. Therefore, they are attributed to possible ancient structures.

Figures 9.18 and 9.19 show different views of the 3D subsurface distribution. The high resistivity anomaly at the western end of the sampled volume reflects the tomb whose entrance was exposed at the commencement of the survey. Ground truth testing in this area is described in the section below concerning excavations at Kastrouli.

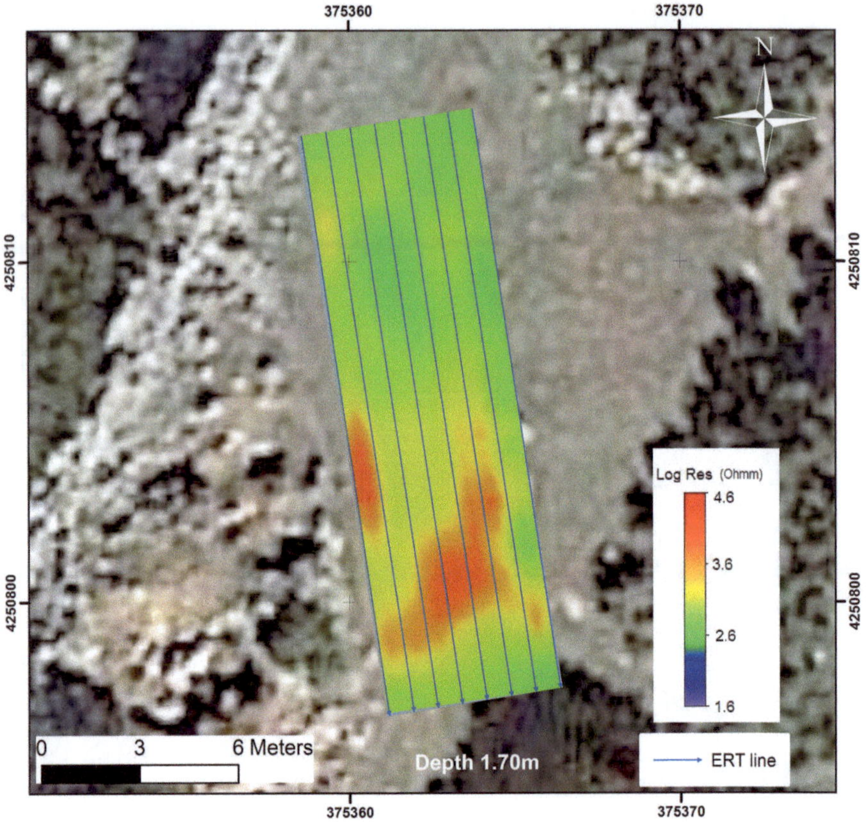

Fig. 9.17 Resistivity distribution (slice) at the depth of about 1.70 m for the "western tomb area"

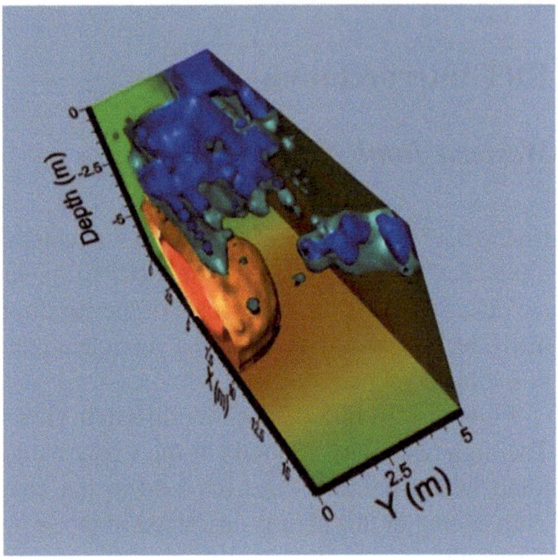

Fig. 9.18 Three-dimensional distribution of the subsurface resistivity at the "western tomb area"

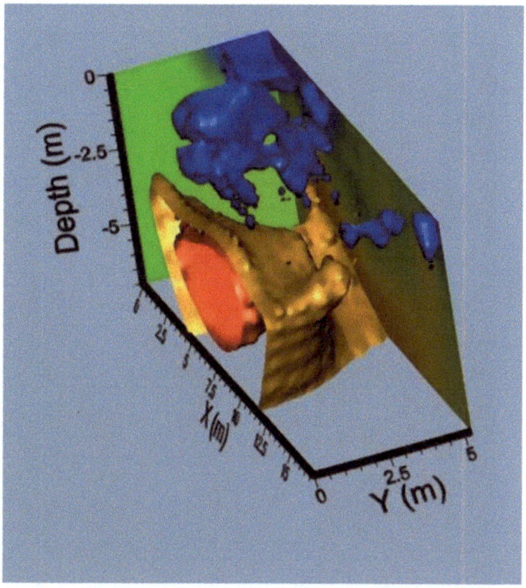

Fig. 9.19 Three-dimensional distribution of the subsurface resistivity at the "western tomb area"

Eastern Circle

Figures 9.20, 9.21 and 9.22 show the resistivity distribution at various depth slices for area at the "eastern circle." These two-dimensional distributions of resistivity at various depths were inferred by slicing the three-dimensional volume of the inverted data. In all figures the depth to which each slice corresponds is marked on the relevant figure, but also it is referred in the captions. Note that the color scale of the variation of the resistivity values is logarithmic.

A pronounced magnetic anomaly is observed in all figures showing the subsurface resistivity at the "eastern circle" area. This anomaly is obviously caused by a

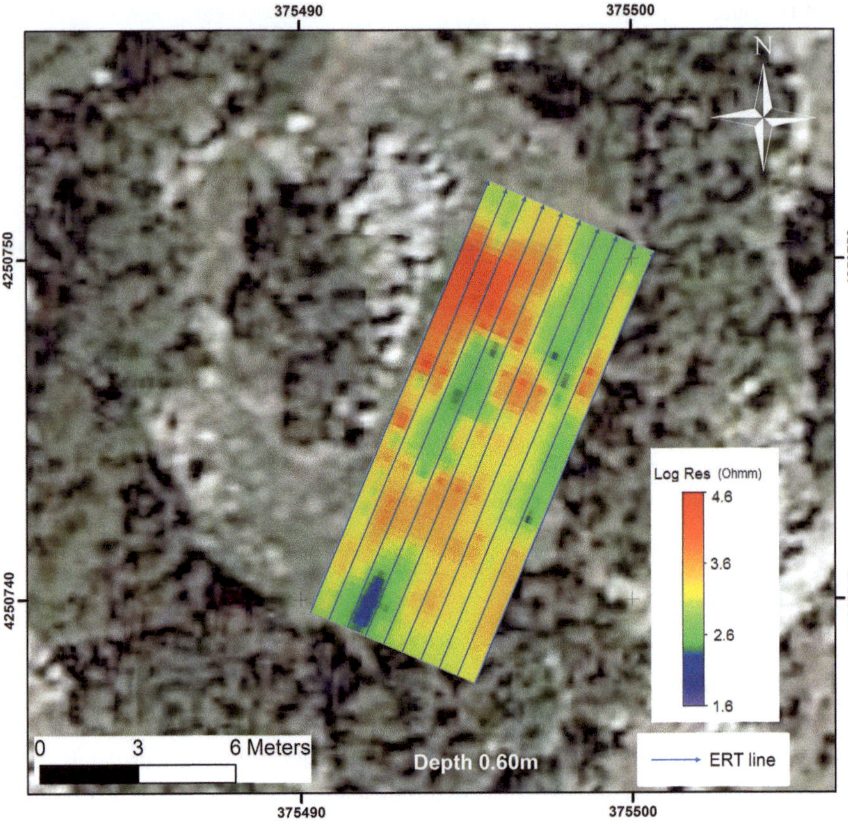

Fig. 9.20 Resistivity distribution (slice) at the depth of about 0.60 m for the area of the "eastern circle"

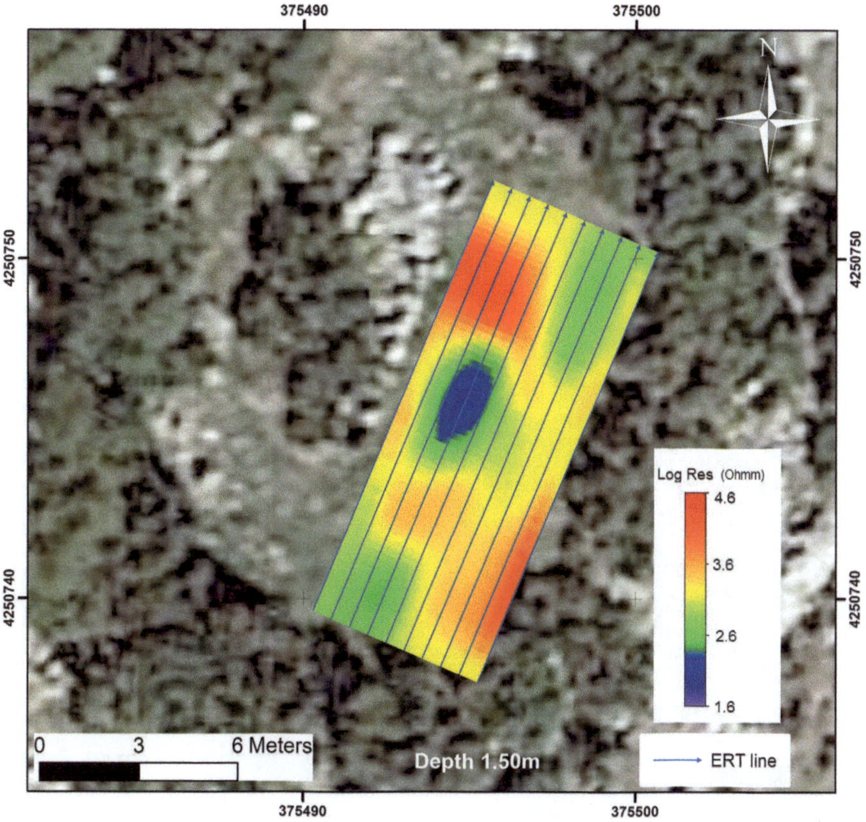

Fig. 9.21 Resistivity distribution (slice) at the depth of about 1.50 m for the area of the "eastern circle"

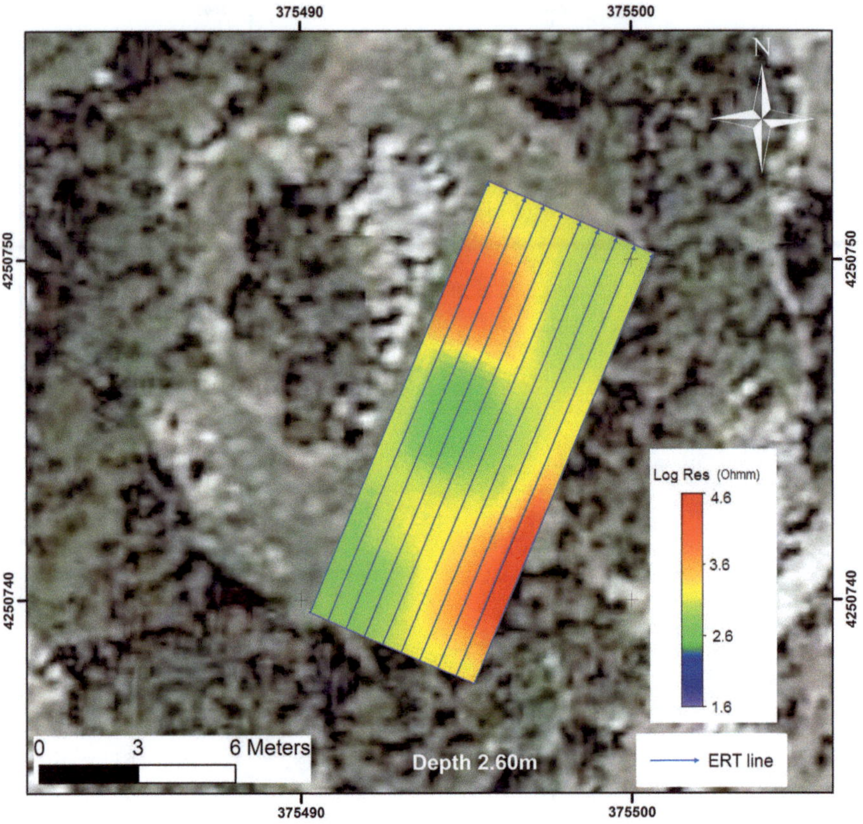

Fig. 9.22 Resistivity distribution (slice) at the depth of about 2.60 m for the area of the "eastern circle"

hole at the resistive bedrock which may be a man-made pit. Figures 9.23 and 9.24 show different views of the 3D subsurface distribution. These images confirm the finding commented previously. The low resistivities are very clearly imaged both in the 2D slices and in the full 3D views suggesting the presence of a void that merits future investigation.

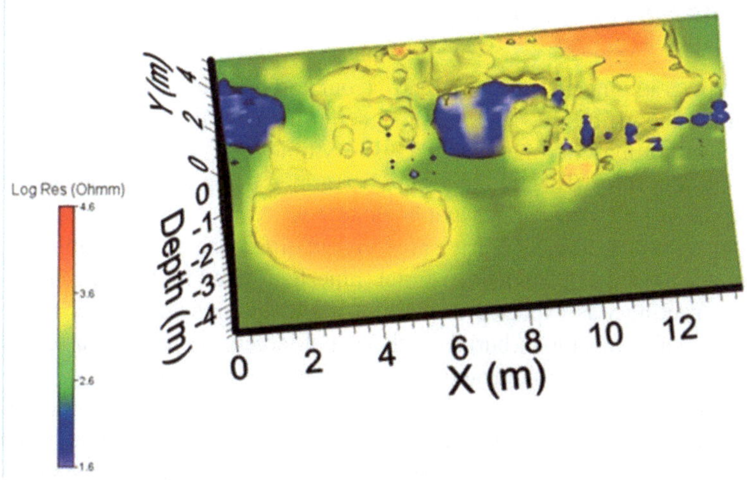

Fig. 9.23 Three-dimensional distribution of the subsurface resistivity at the "eastern circle"

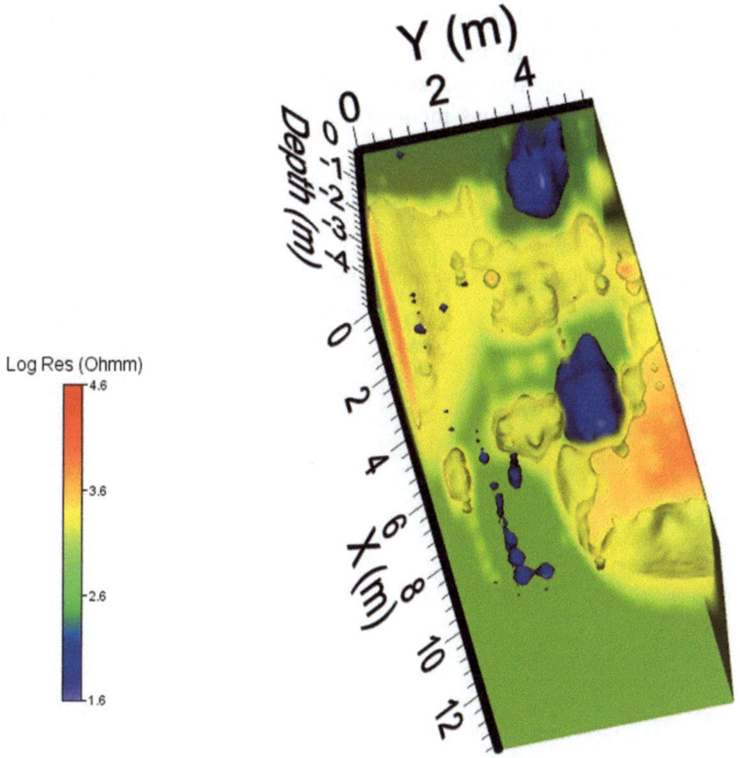

Fig. 9.24 Three-dimensional distribution of the subsurface resistivity at the "eastern circle"

Magnetic Survey in Sector C, Kastrouli

A magnetic gradiometer survey was carried out northern and southern aspects of the site that are shown in Fig. 9.12. Also, magnetic susceptibility readings were carried out on pieces of masonry material (exclusively limestone) but also on the soil hosting the ancient ruins. The readings were performed using a SM-20 κ-meter of *GF Geoinstruments*, and they are shown in Table 9.3.

It is evident from Table 9.3 that a pronounced difference of susceptibilities exists between the topsoil and the main material (limestone) used for building. Thus, magnetic prospecting was expected to produce reasonable results provided that other factors were also favorable (burial depth, size of targets, no ferrous garbage spread on the surface, no archaeological or man-made interferences, etc.).

Several meshes of grids were set on the ground surface at the top of the Kastrouli hill. In each mesh, 10×10 m^2 square cells were established that are shown in Fig. 9.12. The cells were referenced to the Greek Geodetic Reference System 1987 or Hellenic Grid (ΕΓΣΑ 1987). The corners of each cell were marked on the ground by wooden pegs. Then, a 0.5 m × 0.5 m grid was created in each cell using measuring tapes. That is, measurements were taken along traverses spaced 0.5 m apart each from the other, stepwise at 0.50 m intervals. For the square cells K3, K4, K5S, K6S, K7S, and K8S, the measuring step was set at 0.25 m. The orientational variation and zeroing of the instrument were checked initially and periodically after about 1.4 h of operation. Figure 9.25 shows members of the field crew when measuring at Kastrouli.

Table 9.3 Mean values of magnetic susceptibility measurements

Material	No of Samples	Susceptibility (SI)
Stones (masonry material), limestone	4	$7X10^{-6}$
Soil (Terra Rossa)	5	$3.7X10^{-3}$

Fig. 9.25 Member of the field crew taking magnetic measurements

Processing of the Magnetic Data

Data processing started essentially during the fieldwork and was completed afterward at the Laboratory of Exploration Geophysics, Aristotle University of Thessaloniki. The processing sequence was decided after various tests and included the following steps:

- Statistical analysis of the data.
- Transfer of the mean of each traverse to zero (zero mean traverse).
- Despiking by median filter which was performed in 3X3 windows of the data.
- Destagger of the even traverses to correct for small positional shifts between the traverses.
- High-pass filter.
- Interpolation both in the X and Y direction using cubic splines of the form sinX/X (Scollar et al. 1986). This processing step was applied twice.
- Application of Wallis filter (Scollar et al. 1986).
- Creation of gray-scale images in order to have the result in a form which resembles the result that would have been pictured if excavation had taken place (Scollar et al. 1986).
- Transformation of the local coordinate system of each grid to the Greek Geodetic Reference System (1987). That is, the mesh of the geophysical cells was georeferenced.

Result of the Magnetic Survey

Figures 9.26 and 9.27 show the spatial distribution of the processed gradients in the form of gray-scale image. The magnetic susceptibility readings shown earlier imply that the expected anomaly signatures of the buried Mycenaean ruins would have negative character. This is because the susceptibility of the limestone hewn blocks found to have almost negligible values whereas that of the covering soil to be about two orders of magnitude higher. Therefore, in our presentation, the low values appear with dark tones of gray, while the high ones are whiter. The gradients in the range of [−7, 7] nT/0.5 m are shown in Fig. 9.26 which are distributed in the gray-scale levels seen at the left side of the plot. All values that lie out of the defined range are depicted with white color if they are greater than 7 nT/m and black if they are lower than −7 nT/m.

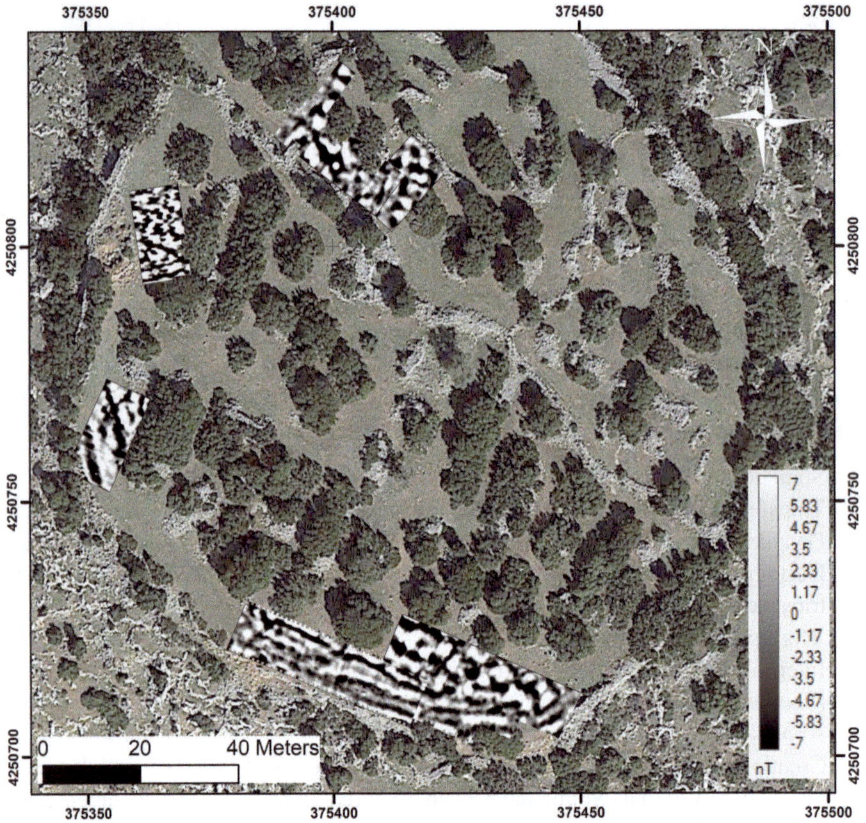

Fig. 9.26 Distribution of the magnetic gradient in the area surveyed. The gradients are clipped to the range [−7,7]. The satellite picture of Google Earth has been used as background. The survey area at the south of the site was sampled in the summer of 2017 and revealed the foundations of a house (Liritzis, personal communication)

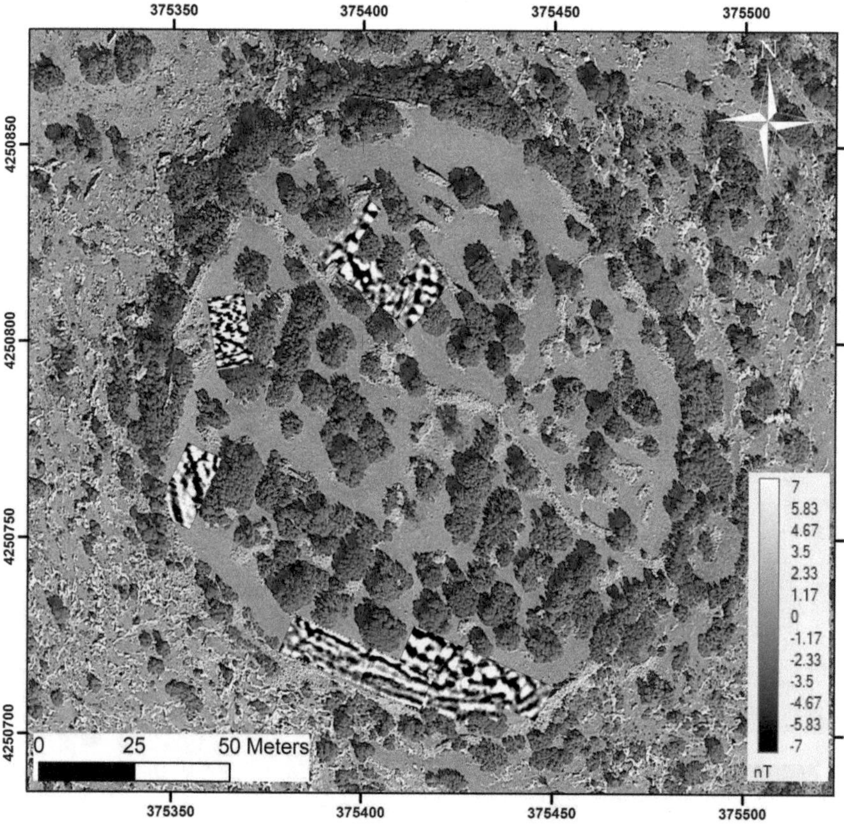

Fig. 9.27 Another view of the distribution of the magnetic gradient. The plotting parameters are identical to those used for Fig. 9.2

The magnetic gradient records as they show up in the maps of figures presented above show that alignments of negative anomalies exist. They are articulated to form geometrical shapes, and therefore they are interpreted as being caused by subsurface ruins of foundation walls. Figs. 9.28, 9.29, 9.30 and 9.31 show parts of the result of the magnetic gradiometer survey.

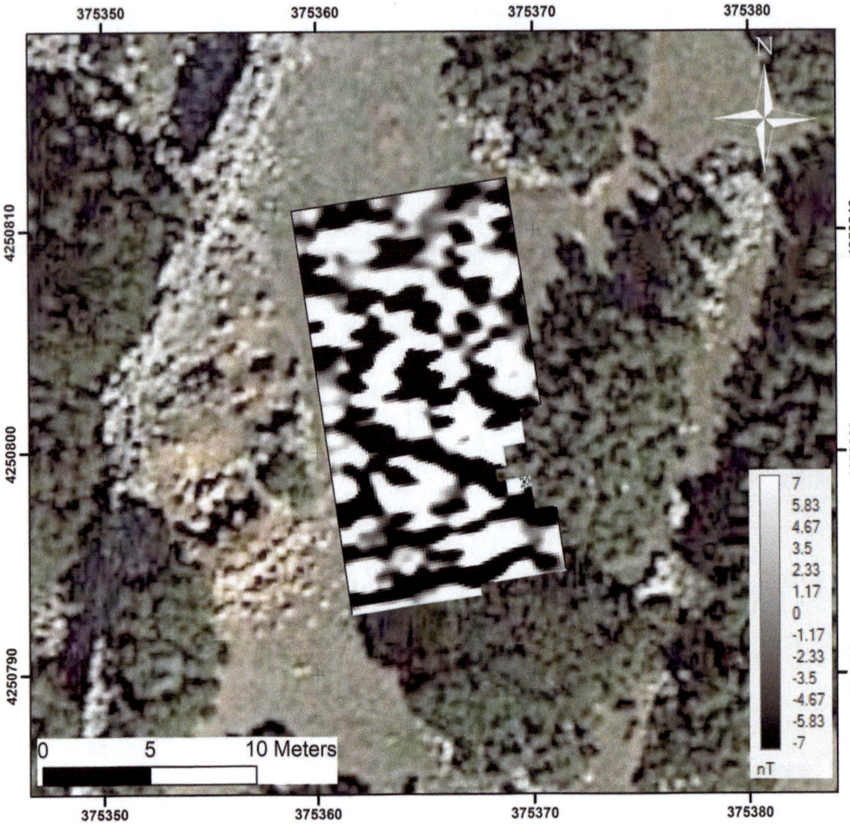

Fig. 9.28 Distribution of the magnetic gradient in the area of the cells K1 and K2. This bit of land is in contact with the open pit that revealed the Mycenaean tomb at the western side of the hill of Kastrouli. The gradients are clipped to the range [−7,7]nT/m. The satellite picture of Google Earth has been used as background

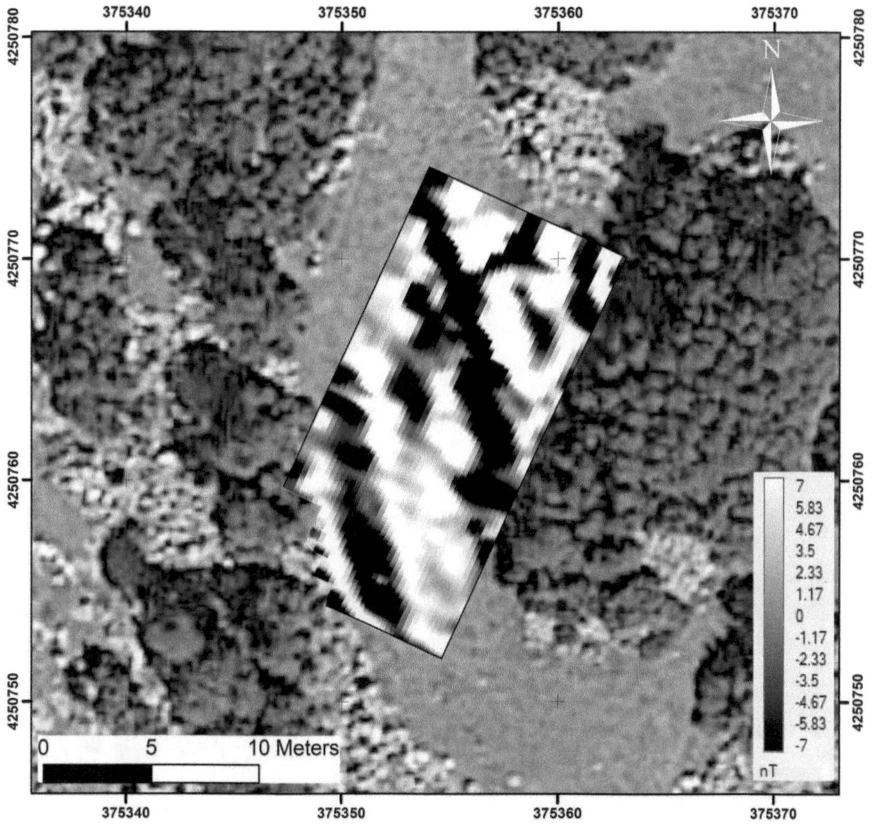

Fig. 9.29 Distribution of the magnetic gradient in the area of the cells K3 and K4. The foundations of a Mycenean building are exposed in the northeastern part of this bit of land. The gradients are clipped to the range [−7,7]nT/m, and the satellite picture of Google Earth has been used as background

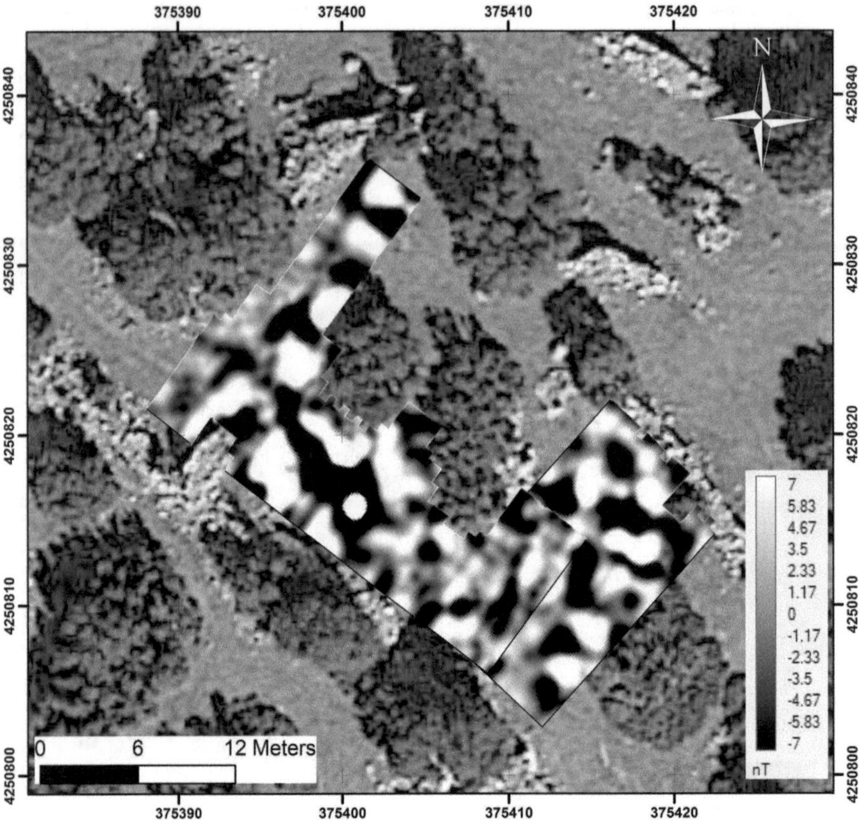

Fig. 9.30 Distribution of the magnetic gradient in the area of the cells KO1, KO2, KO3, KO4, KO5, and KO5B. This bit of land is almost at the top of the Kastrouli hill. The gradients are clipped to the range [−7,7] nT/m, and the satellite picture of Google Earth has been used as background

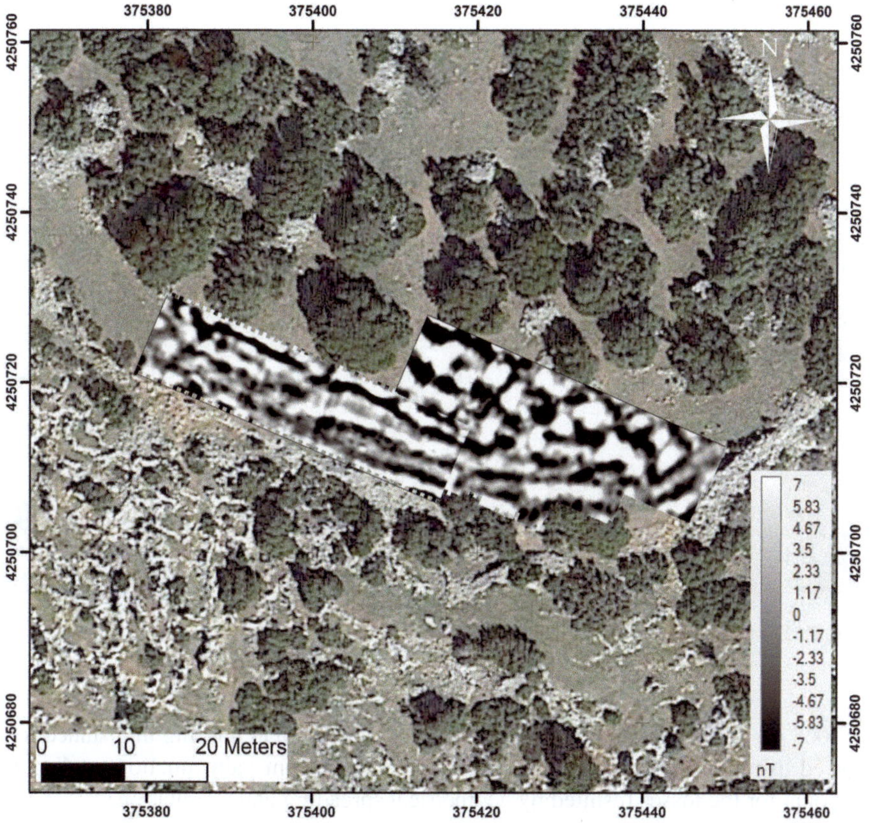

Fig. 9.31 Distribution of the magnetic gradient in the area of the cells K5S, K6S, K7S, K8S, K9S, K10S, K11S, K12S, K13S, and K14S. This bit of land is at the south side of the Kastrouli hill. The gradients are clipped to the range [−7,7] nT/m, and the satellite picture of Google Earth has been used as background

The Ground-Penetrating Radar (GPR) Survey: Data Acquisition and Processing

GPR transects were carried out in cell K1 and K7S (Fig. 9.12), on the same grids that were established on the ground surface for carrying out the resistivity tomographies and magnetic gradiometry. Each transect was placed 0.5 m apart from its adjacent ones. One radiogram was recorded every 0.02 m. Evidently, the case comprises a high-resolution survey. The antennae ABEM RAMAC of MALA Company were used having central frequency at 500 MHz. Figure 9.32 shows members of the crew during the fieldwork. The radiograms subjected to removal of the inductive component (Dewow filtering) by calculating the moving averages into windows of

Fig. 9.32 Members of the field crew carrying out GPR measurements at Kastrouli

15.068 ns. Trace equalization was applied next and median filtering in distance followed using an operator of three traces wide. A custom gain function applied to account for the losses resulted by geometrical spreading and attenuation.

GPR Results

Regarding the "western tomb area," i.e., the cell K1 of the grid established both for magnetics and GPR (Fig. 9.12), the processed radar transects were combined to produce depth slices. Two depth slices showing the subsurface distribution of the amplitude of the electromagnetic waves at about 0.74 and 0.93 m are shown, respectively, in Figs. 9.33 and 9.34. The results are rather pure showing very little signal, a fact that is attributed to the high attenuation rate of the soil in the particular site because of the clay cover. The inadequacy of the method in the specific conditions is pronounced when its results are compared with the respective magnetic and ERT results. Nevertheless, some linear features are revealed also in these slices reinforcing the interpretation of the magnetic gradiometry map. A subterranean hollow identified with GPR was found through ground truth excavations and described in the section below concerning the Tomb A excavation.

Fig. 9.33 The GPR slice at 0.74 m depth

Fig. 9.34 The GPR slice at 0.98 m depth

Respectively, the results in the cell K7S (Fig. 9.12) are shown as depth slice depicting the subsurface distribution of the amplitude of the electromagnetic waves at about 0.99 m in Fig. 9.35 in gray scale. Figure 9.36 shows the same slice but in color scale.

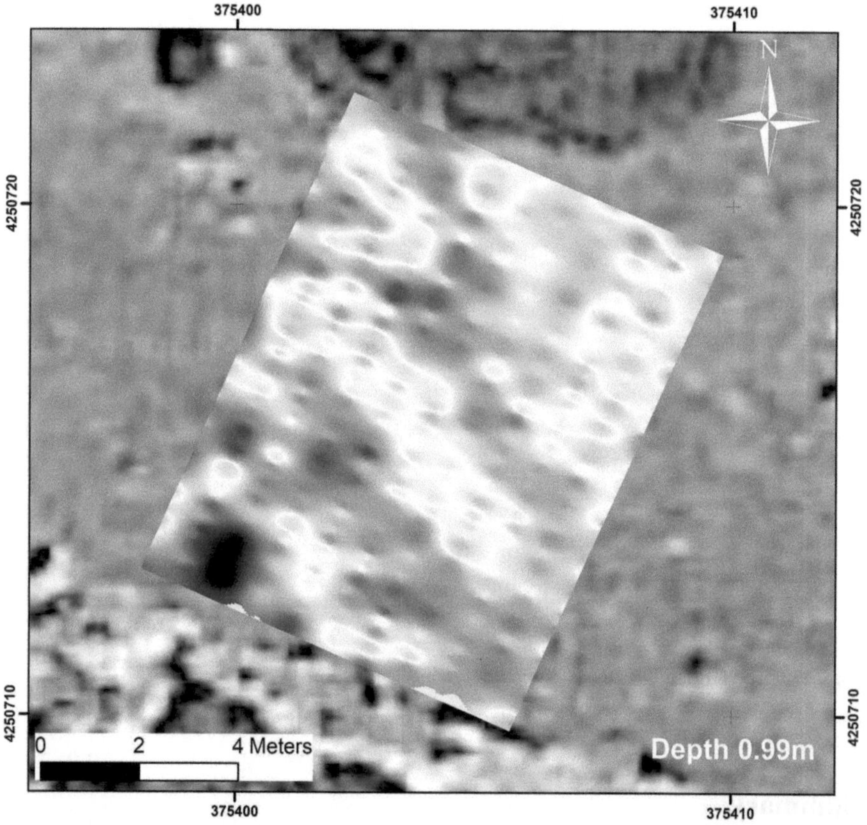

Fig. 9.35 The GPR slice at 0.99 m depth for cell K7S

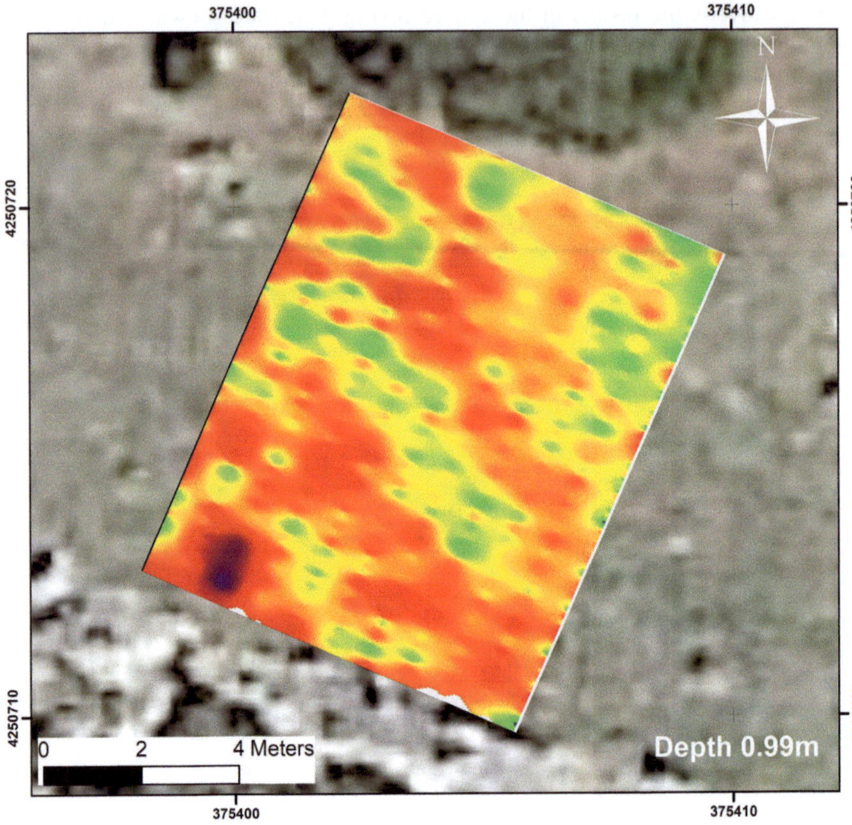

Fig. 9.36 The GPR slice at 0.99 m depth for cell K7S in color scale

Summary

Almost all the existing methods for archaeological prospection were applied at the investigations at Kastrouli. Anomalies of the geophysical fields were detected which were attributed to the presence of concealed ancient remains or structures. In some cases, these anomalies appear with linear shape or tend to create well-defined geometrical shapes. The geophysical images must be seen as a dynamic element, and their interpretation may be altered or complemented with new aspects after the excavations. In other words, the final conclusions should be inferred after the excavation of a part of the surveyed area. Ground-truth excavations confirmed many of the subterranean targets identified with the different geophysical techniques applied at the Kastrouli, Mycenaean settlement. The preliminary results presented here indicate the great potential for extensive excavation at the site and the need for more intensive data processing to facilitate further interpretation.

Excavations at Kastrouli 2016

Excavation at the site was based on an arbitrary site grid, consisting of 5 m × 5 m squares, covering the entire site. Squares were named based on their position in the grid by counting squares in the x and y directions, respectively, and separating these values with a slash (e.g., Square 4/20 is the fourth square east and the 20th square north from the arbitrary origin to the southwest of the site). This was a system determined by A. Sideris. During the 2016 season, excavations took place in three areas: Area A, consisting of excavation in Squares 5/19, 6/19, and 7/19, and two small wall section samples in unnamed areas. One sampling of the northwestern fortification wall of the site occurred in squares 5/21 and 5/22, while a sampling of the southern fortification wall occurred in Square 21/2. Since Tomb A stretched across both Squares 5/19 and 6/19, no balk was established between these squares. During excavation in Area A, a 100% sieving strategy was adopted in order to ensure the collection of material culture missed in excavation or smaller finds not immediately apparent (1 cm mesh for loci outside the tomb and ~3 mm mesh for those within the tomb). All artifact finds and locus boundaries were recorded using a total station (see below for further details).

The contour map of Kastrouli was produced using balloon aerial photography, image-based modeling in Agisoft Photoscan and ArcGIS (Fig. 9.37). Once aerial images of the site were acquired and processed in Agisoft, the dense point cloud was classified to remove vegetation from the 3D model in order to generate a digital surface model (DSM). This DSM was used as the basis for contour generation in ArcGIS. The production of this map took a total of 32 h (balloon photography, 2 h; Agisoft processing, 24 h; point cloud classification and digital surface model (DSM) production, 3 h; final GIS work, 3 h (Map by M. Howland, Center for Cyber-Archaeology and Sustainability, UC San Diego).

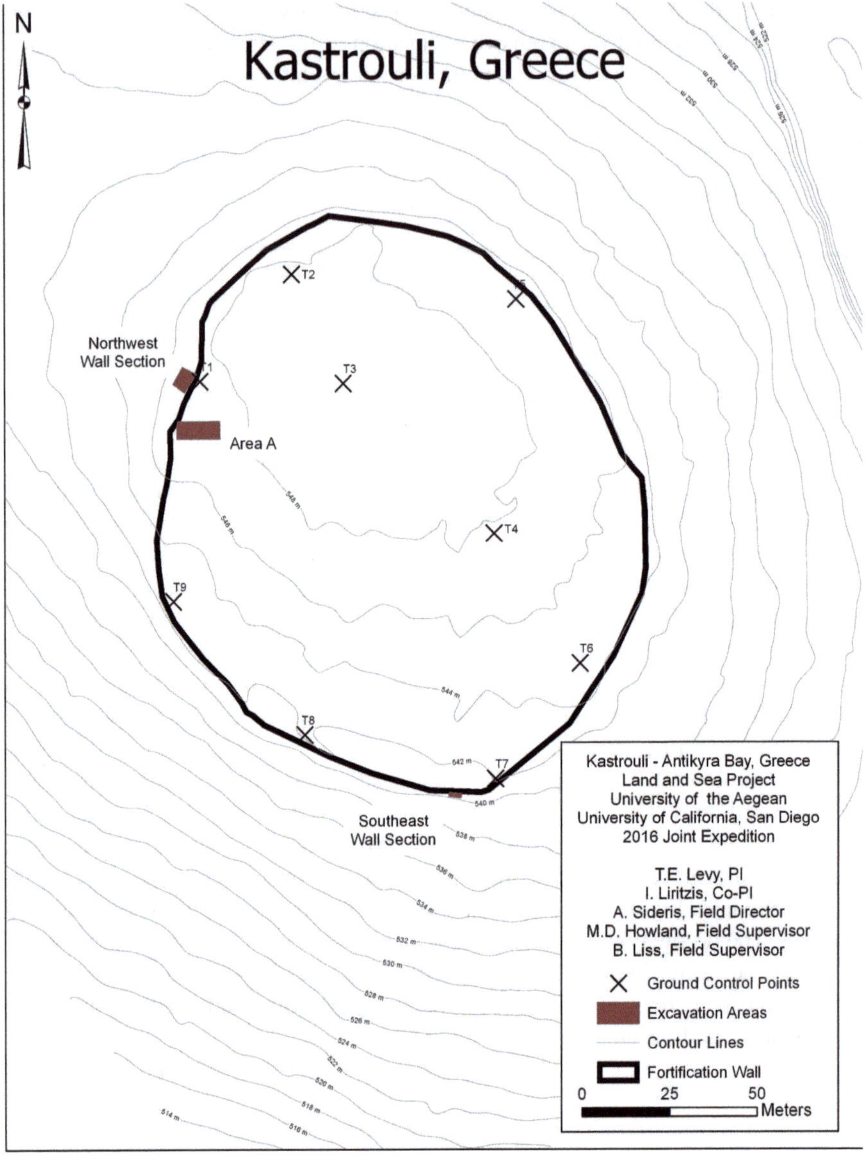

Fig. 9.37 Topographic map of Kastrouli with 2016 excavation areas

Spatial/Context Recording and Artifact Collection

Excavations at Kastrouli employed the fully digital archaeological recording system developed by the Edom Lowlands Regional Archaeology Project (ELRAP) directed by Thomas E. Levy and Mohammad Najjar. The ELRAP on-site digital archaeology (OSDA) 3.0 system (Levy et al. 2010) melds together off-the-shelf technologies and custom computer programs/hardware developed specifically for solving archaeology/cultural heritage problems that researchers face worldwide. The current excavation season utilized several aspects of this spatial recording methodology in order to precisely document the coordinates of archaeological remains at the highest possible spatial resolution in three dimensions. Spatial data was collected with a Leica TS02 total station and the data interface software, *ArchField* (developed by Dr. Neil Smith), that provides real-time data recording and review in the field (the total station was connected to a Microsoft Surface with *ArchField* installed). *ArchField* allows the excavators to record and visualize both points and polygons (i.e., artifact finds and loci) in the field, and the relevant data (i.e., locus type, artifact type, etc.) can be immediately provided and databased. In addition, spatial information collected by *ArchField* is easily exported to a geographic information system (GIS) for further manipulation and analysis (Fig. 9.38). All artifacts collected and recorded with *ArchField* were attributed a unique basket number and bar code to facilitate entry into the *ArchaeoSTOR* artifact database, another custom application allowing for the categorization and sorting of artifacts in the field and in the lab, along with spatial visualization and statistics applications (Gidding et al. 2011). Following field data collection, spatial data linked with artifacts through their basket number/bar code were processed into *ArchaeoSTOR* (Gidding et al. 2014) along with all relevant artifact information (weights, counts, material type, etc.). *ArchaeoSTOR* was recently redeveloped by three undergraduate students from the University of California, San Diego (Rose Smith, Carolyn Breeze, and Taylor Harman) who managed the database and artifact entry in the lab after each day of excavation. Qualitative data regarding archaeological contexts (i.e., loci) was recorded using a Microsoft Access database.

Aerial Photography and Structure from Motion

In addition to the recording of point finds and locus outlines using *ArchField*, the excavation team also adopted an intensive Structure from Motion (SfM) recording campaign in order to document the site in 3D over the course of excavation using the UC San Diego helium balloon system. SfM is a software technology allowing for the creation of highly accurate and photo-realistic 3D models through photogrammetric techniques. The team adopted a two-part approach to SfM data capture: terrestrial and aerial SfM photography. In both approaches, overlapping photographs encompassing the area of interest are captured with complete coverage to facilitate the construction of a 3D model. For aerial photography, a Canon EOS 50D digital single-lens reflex camera (outfitted with a 18 mm lens) is attached by frame to a Kingfisher Aerostat balloon which is walked in overlapping transects over the area of interest. This data collection strategy, an ideal approach to SfM modeling developed through trial and error, was sufficient to develop high-quality 3D models on the site and excavation area scale. The same camera equipment was used terrestrially to capture data used for the production of SfM models at an excavation square scale. In both cases of data capture, these models were subsequently georeferenced,

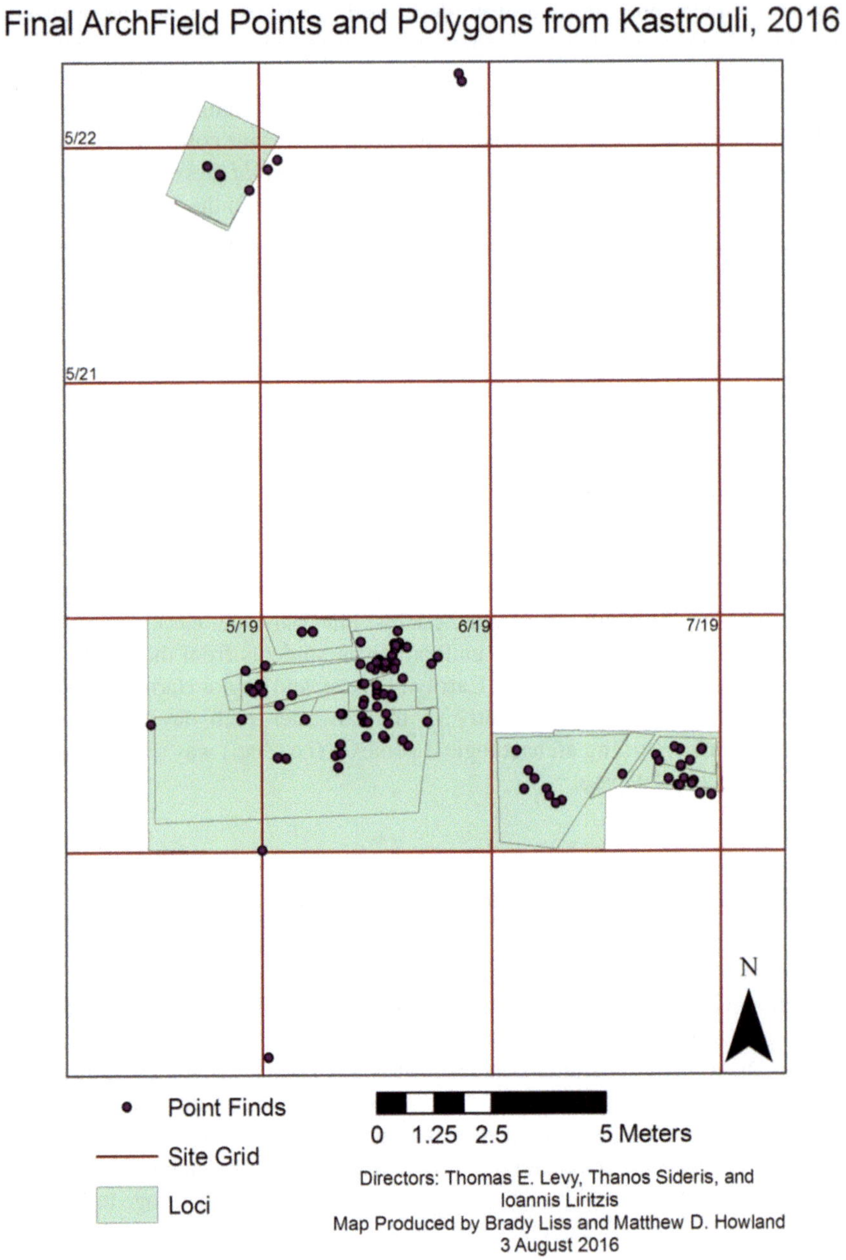

Fig. 9.38 Final export of all *ArchField* points and polygons

facilitating the export of high-resolution orthophotos which serve as an excellent basis for GIS-based digitization of architectural features. This strategy was used for the digitization of top plans. Furthermore, SfM was used for section drawing the walls in the dromos and tomb; orthophotos provided a base for digitization within in GIS rather than hand drawing in the field.

CAVEcam Stereo Photography

Along with SfM, many parts of Kastrouli were documented in 3D using the CAVEcam system (Ainsworth 2012). The CAVEcam is a platform for shooting stereo photography in 360 degrees. The system creates 3D GigaPan images by shooting a grid of photographs across an area of interest with two cameras. To do so, it combines a dual-camera image capture system with a GigaPan EPIC Pro Robotic Controller (Ainsworth 2012). The dual-camera system includes two Panasonic Lumix® GF-1 cameras which provide 12.1 megapixel resolution despite being relatively small for mounting side by side in the controller (Ainsworth 2012: 3). By bracketing the cameras next to each other, they collect two sets of images with slightly differing perspectives to provide stereoscopic vision (much like human eyes). The robotic mount affords automated movement for the cameras in 360 degrees horizontally and up to 180 degrees vertically; this is outfitted with an Ainsworth CC-1 Dual-Camera Controller to automatically capture images from both cameras simultaneously. The GigaPan mount can be programmed to accommodate the desired number of images for the location. Together, the dual cameras and robotic platform create two grids of images (6x12 photos) covering up to 360 degrees from distinct perspectives. These grids of photographs are individually stitched (using the PTGui® Pro software) and displayed to create a single, high-resolution 3D image, which cannot be portrayed in 3D here but represented in Fig. 9.69.

At Kastrouli, CAVEcam photography was captured (by graduate student Tom Holm, University of California, San Diego) at seven locations of interest around the site (Fig. 9.39). Locations 1 and 2 represent two of the excavation areas during the 2016 season, the northern wall section and the tomb excavations, respectively. Location 3 was selected to capture part of the site's fortification wall and the valley in which the site is positioned. Location 4 similarly captured part of the fortification wall but from an outside perspective and some of the terracing around the site. Locations 5, 6, and 7 were all selected to image various architectural features around the center of the site.

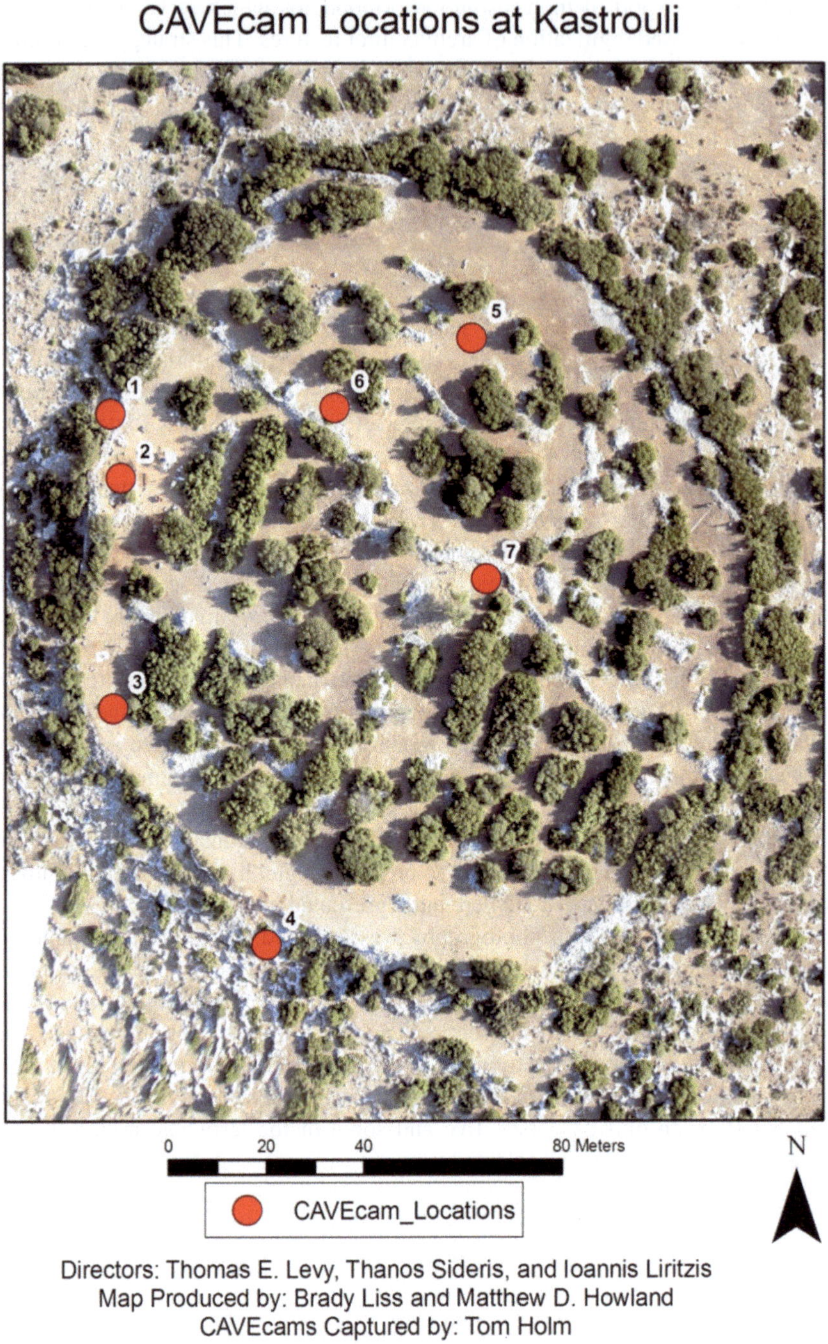

Fig. 9.39 Locations of CAVEcam imagery around Kastrouli (Map by M. Howland Center for Cyber-Archaeology and Sustainability, UC San Diego)

Stratigraphy and Excavation

The 2016 excavations at Kastrouli are preliminarily divided into three strata (Sideris et al. 2017). Surface materials and loci are clearly disturbed by looting, and/or the previous excavations are attributed to Stratum I. The site's fortification wall is believed to be later in date than the tombs based on its close (potentially cutting) construction to the dromos entrance of the tomb. As such, loci associated with the wall section excavations are assigned Stratum II. In addition, undisturbed loci from square 7/19 (Wall 116, Fill 114, and Ashy-Feature 115) are also attributed to Stratum II as it is likely that they are later in date than the tomb (however, this requires further investigation through ceramic typology or other dating methods). Undisturbed loci from within the tomb itself (Loci 112 and 121) are attributed to Stratum III as they are likely the earliest excavated loci. These loci (112 and 121) are associated with the human remains and seem to be the only undisturbed contexts within the tomb.

Area A

Squares 5/19 and 6/19: Tomb Excavation

Stratum I

Stratum I in Squares 5/19 and 6/19 consist of all loci that are considered to have been disturbed by looting, excavation, or by general surface disturbance (Fig. 9.40). These include Loci 100, 101, 102, 104, 107, 108, 109, 110, 111, 119, and 120.

Excavation of Squares 5/19 and 6/19 began with the opening of two general cleaning loci (L100 and L101) (Fig. 9.41), which related to the weeding and cleaning of the surface areas of squares 5/19 (L101) and 6/19 (L100). These loci included the cleaning of some very disturbed fill/topsoil, which was sieved at 100% through 1 cm mesh. Also included in these loci was the cleaning of some disturbed fill inside the tomb.

Following the cleaning of the surface areas of each square and limited cleaning within the tomb, Locus 102 was opened below L100 in order to excavate the area immediately south of the tomb in Square 6/19 and to delineate the southern edge of the largest lintel stone covering the tomb (Fig. 9.42). Excavation in this locus both defined the edge of the large lintel stone and also cleaned and delineated the stones to the south of the lintel. Locus 104 was subsequently opened below L100 on the north end of the lintel stone in order to delineate its northern edge in Square 6/19. The excavated material was disturbed fill from the looting and previous excavation of the tombs. The locus successfully discovered the edge of the lintel stone, resulting in the complete exposure of the two lintel stones still in place over the top of the dromos and the leveling of fill to a height equivalent to the top course of stones in the walls of the tomb. Excavation in Locus 102 and 104 was ceased at this level to avoid destabilizing the tomb walls.

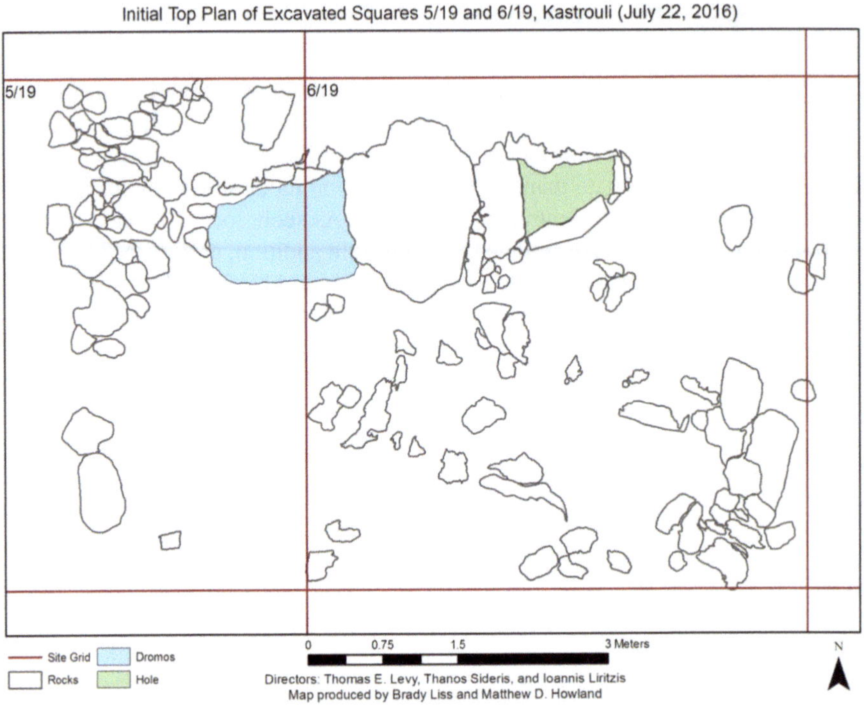

Fig. 9.40 Top plan from the beginning of excavation in Squares 5/19 and 6/19 at Kastrouli

Fig. 9.41 Locus 100 (cleaning locus of Square 5/19) and Locus 101 (cleaning locus of Square 6/19) (Photo – T.E. Levy, Center for Cyber-Archaeology and Sustainability, UC San Diego)

Fig. 9.42 Locus 102 (excavating southern end of lintel stone) and Locus 104 (excavating northern end of lintel stone (Photo – T.E. Levy, Center for Cyber-Archaeology and Sustainability, UC San Diego)

Fig. 9.43 Locus 107 –excavating in eastern access hole to tomb in Square 6/19 (Photo – T.E. Levy, Center for Cyber-Archaeology and Sustainability, UC San Diego)

Locus 107 (Fig. 9.43) was a fill locus in Square 6/19 arbitrarily opened below Locus 100 and contemporary with L108. This locus represents excavation in the interior of the tomb within Square 6/19, accessed through the eastern “opening” to the tomb. The aim of the locus was to remove disturbed fill from the tomb while defining the northern and southern interior walls of the tomb. Excavation in this

Fig. 9.44 Locus 108 – excavating in dromos in Square 5/19 (Photo – T.E. Levy, Center for Cyber-Archaeology and Sustainability, UC San Diego)

locus discovered some fragments of human remains and a stone spindle whorl. While the *ArchField* polygon for this locus represents only the eastern opening to the tomb, the interior of the tomb opens up into a larger area once inside. In practice, the western boundary of this locus was the eastern edge of the eastern lintel, with the entire interior of the tomb east of that line being considered part of L107, resulting in point finds appearing to be outside the locus. A collapsed lintel stone in the tomb was clarified through excavation in this locus. This stone also served as an informal western boundary of the locus in the tomb. This large lintel stone was removed, and a new locus (110) was opened in order to excavate the entire tomb and dromos as a single locus, resulting in the closing of L107.

Locus 108 (Fig. 9.44) was a fill locus in Square 5/19 arbitrarily opened below Locus 101 and contemporary with L107. This locus represented the dromos (western) entrance to the previously looted tomb in Area A. The aim of the locus was to remove disturbed fill from the area of the tomb in Square 5/19 and continue to define the northern and southern walls of the dromos. Excavation in this locus was rapid with large picks and hoes, due to the disturbed nature of the sediment. A conical stone bead was discovered in the sifted material excavated from the locus. This locus was closed after the collapsed lintel stone in the tomb was removed, and a new locus (110) was opened in order to excavate the entire tomb and dromos as a single locus.

Locus 109 (Fig. 9.45) was opened below L100 and contemporary with L102 and L104 in order to remove the disturbed fill material on top of the lintel support stones around the eastern opening to the tomb. The goal of the locus was to delineate the edges of the lintel support stones (i.e., the top stones in the walls of the tomb, just

Fig. 9.45 Locus 109 – excavating around eastern access hole to reveal lintel supports in Square 6/19 (Photo – T.E. Levy, Center for Cyber-Archaeology and Sustainability, UC San Diego)

Fig. 9.46 Locus 110 – excavating across dromos and tomb in Squares 5/19 and 6/19 (Photo – T.E. Levy, Center for Cyber-Archaeology and Sustainability, UC San Diego)

below where the collapsed lintels would have sat) on the north, east, and south edges of the opening. L109 successfully discovered and defined the exterior edges of the lintel support stones, but it was left open in case excavation should continue. The locus was closed on the final day of the 2016 season.

Locus 110 (Fig. 9.46) was originally opened in order to excavate the sediment beneath the collapsed lintel stone (following its removal) within the tomb in square 6/19. Once the sediment immediately beneath the stone was leveled to be consistent with the rest of the tomb (loci 107 and 108), Locus 110 was extended to encompass the entire interior of the tomb and dromos, replacing Loci 107 and 108 and below them. The goal of the locus was to continue to excavate the fill material within the tomb to discover its floor and the founding levels of the walls. During excavation in the locus, a modern safety pin was discovered in the sieve reiterating the disturbed nature of the locus and the tomb. Locus 110 was excavated down to bedrock in the central part of the dromos. At the eastern end of the locus, a vertical slab of worked bedrock was discovered representing the eastern end of the tomb. However, the tomb appeared to have another chamber to the south, and Locus 111 was opened in order to further pursue this possibility, at which time Locus 110 was closed.

Locus 111 (Fig. 9.47) was arbitrarily opened below L110 in Square 6/19 to excavate fill material in the eastern end of the tomb. The locus was opened beneath locus 110 when vertical, worked bedrock was discovered at the eastern edge of the tomb. The goal of the locus was to excavate the fill down to the floor of the tomb which was presumably bedrock and had been discovered in the dromos. During excavations of the locus, a modern fragment of film was discovered in the sieve reiterating the disturbed nature of the locus and the tomb. The locus was closed when a significant concentration of bone was discovered, a comingled secondary burial, which was excavated as Locus 112 (Fig. 9.48; Chovalopoulou et al. 2017).

Locus 119 (Fig. 9.49) was opened to the south of the eastern access hole to the tomb (Square 6/19) in order to excavate the topsoil around the surface of the tomb. While the locus was initially restricted to only the area immediately south of the eastern access, it was subsequently expanded to the south and west, running into Square 5/19. Locus 119 was primarily excavated by three local workers, and it was excavated quickly with large picks. Despite the disturbed nature of the locus, it still

Fig. 9.47 Locus 111 – excavating in eastern end of tomb in Square 6/19 (Photo – T.E. Levy, Center for Cyber-Archaeology and Sustainability, UC San Diego)

Fig. 9.48 Locus 112 – dense collection of human remains, possible secondary burial, in Square 6/19 (Photo – T.E. Levy, Center for Cyber-Archaeology and Sustainability, UC San Diego)

Fig. 9.49 Locus 119 – excavating fill to the south of the tomb in Squares 5/19 and 6/19 (Photo – T.E. Levy, Center for Cyber-Archaeology and Sustainability, UC San Diego)

yielded significant pottery and a broken Phi-figurine. As the locus was excavated to a lower elevation, many large stones were discovered that are potentially part of the tomb architecture. Two large slabs discovered in the southeast corner of Square 6/19 are possibly lintel stones (similar in size and shape to those associated with the tomb), and one is clearly collapsed or disturbed by looters as it is tipped on its side. To the west of these large slabs, many smaller stones (ca. 30 cm in diameter) were discovered that are possible architectural collapse from the tomb(s) as well.

Locus 120, the final locus in Area A attributed to Stratum I, was opened to excavate the fill in the southern chamber of the tomb (Fig. 9.50). This chamber was not

Fig. 9.50 Locus 120 – excavating fill (disturbed by looters) in the tomb in Square 6/19. South section prior to removal of fill to expose full extent of comingled burial (Photo – T.E. Levy, Center for Cyber-Archaeology and Sustainability, UC San Diego)

excavated with the rest of the tomb/dromos, and it appeared to be topped with a large, masoned lintel stone and backed by a vertical, flat slab. This initial locus consisted primarily of fill with some pottery and bone fragments. During excavation, a plastic cup was found, likely indicating that this locus was disturbed by looters or the recent excavations. Locus 120 was excavated down to the possible secondary burials within the tomb across its eastern end and southern chamber (opened as Locus 121 and contemporary with Locus 112).

Stratum II

No loci from Square 5/19 and Square 6/19 were assigned to Stratum II as loci in this stratum are insecure contexts that likely postdate the tomb.

Stratum III

The only loci attributed to Stratum III in Squares 5/19 and 6/19 are Locus 112 and Locus 121. Moreover, these are the only loci that appeared to be from undisturbed contexts; this is evidenced by the well-preserved conditions of the human remains and the compact sediment in which they were embedded. Locus 112 was opened beneath Locus 111 in the eastern end of the tomb in Area A when a significant concentration of human remains was discovered against the worked bedrock. The goal of the locus was to excavate the bones and associated material culture. The human remains did not appear to be articulated but were significant in number (hundreds of complete bones and fragments). It is possible that these bones represent a secondary burial. This locus focused only on the human remains at the eastern extent of the tomb (against the worked bedrock), but the bones continued to the south into a possible second chamber (Locus 121). The locus was closed when all the bones were removed and the bedrock floor was discovered.

Locus 121 (Fig. 9.51) represents the continuation of the bones seen in Locus 112 into the southern chamber of the tomb (below Locus 120). Excavation in this locus uncovered hundreds of human bones (thousands of bone fragments) and many sherds of Mycenaean stirrup jars in situ. Excavation in this locus also recovered a spindle whorl, three figurines (Phi- and Psi-figurines), and a fragment of gold (crumpled gold foil) in situ. In addition a bone bead, a possible seal, and three gold fragments (also crumpled gold foil) were recovered from the sieve. The locus was closed on the final day of excavation; the bedrock beneath the locus was fully exposed, and all of the human remains were excavated. Top plans and section plans of the fully exposed tomb are shown in Figs. 9.52, 9.53 and 9.54.

Fig. 9.51 Locus 121 – dense collection of human remains, probably secondary burial, in Square 6/19 (Photo – T.E. Levy, Center for Cyber-Archaeology and Sustainability, UC San Diego)

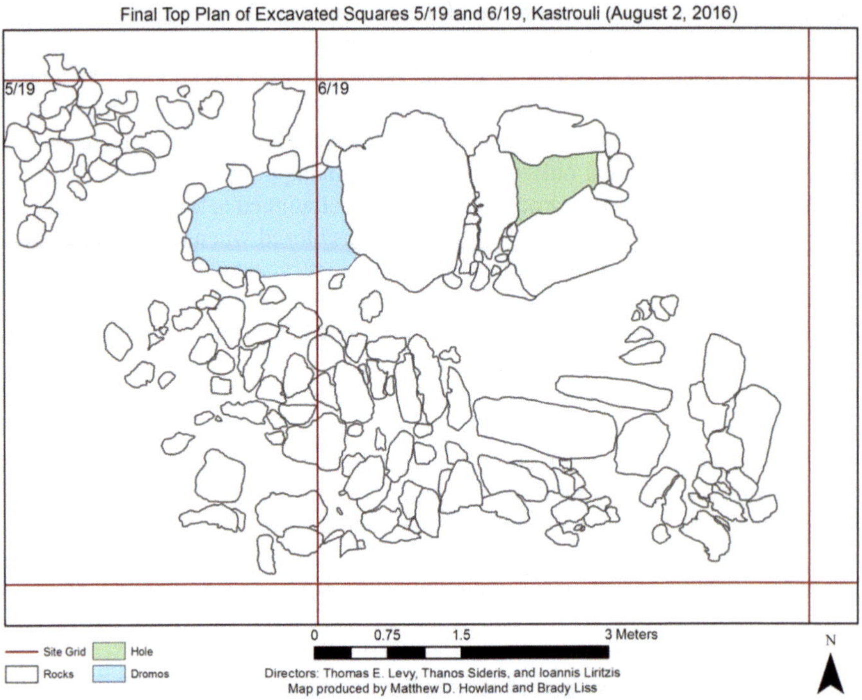

Fig. 9.52 Final top plan from the last day of excavation in Squares 5/19 and 6/19 at Kastrouli

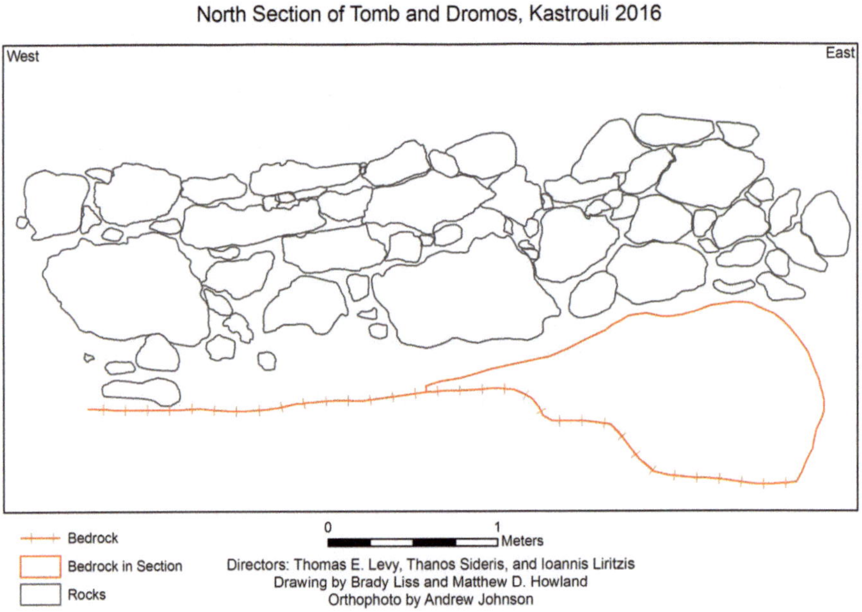

Fig. 9.53 Northern section drawing of tomb and dromos

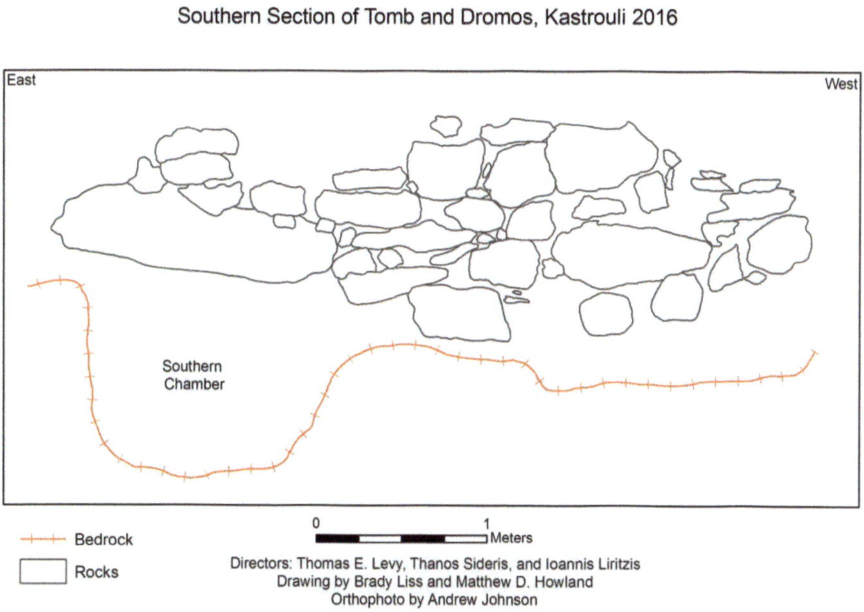

Fig. 9.54 Southern section drawing of tomb and dromos

Interpretation

Tomb A represented the main focus of excavation during the 2016 field season. All loci in squares 5/19 and 6/19 are grouped into Strata I and III, reflecting a general divide in excavated loci between disturbed and undisturbed contexts, respectively. In the area of the tomb, the potential for disturbance was high given the recent occurrence of looting and limited archaeological excavation. Excavation in all loci now grouped in Stratum I corroborates the likelihood of disturbance, given a lack of clear stratification and the limited density of finds. The presence of two fragments of modern debris (a piece of photographic film and a fragment of a plastic cup), the latter of which was found during excavation, also evidence the disturbed nature of these loci. Loci (112 and 121) classified in Stratum III, however, seem to be undisturbed, based on the density of relatively intact human bones interspersed with relatively large fragments of diagnostic pottery sherds. L112 and L121, which represent the same ancient context and are separated only for reasons of excavation process, seem to represent a multiple secondary burial, based on the disarticulation of the bones. The comingled bones of multiple individuals and grave goods with no apparent orientation also suggest that multiple burials in the tomb may have been collected and condensed in one part of the tomb in order to clear space for later burials or activities in ancient times. The discovery of gold foil fragments, figurines, and finely decorated ceramics indicates that at least one of the ancient burials would have contained grave goods of fine quality (Figs. 9.55, 9.56 and 9.57). Diagnostic

Fig. 9.55 Mycenaean stirrup jar sherds found in association with human remains in Locus 121, Square 6/19 (Photo – T.E. Levy, Center for Cyber-Archaeology and Sustainability, UC San Diego)

Fig. 9.56 Psi-figurine found in association with human remains in Locus 121, Square 6/19 (Photo – T.E. Levy, Center for Cyber-Archaeology and Sustainability, UC San Diego)

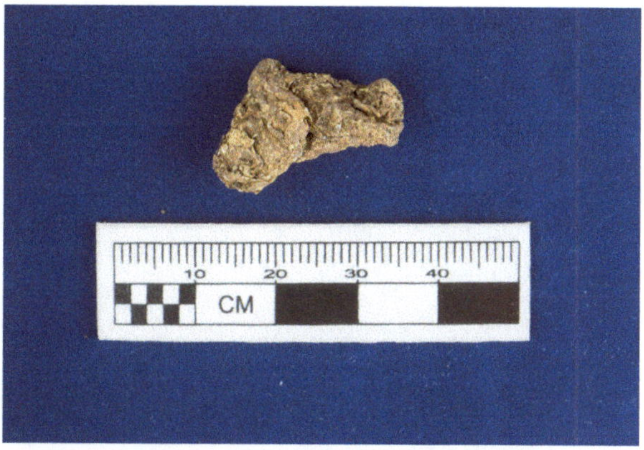

Fig. 9.57 Gold fragment (crumpled foil) found from sieve of Locus 121, Square 6/19 (Photo – T.E. Levy, Center for Cyber-Archaeology and Sustainability, UC San Diego)

figurines and Mycenaean stirrup jar fragments, along with the tomb architecture, also suggest that the tomb was Mycenaean/Late Helladic in date, though verification of this and increasing the precision of the dating depend on subsequent typological and scientific dating (Liritzis et al. 2016).

Square 7/19: Investigation of Geophysical Survey Results (Ground Truth)

Stratum I

Square 7/19 was opened to the immediate east of the tomb excavation with the primary goal of exploring a possible subsurface void in the area detected by geophysical survey (by Grigoris Tsokas and his team). Only the southern half of the square was opened for excavation due to the time constraints of the short season (Figs. 9.58, 9.59 and 9.60). In this square, only Locus 106 and Locus 113 were assigned to Stratum I because they were primarily topsoil (Figs. 9.58 and 9.59). Excavation began in the southwest corner of the square with Locus 106 which was dedicated to excavating the topsoil in this area of the square. The locus was excavated quickly with large picks, and collected material culture consisted mostly of pottery. The top of a large stone was also discovered, but its edges were not fully delineated (it is unclear if this was simply a large stone or a bedrock outcropping). Locus 106 was closed in order to expand excavations to the east (Locus 113, still within the southern half of the square). Locus 113 was a roughly 0.5 m × 3.5 m trench opened to expand excavation across the east-west length of the square. During excavation, 1–2 rows of ca. 5 stones were discovered resembling a possible wall, and at this time Locus 113 was extended an additional 0.5 m to the immediate south. Excavation in this newly expanded portion of locus revealed a continuation to these stones, and it also appeared that this possible wall continued outside the square to the southwest. To the east of the wall feature, excavation in Locus 113 also discovered a possible fire pit feature (Locus 115). With this discovery and the presence of the wall feature

Fig. 9.58 Locus 106 – excavating topsoil in southwestern corner of Square 7/19 (Photo – T.E. Levy, Center for Cyber-Archaeology and Sustainability, UC San Diego)

Fig. 9.59 Locus 113 – expanded excavations in Square 7/19 to the east (Photo – T.E. Levy, Center for Cyber-Archaeology and Sustainability, UC San Diego)

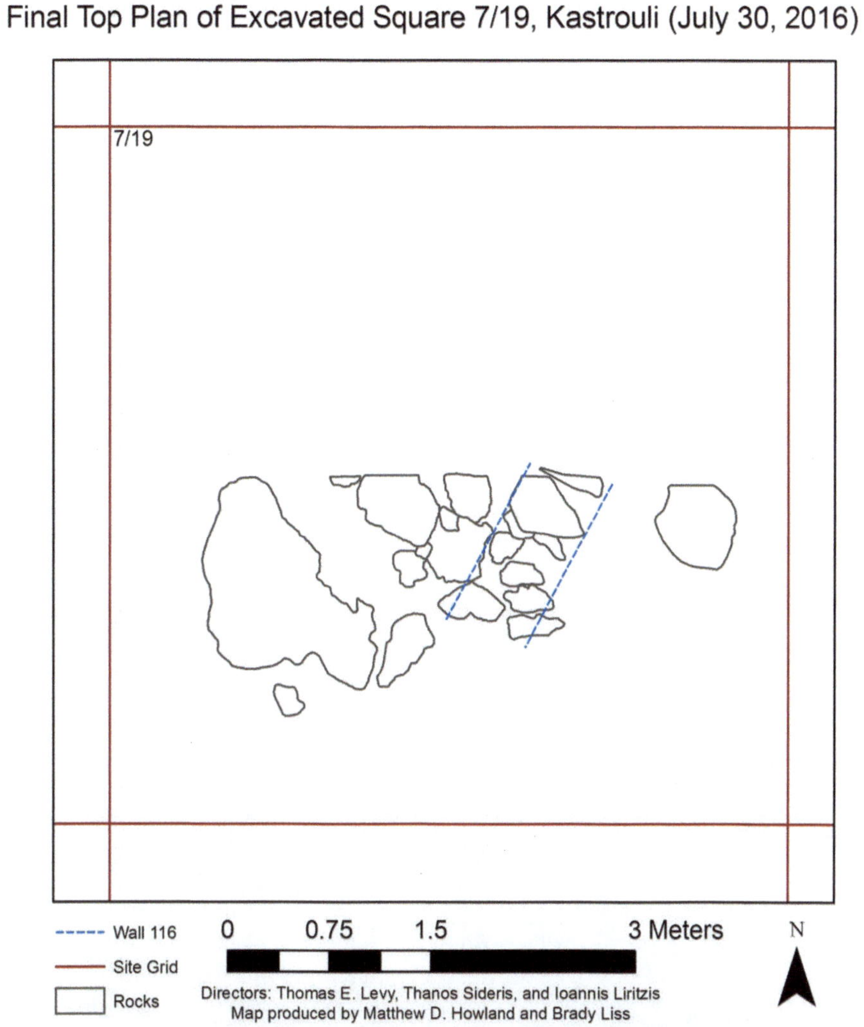

Fig. 9.60 Final top plan from the last day of excavation in Square 7/19 at Kastrouli

(Locus 116), Locus 113 was closed. Material culture collected from the locus included mostly pottery and a highly fired loom weight.

Stratum II

In Square 7/19, Loci 114, 115, 116, and 117 were assigned to Stratum II (Figs. 9.61, 9.62, 9.63 and 9.64). These loci were attributed to Stratum II based on their assumed later date than the tomb, but their undisturbed contexts would be inappropriate to

Fig. 9.61 Locus 114 – excavating to the east of Wall 116, possible structure interior in Square 7/19 (Photo – T.E. Levy, Center for Cyber-Archaeology and Sustainability, UC San Diego)

Fig. 9.62 Locus 115 – excavation of possible fire pit feature in Square 7/19 (Photo – T.E. Levy, Center for Cyber-Archaeology and Sustainability, UC San Diego)

include in Stratum I. Locus 116 represents the wall feature described above which included 1–2 rows and 1–2 courses of unworked stones. Locus 115 (Fig. 9.62) encompassed the fire pit feature (to the east of Wall 116) based on the presence of dark, ashy sediment and unique, possibly worked stones. Locus 114 (Fig. 9.61) was opened in the immediate area around the burn feature and up to Wall 116. The area to the west of Wall 116 (and below Locus 106) was assigned Locus 117. Excavation focused in Locus 115 where some in situ pottery was collected (a possible cup

Fig. 9.63 Locus 116 – Wall feature in Square 7/19 (Photo – T.E. Levy, Center for Cyber-Archaeology and Sustainability, UC San Diego)

Fig. 9.64 Locus 117 – excavating to the west of Wall 116 in Square 7/19 (Photo – T.E. Levy, Center for Cyber-Archaeology and Sustainability, UC San Diego)

base – Basket 20,079) and the possible worked stones around the fire pit feature were excavated (Basket 20,086–20,088). These stones also appeared to be fire cracked reiterating the possible presence of significant heat (the over-fired loom weight from Locus 113 also supports this understanding). Locus 115 was closed with the bottom of the ashy sediment, at which time Locus 114 was excavated to a similar elevation. Locus 114 was closed once level with Locus 115. The excavations in Locus 117 west of the wall continued until the closing of the square, but it was unable to delineate the large stone originally discovered in Locus 106. The square and all associated loci were closed on 29 July in order to focus all excavations within the tomb. The square was covered with a thick plastic sheet and backfilled for protection during the off-season.

Interpretation

Despite the limited excavation in Square 7/19, it is possible that the wall and interior of a structure were partially excavated (Figs. 9.63 and 9.64). While only a small part of the wall (Locus 116) was excavated, it appeared to be in line with several large stones to the southwest of the square suggesting both the wall and possible structure continued in that direction. Loci excavated to the immediate east of the wall were consistent with a possible habitation or activity area, i.e., the interior of the structure. Locus 115 yielded a potential fire pit, and the in situ pottery and loom weight from Loci 115 and 113, respectively, reiterate the possibility of an activity area. In contrast, excavations to the immediate west of Wall 116 in Locus 117 only discovered some pottery and the presence of a large stone or bedrock outcrop; perhaps this area represents the exterior of the structure. However, due to the limited size of the excavation in Square 7/19, these conclusions remain highly speculative but should be further pursued in the future.

Fortification Wall Section Excavations

Squares 5/21 and 5/22

Stratum II

The two wall section excavations (Squares 5/21 and 5/22 and Square 21/2) attempted to discover the founding levels of the fortification wall that surrounds the site to facilitate its dating (Figs. 9.65 and 9.66). Both wall section excavations (Loci 103, 105, and 118) were attributed to Stratum II based on the hypothesis that the wall postdates the tomb. The excavation in Squares 5/21 and 5/22 focused on a northwest section of the wall where there appeared to be two phases of construction. The earlier phase consisted of 2–3 courses of large, unhewn stones (50+ centimeters in diameter), while the later phase was constructed of smaller field stones of 5–6 courses (using the earlier wall as a foundation). It was assumed that the earlier, larger construction can be attributed to the Mycenaean occupation at the site and excavations intended to address this hypothesis. Excavation focused on the exterior side of the wall where much of its construction was visible. Two loci were opened during excavation: Wall Collapse Locus 103 and Fill Locus 105. Locus 103 was dedicated only to removing the wall collapse (no excavation or material culture collected), and it was immediately closed once all stones were cleared. Locus 105 was

Fig. 9.65 Locus 103 (removing wall collapse at northwest wall section excavation) and Locus 105 (excavating fill at northwestern wall section (Photo – T.E. Levy, Center for Cyber-Archaeology and Sustainability, UC San Diego)

Fig. 9.66 Locus 118 – excavating southern wall section in Square 21/2 (Photo – T.E. Levy, Center for Cyber-Archaeology and Sustainability, UC San Diego)

dedicated to excavating the fill abutting the wall to reveal its lowest courses. The locus revealed one additional course of large stones before discovering its foundations directly on the local bedrock. In addition, pottery was discovered within the bottom course of the wall (Basket 20,008), thus providing a secure dating method for its construction. After the bedrock foundation was discovered, Locus 105 was closed with all excavation in this area. For future analysis, samples for optically stimulated luminescence (OSL) were collected by Ioannis Liritzis to date the construction of the wall.

Square 21/2

Stratum II

Excavation in Square 21/2 occurred on the exterior edge of the fortification wall at the southern end of the site and was assigned Locus 118 (Stratum II). The goal of the locus was to discover the founding levels of the site's fortification wall to facilitate its dating. Excavation in this area uncovered stones likely collapsed from the wall embedded in a fine grayish brown fill. These presumably collapsed stones were not removed with excavation. As with the wall section excavated in the northwest, the wall was discovered to be constructed directly on bedrock, which was exposed at the western edge of the locus. The exposed wall consists of five courses of large (ca. 50 cm diameter) stones, with smaller stones placed into the gaps between the large stones. This wall appears to have been constructed in one phase. Excavation did not continue in this area, and Locus 118 was closed following the exposing of bedrock in the western edge of the locus. As with the northwestern wall section, samples for OSL were collected by Ioannis Liritzis to date the construction of the wall.

Interpretation

The excavations at each wall section achieved the goal of discovering the founding levels of the site's fortification wall. In both cases, the wall constructed of large stones was constructed directly on the local bedrock. Post-excavation analysis will be critical in facilitating the dating of the walls. Both the ceramic typology from the pottery collected from Locus 105 and the OSL analysis will be critical in this investigation.

Summary

The 2016 excavation at Kastrouli was successful in achieving the goals of its research design. The exposed tomb in Area A was fully and systematically excavated down to its bedrock surface. All remaining material culture and human remains (following the looting and previous excavations) were excavated and will be critical in interpreting and dating the tomb. At the moment, based on the typology of the ceramics and stratigraphy of the site, the comingled burial represents a use span from ca. 1300 to 1150 BC. In addition, the site's large fortification wall was sectioned in two areas finding the foundations of its construction directly on the local bedrock. These excavations facilitated the collections of OSL samples which will be essential in providing an absolute date for the construction of the wall.

Contextualizing the Mycenaean Coastal World: 3D Documentation of Steno and the Potami Bays

In order to contextualize the interface between the land and sea in this Mycenaean coastal world, the Kastrouli–Antikyra Project captured a portion of the local coastline in 3D using terrestrial and aerial photography methods. The 3D documentation focused on the Potami Bays and the Mycenaean Steno archaeological site (described further below). Steno's unique position atop a rocky outcrop just off the coast provides an ideal vantage point over the Potami Bays suggesting it was an integral component of the coastal world (Figs. 9.67, 9.68 and 9.69). Using the balloon and CAVEcam systems described above, two team members recorded the site and bays over the course of a few hours. The balloon was used for one flight focusing on Steno to produce a 3D model of the site and its extreme topography (Fig. 9.67). The aerial photography was also used to create an orthophoto for future site mapping or other GIS analyses (Fig. 9.68). The CAVEcam was positioned in three locations along the coast of the bays for stereo photography of the entire feature – once in each smaller bay (Potami and Sotira) and once on the small peninsula separating them. An additional panorama was taken from atop Steno to capture the site and its perspective of the coast/bays (Fig. 9.69). Together, these datasets provide a complete digital record of Steno and Potami Bays.

Fig. 9.67 Screenshot of Steno 3D model in Agisoft software created from balloon photography

Fig. 9.68 Orthophoto of Steno created from balloon photography

Fig. 9.69 The 360 degree panorama from the top of Steno with views of the Potami Bays (Captured with the CAVEcam)

Marine Remote Sensing: The Mycenaean Coastal World (from Kastrouli to the Antikyra Bay)

Introduction

In the Antikyra Bay project, we have taken up Thomas Tartaron's (2013) challenge to identify and work up a methodology for the investigation of ancient Mycenaean coastal worlds – the local land and sea interfaces of the Late Bronze Age Aegean. This report describes the fieldwork of a marine remote sensing survey, which was carried out in the coastal zone of Antikyra Bay, Central Gulf of Corinth, in Greece. The survey was planned and carried out between 4th and 9th of August 2016, by the Laboratory of Marine Geology and Physical Oceanography of the University of Patras in cooperation with the University of California, San Diego, under the direction of Prof. Thomas Levy.

The Antikyra marine remote sensing survey is an ongoing research project designed:

- To define the sub-bottom stratigraphy of the recent sediment sequence
- To illustrate the seabed morphology of the survey area
- To collect long (up to 6 m) sediment cores in specific locations based on the results of the marine remote sensing survey
- Besides the selection of the sediment cores, the project aimed:
- To define the evolution of the coastline configuration of the Antikyra Bay over the last 18,000 yrs. BP based on the seismic stratigraphy and the mapping of possible paleo-shoreline features
- To detect targets (surface and subsurface) of potential archaeological interest

Fieldwork

Field activities in the Antikyra Bay during August 2016 survey period included:

- Mapping of the morphology of the seafloor
- Study of the seabed seismic stratigraphy
- Sediment core sampling

The marine remote sensing survey was carried out using a Kongsberg GeoPulse Plus (GeoAcoustics Universal) chirp sub-bottom profiler system and an EG and G side-scan sonar. A Hemisphere V100 GPS system with accuracy of approximately 1.5 m was used for the navigation and the positioning.

In order to meet the objectives of the survey, a 16 m–long wooden vessel (MY LORD, MY LADY) was used (Fig. 9.70). The vessel had been suitably modified to meet the specific needs for the remote sensing survey and the sediment sampling (Fig. 9.71).

Fig. 9.70 My Lord, My Lady research vessel from the University of Patras used for coring expedition in the Antikyra Bay, Gulf of Corinth, Greece, 2016 expedition (Photo courtesy G. Papatheodorou, University of Patras)

Fig. 9.71 The vessel "MY LORD, MY LADY" which was used for the remote sensing survey and the sediment sampling, equipped with (**a**) the sub-bottom profiler (over the side), (**b**) the side-scan sonar, (**c**) acquisition unit, and (**d**) sampling devices (Photo courtesy G. Papatheodorou, University of Patras)

Side-Scan Sonar Survey

The side-scan sonar survey aimed at (i) the mapping of the geomorphological and textural features of the seafloor and (ii) the detection and positioning of targets which may represent man-made features. The side-scan sonar system emits acoustic pulses providing a plan view seafloor acoustic image. The main advantage of a side-scan sonar system is the ability to survey wide seafloor areas at a greater "over the ground" speed. The side-scan sonar system consists of:

- A dual frequency (100 and 500 kHz) towfish 272TD (Fig. 9.72)
- Kevlar cables 50, 150, and 200 m
- Digital recording unit Edgetech 4100P topside (Fig. 9.73)

Over 40 side-scan sonar lines having a length of 40 km and covering a total area of about 2 km^2 were surveyed in the coastal zone of Antikyra at water depths

Fig. 9.72 Dual frequency towfish 272TD with the Kevlar-type cable

Fig. 9.73 The digital recording unit Edgetech 4100P topside (Photo courtesy G. Papatheodorou, University of Patras)

Fig. 9.74 Map of the surveyed areas showing the tracklines of the side-scan sonar and sub-bottom profiling. From right to left – Ag. Isidoros, Potami/Ag. Sotirios, and Valtos (Photo courtesy G. Papatheodorou, University of Patras)

between 3 and 30 m (Fig. 9.74). The side-scan sonar lines were running almost parallel and perpendicular to the central axis of the three small coves, Ag. Isidoros, Potami/Ag. Sotirios, and Valtos up to 30 m water depth (Fig. 9.74). The side-scan sonar survey of the abovementioned areas was carried out with range of 50–100 m each side with the 100 and 500 kHz frequency, in order to achieve the best resolution of the side-scan sonar system. The line spacing was such that the seafloor area covered between two lines was overlapped by 50%.

The excellent quality of the acquired side-scan sonar raw data will provide important information regarding the morphology of the seafloor (Figs. 9.75 and 9.76) and possible man-made targets lying on the seafloor.

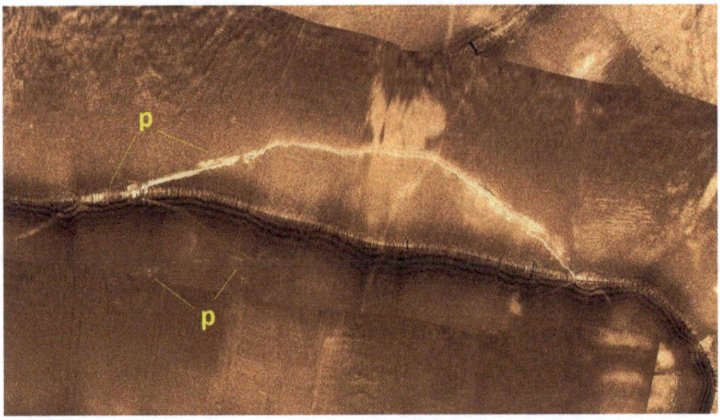

Fig. 9.75 High-resolution side-scan sonar mosaic showing submerged paleo-shorelines (p) in Ag. Isidoros cove. *Light-tone area represents hard substrate and low-tone area seafloor covered by fine-grained sediments* (Photo courtesy G. Papatheodorou, University of Patras)

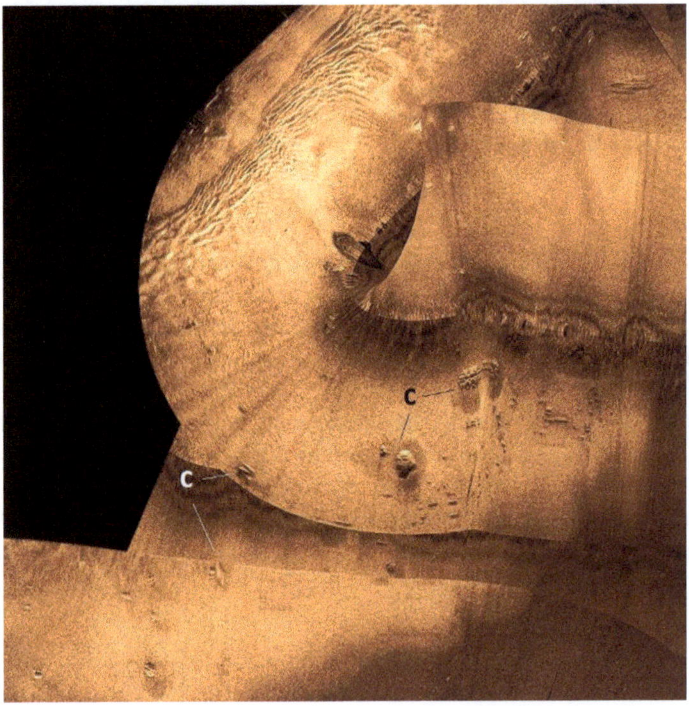

Fig. 9.76 High-resolution side-scan sonar mosaic showing Collagen formations (c) (small reefs) on the seafloor (Photo courtesy G. Papatheodorou, University of Patras)

Sub-Bottom Profiling Survey

The sub-bottom profiling survey at Antikyra Bay was carried out using a chirp sub-bottom profiler. A Kongsberg GeoPulse Plus (GeoAcoustics Universal) chirp sub-bottom profiler system has been used for the examination of the upper (<30 m) seismic stratigraphy of the seabed. The system can operate using various signal waveforms, but for optimum performance a chirp signal with frequency ranges between 1.5 and 11.5 kHz has been used, providing high-penetration, high-resolution data. The penetration of the system can reach up to 80 m in loose sediments, and its resolution is less than 10 cm.

The sub-bottom profiler system emits medium to high frequency acoustic pulse in the form of acoustic conical beams providing a geological profile (seismic profile) of the sub-bottom beneath the path over which the system is towed.

The GeoPulse Plus chirp sub-bottom profiler consists of:

- An over-the-side Transducer Mounting and the trailing single-channel hydrophone (Fig. 9.77)
- The Universal Transceiver (Fig. 9.77)

Fig. 9.77 (**a, b**) O.R.E. Model 132A/132B over-the-side Transducer Mounting (**c**) Universal Transceiver of the chirp system and (**c**) a chirp seismic profile collected from the surveyed area (Photo courtesy G. Papatheodorou, University of Patras)

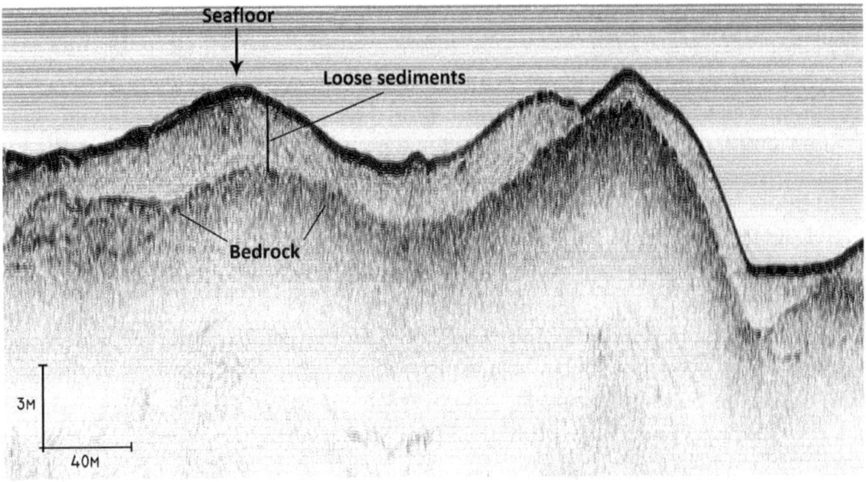

Fig. 9.78 High-resolution chirp seismic profile showing surface loose sediments, 3 m in thickness, overlying the bedrock (Photo courtesy G. Papatheodorou, University of Patras)

- Data acquisition was achieved through Sonarwiz (Chesapeake Technology Inc.) software (Fig. 9.77).

Over 40 chirp sub-bottom profiler lines having a total length of 40 km were surveyed. Additionally, for the reconstruction of the paleogeography and the detection of submerged paleo-shorelines, sub-bottom profiler lines were acquired parallel and almost perpendicular to the shoreline of the surveyed coves (Fig. 9.74).

A time base (TB) of 0.10 sec and a 0.1 msec pulse was used for the sub-bottom profiling survey in the area. The vertical resolution of the system was about 10 cm. The collected chirp raw data is of excellent quality and allows the identification of the stratigraphy of the seafloor of the survey area (Fig. 9.78).

Sediment Core Sampling

A 6 m long corer has been used to collect sediment core samples from the seabed. Richard Norris (Scripps Institution of Oceanography) and Thomas Levy (University of California, San Diego) and students Rishi Sugla and Thomas Holm were responsible for the operation of the corer and the collection of the sediment cores. The sampling positions were chosen after the completion of the geophysical survey and on the basis of the high-resolution chirp seismic profiles. In total nine (9) sediment cores were collected from the three coves, two (2) from Valtos, six (6) from Potami/Ag. Sotirios, and one (1) from Ag. Isidoros (Table 9.4). Table 9.4 presents the geographical coordinates of the collected sediment cores and the thickness of the loose surface sediments above the bedrock at the sampling sites (chirp data).

Table 9.4 Coring sites with coordinates and sediment thickness in study area

Core site	X (latitude)	Y (longitude)	Sediment thickness (m)
Valtos 1	38° 21′ 02.06”	22° 35′ 57.70”	2.5
Valtos 2	38° 21′ 03.18”	22° 35′ 57.08”	2.5
Potami 1 and 3	38° 21′ 29.91”	22° 36′ 16.10”	3.6
Potami 2 and 4	38° 21′ 28.05”	22° 36′ 09.97”	2.9
Agios Sotirios 1	38° 21′ 30.68”	22° 36′ 23.31”	3
Agios Sotirios 2	38° 21′ 29.68”	22° 36′ 20.96”	2.6
Agios Isidoros	38° 21′ 38.30”	22° 37′ 16.17”	2.3

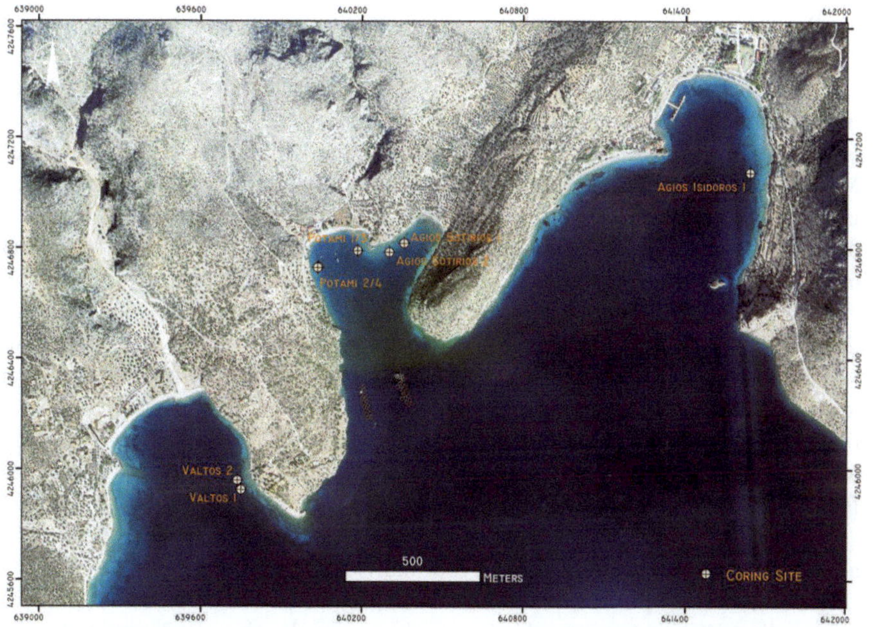

Fig. 9.79 Map of the surveyed areas showing the sediment cores sites (Photo courtesy G. Papatheodorou, University of Patras)

Sediment Core Extraction and Preliminary Study

Sediment cores were collected in four small bays within the larger Antikyra Bay: these include (from west to east) Valtos, Potami, Sotirios, and Agios Isodoros in the Gulf of Corinth (Fig. 9.79). These smaller bays and inlets are characterized by pebble beaches that were and still are used as small harbors for fishing, aqua farming, and recreation. As pointed out by Sideris (2014:176–177), the four small bays studied here can be characterized as follows (from west to east): *Valtos* – is exposed to southern and western winds. No archaeological remains have been found here, but there is a freshwater stream on to NW side of the bay. Only modern occupation evidence is known for this small bay; Potami – there are two small bays here, and they are exposed only to southern winds. Potami has a spring emerging on the beach and a partially filled wetland on the north side of the bay. The area took its name (Greek for "rivers") from the network of small springs that are found less than a hundred meters from the shore. The small western bay is referred to as "Potami," which is where our team carried out most of its coring activities. There is no evidence of antiquities along the Potami shore – only modern occupation linked to a tavern and fish farm. However, the two small Potami bays here (Potami and Sotira) are separated by a small inlet and promontory called Steno that has multiple ancient occupations including from the Mycenaean period. As Steno is situated on a rugged and naturally defended chersonese, it would be an excellent defensive platform for the Potami bays. To the east of Steno is the other tiny gulf in Potami called Sotira bay. Further east, Agios Isidoros is the last bay sampled by our team. On its western side, there is larger beach, with a smaller one on the east. While the larger beach has little shelter, the smaller one is well protected from wind. Along the southern coast of the Agios Isidoros bay is the promontory site of Vroulia where numerous Mycenaean sherds have been collected. There is a small modern marina near Agios Isidoros's eastern beach where our team docked the research vessel each evening during the expedition. There is little question that the Antikyra Bay area rather than the Itea Bay provisioned Kastrouli during the Mycenaean occupation. From a topographic perspective, there are no easily accessible valleys that lead from Kastrouli down to the west and the Itea Bay. On the other hand, almost due south of Kastrouli is gentle topography that leads directly to the Antikyra Bay. The modern road that leads from Kastrouli to the town of Antikyra follows most of this route. The location of the small Potami bays fed by freshwater streams and dominated by the Steno Mycenaean small fort led us to focus the "sea" portion of our Kastrouli–Antikyra Bay project here.

Sediment coring was achieved by the use of a hammer core system operated by a UC San Diego scuba diver team of four individuals, all trained as science divers (Fig. 9.80) and one professional Greek diver (Fig. 9.80 coring underwater). Cores were collected with 6 m length of agricultural supply pipe, 10.2 centimeters in diameter. These core barrels were fitted with stainless steel cutters, and core catchers riveted into place designed and manufactured at the Scripps Institution of Oceanography by Prof. Richard Norris. The cores were driven into the seabed by the use of a stainless steel sliding hammer that seated onto a set of adjustable handles that could be moved along the length of the core barrel as the core penetrated the bottom. Cores were extracted from the bottom by the use of a shipboard boat winch and inflated lift bag. Oxygen refills for scuba tanks were kindly provided by a local fish farm situated in the Potami Bay.

Visual observations of the split cores were combined with core-scanning XRF measurements of major and minor element sediment chemistry. In the Potami Bay, 2–3 m cores typically have an upper 70–100 cm interval of red-brown clayey silt in the core top, overlying 1–2 m of green shelly sand (see Fig. 9.81). The sand is rich in molluscs and often the roots of *Posidonia* seagrasses and sometimes contains fragments of wood and probably charcoal. Thin interbeds of red-brown silty sedi-

Fig. 9.80 Thomas Levy using hammer core system in Potami Bay. The hammer has two handles on the hammer, which is raised by the diver and released to hammer down the core barrel (Photo – Richard Norris, Scripps Institution of Oceanography, UC San Diego)

ment occur within the green shelly sand and are typically 10–20 cm thick. Potami Core 1 (Fig. 9.81) contains a layer about 30 cm thick at the bottom of the core of this red-brown silty sediment. Interbeds almost always have bioturbated boundaries with adjacent layers. We interpret the green shelly sand to represent the normal marine accumulation in the bay. This sediment tends to be coarser grained and has a higher percentage of pebble sand fine gravel in places within the bay that are exposed to the wind and bottom currents. The green shelly sand often contains molluscs such as small bivalves and *Dentalium* that are in life position, suggesting that the sediment is not substantially reworked. The abundance of shell in the sediment is shown by elevated Sr/Ca ratios, reflecting strontium-rich aragonitic mollusc shells.

In contrast, the red-brown clayey silt is much finer grained and has higher K/Fe ratios in XRF records than the green shelly sand (Fig. 9.81). This chemistry is consistent with the clayey silt (high in potassium) as being derived from eroded soils, particularly the terra rosa soils typically developed on carbonate bedrock in the area. The K/Fe ratios are consistent with the records of other lithogenic elements such as Fe, Ti, Ba, Si, and Zr. Therefore, we interpret the record to indicate a shift in recent times (representing the core top) toward soil loss from upland areas. The existence of multiple layers of red-brown clayey silt in most of our Potami Bay cores suggests that the delivery of eroded soil occurred throughout the depositional record represented by our cores and was interspersed with periods of marine sedimentation of additional shelly green sand.

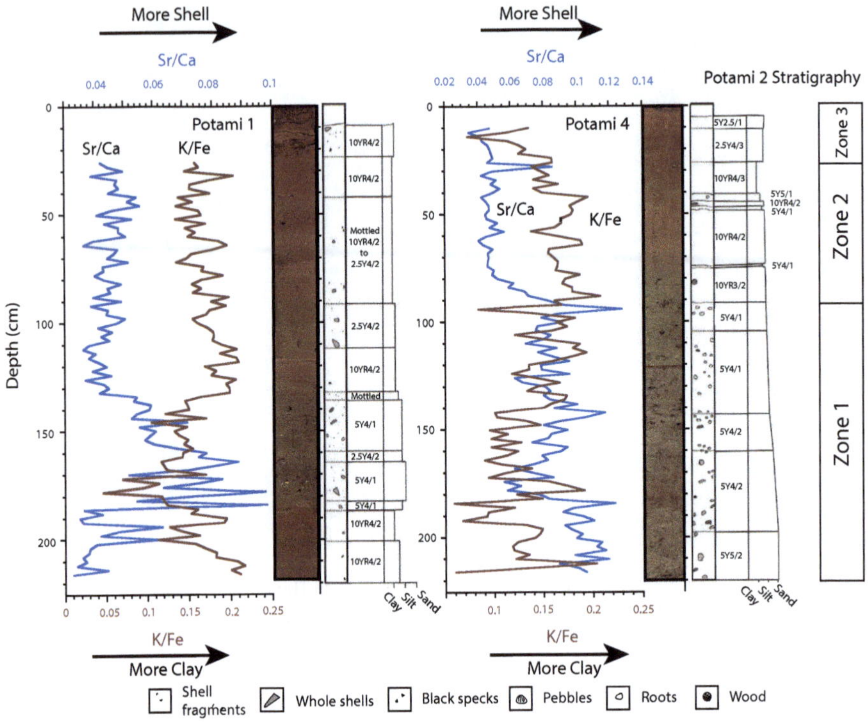

Fig. 9.81 Potomi 4 Core (right) and Potami 1core (left), showing the K/Fe ratio (brown line) and Sr/Ca ratio (blue line) against the core images and core drawings. A drawing is not available for Potami 4, so we show the stratigraphy of Potami 2 (taken within a few meters of the site of Potami 4) for comparison. The K/Fe record reflects clay abundance, with generally higher amounts of clay in the red-brown intervals of the cores. Increases in the Sr/Ca ratio are associated with the shelly green sands suggesting elevated abundance of marine aragonitic shells relative to the red-brown sediment layers. Note the upward increase in abundance of clay-rich sediment, likely reflecting erosion of terra rosa soils from nearby limestone slopes. Similar increased delivery of soil toward the tops of our core records is seen in the other cores collected during the Antikyra coring program consistent with a regional increase in soil erosion in recent times. However, we await dating the cores before we can evaluate the rate and timing of local soil erosion in the area. (Courtesy of R. Norris and I. Rivera-Collazo, as we both contributed to the graph).

During coring operations, we drove the cores into the seabed until they would no longer penetrate further. The core penetration depths (~2–2.5 m) were broadly in agreement with the expected sediment thicknesses obtained from geophysical records derived from a sub-bottom profiler system (see marine geophysics section above). Hence, we expect that our cores have captured the entire recent (late Holocene) record of sedimentation in Potami Bay. The bay is surrounded by exposures of well-cemented pebble and cobble conglomerates associated with alluvial fans of Pleistocene age. Although the start date for sedimentation in our cores has not yet been established, it is almost certainly from no older than early to middle Holocene, after sea level stabilized near its current position.

Geomorphological Implications of the Cores

The preliminary assessment of Potami 1 and 2 provides an initial understanding of the local land and sea conditions. The final interpretation of all cores requires additional laboratory analyses, including high-resolution absolute dating. The sedimentary sequence of both cores accumulated in the marine environment. No in situ paleosols are evident in the record. XRF analysis was performed to Potami 4, but sedimentary assessment was done to Potami 2. These two cores were obtained from the same location, and it is therefore possible to compare the results, but it is also evident that the records are not precisely equal. Additional analyses will be performed to improve understanding of the sedimentary sequences of the basin.

Potami 1 (Fig. 9.81) presents a fine-grained sequence, suggesting a low-energy environment, possibly influenced by the local wetland. The deepest section (Zone 1) records the accumulation of terrigenous sediments, including terra rosa soils. This suggests slope instability and inland erosion. This sequence of reddish clayey silts fines upward to silty clay suggesting even more intense soil erosion. The smaller grain size content, which is yet to be analytically measured, suggests that the erosion could have reached deeper soil horizons, indicating possible intensification of deforestation. This sequence was only briefly interrupted by what seems to be a slight stabilization that also presents increased Sr/Ca ratio and coincides with a stratigraphic break in deposition between ~185-135 cm depth. This short break suggests possible forest recovery or decreased soil erosion, combined with stabilization of the marine environment.

Zone 1 is followed by a coarser sequence of gray sandy silts with high shell content in growth position (Zone 2). The contact with Zone 1 presents the lowest levels of K/Fe of the entire deposit, suggesting a dramatic change in the characteristics of the sediments transported to the embayment. It suggests that erosion decreased dramatically, possibly to the extent that the water column was clear of suspended sediments, fostering a thriving marine environment, as suggested by the in situ mollusc shells. This change could have been caused by reduced precipitation, by stabilization of forests or a combination of both. While more analyses are needed, we are inclined to link this shift to forest recovery, but this still needs to be tested. The uniformity of the deposit suggests that, overall, erosion of soils into the basin dramatically decreased, particularly during the deepest section of this zone. The upper section, between ca. 130 and 160 cm in depth, presents a slightly finer sequence, which coincides with a return to lower Sr/Ca and higher K/Fe readings. While these measures are not as high as those in Zone 1, it is possible that slope soils were again starting to be exposed or available for erosion, but their input to the basin was not significant enough as to cause evident impact. It is possible that sediment suspension was still low. This section is topped off by a mottled layer of grayish and reddish sediments, suggesting mixing and instability.

Zone 3 presents a fining-up sequence that coarsens in the upper 15 cm of the core. In the lower section of the Zone, at the contact with the mottled layer capping Zone 2, the sequence presents reddish clayey silt indicating a return to the erosional conditions that were dominant in Zone 1. K/Fe readings are not as high as before, suggesting that, while the color represents erosion of fresh terra rosa soils, it might not have been as intense as before, or the soils were more immature. The drastic reduction in shell content, together with the very low Sr/Ca readings, indicates that this return to soil erosion on land affected the marine environment, possibly due to suspended sediments in the water column and high mud deposition rates. Sedimentologically, erosional conditions seem to have stabilized slightly, as indicated by a return to grayish sediments and in situ shells between ca. 85 and 105 cm. However, the XRF results suggest that, in contrast with Zone 2, this decrease in terra rosa input was not absolute, as terrigenous sediments continued to be accumulated. A mottled sequence with finer silty clay and a decrease in shell content indicates instability and mixing of the depositional environment, topped by a reddish layer that continues to the present.

Even though located in the same basin, Potami 2/4 presents a very different sedimentary sequence to Potami 1. The first observation is that the sequence is significantly coarser. This makes sense in the context of the geographical location of the sample, near the head of a rocky coastal foreland. Potami 2 begins with coarse to very coarse sands and pebbles with silt inclusions and fines upward to a silty clay layer in Zone 3. The presence of angular and subangular pebbles and grains suggests the local provenience of the sediments, which could not have been transported in long distances. It is possible that the sediment source is the rocky foreland itself, therefore constituting an immediately local record of land conditions.

Zone 1, the deepest section, presents a marine deposit with thick and stable *Posidonia* seagrass ecosystems, evidenced by often dense root systems. Soil input to this sequence was minimal, although the XRF results suggest that terra rosa input could have increased irregularly in the upper section of the zone. Overall, Zone 1 fines upward from very coarse sand to sandy silt. These characteristics suggest overall clear water column and stability of the soils on the slopes immediately around the core collection point. The fining-upward sequence suggests deepening water, possibly indicating increasing sea level.

Zone 1 in Potami 2 core was drastically interrupted by Zone 2, as evidenced by a sharp contact between the layers and sudden color change to reddish brown. This sequence is a reddish deposit of sandy silt that fines upward to silty clay. Potami 4, in contrast, shows a gradational contact between the shelly sand and overlying red-brown clay-rich sediment. While Potami 4 seems to present a fairly uniform sequence. Potami 2 presents a series of gray laminations at 60 cm and again between ca. 35 and 45 cm, which need to be further explored. Zone 2 suggests the sudden exposure of soils to erosion into the basin. The disappearance of *Posidonia* grasses from the sequence and the identification of a well-preserved wood fragment suggest forest clearance and strongly point toward human intervention.

Zone 3, the uppermost deposit, presents a return to slightly coarser sediments (sandy silt). While color is not dramatically different between Zones 3 and 2, the XRF results suggest a significant change in the mineral composition of the transported sediments, which deserves further exploration. It is possible that this change reflects a change in the availability of soils for erosion and transport in the recent past, very near the present.

Absolute dating and additional high-resolution analyses are still required to be able to interpret these results and the relationship in the sedimentary sequences of Potami 1 and Potami 2/4. A cursory assessment suggests that Zone 2 of Potami 1 and Zone 1 of Potami 2/4 might be related, indicating that the deeper sequence of Potami 1 might correspond to an early human intervention in the Potami basin, followed by abandonment and forest recovery, which is evidenced as decreased fine-grained terrigenous sediment input in the basin. Zone 3 of Potami 1 might correspond to Zone 2 of Potami 2/4, indicating a return to intensive intervention with local soils that continues to the present. Zone 3 of Potami 2/4, which suggests a change in terrigenous sediment erosion to the basin, might correspond to the uppermost section of Potami 1 Zone 3 and relate to changes in settlement patterns or population destabilization as recently as the twentieth century or possibly at the end of the Late Bronze Age (cf. Knapp and Manning 2016). Absolute dating of the cores should resolve this issue.

Summary Remarks on the Sediment Cores and Bays

The next step in the analyses will be to extract suitable samples from the cores for radiocarbon or uranium–thorium (U-Th) dating to finalize the chronological history of sediment deposition in Valtos, Potami, Sotirios, and Agios Isodoros bays. U-Th dating may provide the most accurate method of dating the cores from this project. In a recent study by Cramer et al. (2017), U-Th dating of Caribbean reefs provided a high-resolution chronology to monitor changes in fish, coral, and urchin composition and reef accretion rates over a 3000 year period. Working with lake sediments in Macedonia using novel isotopic proxies that track soil erosion and development, Athony Dosseto (personal communication) found an unprecedented erosion event beginning at ca 3500 yr. BP (and culminating at 2500 yr. BP) that would encompass the Late Bronze Age collapse in the Aegean region. These are the kinds of exciting new developments in dating techniques and sedimentology research that will provide new research directions for examining the marine cores collected during the Kastrouli–Antikyra expedition. These methods may provide the kind of temporal resolution needed to link the geomorphological and environmental record revealed in the cores with the settlement history of this part of ancient Phokis during the Late Bronze Age when a number of Mycenaean sites were established along the northern coast of Antikyra Bay (cf. Sideris 2014). The small bays studied here on the northern shore of the Gulf of Corinth have two Mycenaean sites in close proximity.

Conclusion

The Kastrouli–Antikyra Bay Land and Sea Project near Greece's Gulf of Corinth was inspired by a number of interwoven research goals including: (a) applying a range of cyber-archaeology and geophysical tools to address the issue of at-risk cultural heritage in the eastern Mediterranean; (b) using this study to help develop a marine archaeology methodology suitable for studying human coastal adaption during the late Holocene across time and space; (c) focusing on the end of the Late Bronze Age in the Eastern Mediterranean to address the problem of the collapse of Mycenaean, Hittite, and New Kingdom Egyptian civilizations to investigate the role that climate, environmental, and social factors may have played in this process; and (d) finally to engage in the more local problem of understanding the nature of Mycenaean coastal worlds.

As this is a preliminary study, we do not have definitive answers to the issues raised above. This paper has been more of a methodological treatise on how researchers can integrate an archaeological land and sea project using the tools of cyber-archaeology and marine science. By combining transdisciplinary approaches to cyber and marine archaeology within an anthropological analytical context, we believe important new research horizons will unfold. Where do we stand with the four research goals of the project? The Kastrouli–Antikyra Bay Land and Sea Project successfully addressed the issue of "at-risk world heritage," one of the major goals of our University of California Office of the President Catalyst Grant. The site of Kastrouli (Fig. 9.2) was selected for investigation because several late Mycenaean tombs were robbed and in a state of deterioration (Raptopoulos 2012), and it is located approximately midway between Delphi where we have been conducting a major digital heritage project (Liritzis et al. 2016; Liritzis et al. in press), and only 5 km from the Antikyra Bay providing and ideal "land and sea" study area. As Kastrouli had never been systematically investigated, to adequately record the damaged tombs, we used the tools of cyber-archaeology to establish a state-of-the-art research infrastructure based on digital data capture, curation, analyses, and dissemination. As shown above, this included beginning with the establishment of a 3D photogrammetric network of trigonometric points at Kastrouli under the direction of Prof. Andreas Georgopoulos of the National Technical University of Athens (Fig. 9.4). This was followed by mapping the site using SfM aerial photography using helium balloon system (Fig. 9.37) and georeferenced using the trigonometric network linked to the Greek (Hellenic) Geodetic Reference System . These integrated mapping systems provided the spatial foundation on which the Mycenaean tomb was excavated using the cyber-archaeology fieldwork workflow that includes real-time GIS data recording using *ArchField* (Smith et al. 2015; Smith and Levy 2014; Smith and Levy 2012) and *ArchaeoSTOR*, a web-based geospatial database that archives all the digital data collected in the field and lab (Gidding et al. 2011, 2014). As part of the Catalyst project, to enhance the curation of archaeological field data, ArchaeoSTOR has been improved so that the web-based program now feeds field data directly into a permanent archive in the University of California, San Diego Library Digital Collections (http://library.ucsd.edu/dc/). Accordingly, the Kastrouli ArchaeoSTOR records (and any other excavation) can now be uploaded directly from ArchaeoSTOR to the online digital collections (Smith et al. 2017). The full citation for the dataset is Levy, Thomas E; Sideris, Athanasios; Liritzis, Ioannis; Howland, Matthew D; Liss, Brady (2017): Kastrouli Mycenaean

Excavations, Greece 2016. UC San Diego Library Digital Collections. https://doi.org/10.6075/J0NG4NSV. It is our contention that the ultimate repository for digital archaeological data should be in a research university's digital library and the 2016 Kastrouli excavation provides a model for how this can be achieved.

Three days prior to the Kastrouli excavation, to identify additional subterranean features associated with Tomb A and other archaeological targets at the site, a series of detailed geophysical surveys were carried out at the site under the direction of Prof. Gregorios N. Tsokas of the Aristotle University of Thessaloniki that included resistivity tomography, magnetic gradiometry, and ground-penetrating radar (GPR). As described above, from a site perspective, numerous potentially significant archaeological features were located across the site on various flat terrace areas using this complement of geophysical techniques. On the smaller scale, in the vicinity of Tomb A, the electrical resistivity tomography results identified an additional subterranean feature linked to Tomb A that ground-truth excavation showed to be a significant addition to the Mycenaean mortuary architecture at the site. For future work at the site, the geophysical survey results described above may help identify important target areas for excavation.

The 2016 excavation of Tomb A at Kastrouli has been published in detail elsewhere (Sideris et al. 2017). The significance of Tomb A can be summarized as follows. It is a hybrid between a rock-cut chamber tomb and the built tomb types with a dromos passage. Based on the ceramic assemblage (Fig. 9.55) made up of numerous Mycenaean stirrup jars and Psi figurines, the tomb must have been constructed at the beginning of the LH (Late Hellenic IIIA 2 or slightly later period). The tomb contained a large number of human comingled human remains found in a carved depression in the limestone bedrock at the eastern extremity of the tomb. In a preliminary study of the human remains, Chovalopoulou et al. (2017) identified a minimum number of 19 individuals (MNI) in the bone pile: 15 adults, 2 subadults, an infant, and a fetus. Domestic animal bones were also found here including bones and/or teeth of *Gallus gallus domesticus* (chicken), *Bos taurus* (domestic cow), *Sus scrofa domesticus* (domesticated pig), and *Ovis aries*/*Capra hircus* (sheep/goat) (2017:269). As these domestic animal remains were found with the comingled human remains, we suggest that they represent feasting associated with the burial ritual at the site. As shown in the compendium of studies assembled by James Wright (2004) in *The Mycenaean Feast*, the presence of domestic animals related to feasting is common in Late Bronze Age settlement and mortuary contexts. Contemporary with Kastrouli, the Late Helladic IIIA 2 occupation at Tsoungiza at ancient Nemea produced evidence of ceremonial feasting (Dabney et al. 2004). The deposit showed dominance of head and foot bones from MNI 6 cattle, suggesting on-site butchery with possible redistribution for the meat elsewhere (2004:77). Post-mortuary event intrusion by snakes is indicated by a large number of snake vertebrae and different species of gastropod (snail) shells. As Kastrouli is a relatively small isolated Mycenaean site (6 ha), we had assumed it was a relatively poor LH IIIA 2–LH IIIC agricultural site. In addition, based on the SfM mapping of the site and geophysical surveys, there seems to be a cluster of tombs around the northwestern edge of the summit of the site. During the excavation of Tomb A, another mortuary structure was found immediately to the south. Thus, there may be a cemetery in this part of the site providing an ideal locale for investigating the social organization of this LH site. To our surprise, Tomb A with its well-built mortuary structure with large stone slabs and dromos (over 10 m in length), Psi figurines, and gold foil probably associated with prestige goods (textiles, wood?) indicates a much more complex society at Kastrouli than previously assumed. The nature of the complex society at Kastrouli within the Mycenaean "world system" is beyond the scope of this paper.

In terms of Kastrouli's site size (1.67 ha), it is useful to compare it to settlement patterns in other regions of Greece. In spite of the problems associated with estimates for site size in the region of Messenia (and elsewhere in Greece), Simpson (2014:19) uses provisional categories such as "village," "hamlet," and "farm." Accordingly, Mycenaean sites with LH sherd scatters larger than 1.0 ha (i.e., over 10,000 m2) are considered "villages," 0.5–1.0 ha are classified as "hamlets," and sites below 0.5 ha are designated "farms." Settlements that are over 2.5 ha are characterized as "large." When the habitation area, cemetery, and palace are included, the mega site of Pylos (Davis et al. 1997) is ca. 18 ha in size. While there is a Mycenaean Atlas Project (http://www.helladic.info/) that could serve as a platform for coordinating research on ancient site size in a systematic fashion for the whole of Greece and larger Mycenaean world, having the data available in a user friendly Google Earth platform like the Digital Archaeology Atlas of the Holy Land (https://daahl.ucsd.edu/DAAHL/) would expedite settlement pattern studies for this key period. Thus, at 1.67 ha in size, it is justifiable to consider Kastrouli as a "small" site. The discovery of a rich burial assemblage at such a seemingly peripheral site suggests a need for further excavation to clarify the nature of the small Mycenaean coastal world (Sherratt 1993) that linked Kastrouli to the Bay of Antikyra and larger Gulf of Corinth during the Late Bronze Age.

As noted above, the Potomoi bay is the most likely candidate for Kastrouli's maritime access to the larger Mycenaean coastal world. Situated between the Trachilos peninsula in the west and the Pharyngion (Mounta) peninsula in the east (Sidiris 2014:176), the Potami small bays have a number of features that support this hypothesis: (a) extensive pebble beaches suitable for beaching small boats, (b) a number of freshwater springs close to these beaches making the provisioning of boats and human occupation here relatively easy, (c) the natural topography of the drainage system that leads down from Kastrouli to Antikyra but shifts to the west emptying into Potomoi Bay near the Mycenaean site of Steno, and (d) the Steno small fort situated on a promontory overlooking and defending the two small bays of Potami and Sotira. Tartaron (2013:186) has proposed a framework for classifying Mycenaean maritime cultural landscapes that include different spheres of interaction in relation to geographical scale, temporality, operators, typical vessels, some examples of archaeological evidence, and suggestions for typical modes of exchange. The range for local systems to interregional ones includes coastscape, maritime small world, and regional/intracultural maritime spheres to the largest interregional/intercultural maritime spheres. As seen in Fig. 9.3, Steno is one of four coastal Mycenaean occupations (LH II and III sherds have been found at Antikyra, cf. Sidiris 2014:185) around the Antikyra Bay, and there are numerous Mycenaean sites along the northern coast of the Gulf of Corinth in this region of Phokis (http://www.helladic.info/). Thus, the Potami bay and its link to LH III Kastrouli form a coastscape territorial interaction sphere with linkage to the interior as well as a maritime small world that connected many coastscapes around the Gulf of Corinth. For the study presented here, we focus on the local Kastrouli–Potami Bay coastscape. This coastscape would have been the scene of everyday interaction where specialist seafarers, craft specialists, farmers, and other nonspecialists would have interacted. Based on Bronze Age archaeological parallels such as the Akrotiri Flotilla Fresco boats (Marinatos 1974; Strasser 2010), the Mitrou boat (Van de Moortel 2009), Cretan seals (Wedde 2000), and boat models, it is possible that fishing boats, pilot boats, and coasting vessels frequented Potami Bay. Home-based and reciprocity exchange would have characterized the inland and coastal maritime interaction. How this Mycenaean maritime cultural landscape system related to sea level rise, the identification of paleo-beaches in our side-scan sonar survey described above, and environmental change will become more clear once the sediment cores described here are carefully dated. Together, the land and sea approach to Mycenaean coastal advocated here can provide a more holistic way of investigating climate, environmental, and social change on a global scale.

Acknowledgments The authors would like to thank the Ministry of Culture of Greece for granting permission to excavate at Kastrouli and Mrs. A. Tsaroucha, member and representative of the Ephoreia of Antiquities at Phokis (EAPh) in Delphi, for excellent collaboration. All archaeological works and surveys at Kastrouli were supervised by the EAPh's delegate, Anthoula Tsaroucha, and made possible through the constant support of the EAPh and Nancy Psalti, its director. Thanks also to Dr. Nikolaos Petrochilos of the EAPh for his help and support. We thank also Dr. Fotis Dasios for discussing with us the Sykia chamber tomb and its finds. We are grateful to the villagers of Kastrouli for hosting the 2016 expedition in their homes and tavernas with warmth and good will. The Desfina municipality was very helpful thoughout the project, and we are grateful for their help and support of the following: Mr. Babis Kaliakoudas (president of Desfina municipality community) for excellent support prior, during, and after the 2016 fieldwork; Mrs. Panagiota Karamani (conservator) for her assistance; Mrs. Fotini Koukou (the guardian) for excellent cooperation; and Mrs. Alina Levy for her care with logistics and the whole project. At the University of Patras, we would like to thank Nikos Georgiou, MSc, PhD candidate, Laboratory of Marine Geology and Physical Oceanography (LMGPO), Department of Geology; Xenophon Dimas, MSc, PhD candidate, LMGPO; Spyros Sergiou, MSc, PhD candidate, LMGPO; and Nikos Georgrious, professional diver, Patras, Greece. We also appreciate the help of Sophia Margaritis, owner of the Hotel Arimar in Antikyra, which served as our base during the work in that area. For useful suggestions on Aegean archaeology, we warmly thank Eric Cline, Malcolm Weiner, and Assaf Yasur-Landau. Some US graduate student support was provided by the University of California Office of the President through a Research Catalyst Grant for At-Risk Cultural Heritage and the Digital Humanities (Grant ID: CA-16-376911; Lead PI: Thomas Levy, Ph.D.). Tom Levy would like to warmly thank Norma Kershaw for her support, and we are especially grateful to Liz Anne and Phokion Potamianos of La Jolla, California, for their generous support of this project given to Tom Levy and the Scripps Center for Marine Archaeology. Richard Norris would like to thank Dr. Katie Cramer for assistance in organizing the shipment of core pipe and other gear to Greece for this study.

References

Ainsworth, R. A. (2012). *Stereo panoramic photography for virtual reality*. Ridgeway: Ainsworth & Partners.

Aitken, M. J. (1974). *Physics and archaeology*. Oxford: Clarendon Press.

Annan, P. A. (1992). Ground Penetrating Radar: workshop notes. Sensors and Software, Mississauga, Ontario.

Barker, R. D. (1992). A simple algorithm for electrical imaging of the subsurface. *First Break, 10*, 53–63.

Ben-Shlomo, D., Shai, I., Zukerman, A., & Maeir, A. M. (2008). Cooking identities: Aegean-style cooking jugs and cultural interaction in iron age Philistia and neighboring regions. *American Journal of Archaeology, 112*(2), 225–246.

Chovalopoulou, M., Bertsatos, A., & Manolis, S. (2017). Identification of skeletal remains from a Mycenaean burial in Kastrouli-Desfina, Greece. *Mediterranean Archaeology and Archaeometry, 17*(1), 265–269.

Cline, E. H. (2014). *1177 B.C. : The year civilization collapsed*. Princeton: Princeton University Press.

Constable, S., Parker, R., & Constable, C. (1987). Occam's inversion: A practical algorithm for generating smooth models from electromagnetic sounding data. *Geophysics, 52*, 289–300.

Cramer, K. L., O'Dea, A., Clark, T. R., Zhao, J., & Norris R. D. (2017). Prehistorical and historical declines in Caribbean coral reef accretion rates driven by loss of parrotfish. *Nature Communications, 8*, 14160. https://doi.org/10.1038/ncomms14160l:1-8.

Dabney, M. K., Halstead, P., & Thomas, P. (2004). Mycenaean feasting on Tsoungiza at ancient Nemea. In J. C. Wright (Ed.), *The Mycenaean feast* (pp. 77–95). Athens: American School of Classical Studies at Athens.

Davis, J. L., Alcock, S. E., Bennet, J., Lolos, Y. G., & Shelmerdine, C. W. (1997). The Pylos regional archaeological project Part I: Overview and the archaeological survey. *Hesperia: The Journal of the American School of Classical Studies at Athens, 66*(3), 391–494.

Degroot-Hedlin, C., & Constable, S. (1990). Occam's inversion to generate smooth, two- dimensional models from magnetotelluric data. *Geophysics, 55*, 1613–1624.

Edwards, L. S. (1977). A modified pseudosection for resistivity and IP. *Geophysics, 42*, 1020–1036.

Fassbinder, J. W. E. (2015). Seeing beneath the farmland, steppe and desert soil: Magnetic prospecting and soil magnetism. *Journal of Archaeological Science, 56*, 85–95.

Gidding, A., Matsui, Y., Levy, T. E., DeFanti, T., & Kuester, F. (2011, December). *e-Science and the Archaeological Frontier*. In 2011 IEEE Seventh International Conference on eScience (pp. 166–172). IEEE.

Gidding, A., Levy, T. E., & DeFanti, T. A. (2014). ArchaeoSTOR: The development and utilization of a web-based database for the field and lab. *Near Eastern Archaeology, 77*(33), 198–202.

Goodman, D., & Piro, S. (2013). *GPR remote sensing in archaeology*. New York: Springer.

Goodman, D., Nishimura, Y., & Rogers, J. D. (1995). GPR time slices in archaeological prospection. *Archaeological Prospection, 2*, 85–89.

Griffiths, D., Turnbull, J., & Olyianka, A. (1990). 2-dimentional resistivity mapping with a computer controlled array. *First Break, 8*, 121–129.

Knapp, A. B., & Manning, S. W. (2016). Crisis in context: The end of the Late Bronze age in the Eastern Mediterranean. *American Journal of Archaeology, 120*(1), 99–149.

Killebrew, A. E. (2005). Biblical Peoples and Ethnicity – An Archaeological Study of Egyptians, Canaanites, Philistines, and Early Israel, 1300–1100 B.C.E. Atlanta: Society of Biblical Literature.

Langgut, D., Finkelstein, I., & Litt, T. (2013). Climate and the late bronze collapse: New evidence from the Southern Levant. *Tel Aviv, 40*, 149–175.

Langgut, D., Neumann, F. H., Stein, M., Wagner, A., Kagan, E. J., Boaretto, E., & Finkelstein, I. (2014). Dead Sea pollen record and history of human activity in the Judean highlands (Israel) from the intermediate bronze into the iron ages (~2500–500 BCE). *Palynology, 38*(2), 280–302.

Le Borge, E. (1955). Susceptibilite magnetique anormal du sol superficial. *Annales de Geophysique, 8*(11), 399–419.

Levy, T. E., Petrovic, V., Wypych, T., Gidding, A., Knabb, K., Hernandez, D., Smith, N. G., Schlulz, J. P., Savage, S. H., Kuester, F., Ben-Yosef, E., Buitenhuys, C., Barrett, C. J., Najjar, M., & DeFanti, T. (2010). On-site digital archaeology 3.0 and cyber- archaeology: Into the future of the past—New developments, delivery and the creation of a data avalanche. In M. Forte (Ed.), *Introduction to cyber-archaeology* (pp. 135–153). Oxford: Archaeopress.

Levy, T. E., Najjar, M., & Ben-Yosef, E. (2014). *New insights into the iron age archaeology of Edom, southern Jordan – surveys, excavations and research from the Edom Lowlands Regional Archaeology Project (ELRAP)*. Los Angeles: Cotsen Institute of Archaeology Press UCLA.

Linford, N. (2006). The application of geophysical methods to archaeological prospection. *Reports on Progress in Physics, 69*, 2205–2257.

Liritzis, I. Zhengyao, J., Anchuan, F., Sideris, A., & Drivaliari, A. (2016). Late Helladic and later reuse phases of Kastrouli settlement (Greece): preliminary dating results Mediterranean. *Archaeology and Archaeometry, 16*(3), 245–250.

Lipschitz, O., & Maeir, A. M. (2017). *The Shephelah during the iron age: Recent archaeological studies*. Winona Lake: Eisenbrauns.

Liritzis, I., Pavlidis, G., Vosynakis, S., Koutsoudis, A., Volonakis, P., Petrochilos, N., Howland, M., Liss, B., & Levy, T. E. (2016). DELPHI4DELPHI: first results of the digital archaeology initiative for ancient Delphi, Greece. *Antiquity,* Project Gallery On-line December 2016:6 p. http://www.antiquity.ac.uk/projgall/liritzis354

Marinatos, S. N. (1974). Excavations at Thera VI (1972). Athens: Vivliothiki tis en Athinis Archaeologikis Etereias 64.

Papadopoulos, N. G., Tsourlos, P., Tsokas, G. N., & Sarris, A. (2006). 2D and 3D resistivity imaging in archaeological site investigation. *Archaeological Prospection, 13*(3), 163–181.

Parasnis, D. S. (1997). *Principles of applied geophysics* (3rd ed.). London: Chapman and Hall.

Raptopoulos, S. Y. (2012) ΜΥΚΗΝΑΪΚΟΣ ΘΟΛΩΤΟΣ ΤΑΦΟΣ ΣΤΗ ΔΕΣΦΙΝΑ ΦΩΚΙΔΟΣ. In ΑΡΧΑΙΟΛΟΓΙΚΟ ΕΡΓΟ ΘΕΣΣΑΛΙΑΣ ΚΑΙ ΣΤΕΡΕΑΣ ΕΛΛΑΔΑΣ (pp. 1071–1078).

Scollar, I., Weidner, B., & Segeth, K. (1986). Display of archaeological magnetic data. *Geophysics, 51*(3), 623–633.

Sherratt, A. (1993). What would a bronze-age world system look like? Relations between temperate Europe and the Mediterranean in later prehistory. *Journal of European Archaeology Archive, 1*(2), 1–58.

Shima, H. (1990). 2-D automatic resistivity inversion technique using alpha centers. *Geophysics, 55*, 682–694.

Sideris, A. (2014). *Antikyra history & archaeology*. Athens: Municipality of Distomo.

Sideris, A., Liritzis, I., Liss, B., Howland, M., & Levy, T. E. (2017). At-risk cultural heritage: New excavations and finds from the Mycenaean site of Kastrouli, Phokis, Greece. *Mediterranean Archaeology and Archaeometry, 17*(1), 271–285.

Simpson, R. H. (2014). Mycenaean sites in Messenia. In R. H. Simpson (Ed.), *Mycenaean Messenia and the Kingdom of Pylos* (Vol. 45, pp. 15–44). Philadelphia: INSTAP Academic Press.

Smith, N. G., & Levy T. E. (2012). Real-time 3D archaeological field recording: ArchField, an open-source GIS system pioneered in Jordan. *Antiquity, 85*(331):on-line http://antiquity.ac.uk/projgall/smith331/

Smith, N. G., & Levy, T. E. (2014). ArchField in Jordan: Real-time GIS data recording for archaeological excavations. *Near Eastern Archaeology, 77*(3), 166–170.

Smith, N. G., Howland, M., & Levy, T. E. (2015). *Digital archaeology field recording in the 4th dimension: ArchField C++ a 4D GIS for Digital Field Work* (pp. 251–258). Granada: Digital Heritage.

Smith, R. E., Breeze C., Harman T., Gupta A., Reece F., Liss B., Burton M. M., & Levy T. E. (2017). *ArchaeoSTOR: A User-Friendly Archaeological Database*. Poster presentation at the 45th Computer Applications & Quantitative Methods in Archaeology International Conference, March 14–16, 2017, Atlanta, Georgia.

Strasser, T. F. (2010). Location and perspective in the Theran Flotilla Fresco. *Journal of Mediterranean Archaeology, 23*(1), 3–26.

Tartaron, T. F. (2013). *Maritime networks in the Mycenaean world.* New York: Cambridge University Press.

Thomatos, M. (2006). *The final revival of the Aegean bronze age : A case study of the Argolid, Corinthia, Attica, Euboea, the Cyclades and the Dodecanese during LH III C middle*. Oxford: Archaeopress.

Tite, M. S., & Mullins, C. (1971). Enhancement of the magnetic susceptibility of soils on archaeological sites. *Archeometry, 13*(2), 209–219.

Tsourlos, P. (1995). *Modeling interpretation and inversion of multielectrode earth resistivity datasets*. Ph. D. Thesis. University of York.

Tsourlos, P., & Ogilvy, R. D. (1999). An algorithm for the 3-D inversion of tomographic resistivity and induced polarisation data: Preliminary results. *Journal of the Balkan Geophysical Society, 2*(2), 30–45.

Tsourlos, P., Szymanski, J., Dittmer, J. & Tsokas, G. N. (1993). The use of back-projection for fast inversion of 2-D resistivity data. *Proceedings of the 2nd congress of the Greek Geophysical Union, Florina Greece, 5–7 May*, Vol. 1, 71–81.

Tsourlos, P., Dittmer, J. & Szymanski, J. (1995). A study of non-linear techniques for the 2- D inversion of earth resistivity data. Expanded abstracts of the 57th meeting of the EAEG, Glasgow, Scotland, 29 May-2 June.

Tsourlos, P., Szymanski, J., & Tsokas, G. N. (1999). The effect of terrain topography on commonly used resistivity arrays. *Geophysics, 64*, 1357–1363.

Van de Moortel, A. (2009). Middle Bronze Age Boat of Mitrou, Central Greece. *Between continents : proceedings of the Twelfth Symposium on Boat and Ship Archaeology* (pp. 17–26), Istanbul Istanbul: Ege Yayinlari.

Ward, S. H. (1990). Resistivity and induced polarization methods. In: S. H. Ward (Ed.), *Geotechnical and environmental geophysics 1: Review and tutorial (Investigations in Geophysics 5)* (pp. 147–189). Tulsa: SEG.

Wedde, M. (2000). *Towards a hermeneutics of Aegean bronze age ship imagery*. Mannheim: Bibliopolis.

Weiner, M. H. (n.d.). *The impact of climate change, famine, pandemics, and warfare in the collapse of civilizations*. Greece: On file: INSTAP.

Witten, A. (2006). *Handbook of geophysics and archaeology*. London: Equinox.

Wright, J. C. (Ed.). (2004). *The Mycenaean feast*. Princeton: American School of Classical Studies at Athens.

Index

T.E. Levy, I.W.N. Jones (eds.), *Cyber-Archaeology and Grand Narratives*, One World Archaeology, https://doi.org/10.1007/978-3-319-65693-9

I

J

K

L

M

N

O

P

MIX
Papier aus verantwortungsvollen Quellen
Paper from responsible sources
FSC® C105338

If you have any concerns about our products,
you can contact us on
ProductSafety@springernature.com

In case Publisher is established outside the EU,
the EU authorized representative is:
Springer Nature Customer Service Center GmbH
Europaplatz 3, 69115 Heidelberg, Germany

Printed by Libri Plureos GmbH
in Hamburg, Germany